iOS SDK
Programming:
A Beginner's Guide

About the Authors

James A. Brannan is a senior developer with more than 15 years of experience. He has developed using everything from AWK, to Visual Basic, to Java. His current interests are iOS, Blackberry, Android, and Adobe Flex/Flash. He is only $999,000 short of being the next app store overnight millionaire. He lives in Gaithersburg, Maryland, with his wife, two kids, two Macs, and bicycle.

Blake Ward has a PhD in Computer Science from Carnegie Mellon University and has spent more than 30 years programming and managing software development. He has developed for a wide variety of mobile devices, ranging from the Apple Newton and Palm Pilot to RIM's Blackberry, the iPhone and iPad, and Android phones. Blake has worked as a researcher and in management at Apple, Xerox PARC, and numerous startups. He is currently an independent iPhone and Android developer, available through www.iphoneappquotes.com.

About the Technical Editor

Born to golf, forced to work, **Steven Weber**, a Java Web Applications engineer, has ten years application development under his belt. He's dabbled in iOS application development and released one corporate application since the launch of Apple's App Store. He's currently living it up in the Colorado Rockies.

iOS SDK Programming:
A Beginner's Guide

James A. Brannan
Blake Ward

New York   Chicago   San Francisco
Lisbon   London   Madrid   Mexico City
Milan   New Delhi   San Juan
Seoul   Singapore   Sydney   Toronto

The **McGraw·Hill** Companies

Cataloging-in-Publication Data is on file with the Library of Congress

iOS SDK Programming: A Beginner's Guide

1234567890   DOC DOC   10987654321

ISBN 978-0-07-175908-3
MHID   0-07-175908-5

Sponsoring Editor   Roger Stewart
Editorial Supervisor   Jody McKenzie
Project Manager   Vastavikta Sharma, Glyph International
Acquisitions Coordinator   Joya Anthony
Technical Editor   Steven Weber
Copy Editor   Bob Campbell
Proofreader   Claire Splan
Indexer   Jack Lewis
Production Supervisor   George Anderson
Composition   Glyph International
Illustration   Glyph International
Art Director, Cover   Jeff Weeks
Cover Designer   Jeff Weeks

For Timothy Hill and Doctor Ronald Holt. This book is not some lofty political or anthropological treatise, but it was fun writing.
—James

For Bryce—the real author in our family.
—Blake

Contents at a Glance

Contents

Acknowledgments

Thanks to the technical editor, Steven Weber, and everybody at McGraw-Hill, particularly Roger Stewart, Joya Anthony, Jody McKenzie, Vastavikta Sharma, and Bob Campbell. Special thanks to Everaldo and his Crystal Project Icons licensed under the LGPL. These icons have made the examples much more visually appealing in both this book and others. And of course, thanks to Neil Salkind, our book agent, who introduced us to computer book writing and kept the ship navigating straight despite some stormy moments. Finally, thanks to the iPhone SDK Forum (www.iphonesdk.com). In no small part, the idea for a tutorial-based approach for this book came directly from your video tutorials offered on your site.

Introduction

Response to the iPhone, the iPod touch, and now the iPad has been nothing short of overwhelming. The App Store has captured the hobbyist's imagination like no other platform in recent memory. Hobbyists have made—and will continue to make—money from their creations sold on the App Store. And we aren't necessarily talking about high-minded technical innovations. The media has reported that apps that make your iPhone pass gas have made folks hundreds of thousands of dollars. Rival farting App developers have even gone so far as to sue one another over the App Store's precious revenue. The iOS family of devices and the App Store are here to stay—and there's still plenty of opportunity for you to create the next great app.

As proof of this popularity, after posting a few tutorial videos on Vimeo, James heard from people from Asia, Europe, and South America about those videos. So, when we decided to write this book, we kept in mind that iOS devices have significant international appeal. We have tried to make this book as accommodating as possible for as wide an audience as possible. We have kept colloquialisms to a minimum, for instance. But more important than avoiding colloquialisms, this book relies upon discrete, numbered steps that illustrate each major concept. Rather than a lot of prose describing the iOS SDK, we show you the SDK in action.

The Book's Focus

This book has three goals. The first of these is to get you comfortable with using the iOS's user interface controls in Interface Builder. Interface Builder is a useful tool that removes much of the complexity of creating and laying out the user interface for iOS apps. Once you master this tool, building a graphical user interface (GUI) using Interface Builder is quicker and more intuitive than using code.

The second goal of this book is to brush up your C language programming skills and introduce you to Objective-C. Most likely you haven't used C since college, and chances are good you have never used Objective-C. However, because Objective-C is the language used for Cocoa and Cocoa Touch programming, you must understand Objective-C if you wish to create iPhone and iPad apps. After refreshing your memory on C, this book moves on to Objective-C with a two-chapter tutorial that will give you a foundation for getting started with the iOS SDK.

The third goal of this book is to cover all of the most useful functionality of the iOS SDK so that you're ready to create your own iOS apps for the App Store. We cover using the latest version of Apple's development environment, XCode 4, and most of the features introduced in the latest versions of the SDK for the iPad and the iPhone 4.

NOTE
This book's code examples can be downloaded at:
www.mhprofessional.com/computingdownloads.

The Book's Content

This book assumes no prior C or Objective-C knowledge. Although not comprehensive, chapters on C and Objective-C should provide enough detail to understand the book's remaining chapters. The book starts with the prerequisites. Both C and Objective-C are prerequisites to programming iOS applications. You don't need to be a C expert to use Objective-C, but you should remember C's basics. After providing a C refresher, the book has two chapters on Objective-C. These chapters introduce a lot of concepts quickly, but Objective-C is the language used for Cocoa Touch, so you'd be advised to learn it. After covering Objective-C, the book provides a chapter on installing an iOS application on an iPhone, iPod touch, or iPad device. It also provides a tutorial on debugging and testing your application.

Chapter 6 finally begins the book's UIKit coverage. Chapters 6 through 10 discuss the UIView subclasses you use when laying out an iOS application. Chapter 11 discusses alerts, action sheets, and application badges. Chapters 12 and 13 discuss the many controls available for an iOS user interface. Chapter 13 also discusses how to use the photo library and the camera built into the iPhone.

After describing the UIKit, the book then moves on to discuss several other essential iOS application programming topics. Chapter 14 discusses setting your application's preferences using the Settings application. Chapter 15 discusses file I/O, property lists, and archiving objects. Chapter 16 discusses using the iOS's built-in database, SQLite. Chapter 17 builds a more complex iOS application and discusses Core Data, by far the easiest persistence framework you can use while programming with iOS. Chapter 18 discusses using iTunes music in your application.

Finally, Chapter 19 discusses the new SDK functionality available for the iPad and shows you how to create a universal application that will run on the iPhone or iPod touch but also take full advantage of the larger display on the iPad when available. All of the framework functionality described in the earlier chapters applies to the iPad and the new iPhone 4, so this chapter focuses on how to layer new iOS 4 functionality on top of the skills that you've already learned.

This book doesn't require any prior knowledge of C, Objective-C, or Cocoa Touch and the iOS frameworks, so provided you have some prior programming experience and you work through all of the exercises in the book, you should be ready to start working on your own iPhone applications when you've finished the book. However, even if you eventually decide to hire an independent developer to help build your application (via a web site like www.iphoneappquotes.com), everything you've learned working through the exercises will be invaluable when it comes time to turn your ideas into a design and work with others to implement them.

Chapter 1

The iOS Software
Development Kit (SDK)

Key Skills & Concepts

- Understanding the App Store
- Understanding how to obtain Xcode and the iOS SDK
- Deciding if this book is right for you
- Understanding Xcode's help and Apple's online documentation

So why do people pay over $100 a month for an iPhone? Or more than $500 for an iPad? Simple—they're useful tools *and fun toys*. If you get lost, just start the Maps application, and within seconds, it has located your position and provided you with a map. You can check your e-mail anywhere, listen to music, and every once in a while even answer a phone call. The built-in functionality of the iPhone, iPod Touch, and iPad is undeniably useful, but the real magic of these devices is the App Store. There you can find more than a quarter of a million applications that turn your iPhone from a useful general device to a tool specialized for exactly what you want to do.

Apple's App Store has created a new phenomenon—millions of people think of buying cheap apps the same way they think about picking up a latte on the way to work; it's an impulse buy they do several times a week. Unlike other smartphone users, iPhone users buy apps, lots of them! There may already be a staggering number of apps in the App Store, but the opportunities are still endless for turning your ideas into profitable apps.

NOTE

Apple reviews every app before publication in the App Store, and you should read their current guidelines for acceptance before starting on your app. Obvious categories like gambling and pornography aren't allowed, but even apps that show scantily clad models risk rejection from the App Store. But don't worry too much; if your app is bug free and follows the guidelines, it will probably be approved within a week.

The App Store

The App Store is a unique concept. The App Store is an Apple application on the iPhone, iPod Touch, and iPad. You use the App Store to browse and download applications from Apple's iTunes Store. Some applications are free, while others have a (usually) nominal charge. Using your iTunes account, you can download applications directly to your iPhone, iPod Touch, or iPad (your device). What we like is that anyone can use an iTunes Gift Card that you buy at your local grocery store; no credit card needed.

Don't know what to buy? You can go to one of the many web sites dedicated to reviewing applications on the App Store. For instance, www.appstoreapps.com (Figure 1-1) provides independent reviews of both free and paid applications. The App Store itself also includes customer ratings and reviews. Many applications are junk, but lots are quite amazing.

Downloading applications from the App Store is both easy and inexpensive. That makes it a lucrative market for independent developers wishing to take advantage of the iTunes Store's large user base. Independent developers can develop applications for the App Store by downloading the iOS SDK, developing an application, and joining the iOS Developer Program. Apple then reviews your application, and once it passes the review process, it is added to the iTunes Store. Apple deals with the customers, distribution, and collecting payments, and you get 70 percent of the proceeds.

Figure 1-1   The appstoreapps.com web site reviews most App Store applications.

The Software Development Kit (SDK)

So you have decided to try your hand at developing applications for the App Store. The first thing you need to do if you want to become an iPhone/iPad developer is register as a member at the iPhone Dev Center at http://developer.apple.com/iphone. Membership is free and allows downloading the SDK and viewing all of the Apple documentation.

Once you've signed up, download and install Xcode and the iOS SDK from Apple's Developer Connection. Step-by-step installation instructions are available on Apple's web site. After installing the iOS SDK, the absolute next thing you should do is start Xcode and download the documentation—all the documentation (Figure 1-2). It will take a while, but it is well worth it.

NOTE

You will find Apple's documentation surprisingly complete and well written. We refer to their documentation often in this book, so it is best to download it before continuing.

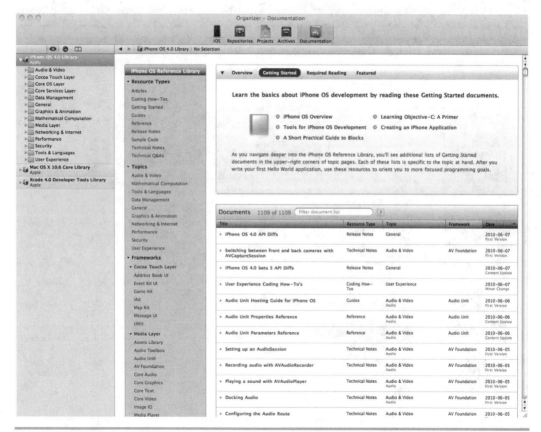

Figure 1-2 The iOS Reference Library in Xcode

Paid Membership

You can install the SDK, write apps, and run them in the simulator with a free membership. However, testing applications on a device and selling applications on the App Store require that you register with the iPhone Developer Program. This membership is different from membership to the iPhone Dev Center. The iPhone Developer Program for individuals costs $99/year and entitles you to the tools needed to test on a device. It is also how you submit and distribute your application to the App Store, and Apple distributes any profit you might earn through your iPhone Developer Program membership.

Objective-C, Foundation Framework, Cocoa Touch, and UIKit

Apple describes the iPhone and iPad device's technology as layers. The base layer is the Core OS layer. On top of that is the Core Services layer. On top of the Core Services is the Media layer. The topmost layer is Cocoa Touch (Figure 1-3).

You can simplify the iPhone operating system (iOS) even more; think of it as two layers—a C layer and a Cocoa layer (Figure 1-4). The C layer comprises the operating system's layer. You use BSD UNIX–style C functions to manipulate this layer. This layer consists of things like low-level file I/O, network sockets, POSIX threads, and SQLite.

Cocoa Touch
Media
iPhone OS
Core Services

Figure 1-3   The iPhone and iPad device's technology layers

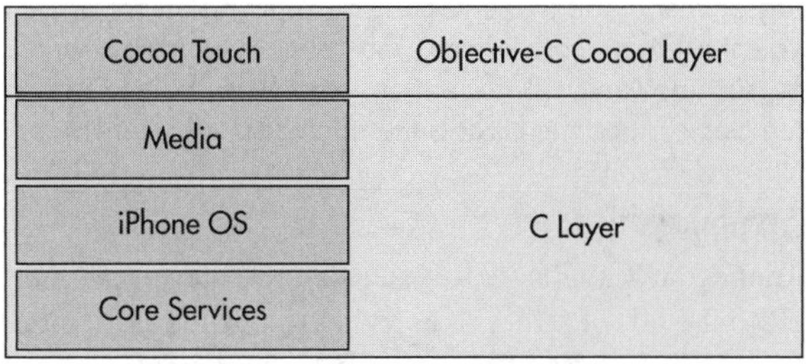

Cocoa Touch	Objective-C Cocoa Layer
Media	
iPhone OS	C Layer
Core Services	

Figure 1-4   The iPhone and iPad device's programming layers

The Media layer is also rather low-level and contains C application programming interfaces (APIs) like OpenGL ES, Quartz, and Core Audio. The Cocoa layer overlays the C layer, and it simplifies iOS programming. For instance, rather than manipulating C strings, you use the Foundation framework string, NSString.

Cocoa Touch

On the iPhone and iPad, Cocoa is called Cocoa Touch, rather than simply Cocoa, because the iOS contains touch events. If you have ever tapped, flicked, swiped, or pinched your device's display, you know what touch events are. Touch events allow you to program responses to a user's touching the screen with his or her fingers.

Cocoa Touch also provides the primary class libraries needed for development. The two Cocoa Touch frameworks you will use in every application you write are the Foundation framework and the UIKit framework. A framework is collection of code devoted to a similar task. The Foundation framework is dedicated to standard programming topics, such as collections, strings, file I/O, and other basic tasks. The UIKit is dedicated to the iPhone and iPad device's interface and contains classes such as the UIView. In this book, you spend most of your time learning the UIKit.

Foundation Framework

The Foundation framework contains Objective-C classes that wrap lower-level core functionality. For instance, rather than working with low-level C file I/O, you can work with the NSFileManager foundation class. The Foundation framework provides many useful classes that you really should learn if you want to program robust iOS applications. The Foundation framework makes programming using collections, dates and time, binary data, URLs, threads, sockets, and most other lower-level C functionality easier by wrapping the C functions with higher-level Objective-C classes.

TIP

See Apple's Foundation Framework Reference for a complete listing of the classes and protocols provided by the Foundation framework.

NOTE

If you are a Java programmer, think of the iOS's programming environment like this: Objective-C is equivalent to Java's core syntax. The Foundation framework is equivalent to Java's core classes, such as ArrayList, Exception, HashMap, String, Thread, and other Java Standard Edition classes, and the UIKit is the equivalent of SWING.

The iOS Frameworks

Table 1-1 lists the frameworks available to you as an iOS developer. Of these frameworks, this book dedicates itself to the UIKit rather than trying to cover a little bit of every framework. Once you've mastered UIKit, adding functionality to your app from the other frameworks is relatively straightforward.

Framework	Purpose
Accelerate	Accelerating math functions
AddressBook	Accessing user's contacts
AddressBookUI	Displaying Addressbook
AssetsLibrary	Accessing user's photos and videos
AudioToolbox	Audio data streams; playing and recording audio
AudioUnit	Audio units
AVFoundation	Objective-C interfaces for audio playback and recording
CFNetwork	WiFi and cellular networking
CoreAudio	Core audio classes
CoreData	Object-oriented persistent data storage
CoreFoundation	Similar to Foundation framework, but lower level (don't use unless you absolutely must)
CoreGraphics	Quartz 2D
CoreLocation	User's location/GPS
CoreMedia	Low-level audio and video routines
CoreMotion	Accelerometer and gyro functions
CoreTelephony	Telephony functions and routines
CoreText	Advanced text layout and rendering
CoreVideo	Pipeline model for digital video
EventKit	Accessing user's calendar
EventKitUI	Displaying standard system calendar
ExternalAccessory	Hardware accessory communication interfaces
Foundation	Cocoa foundation layer
GameKit	Peer-to-peer connectivity
iAd	Displaying advertisements
ImageIO	Reading and writing image data
IOKit	Low-level library for developing iPhone hardware attachments
MapKit	Embedding map in application and geocoding coordinates
MediaPlayer	Video playback
MessageUI	Composing e-mail messages
OpenAL	Positional audio library

Table 1-1   Frameworks in iOS

Framework	Purpose
OpenGLES	Embedded OpenGL (2-D and 3-D graphics rendering)
QuartzCore	Core animation
QuickLook	Previewing files
Security	Certificates, keys, and trust policies
StoreKit	In App purchasing
SystemConfiguration	Network configuration
UIKit	iOS user interface layer

Table 1-1   Frameworks in iOS (*continued*)

iPhone/iPad Limitations

If you have never programmed for a small device like an iPhone, there are some limitations you should be aware of before you begin programming. Memory and processor speed are constrained, and the screen is small. Security is also tight in iOS, and applications are limited in what they can do.

Memory and Processor Speed

An iPhone's memory and processor speed are constrained compared to your desktop computer, and you'll want to keep that in mind as you develop your application. You'll want to think carefully about what information you need, whether it should be cached, the amount of memory needed, and freeing up memory when you no longer need it. iOS provides functionality to warn your application when memory is running low, so you can write your application to deal gracefully with the constraints of any iOS device it's currently running on.

CAUTION

If your application uses too much memory, your device's operating system may abruptly terminate your application to prevent a system crash.

Small Screen

The original iPhone screen and the iPod Touch's screen measure only 480 × 320 pixels. That's not much room to work with. Of course, controls such as buttons are smaller on an iPhone, but the layout space is still significantly constrained. If you are accustomed to programming user interfaces on a 1280 × 800 pixel display, you must adjust your thinking. Screen size is limited.

The iPad's screen is 1024 × 768. Now, if you're an older programmer, this isn't problematic, as we remember the days when we programmed for 800 × 600 desktop displays, or even worse, 640 × 480. However, the interface is still small compared to a modern desktop's display. If you pack too much information onto an iPad's screen, it is going to be difficult for users to read and digest it all.

The resolution of the new iPhone 4 is double that of the original at 960 by 640 pixels, but most of the time you'll still develop your apps for a 480 × 320 coordinate system and the system layers will just take care of mapping that to the higher-resolution screen for a sharper appearance.

The small screen size also results in only one window being visible at a time on an iPhone or iPod Touch. The iPad adds support for a single pop-up window, but you'll still want to think in terms of having a single window and swapping views based on interaction from your user.

Security

You can only read or write to directories that are part of your application's bundle or your application's documents directory. Areas accessible to your application are said to be in your application's sandbox. You cannot read files created by other applications unless the application places the files in its documents folder and explicitly indicates to iOS that it wishes to share its documents directory. Other applications can only access the documents in a shared documents folder. Users can also access documents placed in a shared documents directory when they synchronize their device with their desktop using iTunes. You will see how to accomplish sharing using the documents directory in Chapter 15.

Short-Lived Applications

Until iOS4, applications could not be memory-resident. A memory-resident application can run in the background while a user runs other applications. As of iOS4, applications can perform some rudimentary background processing. However, you should note it is still very limited. You cannot run multiple applications "full-throttle" and then switch between them while they are still processing, as you can on a desktop, a Blackberry, or a device running Android.

iOS apps can request additional processing time from iOS when being moved to the background. However, this processing must be short and quick, or else iOS will terminate the app. After processing, iOS suspends the app. You learn more about Apple's rudimentary multitasking in Chapter 6. In general, though, Apple prevents developers from writing applications that run in the background.

Manual Memory Management

Garbage collection is one of the nicest features of Java and one of the big improvements in Objective-C 2.0 running in Mac OS desktop apps. Garbage collection frees developers from having to worry about memory management; you simply create objects as needed and the system takes care of freeing them when they're no longer needed. But iOS, with its limited resources, does not include Objective-C 2.0 garbage collection, and you must manage memory yourself. Although manual memory management can be a pain, it is not a huge limitation. Just be aware that forgetting to release an object is all too easy a mistake to make. As you will see in Chapter 5, there are tools to help you track down and fix these errors.

Relevant Documentation

Apple provides considerable online documentation. You have access to that documentation both through your Developer Connection membership and through Xcode's help. You should refer to that documentation often. Most documentation is also available as PDF documents. The first three documents you should download and keep handy are the iOS Application Programming Guide, iOS Development Guide, and iPad Programming Guide. You might then consider downloading the Cocoa Fundamentals Guide. You will also find documents on Objective-C and various Cocoa classes. If you followed this chapter's earlier recommendation and downloaded the documentation, you will find that all this information is at your fingertips using Xcode's help. This book tries not to duplicate these online and desktop sources, but rather complement them by providing step-by-step examples illustrating how to do things. Once you understand how, the online documentation shows you more options to expand upon this book's tutorial.

Try This Getting a Quick Start on iOS Development

To whet your appetite, this chapter ends with a quick-start example. The next four chapters will cover prerequisites that you should have prior to learning the iOS's UIKit and Cocoa Touch. But you probably want to get a feeling for what writing an app for the iPhone will be like, so we'll end this chapter with a simple iOS application. This quick start will familiarize you with the main tools of iOS development by showing you how to connect a graphical interface created with drag-and-drop in the Interface Builder to your Objective-C classes written using Xcode.

1. Open Xcode. From the menu select File | New Project and the New Project dialog appears (Figure 1-5).

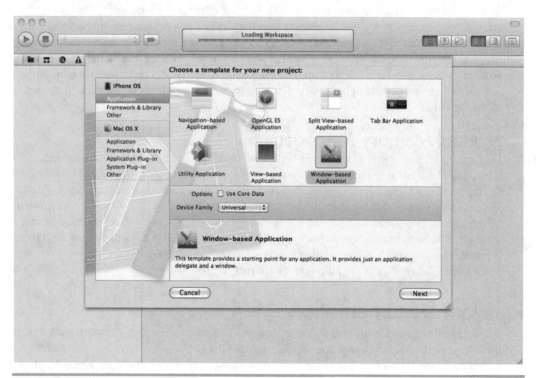

Figure 1-5 New Project dialog

2. Select View-based Application and ensure iPhone is selected in the Product drop-down. Click Next. In the Choose Options dialog, give the application the name **QuickStart** (Figure 1-6). In the Company Identifier field you'll need to enter the company name that you used when creating a provisioning profile on the Apple Developer Connection site.

3. Xcode should create the project. In the Groups & Files pane, expand the Classes and Resources folders and click on MainWindow.xib. Select View | Utilities | Object Attributes from the main menu. Select View | Show Debugger Area from the main menu. You now have all of the main areas of the Xcode interface visible (Figure 1-7). Familiarize yourself with the layout of information and controls.

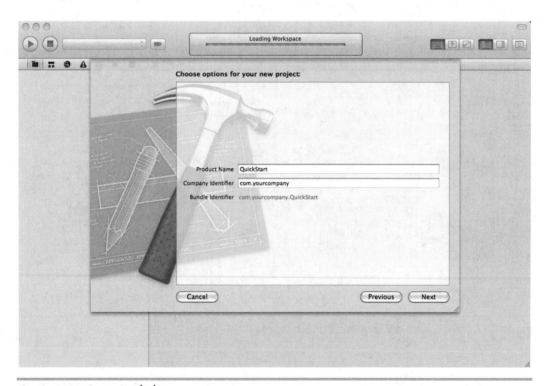

Figure 1-6   Save As dialog

(continued)

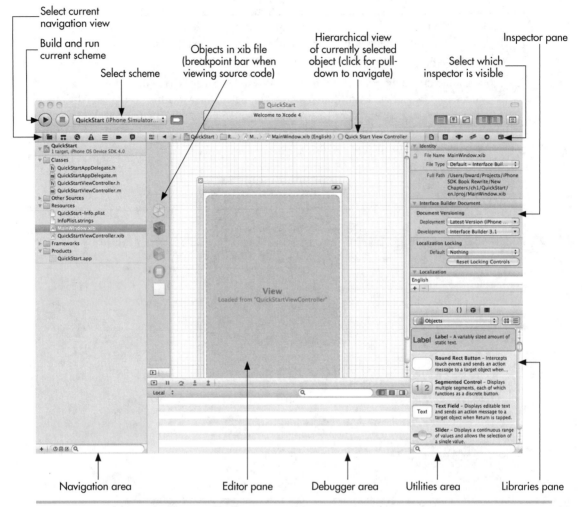

Select current navigation view

Build and run current scheme

Select scheme

Objects in xib file (breakpoint bar when viewing source code)

Hierarchical view of currently selected object (click for pull-down to navigate)

Inspector pane

Select which inspector is visible

Navigation area

Editor pane

Debugger area

Utilities area

Libraries pane

Figure 1-7 The Xcode 4 IDE with all panes visible

4. Click QuickStartViewController.xib to open it in Interface Builder. Starting with Xcode 4, the Interface Builder is now built in, so you can edit your interface directly in the project window.

5. You should see a canvas like the one shown in Figure 1-8. Click the View button in the middle of the window (square with a dotted outline) and a view will appear on the canvas (Figure 1-9).

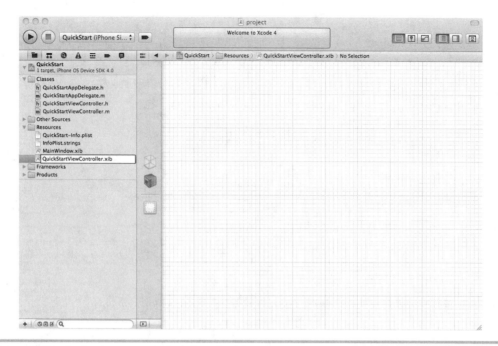

Figure 1-8   A view's canvas in Interface Builder

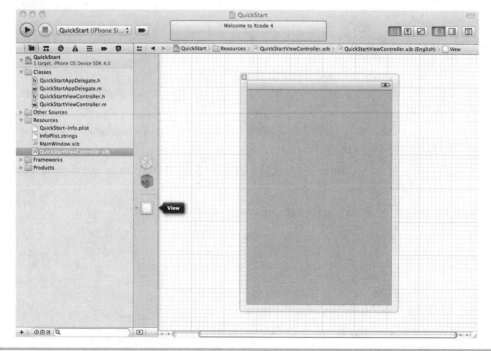

Figure 1-9   Canvas with the view displayed   *(continued)*

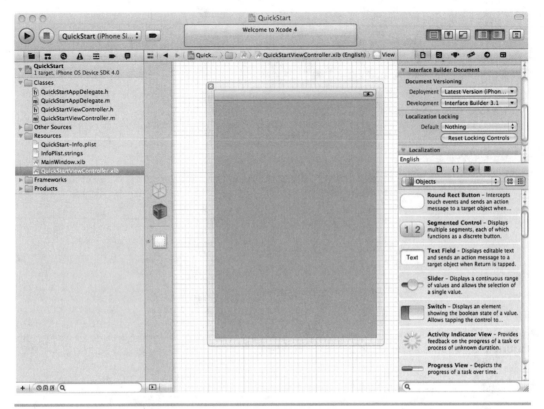

Figure 1-10   The object library

6. Make the object library visible by selecting View | Utilities | Object Library from Interface Builder's main menu (Figure 1-10).

7. Scroll through the controls until you find a Round Rect Button. Drag and drop the button to the canvas (Figure 1-11).

8. Double-click the button on the canvas, and give the button a title.

9. Drag a label from the library to the canvas (Figure 1-12).

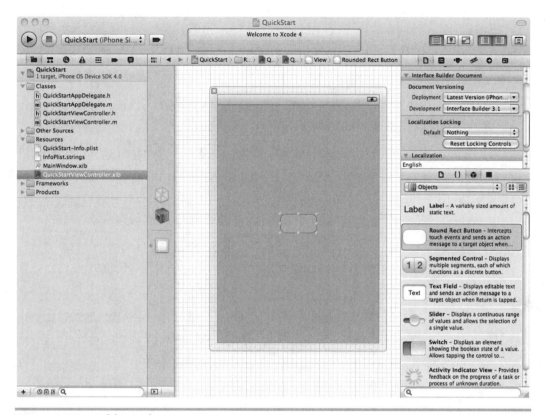

Figure 1-11   Adding a button

10. Select File | Save to save your interface changes. You can select View | Utilities | Hide Utilities from the main menu to hide the object library for now.

11. Select QuickStartViewController.m in the Classes folder in Groups & Files. Xcode should display the file in the editor pane (Figure 1-13).

12. Open QuickStartViewController.h and modify the file so that it matches Listing 1-1.

(continued)

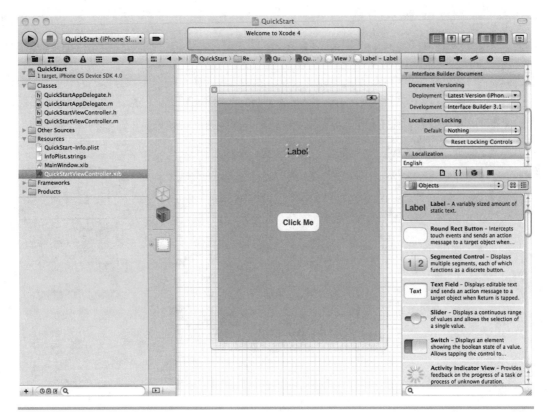

Figure 1-12 Adding a label

Listing 1-1 QuickStartViewController.h

```
#import <UIKit/UIKit.h>
@interface QuickStartViewController : UIViewController {
IBOutlet UILabel * myLabel;
}
@property (nonatomic, retain) IBOutlet UILabel * myLabel;
-(IBAction) sayHello: (id) sender;
@end
```

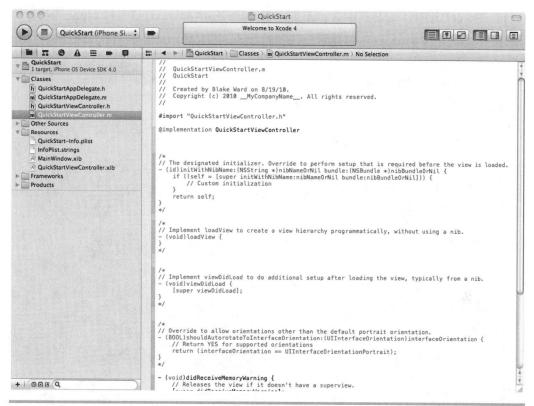

Figure 1-13 Xcode displaying QuickStartViewController.m

13. Change QuickStartViewController.m so that it matches Listing 1-2.

Listing 1-2 QuickStartViewController.m

```
#import "QuickStartViewController.h"
@implementation QuickStartViewController
@synthesize myLabel;
-(IBAction) sayHello: (id) sender {
NSLog(@"Hello....");
self.myLabel.text = @"Hello";
}
-(void) dealloc {
[super dealloc];
[myLabel release];
}
@end
```

(continued)

14. Select Product | Build "QuickStart" from Xcode's main menu to build the application.

15. Click QuickStartViewController.xib in the Resources folder to display the Interface Builder again.

16. Select the button on the canvas. Select View | Utilities | Connections from the main menu to show the object's connections (Figure 1-14).

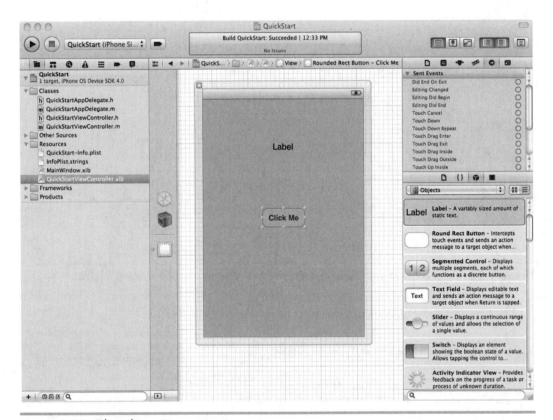

Figure 1-14 The Object Connection Inspector

17. Next to Touch Up Inside, click and hold on to the little circle. Move your cursor to File's Owner in the document window and release. Select sayHello: from the pop-up window (Figure 1-15).

18. Click the label on the canvas, and the Inspector's content should change to match the label. Click the circle next to New Referencing Outlet, and drag and drop on the File's Owner (Figure 1-16). Select myLabel from the pop-up window. Be careful not to select View.

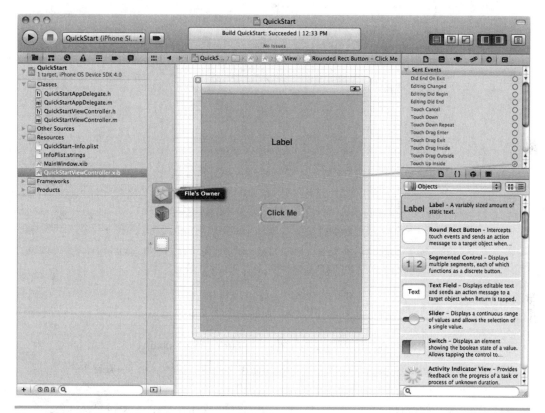

Figure 1-15 Connecting a button to an IBAction

(continued)

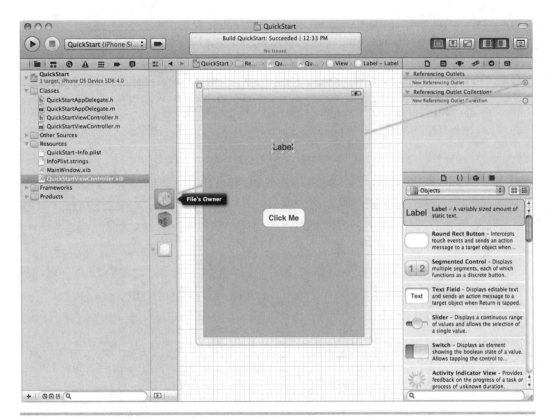

Figure 1-16 Connecting the label to an IBOutlet

19. Select File | Save from the main menu to save your interface changes.

20. In Xcode, ensure the Active SDK shows the iPhone Simulator option selected (Figure 1-17).

21. From Xcode's main menu, select Product | Run "QuickStart". Xcode should start the simulator, install your application in it, and start your application (Figure 1-18).

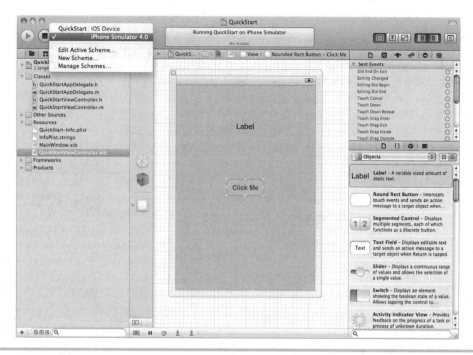

Figure 1-17   Ensuring Active SDK shows the Simulator selected

Figure 1-18   The application running in the iPhone Simulator   *(continued)*

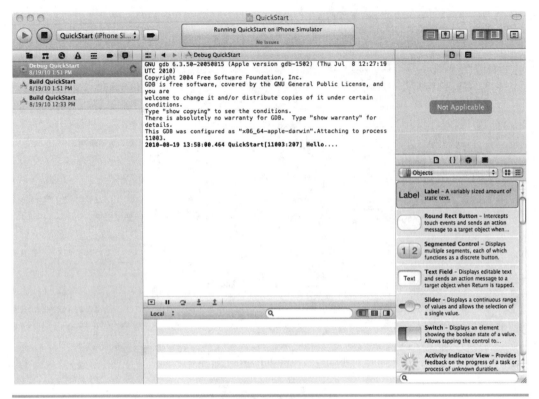

Figure 1-19 The debugging console after clicking the button

22. Select View | Navigators | Log and then click the Debug QuickStart entry in the left column to show the Debugger Console.

23. Click the button, and the label's text changes to Hello and the console displays the log (Figure 1-19).

You've just completed a lot of steps with no explanation. But what you did in this Try This will be second nature by this book's end. Apart from just experiencing the whole process of creating a new iPhone app, the biggest concept you should take away from this simple example is using the IBAction and IBOutlet keywords.

IBAction and IBOutlet are covered several times later in this book. IBActions are how you connect methods in classes in Xcode to events fired by components created using Interface Builder. IBOutlets are how you connect properties in classes within Xcode to graphical components created using Interface Builder.

These graphical components reside in a nib file, so a more correct explanation would be that IBActions and IBOutlets connect code to components in a nib file. For instance, you connected the button's Touch Up Inside event to the sayHello: action. The button lives in the nib, while the sayHello method lives in the compiled class. Making the sayHello method an IBAction connects the two. Like the button, the label also lives in the nib, while the myLabel property lives in the compiled class. Making the myLabel property an IBOutlet in the class file and then connecting the two in Interface Builder allows the class to manipulate the label via the myLabel property. Don't worry if this is still somewhat confusing—it won't be by the book's end. If you must know more now, Chapter 7 has a more "official" explanation of IBOutlets and IBActions.

Summary

This chapter introduced you to this book's content. Anyone with basic programming skills can write and release an application on Apple's App Store. Moreover, he or she can make money selling the application. Although the obvious, easy applications may have all been released, there is room for high-quality applications on the App Store. All it takes is for Apple to feature your application on its web site, and you are looking at a few thousand dollars for your efforts.

We love iOS programming and find Objective-C to be a beautiful, elegant language. We're certain that by the end of this book, you will too.

Chapter 2

A C Refresher

Key Skills & Concepts

- Creating simple C command-line programs

- Using C comments

- Understanding headers, import, and include

- Understanding preprocessor statements

- Reviewing data types and operators

- Understanding C functions, basic C syntax, and using pointers

Like almost every modern operating system, language, and programming tool of any importance, Mac OS X and the iOS operating system were built using the C programming language. Not the Objective-C programming language and Cocoa framework, not the C++ programming language, but C. Objective-C is an object-oriented language built using C. Cocoa is a framework that hides difficult C programming tasks with easy-to-use objects programmed in Objective-C. But behind every Cocoa object you construct, you find C code defining the construct.

NOTE

The computer scientists Dennis Ritchie and Brian Kernighan developed C at Bell Laboratories in 1978.

You must know at least some C if you want to program using Objective-C. In this chapter, we will review basic C. This chapter assumes some programming experience—for instance, we assume you know what a method, an integer, a function, and other basic programming constructs are. Ideally, you have had at least one university course using Java or a year's experience using Java. Experience using C# also suffices, as the language is remarkably similar to Java. As most universities teach Java these days, and Java seems to be the most prevalent language for systems developers, in this book we assume some very basic Java programming experience.

TIP

If you have never programmed before, a good reference is the *Absolute Beginner's Guide to C, Second Edition,* by Greg Perry (Sams, 1994). It teaches programming and C at about the right level needed for this book. *Objective-C for iPhone Developers: A Beginner's Guide* by James Brannan (McGraw Hill, 2010) also covers C and basic C constructs such as loops more thoroughly than this book. A good free reference on C is the online tutorial "How C Programming Works" on the howstuffworks web site (http://computer.howstuffworks.com/c.htm).

C Command-Line Programs

Like Java programs, C programs start with a main function. The C main function takes an integer and a pointer to a character array as inputs and returns an integer.

```
int main (int argc, const char * argv[])
```

The returned integer typically indicates the program's success or failure. Zero usually indicates success, while a number indicates failure. Often programmers return different values as error codes. Program users can then determine what went wrong by looking up the error code in the application's documentation.

The main function can only be implemented once in your program. When your program runs, OS X finds the main function and uses it as your program's starting point.

Try This Creating a Simple C Program Using Xcode

1. Open Xcode, Apple's integrated development environment (IDE). You'll be using Xcode for all of your iOS programming, and by the end of this book, you'll be very familiar with its features. We'll introduce Xcode functionality as it's needed, but it can be worthwhile to take a little time to create a dummy project and play around with all of the buttons, navigation, and views that can be hidden or shown in Xcode's single window interface.

2. Create a new project in Xcode by selecting File I New I New Project from the main menu. Highlight Application under Mac OS X and then select Command Line Tool, select C from the Type drop-down, and click Next . Name the project **C Main Project** (Figure 2-1).

3. Open main.c and note the function created by Xcode. It even created the "Hello World" message for you (Listing 2-1). Run your new application by selecting Product I Run "C Main Project" from the main menu, or by simply clicking the Run button (circular button with a black triangle) in the upper-left corner of the window. Select View I Show Debugger Area in the main menu to display the Debugger. The console output is in the lower-left pane; you'll see "Hello World!" printed there.

Listing 2-1 The main function in a C program

```
#include <stdio.h> int main
(int argc, const char * argv[]) {
  // insert code here...
  printf("Hello, World!\n");
  return 0;
}
```

(continued)

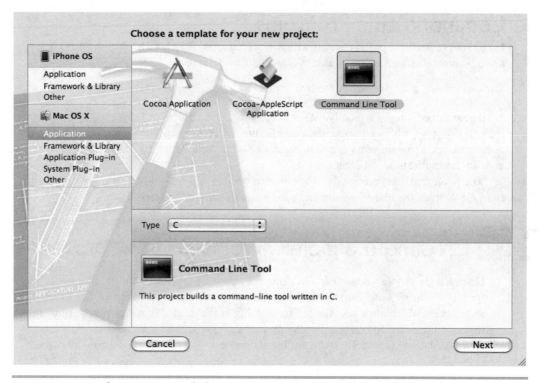

Figure 2-1 Xcode New Project dialog

C Comments

C's comment syntax is the same as Java's. A double forward slash indicates everything following on the same line is a comment. A slash followed by an asterisk indicates everything following until the next asterisk and slash is a comment. For instance, the following are both comments. The first is a single-line comment, while the second is a multiline comment.

```
// This is a comment in C code.
/* This is a multiline comment in C Code.
This comment can be multiple lines. */
```

Comments are, of course, ignored by the compiler and are ways for you to provide code explanation for future programmers who might debug or modify your code.

Understanding Headers, Import, and Include

A header file ends with an .h file extension and contains function prototypes and preprocessing statements. A *prototype* is a function's signature. A *signature* is a function name, a return type, and parameters, with no body. Compilers use prototypes so that functions in other files can "see" the function.

You can also say a header file declares functions. Declaring a function means you are telling the compiler you intend to define a function with the same signature as the declaration.

Code including or importing a header file declares to a compiler it might use that header file's functions. Through the compiler's magic, the compiler combines all files and resolves references to functions in different files, provided they all play fair and include or import the needed header files.

TIP

In standard C programs, you usually see headers included in other files. You use the #include directive when including a file in another file. In Objective-C, you typically see headers imported in other files. You use the #import directive when importing a file in another file. When importing a header file, the compiler ensures the header is only included once in your application. When including a file, no such protection is provided. Don't worry if you don't really understand the difference—understanding the difference is not important. Just know that when programming for iOS, use #import.

Try This Creating a Header File

1. Create an iPhone application using the View-based Application template. Be certain you select iPhone in the Product drop-down. Name the application CreateHeaderFile.

2. In the navigation pane on the left, CTRL-click the project name and select New Group to create a new group (folder) named C Files. Add a C file to the group using the New File dialog (Figure 2-2). Name the file cwork.c, and add it to the project.

NOTE

You can use a view-based iOS application to illustrate using C in an iOS application because you can freely mix Objective-C and C in iOS programs, as Objective-C is a superset of C.

3. Type the code in Listing 2-2 into the cwork.c file. Be certain you add the function's signature to cwork.h (Listing 2-3).

(continued)

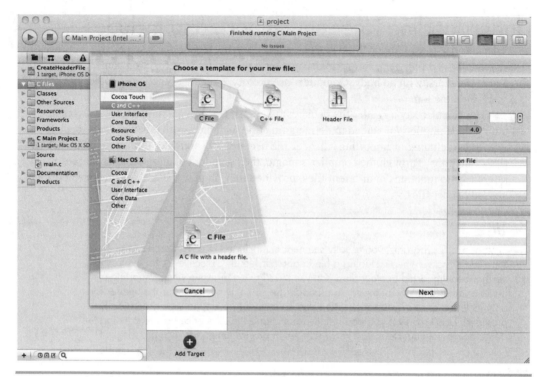

Figure 2-2 Adding a C file to the project using the New File dialog

---

Listing 2-2 The sayHello function defined in cwork.c

```
#include "cwork.h"
void sayHello() {
printf("hello programmer....\n");
}
```

Listing 2-3 The sayHello function declared in cwork.h

```
#include <stdio.h>
void sayHello();
```

The sayHello function is declared in cwork.h and defined in the cwork.c file. The sayHello function returns no value, and so its return type is void. The printf statement is declared in the standard input and output header, and so you include the stdio.h header file. Note the angle brackets; you include system libraries using angle brackets. You include headers exclusive to your project using double quotes.

4. Open main.m, import cwork.h, and add the sayHello function to the file (Listing 2-4).

Listing 2-4   The sayHello function added to main.m in the sample project

```
#import <UIKit/UIKit.h>
#import "cwork.h"
int main(int argc, char *argv[]) {
 NSAutoreleasePool * pool = [[NSAutoreleasePool alloc] init];
 sayHello();
 int retVal = UIApplicationMain(argc, argv, nil, nil);
 [pool release];
 return retVal;
}
```

5. If you have more than one project in Xcode, make sure "C Main" is the selected project in the pull-down menu and then click the Run button next to the pull-down (round button with a black triangle). The message "hello programmer...." will output to the console. You'll probably have to select View | Navigators | Log and then pick the "Debug C Main Project" log from the list to see the output.

6. Click the button with a black square to stop the program from running.

Preprocessor Statements

The #include and #import statements are *preprocessor* statements. When compiling a program, the compiler processes all statements with a # sign before compiling the program; hence, the term preprocessor statement. The compiler replaces the preprocessor statements with their actual values.

Try This   Using Preprocessor Statements

1. Open the cwork.h header file from the preceding section's project, CreateHeaderFile.

2. Type **#define MYNUMBER 20** in cwork.h and save the file.

3. Modify the sayHello function to the code as in Listing 2-5. Notice that you change the sayHello function to return an integer. You must also change the cwork.h file (Listing 2-6).

(continued)

Listing 2-5 The sayHello function modified to include a preprocessor statement

```
int sayHello() {
  printf("hello programmer....%d\n", MYNUMBER);
  return 0;
}
```

Listing 2-6 The cwork.h file

```
#include <stdio.h>
#define MYNUMBER 20
int sayHello();
```

4. Make sure your new project is selected in the pull-down and then click the Run button to run the application. The console should now echo the message with the number defined in cwork.h.

NOTE
You define constants in header files using the #define preprocessor directive. You don't include a constant's type when defining a constant.

You defined a constant in cwork.h; then when you compiled, the compiler first resolved any defined constants, replacing the constant with the literal value.

Data Types and Operators
C's basic data types are the same as Java's and should appear familiar (Table 2-1).

Data Type	Description
char	An eight-byte ASCII character
short	A small integer
int	An integer
long	A large integer
float	A floating point number, single precision
double	A floating point number, double precision

Table 2-1 C's Basic Data Types

Operator	Operator Character(s)
Assignment	=
Addition	+
Subtraction	−
Division	/
Multiplication	*
Remainder (mod)	%
Unary ++ and --	x++ or x-- ++x or --x
Equal	==
Not Equal	!=
Greater Than	>
Less Than	<
Greater Than or Equal	>=
Less Than or Equal	<=
Boolean Not	!
Boolean And	&&
Boolean Or	||

Table 2-2   C's Basic Operators

C's common operators should also appear familiar (Table 2-2). Note the table excludes the less commonly used bitwise and shift operators.

Control, Functions, and Conditional Statements

Control statements, functions, and conditional statements all have the same syntax as their Java counterparts. Conditional if statements are the same as used in Java (Listing 2-7).

Listing 2-7   Using if statements in C

```c
if(myInt < 2) {
  printf("the value is not equal");
  myOtherInt = 3;
} else if (myInt == 5) {
  myOtherInt = 7;
} else {
  myOtherInt = 3;
}
```

Switch statements are also equivalent to a Java switch statement (Listing 2-8).

Listing 2-8   C's switch statement

```c
switch (myInt) {
  case 1:
    myOtherInt = 3;
    printf("case one");
    break;
    case 2:
    myOtherInt = 5;
    break;
  default:
    myOtherInt = 4;
}
```

Loops should prove familiar if you know Java, as should the do-while loop and the for loop (Listing 2-9).

Listing 2-9   The while, do-while, and for loops using C

```c
int i = 0;
while(i < 20) {
  printf("loop%d", i);
  i++;
}
do {
  printf("loop%d", i);
  i--;
} while(i > 0);
for(int i = 0; i < 20; i++) {
  printf("loop%d", i);
}
```

Arrays and Structures

C arrays are similar to Java arrays. You declare arrays the same way, but C has no *new* keyword; you simply start using the array (Listing 2-10).

Listing 2-10   Using a C array

```
int myArray[100];
myArray[0] = 1;
myArray[1] = 2;
```

C has structs; Java doesn't have a struct data type. In C, a *struct* is similar to a class, but has no functions or inheritance (Listing 2-11).

Listing 2-11   A C struct

```
struct myBox {
    int length;
    int width;
}
```

Arrays can hold structures; for instance, you might declare an array to hold 100 myBox instances (Listing 2-12).

Listing 2-12   Using a C struct in an array

```
struct myBox myBoxes[100];
myBoxes[0].length = 10;
myBoxes[0].width = 2;
```

Functions

You declare functions the same way using C as you do using Java, only C does not restrict a function's visibility. C has no public or private functions. As in Java, you declare a C function with a return type, a name, and argument list. You write function declarations in header files. You write function definitions in C source files. Functions that don't return anything use void as their return type. If a function takes no arguments, you can optionally list the arguments as void.

```
void sayHello(void);
```

Although you can't declare a function private, you can declare a function static. But a static function in C is very different from a static function in Java. In C, declaring a function static is similar to declaring a function private in Java. In C, only functions declared in the same file can use a function declared static. Static functions are useful for utility functions that won't be used elsewhere in a program.

```
static void sayHello(void){ printf("hello\n");}
```

Note that you don't declare the static function's prototype in a header file. You simply write the function in the source file using the function.

The printf Statement

C uses the printf statement for outputting to the standard output stream. Its declaration is as follows:

```
int printf( const char *format, arg1, arg2, ..., argn);
```

The statement takes a pointer to the characters you wish to send to the standard output stream and zero or more items for formatting. For instance, consider the following printf statement:

```
printf("Hello world...%d times", 22);
```

This statement results in the following output:

```
Hello world...22 times
```

Another common argument is %s for character strings. For instance, the following code defines a character array and then prints it.

```
char * hello = "hello turkey";
printf("%s\n", hello);
```

Pointers

Java does away with pointers; however, Objective-C relies extensively upon pointers. A *pointer* is a reference to another variable, or more technically, a pointer is a variable that references another variable's memory space. Think of your computer's memory as one large cubbyhole block. A variable occupies a cubbyhole. A pointer points to the particular cubbyhole, but the pointer's value is not the value in the cubbyhole; the pointer's value is the cubbyhole's address.

In Figure 2-3, the cubbyhole n is located in row 2, column 5, and its value is 12. Cubbyhole n's value is 12, and its address is second row, fifth column. Pointer p points to n's location, which is second row, fifth column. Pointer p's value is not 12, but rather, second row, fifth column. This is an important distinction.

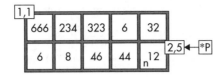

Figure 2-3   Pointers as cubbyholes

You indicate pointers using the asterisk (*). Pointers point to a location in memory of another variable. The ampersand (&) indicates a variable's address in memory.

Try This   Using Pointers

1. Create a new C command-line application, and name the application **Using Pointers**.

2. Modify main.c file so that it appears like Listing 2-13.

3. Select the project in the pull-down and click the Run button.

Listing 2-13   C program illustrating pointers

```
#include <stdio.h>
int main (int argc, const char * argv[]) {
    int anIntVal = 10;
    int *pavalue = & anIntVal;
    printf("address:%p value:%d\n", pavalue, *pavalue);
    return 0;
}
```

In this listing, anIntVal's value is 10, pavalue points to anIntVal's memory address, and the printf statement prints anIntVal's address followed by anIntVal's value; pavalue points to anIntVal's address while *pavalue is anIntVal's value.

NOTE

If you are following along in Xcode, realize your address values will be different from those listed in this chapter's example code results.

```
address:0xbffff628 value:10
```

4. Modify main so that the first two lines appear as follows:

```
//int avalue = 10;
int avalue;
```

(continued)

5. Add the following line to just before the function's return statement:

```
printf("value's actual value:%d\n", avalue);
```

6. Compile and run. Listing 2-14 contains the incorrect output.

Listing 2-14 Output from C command-line program

```
address:0xbfffff764 value:0
value's actual value:0
Program exited with status value:0.
```

Initializing a variable only reserves memory space; it does not assign the variable a value. When you refer to an uninitialized variable, you could get any result. You must initialize a variable with a value before using it.

7. Change the function so that anIntVal is initialized to 10 and then click Build And Go. The debugger console echoes 10, as expected.

Dereferencing a Pointer

You can also dereference a pointer by assigning the pointer's location a new value. You do this through what's called *dereferencing* the pointer. Consider the code in Listing 2-15.

Listing 2-15 Dereferencing a pointer

```
int a = 10;
int *b = &a;
*b = 52;
printf("value:%d value:%d",*b,a);
```

The third line sets the content of the memory at the address pointed to by the pointer b to the integer value 52. The address pointed to by pointer b happens to be the variable a, so changing the content changes a's value too, as it is the location pointed to by b. Running this code results in both values printing as 52. Note that a common error is to use an uninitialized pointer or a modified pointer to accidentally corrupt memory in an unintended location in your program (for instance, accidentally using b = 52 rather than *b = 52 would change the pointer and lead to corruption if the pointer were used again later).

Pointers and Arrays

One place where pointers are useful in C programming is arrays. A common technique is to iterate through an array using a pointer as an iterator to the array's elements. The following project illustrates this technique.

Try This Using an Array with Pointers

1. Create a new command-line application called **C Pointer Array**.

2. Modify main in main.m to appear like Listing 2-16.

Listing 2-16   A C program iterating through a pointer array

```
#include <stdio.h>
int main (int argc, const char * argv[]) {
    int values[10];
    int *iterator;
    for(int i = 0; i < 10; i++) {
        values[i] = i * 2;
        printf("value: %d ", values[i]);
    }
    iterator = values;
    for(int i = 0; i < 10; i++) {
        printf("value(%d):%d ", i, *(iterator+i));
    }
    *(iterator+4) = 999;
    printf("\nvalue of element at 4: %d", values[4]);
    return 0;
}
```

3. Select the project in the pull-down and click the Run button. Listing 2-17 is the debugger's output.

Listing 2-17   Debugger Console output

```
[Session started at 2008-09-05 21:57:35 -0400.]
value: 0 value: 2 value: 4 value: 6 value: 8 value: 10 value: 12
value:14 value: 16 value: 18 value(0):0 value(1):2 value(2):4
value(3):6
value(4):8 value(5):10 value(6):12 value(7):14 value(8):16 value(9):18
value of element at 4: 999
The Debugger has exited with status 0.
```

(continued)

What you did in this example was use a pointer to iterate through an array. The iterator points to the array's address. The iterator first points to the element at index zero. The iterator + 1 points to the element at the first position. And iterator + n points to the element at the *n*th position. As you iterate through the array's values, you can use the value at the address to which the iterator points.

Summary

This chapter did not provide enough detail for you to completely learn C. In fact, this chapter hardly scratched C's surface. But it did provide you with enough information to understand the rest of this book. You must know basic C to understand Objective-C and iOS programming. Hopefully, this chapter refreshed your memory enough to begin the next chapter. If you are familiar with Java's basic programming structures, C header files, and C pointers, you should have no trouble understanding the next two Objective-C chapters. If you are still uncertain, you can find many free online C tutorials using Google. But don't worry—C is kept to a minimum in this book.

NOTE

If new to programming and C programming, you might benefit from buying the book: *The C Programming Language, Second Edition,* by Brian W. Kernighan and Dennis M. Ritchie (Prentice Hall, 1988).

Chapter 3

Just Enough Objective-C: Part One

Key Skills & Concepts

- Understanding Objective-C classes and objects

- Understanding an interface and an implementation

- Understanding simple messaging

- Understanding alloc and init

- Managing memory using retain and release

- Managing memory using autorelease

iOS applications use Cocoa classes, and these classes use the Objective-C programming language. So you must know Objective-C if you wish to program iOS devices. At first glance, Objective-C's syntax might seem strange and difficult. But don't worry—the language is easy and its strangeness will give way to an elegance I'm sure you will appreciate. In this and the next chapter you learn enough Objective-C to begin iOS programming.

CAUTION

If coming from a .NET or Java background, pay particular attention to the sections on memory management. Unlike these languages, memory management is not automatic on iOS devices. You must manage memory manually.

Objective-C Classes and Objects

Objective-C classes are the same as classes in any other object-oriented programming language. A class encapsulates both state (properties) and behavior (methods), and forms an object-oriented program's basic building blocks. An object-oriented application functions by objects sending messages between each other. For instance, in a typical Java command-line application, you begin the program by calling a static method called main in a class. This main method instantiates one or more objects, and the application's remaining functionality consists of messages between those objects instantiated in the main method, as well as any objects they might in turn instantiate.

Class Interface and Implementation

Objective-C separates a class into an interface and an implementation. An *interface* declares instance variables and methods. It is a standard C header file and doesn't provide any method definitions. The *implementation* contains the method definitions for the class. It is a file with its own .m extension rather than a .c extension.

Try This   Generating an Objective-C Class' Interface and Implementation

1. Create a new View-based Application. Only this time, rather than selecting iPhone from the Product drop-down, select iPad. Name the project **ChapThree**.

2. In Groups & Files, right-click Classes and select New Group from the pop-up menu. Name the group **Objective-C**.

3. Right-click the newly created Objective-C folder and select New File from the pop-up menu. From the New File dialog, highlight Cocoa Touch and select Objective-C Class. Ensure the Subclass says NSObject (Figure 3-1). Click Next.

4. On the next dialog screen, name the class **Simple**.

   The template generates Simple for you, writing its interface in Simple.h (Listing 3-1) and its implementation in Simple.m (Listing 3-2).

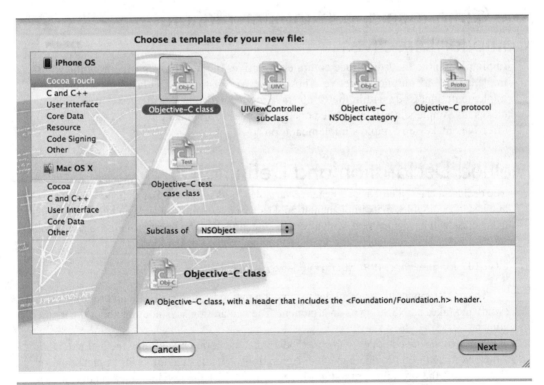

Figure 3-1   Selecting a new Objective-C class using Xcode's New File dialog

(continued)

Listing 3-1   Objective-C interface

```
#import <Foundation/Foundation.h>
@interface Simple : NSObject {
}
@end
```

Listing 3-2   Objective-C implementation

```
#import "Simple.h"
@implementation Simple
@end
```

The @interface and @implementation Compiler Directives

In Simple.h, note the @interface compiler directive. In the Simple.m file, note the @implementation compiler directive. These directives distinguish a class' interface from its implementation. Code within the @interface and @end compiler directives in Simple.h makes up Simple's interface, while code within the @implementation and @end compiler directives makes up Simple's implementation.

Method Declaration and Definition

You declare a class' methods and instance variables in its interface. You define a class' methods and instance variables in its implementation. Declaring a method means you tell the compiler that a class will have a method, with a certain signature, but you don't provide the actual code for the method. For instance, consider the following method declaration.

```
-(void) sayHello: (NSString*) name;
```

The declaration tells the compiler to expect a method called sayHello that returns nothing (void) and takes an NSString as an argument. The declaration says nothing about the method's content.

You provide the compiler with a method's implementation by defining the method. Defining a method means you provide a method declaration's actual behavior, or its implementation. For instance, the sayHello method in Listing 3-3 provides the sayHello method declaration's behavior.

Listing 3-3   A simple Objective-C method implementation

```
-(void) sayHello: (NSString*) name {
  NSMutableString *message = [[NSMutableString alloc]
        initWithString:@"Hello there "];
  [message appendString:name];
  NSLog(message);
  [message release];
}
```

Try This Adding SayHello to the Simple Class

1. Open the last section's project, ChapThree. Add the sayHello method from Listing 3-3
   to Simple.m (Listing 3-4). Don't forget to add the method's declaration to Simple.h
   (Listing 3-5).

Listing 3-4   Simple.m modified to declare sayHello

```
#import "Simple.h" @implementation Simple
-(void) sayHello: (NSString *) name {
NSMutableString *message = [[NSMutableString alloc] initWithString:
@"Hello there "];
  [message appendString:name];
  NSLog(message);
  [message release];
}
@end
```

Listing 3-5   Simple.h modified to declare sayHello

```
#import <Foundation/Foundation.h>
@interface Simple : NSObject {
}
-(void) sayHello: (NSString *) name;
@end
```

2. Open main.m in the Other Sources folder and import Simple. Then in main, create a
   Simple instance and call it the sayHello method (Listing 3-6).

(continued)

Listing 3-6   The file main.h modified to call the sayHello method

```
#import <UIKit/UIKit.h>
#import "Simple.h"
int main(int argc, char *argv[]) {
  NSAutoreleasePool * pool = [[NSAutoreleasePool alloc] init];
  Simple * mySimple = [[Simple alloc] init];
  [mySimple sayHello:@"James"];
  [mySimple release];
  int retVal = UIApplicationMain(argc, argv, nil, nil);
  [pool release];
  return retVal;
}
```

  3. Build and run the program, and the hello message will appear in the debugger console.

Interface Anatomy

A class' interface consists of import statements, a class declaration, any instance variables, and method signatures. Review Simple's interface in the Simple.h file. Objective-C classes import or include other libraries and headers just like C (just a reminder, always use import, as this assures you won't include the header file twice). The following line declares to the compiler an Objective-C class named Simple that extends NSObject:

```
@interface Simple : NSObject
```

   Opening and closing braces follow the class declaration. Instance variables go between these braces. Below the closing brace, you add class method declarations. Following any method declarations, the interface ends with the @end directive, which signifies the interface's end. Figure 3-2 summarizes an Objective-C interface's anatomy.

Implementation Anatomy

An interface is only half an Objective-C class, though. A class' implementation is as important as its interface. Review Simple's implementation in the Simple.m file. This file begins by importing the class' interface. Simple's implementation then begins with the @implementation compiler directive.

```
@implementation Simple
```

   Simple's implementation ends with the @end compiler directive. Method definitions go between the two directives. Figure 3-3 summarizes an Objective-C class implementation.

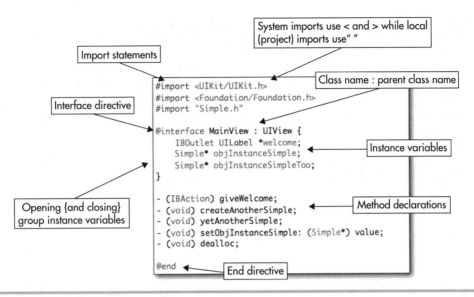

Figure 3-2 An Objective-C interface summary

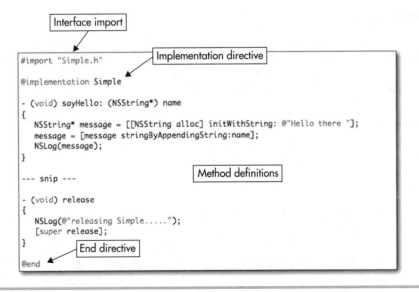

Figure 3-3 An Objective-C implementation summary

Public, Private, and Protected Instance Variables

Classes can set instance variables to be private, protected, and public. You use the compiler directives @private, @protected, and @public to declare instance variable visibility. The *private* directive ensures variables marked as private are only visible to the class that declares the instance variable. The *protected* directive ensures protected variables are only visible to the declaring class and its descendants. The *public* directive allows any class access to the public variables.

Consider the interface code snippet in Listing 3-7.

Listing 3-7   Public and private methods

```
@public
  NSString* groupName;
  int intGroupSize;
@private
  NSString* otherGroupName;
  int intOtherGroupSize;
```

In this interface declaration, the instance variables groupName and intGroupSize are public, while otherGroupName and intOtherGroupSize are private.

Understanding Simple Messaging

Objective-C methods look substantially different from Java methods. Although the syntax is confusing at first, it's not difficult once you become used to it. Note that you don't say that you "call a method" when using Objective-C. Instead, you "send a message to a receiver." For instance, using Java you might type the following:

```
objMyObject.getFooUsingID(33);
```

When describing this line, I write that I am calling objMyObject's getFoo method and passing the argument 33. In Objective-C, the same message appears as follows:

```
[objMyObject getFooUsingID : 33];
```

When describing this line, I write that I am sending a getFooUsingID message, passing the argument 33, and objMyObject is the receiver.

The difference between calling a method and sending a message isn't Objective-C's only difference from Java, C++, and other dot-notation languages. Objective-C uses what's called infix notation. Infix notation mixes operands and operators. You don't really need to fully understand infix notation, other than it means Objective-C looks substantially different from Java and C++. An Objective-C message begins with an opening square brace and ends with a closing square brace followed by a semicolon. The object's name follows the opening brace, followed by a space, followed by the message. Arguments passed to the message follow a colon.

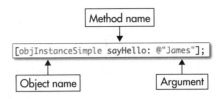

Figure 3-4   A simple Objective-C message

You can, of course, have multiple-argument methods, as you will see in the next chapter. For now, though, just consider single-argument methods. Figure 3-4 summarizes an Objective-C message with a single argument.

Using self in a Message

The term *self* refers to an object when sending a message, and it is also the receiver. For instance, you might make a mental note to yourself to pick up milk on the way home from work (Listing 3-8).

Listing 3-8   A method using the self keyword

```
-(void) goHome {
  Milk * myMilk = [self pickupMilk];
}
-(Milk*) pickupMilk {
  // pick up milk logic
}
```

Both methods are in the same object, and so the goHome method sends the message pickupMilk to itself, or self.

Nested Arguments

As when programming in Java, you can nest Objective-C messages. For instance, using Java, you might write the following:

```
objMyObject.getFoo(objMyFooIdentifier.getID());
```

In Objective-C, you would write the same statement as follows:

```
[objMyObject getFoo: [objMyFooIdentifier getID]];
```

Using Java, you might nest an object's constructor in another method.

```
objTester.testFubar(new Fubar(33));
```

In Objective-C, you can also nest object constructors in other methods.

```
[objTester testFubar[[Fubar alloc] initWithInteger : 33]]];
```

In this method, a new Fubar instance is first allocated and then initialized with 33, and the resulting object reference is sent as an argument to the testFubar message.

Class and Instance Methods

As discussed earlier, you declare methods in a class' interface and define methods in a class' implementation. Just as in C, a method declaration consists solely of the method's signature, while the definition is the method's actual implementation. In both files, there are two method types: instance and class methods. *Instance* methods begin with a minus sign, while *class* methods begin with a plus sign. A class method is similar to a Java static method, meaning you don't need to create a class instance to use the method. For instance, the following is an instance method.

```
-(void) sayHello: (NSString*) name
```

Using the method requires creating a class instance first. Although not required, you should also initialize the class. Remember, all classes extend NSObject, which has an init method, so every Objective-C class is guaranteed to implement init.

```
Simple *objSimple = [[Simple alloc] init];
[objSimple sayHello:@"James"];
```

Now consider class methods. Class methods begin with a plus sign.

```
+ (void) sayGoodBye;
```

A class method doesn't require creating a class instance before using the method. For instance, when first allocating space for an object instance, you call a class' alloc method. If the class doesn't implement the alloc method, the runtime traverses up the class' inheritance hierarchy until it finds an alloc method or it reaches NSObject's alloc method and calls it.

```
Simple *mySimple = [Simple alloc];
[mySimple init];
```

The alloc method is a class method example. You don't instantiate a class instance before calling alloc; rather, you call alloc directly using the class. You create and use class methods just like Java static methods. And Objective-C class methods have the same restrictions as Java static methods. You can't reference that class' instance variables from a static method, as the instance variables haven't been initialized. You also can't refer to other instance methods from the same class as the class method. Remember, as with a Java static method, you are using an uninitialized class, not an initialized object. If your class method relies upon a class being initialized, runtime errors will result.

Try This   Adding sayGoodBye as a Class Method

1. Open the last example's project in Xcode. Open Simple.h and add the sayGoodBye method declaration to it (Listing 3-9). Be certain to use a + and not a − in the method's signature.

Listing 3-9   Simple.h modified to include sayGoodBye declaration

```
#import <Foundation/Foundation.h>
@interface Simple : NSObject {
}
+ (void) sayGoodBye;
-(void) sayHello: (NSString *) name;
@end
```

2. Add the method's definition to Simple.m (Listing 3-10).

Listing 3-10   Simple.m modified to include sayGoodBye definition

```
#import "Simple.h"
@implementation Simple
+ (void) sayGoodBye {
  NSLog(@"Goodbye...");
}
-(void) sayHello: (NSString *) name {
  NSMutableString *message =
    [[NSMutableString alloc]initWithString:@"Hello there"];
  [message appendString:name];
  NSLog(message);
  [message release];
}
@end
```

(continued)

3. Have main.m call the sayGoodBye method as in Listing 3-11.

Listing 3-11 The main.h file modified to call sayGoodBye

```
int main(int argc, char *argv[]) {
  NSAutoreleasePool * pool = [[NSAutoreleasePool alloc] init];
  Simple * mySimple = [[Simple alloc] init];
  [mySimple sayHello:@"James"];
  [mySimple release];
  [Simple sayGoodBye];
  int retVal = UIApplicationMain(argc, argv, nil, nil);
  [pool release];
  return retVal;
}
```

4. Build and run the application, and "Goodbye..." will be written to the debugger console (Listing 3-12).

Listing 3-12 Debugger console after running ChapThree

```
[Session started at 2010-12-17 21:33:38 -0500.]
2010-12-17 21:33:40.498 ChapThree[851:20b] Hello there James
2010-12-17 21:33:40.501 ChapThree[851:20b] Goodbye...
```

The alloc and init Methods

The alloc method is how you create class instances for all Objective-C classes. This method allocates memory space for the new object instance. It is inherited from the NSObject class, so you don't really need to implement this method yourself.

The init method is how you initialize a class once allocated. Unlike the class method alloc, the init method is an instance method. The init method is also a method in NSObject. If a class has no specific initialization requirements, you don't need to override init, nor are you required to call it when instantiating a class. However, if you have specific initialization requirements, you should override this method. Good programming practice, though, is to always call init, usually on the same line as the allocation.

The init method returns an id. An id is an Objective-C type that is a pointer to the object instance's address. The id is weakly typed, though, and the runtime treats all ids the same. Overriding an init method should always call the class parent's init method (Listing 3-13).

Listing 3-13 A simple init implementation

```
-(id) init {
  if (self = [super init]){
    magicNumber = 5;
  }
  return self;
}
```

In Listing 3-13, the method assigns itself to its parent's id. If the parent's init method fails, it returns a nil value and the if statement fails. If it succeeds, the evaluation is true and the instance variable, magicNumber, is set to five. The init method ends by returning itself.

You can also initialize an object by passing arguments. By convention, initialization methods that take arguments are named init, followed by the data type of the argument. For instance, you could modify the init method in Listing 3-13 to Listing 3-14 if you wanted to initialize with an integer passed as a parameter.

Listing 3-14 A simple init method

```
-(id) initWithInt : (int) value {
  if (self = [super init]) {
    magicNumber = value;
  }
  return self;
}
```

Managing Memory Using Retain and Release

Unlike in Java or C#, when programming for iOS, you manage memory manually; there is no garbage collection on iOS devices. Although as of OS X 10.5, Cocoa includes an option to use automatic garbage collection, this option is not available on iOS devices. Table 3-1 summarizes Objective-C's memory management methods.

Objective-C uses reference counts to determine if memory should be released or retained. When you create a class instance, the runtime allocates memory for the object and assigns that object a reference count of one. For instance, suppose you had a class named Simple. You first allocate space for it using NSObject's alloc method.

```
Simple *objSimple = [[Simple alloc] init];
```

You then use the object.

```
[objSimple sayHello:@"James"];
```

When finished, you call its release method. If no release method is found, the runtime moves up the classes' inheritance hierarchy until it finds a release implementation.

Memory-Related Method	Description
+alloc	Allocate memory for new object and assign the object reference count of one.
−autorelease	Add receiver to autorelease pool.
−dealloc	Deallocate memory for an object with zero reference count.
−release	Decrease object's reference count by one.
−retain	Increase object's reference count by one. Returns the object as an id.
−copy	See documentation.

Table 3-1   NSObject Memory Management–Related Methods

As all classes extend NSObject, if no release instance is found, the runtime calls NSObject's release method.

```
[objSimple release];
```

When an object's reference count reaches zero, the runtime calls the object's dealloc method to deallocate the object. As with release, if the runtime doesn't find a dealloc method, it moves up the inheritance hierarchy until it finds one. If no dealloc method is found, the runtime calls NSObject's dealloc method and the object is deallocated so that the memory can be reclaimed.

You've already seen how alloc, release, and dealloc work; you allocate memory for an object and assign it a reference count of one using the alloc method, and you decrement the reference count by one when calling release. When an object's reference count reaches zero, the program calls NSObject's dealloc method.

The retain method increments an object's reference by one and returns the object reference as an id. Unlike Java, this referencing isn't automatic; you must explicitly call retain to increase an object's reference count. For instance, consider the following Objective-C code (Listing 3-15).

Listing 3-15   Using retain

```
Simple *objSimple = [[Simple alloc] init];
Simple *objSimpleTwo = objSimple;
NSLog(@"retaincount: %d", [objSimple retainCount]);
[objSimple release];
//the next line causes an error because objSimpleTwo is released
[objSimpleTwo sayHello:@"James"];
```

NOTE

Typically, there is no reason to call retainCount. In this chapter, I use retainCount to illustrate Objective-C memory management.

The first line allocates objSimple, and the runtime assigns the object a reference count of one. The second statement creates a new pointer to the objSimple object; both objSimple and objSimpleTwo point to the same physical object in memory. But because the code doesn't call retain, the physical object's reference count is not incremented. When the object is then released, the reference count is decremented by one and the reference count for the object becomes zero. The object is deallocated, so the next line fails, as objSimpleTwo is pointing to deallocated memory space.

Instead, the code should have explicitly retained objSimpleTwo.

```
[objSimpleTwo retain];
```

Retaining objSimpleTwo would have incremented the object's reference count by one, bringing it to two. Then, when objSimple was released, the object's reference count would still be one and the object would not be deallocated. The subsequent call to sayHello would work just fine, as the object that objSimpleTwo pointed to would still exist. Note, this is a somewhat unrealistic example, as you will never write code like Listing 3-15, but it illustrates retain and release.

You can override the NSObject's retain, release, dealloc, and alloc methods. But if you do, be certain to call the object's super method version. The method call for these methods must make it up the inheritance hierarchy to NSObject for memory management to function correctly.

Try This Using Manual Memory Management

1. Open the previous Try This project and implement dealloc, retain, release, and alloc in Simple.m (Listing 3-16). Note that retain returns an id, and that all these methods are declared in NSObject and don't require you to add their signatures to Simple.h.

Listing 3-16   Simple.m modified to include memory management methods

```
#import "Simple.h" @implementation Simple
+ (void) sayGoodBye {
  NSLog(@"Goodbye...");
}
-(void) sayHello: (NSString *) name {
  NSMutableString *message = [[NSMutableString alloc]
        initWithString:@"Hello there"];
  [message appendString:name];
  NSLog(message); [message release];
}
-(void) dealloc {
  NSLog(@"deallocating Simple....");
  [super dealloc];
}
```

(continued)

```
-(id) retain {
  NSLog(@"retaining Simple.....");
  return [super retain];
}
-(void) release {
  NSLog(@"releasing Simple.....");
  [super release];
}
+(id) alloc {
  NSLog(@"allocating Simple....");
  return [super alloc];
}
@end
```

2. Modify main.m to write log statements of the Simple's retainCount (Listing 3-17).

Listing 3-17   The main.h file modified to include retainCount logging

```
#import <UIKit/UIKit.h>
#import "Simple.h"
int main(int argc, char *argv[]) {
  NSAutoreleasePool * pool = [[NSAutoreleasePool alloc] init];
Simple * mySimple = [[Simple alloc] init];
  NSLog(@"retainCount: %d", [mySimple retainCount]);
  [mySimple sayHello:@"James"];
  [mySimple release];
  [Simple sayGoodBye];
  int retVal = UIApplicationMain(argc, argv, nil, nil);
  [pool release];
  return retVal;
}
```

3. Build and run the application. The debugger includes the logging added in Listing 3-16 (Listing 3-18).

Listing 3-18   Debugger console echoing memory management logging

```
[Session started at 2010-12-17 22:30:02 -0500.] 2010-12-17 22:30:03.894
ChapThree[1062:20b] allocating Simple.... 2010-12-17 22:30:03.895
ChapThree[1062:20b] retaincount: 1 2010-12-17 22:30:03.899
ChapThree[1062:20b] Hello there James 2010-12-17 22:30:03.903
ChapThree[1062:20b] releasing Simple..... 2010-12-17 22:30:03.904
ChapThree[1062:20b] deallocating Simple.... 2010-12-17 22:30:03.904
ChapThree[1062:20b] Goodbye...
```

In main.m, the main method first allocates a new Simple instance and assigns the pointer (mySimple) to point to the newly allocated and initialized object.

```
Simple *mySimple = [[Simple alloc] init];
```

The reference count to the object mySimple points to is one, and the debug statement in Listing 3-17 prints a retainCount of one.

Instance Variables and Memory

In Chapter 4, you will learn about properties. You should use them and their accessor methods. If you do, you avoid this section's complications. But you should still understand a little about instance variables and how they are handled in memory. Suppose you have an instance variable, personName, you wish to set, as in Listing 3-19.

Listing 3-19   An instance variable in Simple.h

```
#import <Foundation/Foundation.h>
@interface Simple : NSObject {
  NSString * personName;
}
-(void) sayGoodBye;
-(void) sayName;
-(void) sayHello: (NSString *) name;
@end
```

Now suppose you modified sayHello to set personName, as in Listing 3-20. You must retain the variable; otherwise, when the caller of sayHello releases the string, it will go away and the personName instance variable will be pointing to unallocated memory.

Listing 3-20   Retaining an instance variable

```
-(void) sayHello: (NSString*) name {
  NSMutableString *message = [[NSMutableString alloc]
        initWithString:@"Hello there "];
  [message appendString:name];
  NSLog(message);
  personName = [name retain];
  [message release];
}
```

Note that by retaining name, you are increasing its reference count by one, returning it, and then setting personName to it. This ensures that the string pointed to by personName will not be deallocated until Simple is finished with it. Not retaining a variable when assigning it to another variable, as in Listing 3-20, is a good example of the type of problem you might encounter when not using properties. When the name variable pointer is passed to sayHello, assume there is only one other pointer pointing to name (a retainCount of one). Then, after assigning personName to name, the retainCount remains one. The personName pointer is now at the mercy of the pointer that originally pointed to name outside the sayHello method. When the pointer external to Simple releases the object name points to, the object is deallocated. So the personName pointer now points to deallocated memory space and an error occurs. To correct this problem, you call retain on the instance variable as in Listing 3-20. Anytime you set an instance variable, you should retain it. That way, you ensure that it will not reach a zero reference count while the instance variable still points to the object. Of course, the better solution is to always use accessor methods combined with properties. You learn about accessor methods and properties in the next chapter.

NOTE
You could have written the code in Listing 3-20 using one of NSString's class methods. But using stringWithString would not illustrate using retain.

```
personName = [NSString stringWithString:name];
```

Managing Memory Using Autorelease

Managing reference counts manually is tiresome and error-prone. NSObject's autorelease method manages an object's reference count for you. The autorelease method uses what's called a release pool to manage an object's references. Refer to Listing 3-17 and note that this method's first step is allocating an NSAutoreleasePool. Its second-to-last step is releasing that pool. Calling autorelease adds the object to the pool, and the pool retains the object for you. Consider the sayHelloTom method in Listing 3-21.

Listing 3-21   A method using autorelease

```
-(void) sayHelloTom {
  Simple *objSimple = [[[Simple alloc] init] autorelease];
  [objSimple sayHello:@"Tom"];
}
```

The method allocates a Simple instance and then calls autorelease, assigning objSimple to the autorelease pool. When the method finishes executing, the autorelease pool is deallocated and the Simple instance is subsequently released.

NOTE

The iOS operating system creates an autorelease pool for every event loop and releases it when the loop completes.

Using autorelease and accepting the default autorelease pools makes memory management easy. However, the problem is that there's a penalty: The objects persist for the release pool's lifetime. There is one solution, and that is to manage the NSAutoReleasePool yourself. For instance, you could modify Listing 3-22 to manage its own autorelease pool.

Listing 3-22   The sayHelloTom method managing its own autorelease pool

```
-(void) sayHelloTom {
  NSAutoreleasePool *pool = [[NSAutoreleasePool alloc] init];
  Simple *objSimple = [[[Simple alloc] autorelease] init];
  [objSimple sayHello:@"Tom"];
  [pool release];
}
```

When the pool is released and deallocated, the pool releases the object pointed to by objSimple. When the physical object pointed to by objSimple is released, the reference count is zero, so the runtime deallocates the object. You should note, though, that in this example, the results are exactly the same as if you had used the default autorelease pool. Unless creating many objects, it's probably best to stick to the default NSAutoreleasePool rather than trying to manage it yourself. However, given the constrained resources of many iOS devices, the preferred way to manage memory is to do it manually.

Summary

You're not finished with Objective-C yet. We still haven't learned about properties, multiple-argument messages, Objective-C's dynamic binding and typing, inheritance, composition, categories, protocols, or handling exceptions. While this might seem like a lot that you still need to learn, Objective-C is a full-featured object-oriented language and you will eventually want to take advantage of all of its capabilities while developing for iOS. Despite the length of this and the next chapter, realize you are only scratching the surface of Objective-C.

Chapter 4

Just Enough Objective-C: Part Two

Key Skills & Concepts

- Using properties

- Understanding multiple-argument messages

- Understanding the id variable type, dynamic typing, and dynamic binding

- Understanding inheritance

- Using composition

- Using categories

- Using protocols

- Handling exceptions

In the last chapter, you learned about Objective-C classes, simple message syntax, and managing memory. In this chapter, you learn about properties, multiple-argument messages, dynamic binding, polymorphism, the id type, and inheritance. You also learn about categories and protocols. And finally, you learn about Objective-C exception handling.

Properties

In the last chapter, you had to manage memory when setting an object's instance variable. For instance, if using retain and release, you would write a setter method that explicitly retained the passed value (Listings 4-1 and 4-2).

Listing 4-1   Writing a method that sets an instance variable (interface)

```
@interface MyClass : NSObject {
  Simple * objInstanceSimple;
}
-(void) setObjInstanceSimple: (Simple*) newValue;
@end
```

Listing 4-2   Writing a method that sets an instance variable (implementation)

```
@implementation MyClass
-(void) setObjInstanceSimple: (Simple*) newValue {
  [newValue retain];
```

```
    [objInstanceSimple release];
    objInstanceSimple = newValue;
}
@end
```

Remember, when using Objective-C objects, you are simply manipulating pointers. Pointers point to memory space. When changing an instance variable whose type is inherited from NSObject, you are changing the memory space it points to. Changing the memory space a variable points to without using retain or release almost always results in errors. In Listing 4-2, you explicitly set MyClass's instance variable, objInstanceSimple. The method first retains newValue. The method does this to prevent newValue from being deallocated, should the object later release the newValue. The method then releases objInstanceSimple. It does this to prevent a memory leak when changing objInstanceSimple to point to the memory space pointed to by newValue. After releasing objInstanceSimple, it changes objInstanceSimple to point to newValue.

Managing memory when getting and setting an object's instance variables is a pain. Objective-C 2.0 makes instance variables easier by using *properties*. Properties are shortcuts for creating instance variable accessors. You create properties using compiler directives. The @property directive declares a property, @synthesize tells the compiler to generate accessors, and @dynamic tells the compiler you will provide the accessor methods. A property directive also has one or more attributes. Table 4-1 summarizes the most common attributes.

The readonly attribute indicates the property is read-only, and the synthesize directive only creates a getter for the property. Retain instructs the compiler to create the setter so that it retains the object.

Property Attribute	Description
assign	Setter assigns instance variable to object.
copy	Setter copies object to instance variable.
nonatomic	Setter and getter won't guarantee a complete, viable value is returned in a threaded environment. Faster than atomic and generally what you want to use when programming for iOS.
readonly	Instance variable is read-only; cannot set its value.
readwrite	Instance variable has a getter and setter (default).
retain	Setter assigns instance variable to object and calls retain.

Table 4-1   Property Attributes Covered in This Chapter

Retain

When using a property with retain and managing memory yourself, you must release the temporary variable. For instance, suppose you set an instance variable called objSimpleRetain and this instance variable's property had a retain attribute.

```
@property(retain) Simple objSimpleRetain;
```

When setting this property, you must release whatever temporary instance you might create. Consider the following method that sets objSimpleRetain.

```
-(IBAction)giveWelcome {
  Simple* temp1 = [Simple alloc];
  self.objSimpleRetain = temp1;
  [objSimpleRetain sayHello:@"Mike"];
  NSLog(@"retaincount (mike): %d", [objSimpleRetain retainCount]);
  [temp1 release];
}
```

The temp1 reference is released at the method's end. If you ran the giveWelcome method, NSLog would print two as the retain count. The retain count of two is because the method first allocates temp1, which sets the object's retain count to one, and then the method sets the property; because the property specified retain, the object's retain count becomes two. Finally, the method releases temp1 and the retain count returns to one.

Note that you could have just as easily used autorelease and let the runtime release the temporary object at the event loop's end by writing the method as follows:

```
-(IBAction)giveWelcome {
  Simple* temp1 = [[Simple alloc] autorelease];
  self.objSimpleRetain = temp1;
  [objSimpleRetain sayHello:@"Mike"];
  NSLog(@"retaincount (mike): %d", [objSimpleRetain retainCount]);
}
```

Assign

You can also specify a property use assignment by using the assign attribute.

```
@property(assign) Simple objSimple;
```

Specifying assign is equivalent to simply assigning a pointer to an object without increasing its retain count. You must take care to not call autorelease or release a temporary object, as the assigned property simple points to the temporary object. I generally avoid using assign for objects.

Where assign is appropriate is for creating primitive properties. For instance, you might make an integer a property of a class. An integer is a primitive, and so you assign values to the property; you do not assign a pointer to the integer.

```
@property (assign) int myInteger;
```

Copy

Sometimes you might wish to obtain an independent object copy. You accomplish this using the copy attribute. When you use the copy attribute, the setter creates a new object and the original object is duplicated. This property is an independent object, not related to the original. There are two copy types: shallow and deep.

A *shallow* copy is when you only duplicate an object's references to its instance variables, while a *deep* copy is when you make a copy of those instance variables as well. Making a shallow copy is easy—a deep copy, not so easy.

To copy your own custom class, your class must implement the NSCopying protocol. You learn more about protocols later; a comprehensive discussion on writing your own class that implements the NSCopying protocol is beyond this chapter's scope and would needlessly complicate it. However, in Chapter 15, this book does briefly discuss the NSCopying protocol. Look up the NSCopying online documentation for more information.

However, copying a Cocoa class that already implements the NSCopying protocol is not beyond this chapter's scope. For instance, copying an independent string seems a reasonable enough requirement. Consider the class, Foo, in Listings 4-3 and 4-4, and a method that uses Foo (Listing 4-5).

Listing 4-3   Foo's interface

```
#import <Foundation/Foundation.h>
@interface Foo : NSObject {
  NSMutableString * myString;
}
@property(copy) NSMutableString *myString;
@end
```

Listing 4-4   Foo's implementation

```
#import "Foo.h"
@implementation Foo
@synthesize myString;
@end
```

Listing 4-5   A method that uses Foo

```
-(IBAction)giveWelcome {
  Foo * myFoo = [[Foo alloc] autorelease];
  NSMutableString* message = [[[NSMutableString alloc]
        initWithString: @"A copied string."] autorelease];
  myFoo.myString = message;
  [message appendString:@" More added to end of string."];
  NSLog(myFoo.myString);
}
```

The giveWelcome method creates a Foo instance (myFoo), creates a new string (message), and then sets myFoo's myString property to message. Because Foo's interface declared that myString uses copy, myFoo creates a copy of the new string when giveWelcome sets myString. When giveWelcome changes the message string, myFoo.myString remains the same value. Had you used retain or assign, the myFoo.myString's value would have changed as well.

Releasing Properties

Remember, every class you define should ultimately inherit from the NSObject class. The NSObject class contains a dealloc method. You use this method to release any instance variables and perform other cleanup tasks. When you declare properties in your class, you should always override this method by declaring your own dealloc method in your class. You will see this over and over again in the remainder of this book. In fact, to avoid memory leaks, remember this one rule: when using properties with the attributes nonatomic and retain, always release the properties in a dealloc method. For instance, in Listing 4-3 you declare a property named myString in the class Foo. To prevent a memory leak, Foo should have a dealloc method like Listing 4-6. As you progress through this book, the dealloc method should become second nature.

Listing 4-6   A simple dealloc method

```
-(void) dealloc {
  [myString release];
  [super dealloc];
}
```

NOTE

A common technique you will see used is to set a property to nil rather than releasing it. By setting the property to nil, the generated setter releases the previously allocated object instance and assigns the property to nil.

```
-(void) dealloc {
  self.myString = nil;
  [super dealloc];
}
```

Multiple-Argument Messages

As with Objective-C's other language constructs, multiple arguments will probably appear strange at first; however, once you become accustomed to them, you will find the syntax easier than Java, C++, and other dot-notation languages. Why are we so confident that you will love Objective-C's syntax for multiple arguments? In a word, readability. How many times have you seen code like this in a Java program?

```
objMyClass.startPlay("Adventures of Tom Thumb", 44,
    new CherryPie( ), "Jack Sprat", 77);
```

What exactly do the arguments mean? What are you sending to the startPlay method in objMyClass? Now consider the same method using Objective-C.

```
[objMyClass startPlay: @"Adventures of Tom Thumb" audienceMembers:44
    pie: [[CherryPie alloc] init] supportingActor:@"Jack Sprat"
    extrasNeeded:77];
```

You know exactly what the arguments sent to the method mean when using Objective-C. You are starting a play entitled "Adventures of Tom Thumb" that has 44 members in the audience, needs a cherry pie, has a supporting actor named Jack Sprat, and requires 77 extras.

The signature of the method called in the previous message has a syntax as follows:

```
-(void) startPlay: (NSString*) title audienceMembers: (int) value
    pie: (CherryPie*) pievalue supportingActor: (NSString*) actorvalue
    extrasNeeded: (int) extrasvalue;
```

The first argument is unnamed. The second and any further arguments are distinguished by a space followed by an argument name and colon, followed by the type in parentheses, followed by a parameter name to hold the value.

Now, here's the tricky part: When referring to a multiple-argument method, when calling the method, you refer to its named arguments. An argument's named argument is the name prior to the argument's data type. When using the argument within the method's implementation that the argument is a part of, you refer to the actual parameter name, not the argument name. So, for instance, in the startPlay method's implementation, you refer to title, value, pievalue, actorvalue, and extrasvalue. When calling the method, you refer to startPlay's named arguments: audienceMembers, pie, supportingActor, and extrasNeeded.

Try This   Creating a Simple Multiple-Argument Message

1. Create a new View-based Application. Name the project **SimpleMultiArg**.

2. Create a new NSObject subclass called Simple. Xcode generates the Simple.h and Simple.m files.

3. Open Simple.h and add a method declaration for startPlay (Listing 4-7).

(continued)

4. Open Simple.m and add the method's implementation (Listing 4-8).

5. Modify main.m to use Simple so that it appears like Listing 4-9.

6. Build and run the application. The Debugger Console should echo the same logging as Listing 4-10.

Listing 4-7   Simple's interface

```
#import <Foundation/Foundation.h>
@interface Simple : NSObject {
}
-(void) startPlay: (NSString*) title audienceMembers: (int)
value supportingActor: (NSString*) actorvalue extrasNeeded: (int)
extrasvalue;
@end
```

Listing 4-8   Simple's implementation

```
#import "Simple.h" @implementation Simple
-(void) startPlay: (NSString*) title audienceMembers: (int)
value supportingActor: (NSString*) actorvalue extrasNeeded: (int)
extrasvalue {
  NSLog(@"The title: %@", title);
  NSLog(@"Audience: %d", value);
  NSLog(@"Supporting actor: %@", actorvalue);
  NSLog(@"Extras needed: %d", extrasvalue);
}
@end
```

Listing 4-9   The main.m file modified to call Simple's startPlay method

```
#import <UIKit/UIKit.h> #import "Simple.h" int main(int argc, char
*argv[]) {
  NSAutoreleasePool * pool = [[NSAutoreleasePool alloc] init];
  Simple * objSimple = [[[Simple alloc] init] autorelease];
  [objSimple startPlay:@"Peter Pan" audienceMembers:500
    supportingActor:@"John Doe" extrasNeeded:55];
  int retVal = UIApplicationMain(argc, argv, nil, nil); [pool release];
  return retVal;
}
```

Listing 4-10	Debugger console output from running program

```
[Session started at 2010-12-29 18:49:55 -0500.]
2010-12-29 18:49:57.242 SimpleMultiArg[3132:20b] The title: Peter Pan
2010-12-29 18:49:57.243 SimpleMultiArg[3132:20b] Audience: 500
2010-12-29 18:49:57.244 SimpleMultiArg[3132:20b] Supporting actor:
John Doe 2010-12-29 18:49:57.245 SimpleMultiArg[3132:20b] Extras
needed: 55
```

NOTE

Here, startPlay is not the method's true name. In Objective-C, if a method has more than one parameter, the method's parameters (other than the first parameter) are part of the method's name. By this book's end, you should be familiar with this naming convention, as many of the methods you use will have multiple parameters. For instance, the startPlay method's name is actually the following:

```
startPlay:audienceMemebers:supportingActor:extrasNeeded:
```

Understanding the id Variable Type, Dynamic Typing, and Dynamic Binding

Objective-C is a dynamically typed language. Like Java, Objective-C permits object types to be determined dynamically at runtime rather than statically at compile time. Objective-C accomplishes this dynamic typing using the id data type.

The id Type

The id variable is a data type that represents an object's address. Because it's just an address, id can be any object, and because its type is a pointer, you don't need to include the * symbol, as the * symbol signifies a pointer to a specific type. For instance,

```
Foo * myFoo;
```

is a pointer to a Foo object. The compiler knows the pointer points to an address that contains an object of type Foo. However, the following,

```
id myFoo;
```

provides no such information to the compiler. The compiler only knows that myFoo is a pointer—the compiler knows where the pointer is pointing, but it doesn't know the data type of what myFoo points to. Only at runtime can it be determined what myFoo actually points to.

Dynamic Binding and Dynamic Typing

Objective-C accomplishes dynamic behavior using what's called dynamic typing and dynamic binding. Dynamic typing means that an object's type is not determined until runtime. For instance, a method that takes an id or an instance variable of type id has no way of knowing the object's type until the object is actually sent to the method or assigned to the instance variable.

Dynamic binding means that the method to invoke is not determined until runtime. And, unlike Java, Objective-C often doesn't require casting an object to its specific data type before being used.

Understanding Inheritance

You have already seen how Objective-C classes inherit from parent classes. In the interface, you specify that a class inherits from another class by placing the parent's name after the class's name and a colon.

```
@interface SimpleChild : Simple
```

Like any object-oriented language, Objective-C sets up classes to extend ancestors further up its hierarchy, with new methods and instance variables. Objective-C child classes can also redefine an ancestor's method. But, like Java (and unlike C++), Objective-C allows a class to inherit from only one parent; Objective-C doesn't support multiple inheritance.

Overriding Methods

Objective-C inheritance allows overriding methods, but not instance variables. You already saw an example of overriding methods when you overrode NSObject's dealloc, retain, and release methods in the class Foo.

```
#import "Foo.h"
@implementation Foo
-(void) dealloc {
  NSLog(@"deallocating Foo....");
  [super dealloc];
}
---snip--
@end
```

Instead of calling NSObject's methods, the runtime first calls Foo's. Since Foo's methods also call the parent's version of each method, the runtime looks up Foo's inheritance hierarchy for a version of the method until it finds NSObject's version.

NOTE

The term "super" refers to the class's parent. For instance, you might have a method called doIt that overrides the parent's doIt method. If your doIt method adds functionality rather than replacing the parent's functionality, you should call the parent doIt method as well.

```
-(void) doIt {
  [self doMyStuff];
  [super doIt];
}
```

Overloading Methods

Unlike Java, you cannot overload methods when using Objective-C. In Java you overload a method when you provide a method with the same name but a different signature in the same class. For instance, you could define two methods like the following. The two methods are treated as distinct methods by the Java runtime.

```
public void myMethod(String name);
public void myMethod(int age);
```

Not so when using Objective-C—when faced with two methods like these next ones, the compiler issues an error and will not compile your class.

```
-(void) myMethod: (NSString *) name;
-(void) myMethod: (int) age;
```

Because Objective-C does not support overloading, in the Objective-C programming community, it is common practice to add the argument's name to the method name.

```
-(void) myMethodString: (NSString *) name;
-(void) myMethodInt: (int) age;
```

Finally, you should note that for multiple argument methods, Objective-C's lack of method overloading is not problematic if any argument other than the first is different. Remember, a method's name includes its argument names. The following two method names are not the same:

```
-(void) myMethod: (int) age name: (NSString *) theName;
-(void) myMethod: (NSString *) name age: (int) theAge;
```

The compiler treats these methods as distinct because their names are actually myMethod: name: and myMethod:age: and not simply myMethod. Get used to this naming convention; it might seem strange at first, but it honestly makes Apple's documentation much easier to use.

Using Categories

Categories allow other classes to be extended without requiring inheritance. A category can contain both new methods and methods that override a class's methods. Categories are most useful when you find yourself in a situation where a supplied class doesn't provide functionality you want. To use a category, you create an interface and an implementation that specifies the class you wish to add a category to, followed by the category's name in parentheses. For instance, if you wished to add a category named FooCategory to NSString, you would type the following in the FooCategory.h file:

```
@interface NSString (FooCategory)
```

In the FooCategory.m file, you would type the following:

```
@implementation NSString (FooCategory)
```

followed by whatever methods you wished to add to NSString. Then, in the class you wished to use the category's methods, simply import the category and the runtime automatically resolves calls, such as,

```
[objMyString aMethodIAdded];
```

to the category rather than NSString.

NOTE
You can't add instance variables to a class using a category.

NOTE
In the category's header file, you must import the header file containing the class the category is extending.

Using Protocols

Protocols are similar to Java interfaces. In Java, an interface specifies the methods that a class that implements the interface must have. This is often called a contract. A class claiming to implement an interface should implement that contract—the class is promising it contains implementations for all of the interface's method declarations. So when you write a method like the following, you can rest assured the object has the called method implementation.

```
-(void) handleDoIt : (id <DoerProtocol>) objADoerImpl {
  [objADoerImpl doSomething];
}
```

The method handleDoIt takes an id specified to implement the DoerProtocol as an argument. Then when handleDoIt calls doSomething (a method declared in DoerProtocol), the runtime automatically, using dynamic binding, finds the correct object method implementation and calls it.

The code in the method that takes a protocol as an argument can then call protocol methods, knowing that the class that adopts the protocol has the specified methods. It's not until runtime that the actual class method is dynamically bound to the interface method.

Consider a method that takes a protocol as an argument. At compile time, the compiler only knows that the method takes an instance of the protocol. The compiler doesn't know the actual object's data type. If the method calls a protocol method, the compiler only assumes the method is declared by the protocol. The compiler doesn't know the method definition. At runtime, though, you pass an actual object to the method. When the object is passed to the method, it is dynamically typed. Then, when the method calls the protocol's method, the protocol's method is dynamically bound to the object's method. Thus, just like Java, Objective-C lets you specify generic methods that take a protocol as an argument and then let the runtime dynamically type and bind the object when running the application.

You define a protocol using the @protocol compiler directive combined with an @end directive. You define method declarations between the two directives. For instance, the following code defines a protocol named MyProtocol.

```
#import <Foundation/Foundation.h>
@protocol MyProtocol
-(NSNumber*) myMethod;
@end
```

You specify a class conforms to a protocol by adding the protocol's name in the class's declaration in its header file.

```
@interface Foo : NSObject <MyProtocol>
```

Specifying a protocol in a class's declaration guarantees that class implements the methods declared in the MyProtocol protocol.

Protocols allow adding optional method declarations in addition to required method declarations. You specify optional methods using the @optional compiler directive and required methods using the @required compiler directive. The default for methods is required. For instance, you could modify MyProtocol to have an optional myMethodTwo method.

```
#import <Foundation/Foundation.h>
@protocol MyProtocol
-(NSNumber*) myMethod;
@optional
-(void) myMethodTwo;
@end
```

Of course, having a Java programmer's perspective, we question the logic behind a contract with an optional method declaration—if you write code against a protocol, you want to be darn sure the method is going to be there.

You use the protocol similar to a class, only there is a subtle difference. When passing a class, you aren't actually passing the class, but rather a pointer. For instance, in the sayHello method, you are not passing a string called name as a parameter, but rather a pointer to a string.

```
-(void) sayHello: (NSString*) name;
```

But a protocol isn't a class; it's merely a header file with declarations (not definitions). Instead, either you must pass just the protocol itself (and the id is automatically understood) or you must pass an id.

Using a protocol rather than an id, you would specify something similar to the following in the interface of the class using your protocol. Suppose you wished to define a protocol for thermometers. There are many different ways a thermometer might be implemented. However, they all must tell the user his or her temperature. So if you created a Doctor class, although you know it should tell the patient his or her temperature, you do not know the specific type of thermometer the Doctor will use. So you use a protocol.

```
-(void) sayTemp : (<ThermProtocol>) objTherm;
```

You declare that a method takes a protocol as an argument. You don't specify the object's class, though. For instance, in the sayTemp method, you only know objTherm adopts the ThermProtocol. You do not know objTherm's actual class type.

When using an id—incidentally, this is the preferred syntax you see in Apple's documentation—you would specify something similar to the following:

```
-(void) sayTemp : (id <ThermProtocol>) objTherm;
```

In this example, you declare that sayTemp takes any class that implements the ThermProtocol. Actually, the first method signature without the id is also stating that sayTemp takes any class that implements the ThermProtocol; only the id is left implicit. Both method signatures work equally well, but by convention the second signature is what most programmers write.

Handling Exceptions

Objective-C's exception handling is similar to Java's and C++'s. Like Java and C++, Objective-C provides a try-catch block. Code that might raise an exception is wrapped in a try block, followed immediately by a catch block. The @try compiler directive defines a code block that might throw an exception. The @catch directive defines a code block that handles the immediately preceding try block. The @finally directive defines a code block that is always executed, regardless if an exception was thrown.

```
@try { } @catch(NSException *e) { } @finally { }
```

The most general exception is an NSException. All exceptions inherit from this Cocoa class. Like Java, you can throw an exception. In Objective-C, you use the @throw compiler directive.

NOTE

Apple recommends using the NSError Foundation Framework class rather than NSException for handling expected errors. See Apple's "Introduction to Error Handling Programming Guide for Cocoa" and also "Introduction to Exception Programming Topics for Cocoa" for more information on both classes. You will see instances of NSError and NSException scattered through this book's examples.

Summary

This chapter covered a lot of topics in not very many pages, so it's okay if you're slightly overwhelmed. If you understood half of this chapter's topics, you should do okay for the remainder of the book. If you wish, you might consider reading Apple's "Object-Oriented Programming with Objective-C," available from the iOS Developer's site. It's terse and provides a good introduction to object-oriented programming concepts using Objective-C. Because you already know Objective-C's basic principles, understanding that document should prove easier. Also, although produced by a different publisher, we also recommend the book *Programming in Objective-C 2.0* by Stephen G. Kochan (Addison-Wesley Professional, 2009). This book is clear, concise, and will teach you everything you could ever want to know about Objective-C. However, these two chapters should provide you with everything you need to know so that you can understand the remainder of this book and get started with your own iOS apps. James also has a separate Objective-C book entitled *Objective-C for iPhone Programmers: A Beginner's Guide* (McGraw-Hill, 2010).

For now, continue reading this book and then before pursuing advanced iOS topics, consider quickly working through a specific Objective-C book or at least keeping one handy for reference. Objective-C is not hard once you get past the different syntax. If you understand properties, protocols, and releasing instance variables in the dealloc method and also Objective-C's basic syntax, then you should feel comfortable moving to the next chapter. If you have a basic understanding, trust us when we say that, by this book's end, Objective-C's syntax will seem natural.

Chapter 5

Deploying to an iPhone, Debugging, and Testing

Key Skills & Concepts

- Registering for iOS developer membership

- Obtaining a certificate and provisioning

- Debugging an iPhone application

- Using zombies to debug

- Finding memory leaks

We won't be covering the iOS's UIKit or Cocoa Touch quite yet, but have patience, you begin these topics in the next chapter. Do not skip to the next chapter, though; this chapter is important. First, we'll get you set up with Apple's iOS Developer Program—a necessary step to install and test your app on any iOS device and submit your app to the iTunes App Store. You will also become familiar with many basic tasks required for compiling, debugging, and installing your app on an iOS device.

Throughout the next few chapters, we will talk about creating and running iPhone apps, but everything covered applies equally to any iOS device: all models of the iPhone as well as the iPod Touch and iPad. The deployment and debugging process and most of the UIKit functionality is the same for all iOS devices. In Chapter 19 we'll cover how to create a universal application that recognizes and takes advantage of the larger screen and additional features of the iPad. Where it's relevant, we'll also talk about the differences in the iPhone 4 like the higher resolution display and how to take advantage of them while still running correctly on other iOS devices.

This chapter is not comprehensive, but it does show you the debugger, Xcode 4's major features, and how to get your app on your device for debugging. This chapter covers two topics: installing applications on an iPhone or iPod touch and debugging iOS applications. Although you can perform basic debugging using the iPhone Simulator on your computer, truly debugging and testing your application requires installing and running it on an iPhone, iPod touch, or iPad. For instance, consider memory limitations. On your desktop computer, memory is virtually unlimited. Moreover, you probably have a dual-core, blazing-fast processor. Not so on your iPhone. The iPhone, iPod touch, and iPad all have fewer resources available than the iPhone Simulator, so you should test your applications on an actual device.

NOTE

You must have an iPhone Developer membership to complete some tasks in this chapter. If you do not, you can follow along, but we'd recommend getting membership as soon as possible.

This chapter briefly reviews obtaining membership to the iPhone Developer's program. It then covers obtaining a certificate and provisioning for your application. This chapter's coverage is not comprehensive, though, as the iPhone web site practically holds your hand through the certificate and provisioning process, and there is no need to duplicate its hand-holding here. After installing an application on an iPhone or iPod touch, you can truly debug and test the application. This chapter's second half introduces you to debugging in Xcode and testing for memory leaks using Instruments. As with the certificate and provisioning discussion, this chapter's debugging and testing coverage is not comprehensive, but it should be enough to make you comfortable with performing both tasks.

Ask the Expert

Q: **Why should I care about getting my app on my device right now? Shouldn't I wait until I know how to develop before I spend any money and sign up for iPhone Developer Program membership?**

A: No. You should obtain membership as soon as possible. Some code will work on the iPhone Simulator but not on an actual iOS device. Moreover, the converse is also true. Some hardware features of iOS devices like special gestures, geolocation, the accelerometer, etc. either can't be mimicked effectively in the simulator or won't behave the same as on an actual device. You'll also find it tremendously fulfilling to see your app running on your iPod or iPhone. And you can show off your development efforts to friends and family.

Installing Applications on an iPhone

Installing an application on an iPhone or iPod touch requires iPhone Developer membership. After you have a membership, installing an application is not difficult, as Apple's Developer Portal provides step-by-step instructions.

NOTE

Apple's "iPhone Development Guide," available online, provides a good introduction to installing applications on an iPhone or iPod touch. The examples here illustrate installing an application as of fall 2010. Undoubtedly there will be differences in the web application by the time you read this chapter. The process's fundamentals remain the same, though.

Membership

A basic membership in the iPhone Dev Center on the Developer Connection web site is a prerequisite to downloading the iPhone SDK, and you probably signed up for that while reading Chapter 1. However, to install applications and eventually sell applications on the App Store requires membership in the iPhone Developer Program. Apple offers two membership types: corporate and individual. You must apply, pay a $99 fee, and receive acceptance before becoming a full individual member. After becoming a member, you are granted access to the iPhone Developer Program's Portal. This site is where you obtain certificates, assign new devices, create application IDs, create provisioning profiles, and submit an app to the App Store for approval.

If you are not a registered, paid iPhone developer, you should become one now. Go to the iPhone Dev Center (http://developer.apple.com/programs/iphone/) for complete instructions. You cannot debug apps on your device until you register.

Certificates, Devices, Application IDs, and Provisioning

A certificate is the first thing that is required. Log in to your iPhone Developer Program account and click the iPhone Provisioning Portal link. The Provisioning Portal is where you'll create a signing certificate, register devices, create provisioning certificates, and more (Figure 5-1). Apple has provided lots of online help, including videos, for the Provisioning Profile. Take a little time to go through their documentation before proceeding.

You obtain your certificate by following the instructions on the How To tab in the portal's Certificates tab.

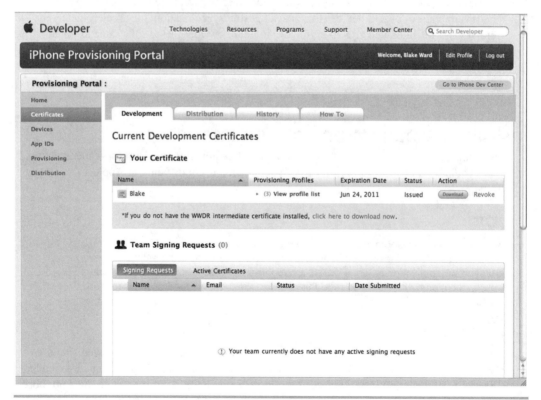

Figure 5-1 The Certificates tab

After obtaining the certificate, you must register the devices you wish to use for debugging. You'll need brief access to each of these devices to retrieve its unique device ID, but otherwise these could be iOS devices that belong to your friends or anyone you want to use for testing your new app (Figure 5-2). As with certificates, complete instructions are provided on the How To tab.

After registering your devices, the next step is to create an App ID for each of your applications. Any application you wish to test on a device must have an App ID (Figure 5-3). If an app will use Apple's Push Notifications or require In App purchasing, then it must have a unique App ID. For other applications you can create a wildcard App ID that ends with a * and use it for multiple apps.

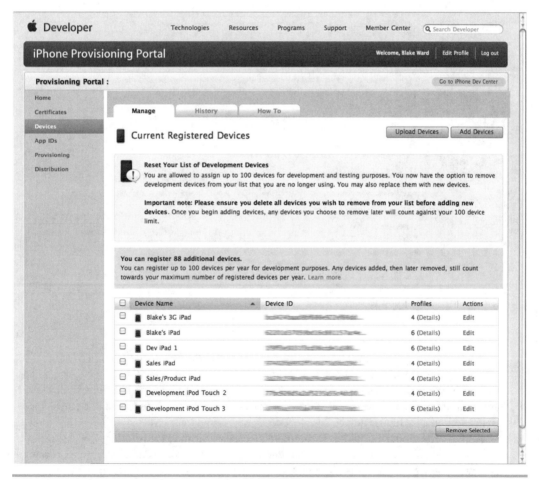

Figure 5-2   The Devices tab

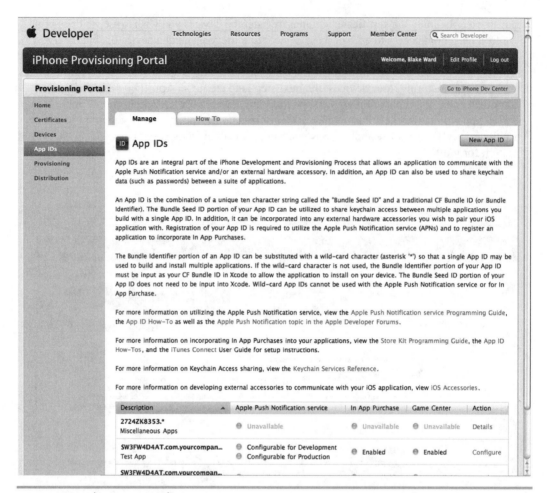

Figure 5-3 The App IDs tab

After obtaining the App ID, you must obtain a provisioning profile (Figure 5-4). A provisioning profile essentially bundles together a signing certificate, a set of devices, and an App ID. It will be installed on your device so that your app can be installed and tested. The provisioning profile will be installed on your device(s) and allows you to install a particular application on a particular device.

Apple's Developer Portal has a complete discussion of the provisioning process; the process is not difficult. What you can do when learning the process is to open two browser windows, one where you work through the steps and the other to skim the instructions as needed. In the following example, we take you through registering and installing a simple application on an iPhone.

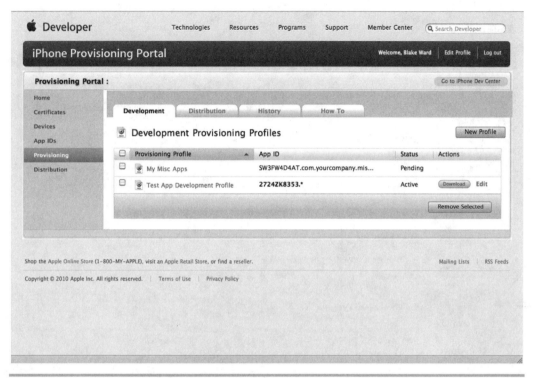

Figure 5-4 The Provisioning Profile tab

Try This Deploying an Application to iPhone

1. Create a new View-based Application named OnMyPhone. Keep track of the Company Identifier and Product Name so that you can create an App ID in the iPhone Provisioning Portal that matches.

2. Log in to the iPhone Developer Program Portal.

3. Click the Certificates tab. If you haven't installed your certificate, do so now. These steps assume a certificate (see Figure 5-1).

4. Click the Devices tab. If you haven't installed your devices, do so now. These steps assume a registered device (see Figure 5-2).

(continued)

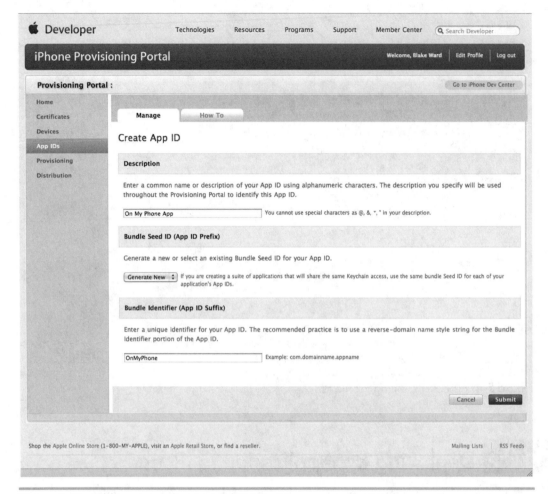

Figure 5-5 Adding an application to the App IDs

5. Click the App IDs tab and add the application (see Figure 5-3). Click the Add ID button on the page's right, and add the OnMyPhone application (Figure 5-5). You'll need to match the Bundle Identifier to what you used in Step 1.

6. Click the Provisioning tab and click the New Profile button on the page's right (see Figure 5-4). Complete the form; be certain you select the certificate and the device you want to provision (Figure 5-6).

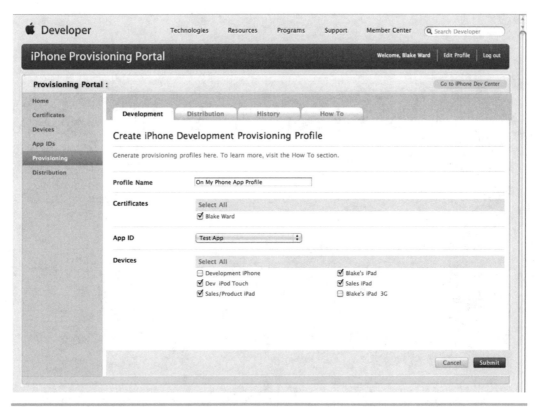

Figure 5-6   Provisioning the OnMyPhone application

7. Click Submit, and you return to the Provisioning page. The Provisioning Profile's status for My On My Phone Profile should say "Pending." Refresh the page until the status has an "Active" status. You are usually quickly granted a profile.

8. Download the profile by clicking the Download button next to the profile. The profile should have a title like "On_My_Phone_Profile.mobileprovision." Move it to a safe location.

9. Ensure your device is connected to your computer.

10. Return to Xcode. From the Window menu, select Organizer. If your device is attached, it should appear under DEVICES (Figure 5-7).

(continued)

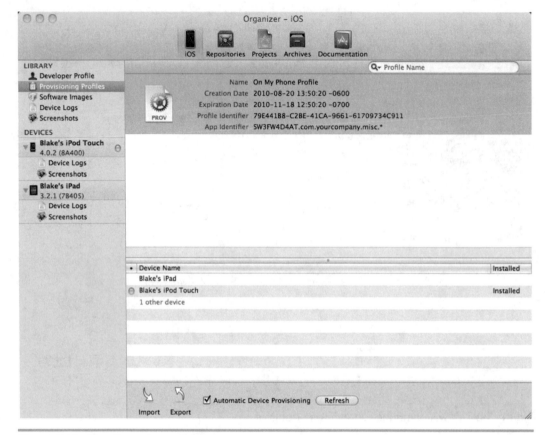

Figure 5-7 The Organizer window

11. Drag the provision file to the Provisioning list.

12. With your iOS device attached, Xcode will probably default to building/running on your device. If not, choose OnMyPhone(*your device name*) from the pull-down menu at the top of the project window instead of OnMyPhone (iPhone Simulator 4.2).

NOTE

With new projects, Xcode will default to building for the latest version of the SDK. This is almost always what you'll want. You should build your app for the latest SDK version but still specify in the build settings that it will run on a range of iOS versions older than the SDK if you don't absolutely require a new feature only available in the latest OS.

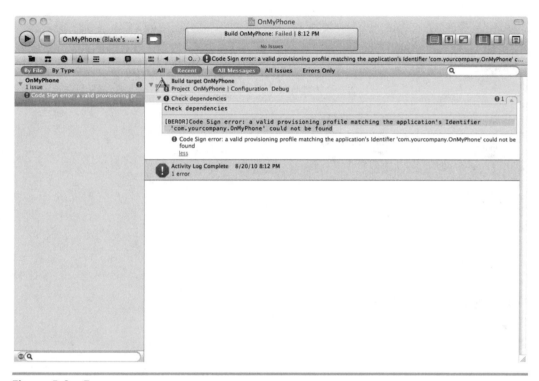

Figure 5-8   Error message

13. You might receive an error the first time. If the build fails, click the Issues button in the navigation pane (the one with an exclamation point) and then click the issue to see details (Figure 5-8). If the application identifier that you chose when you created the project doesn't match the one in the App ID of the provisioning profile, you'll get a signing error. If that happens, you can change the application's identifier by editing the file OnMyPhone-Info.plist (Figure 5-9) or you can go back to the Provisioning Portal and edit to create a new App ID or profile.

14. Close the Project Info window and open Info.plist. Change the bundle identifier to OnMyPhone.

15. Click Run, and the application should install and run on your device.

(continued)

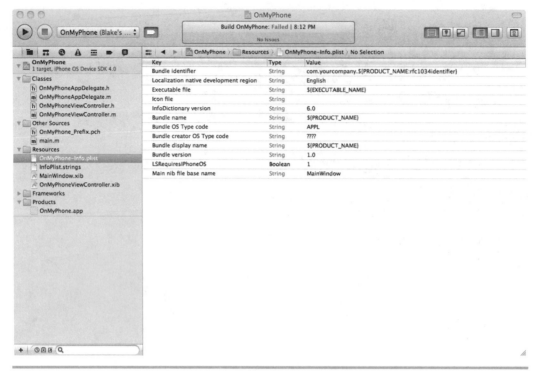

Figure 5-9 Changing the application bundle identifier

NOTE

For more information on provisioning, obtaining App IDs, and other program portal topics, refer to Apple's "iPhone Developer Program User Guide."

Debugging

Debugging and testing your application is paramount if you wish to provide users with a robust application. Xcode provides several excellent tools for debugging and testing your applications. In this section, you explore basic debugging using Xcode's graphical front end to the GNU debugger.

NOTE

For a more complete introduction to debugging, refer to Apple's "Xcode Debugging Guide," available online.

Using the Debugger

Xcode's visual debugger makes it easy to step through the execution of your app, examine variable values, etc. When you select View | Navigators | Debugger from the main menu, you'll see the debugger's panes (Figure 5-10). The left (navigation) pane shows the app's threads and the call stack for each. This tells you where your application is currently at in any point in the application's processing. The main pane on the right is the Text Editor pane, which displays the source code for the method, lets you set/remove breakpoints, and also permits you to view the values of variables by hovering over them. If you select View | Show Debugger Area from the main menu, you'll see the debugger area at the bottom of the window. This pane lets you control execution of your app, see/edit the current function's variable values, and view the contents of the console (log file).

Along the top of the debugger area, notice the buttons that control the debugger. From left to right, they are Continue, Step Over, Step Into, and Step Out. To the right of them you'll see the current stack. Table 5-1 summarizes each button's purpose.

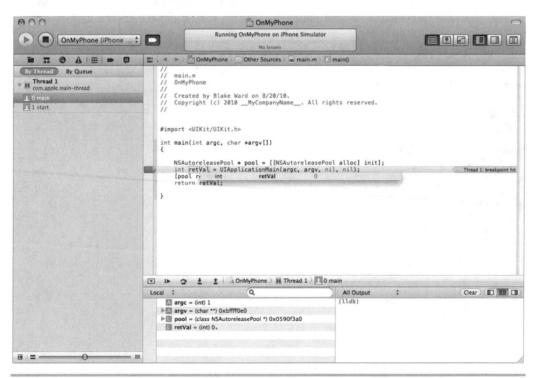

Figure 5-10   The debugger window

Button	Function
Pause/Continue	Pauses the application running in the debugger. Note, when the application is paused, this button says Continue. Continue "un-pauses" the application and resumes processing.
Step Over	Processes the next line of code. If the next line is a function call, it executes the function, proceeding to the next line.
Step Into	Processes the next line of code. If the line is a function call, it jumps to the code inside the function.
Step Out	Processes until the current function exits and stops in the function that called it.

Table 5-1   Debugger Area Buttons

Breakpoints

Breakpoints tell the debugger where to pause. If you set no breakpoints and then run the application in the debugger, nothing unusual happens, as you didn't tell the application to pause. There are several ways to set a breakpoint, but the easiest is to click in the Editor window's gutter next to the line of code you wish the debugger to stop at (Figure 5-11). If you wish to disable the

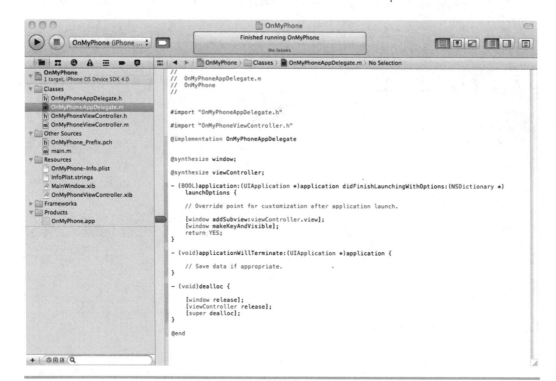

Figure 5-11   Setting a breakpoint

breakpoint, click it again and it turns light blue, indicating it is disabled. If you wish to remove the breakpoint, CTRL-click and select Remove Breakpoint from the pop-up menu. Alternatively, you can drag the breakpoint off the gutter to remove it. When you run the application in the debugger, it will pause processing at the first encountered breakpoint.

Stepping Through Code

When an application pauses at a breakpoint, you can step through your code's execution. Step Over moves directly to the next line, executing any function and stopping on the next line. Step Into also moves to the next line, but if the next line is a function, it jumps to the function's first line, and you can either step through the function line by line or step out of the function. If you choose Step Out, the debugger jumps to the first line after the function call.

Debugger Datatips

One thing you can do while debugging is obtain a variable's value and modify it while debugging. You can move your cursor over the variable in the source code, and a datatip appears with the variable and its value (Figure 5-12). You can even modify the value if desired.

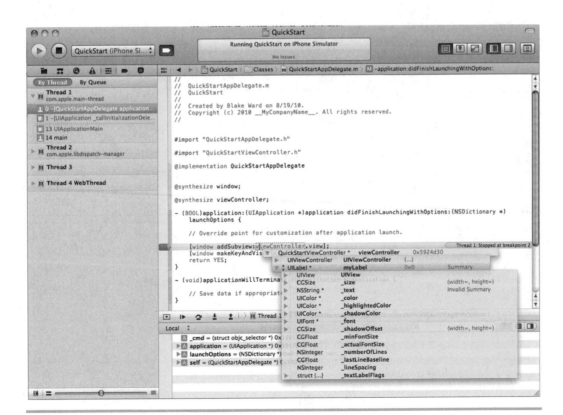

Figure 5-12   The Debugger datatips

Watchpoints

Sometimes you might be interested in having the program pause when a value changes. A *watchpoint* pauses the program when the watched item's value changes. Setting a watchpoint is tricky the first time, but then it becomes easy. To set a watchpoint, start the application in the debugger, and when the application pauses at a breakpoint, select the variable in the debugger window's variable list. Right-click it and select "Watch address of" from the shortcut menu (Figure 5-13). After you click Continue, if the value changes, the debugger notifies you and pauses (Figure 5-14). It's worth noting that watchpoints are not persisted across debugging sessions. Every application launch requires that you reestablish your watchpoints.

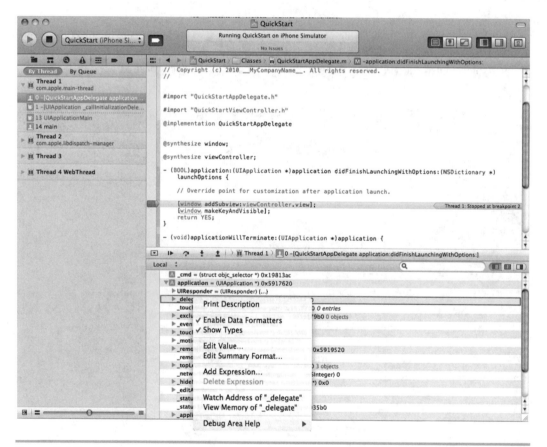

Figure 5-13   Setting a watchpoint

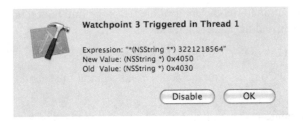

Figure 5-14   The debugger notifies you when a watchpoint's value changes.

Try This   Debugging an Application

1. Create a new Utility Application named Debug.

2. Select FlipsideView.xib to edit it in the Interface Builder. Select View | Utilities | Show Utilities if necessary and then click the Connections button (tiny arrow in a circle). Remove the connection between the view and the File's Owner by clicking the tiny X next to Files's Owner (Figure 5-15).

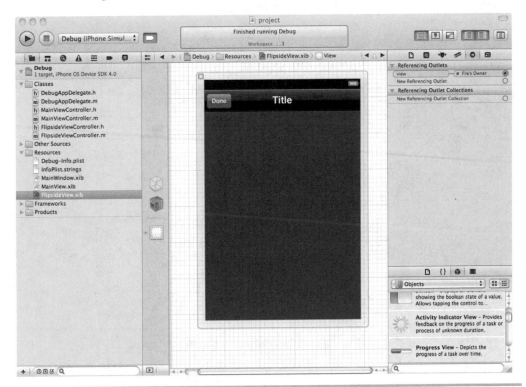

Figure 5-15   Remove the view from the view controller.

(continued)

3. Click the Run button to run the application. Click the Info button in the lower right of the simulator screen, and the application crashes.

4. Quit the iPhone Simulator and return to Xcode.

5. Open MainViewController.m and add a breakpoint at the second line in showInfo (Figure 5-16).

6. Click the Run button again to run the application. If the Debug Area is not visible, select View | Show Debugger Area.

7. Try stepping over the next few lines and the application crashes. You now know exactly which line in your code causes the application to crash. Something about presenting the FlipsideViewController caused the crash.

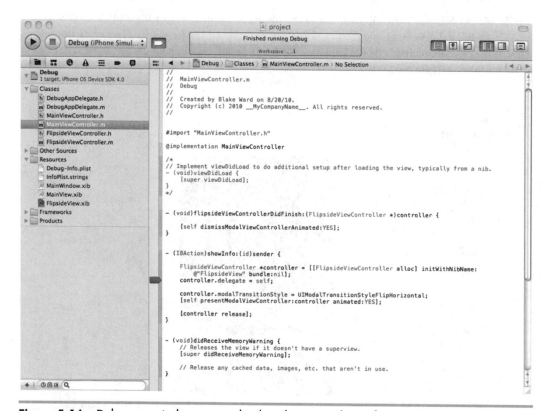

Figure 5-16 Debugger window stopped at breakpoint in showInfo

TIP

Forgetting to set a File's Owner view outlet is a common mistake.

8. Stop the iPhone Simulator and return to Xcode. Remove the breakpoint.

9. From the main menu, select View | Navigators | Breakpoint.

10. Click the + in the lower-left corner to create a new breakpoint and select Add Symbolic Breakpoint from the pop-up menu. Type **objc_exception_throw** for the symbol and click Done (Figure 5-17). You've now set a breakpoint in the code that's called at the moment the error occurs.

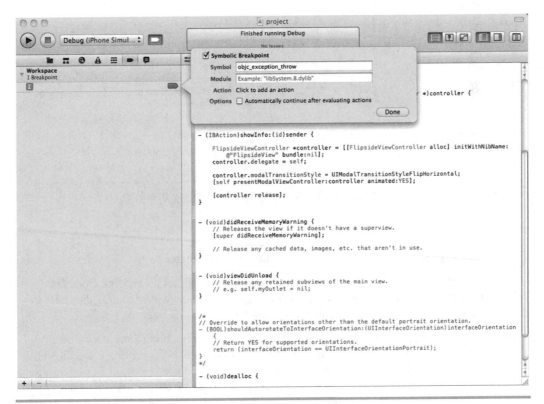

Figure 5-17   Adding objc_exception_throw as a breakpoint

(continued)

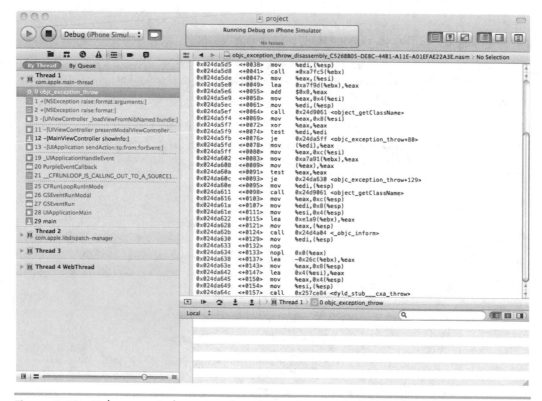

Figure 5-18 Debugger window paused at objc_exception_throw breakpoint

11. Click the Run button to launch the application in the debugger.

12. Click the Info button, and the application halts at the newly set breakpoint. Open the debugger area, if it is not already open (Figure 5-18). You may want to drag the slider in the lower left of the window to increase the detail in the stack trace.

13. Notice the upper-left window. This contains the stack listing. Follow the stack down several items, and you see the last thing to occur prior to an NSException is loading the view from the nib. Follow the stack to row 12, click it, and you see the line of code in the view controller that was executed in the right pane (Figure 5-19). So you know trying to load the view from the nib caused the crash.

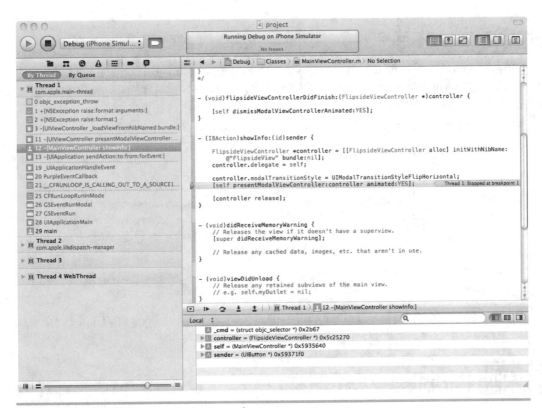

Figure 5-19 Following the stack trace takes you to an error's source.

NSZombieEnabled

When an object is deallocated, if there are any objects with a reference to the deallocated object, they are no longer referencing a valid object. Any messages sent to the deallocated object result in errors. Often, the error is rather cryptic. For instance, the following code fragment is obviously an error.

```
FooBar * myFooBar = [[FooBar alloc] init];
NSMutableArray *myArray = [[NSMutableArray alloc] initWithObjects:

    myFooBar,nil];
[myFooBar dealloc];
[[myArray objectAtIndex:0] sayHello];
```

FooBar is allocated, initialized, and added to myArray. There are two references to myFooBar, so its retainCount is two. However, deallocating myFooBar makes both references invalid, pointing to deallocated memory space. The sayHello message is sent to the first object in myArray—the problem is that the object no longer exists. Although in this simple example it is easy enough to surmise the cause of the error message, in a real application, finding this type of error's source is often difficult.

```
objc[1289]: FREED(id): message sayHello sent to freed

    object=0x521a90 Program received signal: "EXC_BAD_INSTRUCTION".
```

Zombies help avoid this nebulous error, helping you track down an error's source. You enable zombies by setting the NSZombieEnabled environment variable in Xcode. Then, when debugging the application, rather than releasing an object, the debugger creates a zombie object. The zombie knows its original identity before joining the undead. The result is that you usually receive a more descriptive error message.

```
2009-02-28 12:28:38.749 Zombie[1316:20b] *** -[FooBar sayHello]:
    message sent to deallocated instance 0x52c6a0
```

Again, in this simple example, the difference is trivial; in a real-world project, the difference is not trivial. The following task illustrates using NSZombieEnabled.

Try This Enabling Zombies

1. Create a new View-based Application named Zombie.

2. Create a new Objective-C class called FooBar.

3. Create one method called helloThere (Listing 5-1). Don't forget to put the method's signature in FooBar's interface (Listing 5-2).

Listing 5-1 FooBar.m

```
#import "FooBar.h"
@implementation FooBar
-(void) sayHello {
 NSLog(@"Hello there...");
}
-(void) dealloc {
[super dealloc];
}
@end
```

Listing 5-2   FooBar.h

```
@interface FooBar : NSObject {
}
-(void) sayHello;
@end
```

4. Modify application:didFinishLaunchingWithOptions in ZombieAppDelegate (Listing 5-3). Don't forget to import FooBar.

Listing 5-3   ZombieAppDelegate.m

```
#import "ZombieAppDelegate.h"
#import "ZombieViewController.h"
#import "FooBar.h"
@implementation ZombieAppDelegate
@synthesize window;
@synthesize viewController;
- (BOOL)application:(UIApplication *)application
         didFinishLaunchingWithOptions:(NSDictionary *)launchOptions {
    FooBar * myFooBar = [[FooBar alloc] init];
    NSMutableArray * myArray = [[NSMutableArray alloc]
         initWithObjects:myFooBar,nil];
    [myFooBar dealloc];
    [[myArray objectAtIndex:0] sayHello];

    [window addSubview:viewController.view];
    [window makeKeyAndVisible];
    return YES;
}

- (void)applicationWillTerminate:(UIApplication *)application {
    // Save data if appropriate.
}

-(void)dealloc {
    [viewController release];
    [window release];
    [super dealloc];
}
@end
```

(continued)

5. Click the Run button to build and debug the application. Notice the first time you run the application you may not get an error at all (even though we sent a message to a deallocated object). This is part of what makes finding and fixing errors like this so hard—if the memory didn't happen to get used for anything else in the meantime, it might remain valid for an unpredictable amount of time. Even if you do get an error message, it is not all that descriptive (Listing 5-4). The debugger only knows the sayHello message was sent to an object already freed. The debugger doesn't know the object's identity. To change this, you must enable zombies.

Listing 5-4   Debugger Console error logging when zombies are not enabled

```
Attaching to program: '/Users/bward/Library/Application Support/iPhone
Simulator/User/Applications/05688B53-AF22-4F21
-95D3AFFE2682A6EA/Zombie.app/Zombie', process 1351.
objc[1351]: FREED(id): message sayHello sent to freed object=0x521bd0
Program received signal: "EXC_BAD_INSTRUCTION".
```

6. In the pull-down menu next to the Run button, select Edit Active Scheme. Select Launch in the left column and then click the Arguments tab. This should let you edit the arguments passed to the app on launch (Figure 5-20).

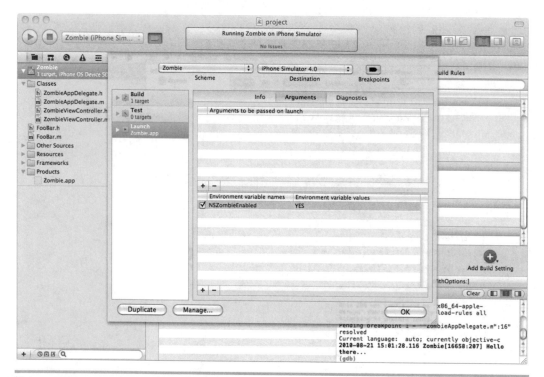

Figure 5-20   The Executable Info window

7. Click the + and add the NSZombieEnabled variable to the environment variable list. Assign it the value YES and click OK.

8. Run the app again. Now the error message is more descriptive (Listing 5-5).

Listing 5-5   Debugger Console output after zombies are enabled

```
2010-08-21 15:10:57.345 Zombie[16692:207] *** -[FooBar sayHello]:
    message sent to deallocated instance 0x592b640
```

Instruments—Leaks

Instruments is a powerful suite of debugging and testing tools. This chapter cannot possibly cover it adequately. Tools include Activity Monitor, CPU Sampler, Leaks, Object Allocations, Core Animation, OpenGL ES, and System Usage (Figure 5-21).

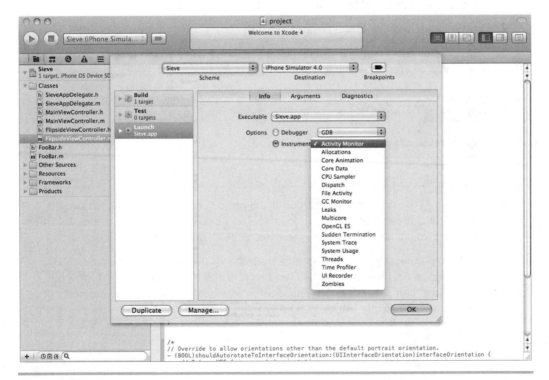

Figure 5-21   Instruments

NOTE

For more information on Instruments, refer to Apple's documentation "Instruments User Guide," available online or via the Instruments Help menu.

However, one tool worth introducing you to here is Leaks. You can use Leaks without knowing much about it. The Leaks instrument allows you to easily find memory leaks in your application. It tells you how many leaks occurred, each leak's size, the address of the leak, and the leaked object's type. Using Leaks is fairly intuitive—rather than explaining, let me simply explain by example through the following application.

Try This ▏ Find a Memory Leak

In the following task, you find memory leaks using the iPhone Simulator. If you didn't do the OnMyPhone exercise in this chapter's beginning, do so now.

Find a Memory Leak on iPhone Simulator

1. Create a new Utility application named **Sieve**.

2. Create a new Objective-C class named **FooBar**.

3. Open FlipsideViewController.m and implement the viewDidAppear method (Listing 5-6). Don't forget to import FooBar.h.

Listing 5-6 ▏ The viewDidAppear method

```
-(void) viewDidAppear:(BOOL) animated {
    FooBar * myFooBar = [[FooBar alloc] init];
}
```

4. Select Edit Active Scheme from the pull-down menu. Click Launch in the left column; then select the Instruments radio button and select Leaks from the pull-down menu. Click OK to save your changes to the scheme.

5. Run the application. Ignore the warning informing you that you never use the FooBar instance in viewDidAppear. Note that when you're using Instruments, Xcode will run the iPad Simulator rather than the iPhone Simulator. You'll also see the Instruments application automatically launch.

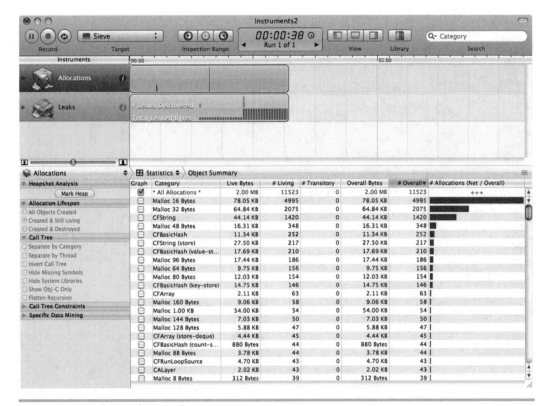

Figure 5-22   The Leaks panel

6. Click Info and Done repeatedly for about 30 seconds. When finished, click Stop in the Instruments window (Figure 5-22).

7. Click Leaks, and a detailed list of the leaked objects appears. Click one of the leaked objects.

8. Select View | Extended Detail from the main menu, and a call stack appears on the window's right (Figure 5-23).

9. Double-click one of the leaks, and the source code will display with the line allocating and initializing FooBar (Figure 5-24).

(continued)

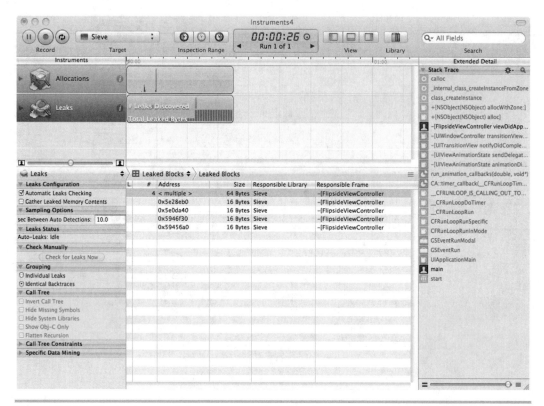

Figure 5-23 The Leaks panel showing extended details

Distributing Your Application

After debugging and testing in the iPhone Simulator and on your own device(s), you'll want to build a deployment version of your app for ad hoc testing by your beta testers (friends, family, etc.) and then a final version for submission to the iTunes App Store. The details of these deployment steps are beyond the scope of this book, but we'll summarize them briefly here. For comprehensive instructions, refer to the Apple documentation and the built-in help on the Provisioning Portal web site.

Ad Hoc Deployment and Testing

Once you've tested your app as much as you can, the next step is to hand it off to some additional beta testers to make sure they understand how to use it and don't stumble across any bugs. Apple's number one reason for rejecting apps submitted to the App Store is crashing bugs they

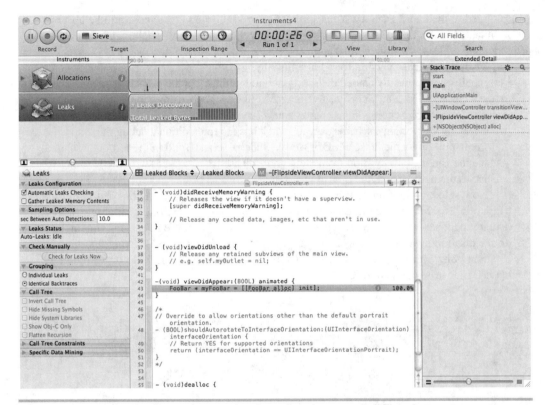

Figure 5-24   Leaks showing source code where the object was allocated

find during the review process—it's worth your time to make sure your app is rock solid before submitting it.

The first step in doing ad hoc testing is to collect the device IDs for each of the test devices and add them in the Provisioning Portal. Note that you're only allowed 100 ad hoc test devices and they only reset once a year, so make sure that you're signing up people who will be available to test all of your applications. Once you've got the device IDs added, you'll need to create a Distribution Certificate and use it to create an Ad Hoc Provisioning Profile that includes all of the device IDs. Download that profile and save it someplace safe—you'll be sending it to each of your testers along with your app.

All of the nifty debugging tasks that you accomplished in this chapter were because your app was compiled for debugging with additional information embedded in the app. You don't want this extra stuff in your released application; it will slow it down or worse. For instance, suppose you left the NSEnableZombie environment variable set to YES. Now when the application ran, released objects would be turned into zombies rather than the objects being returned to available memory. Your application would be sluggish and could be abruptly terminated by the device's operating system. We get rid of this extra debugging information by building a release version of your app.

To build a release version for ad hoc distribution, you'll want to create a new scheme (essentially a conveniently named collection of build settings). In the pull-down menu at the top of the window, select New Scheme, give it a name like "Ad hoc distribution," and pick Launch Scheme from the two choices. This creates a new scheme where we'll change some build settings, while leaving your original scheme easy to switch back to for additional debugging builds.

In the pull-down menu, select Edit Active Scheme, click Build in the left column, and change the Build Configuration from Debug to Release (Figure 5-25). Click OK to save the change to the new scheme.

Now select your app in the navigation panel on the left and then click Build Settings (Figure 5-26). Make sure the Base SDK is set to the most recent one available. Under Deployment set the Targeted Device Family to "iPhone". Set the iOS Deployment Target to the minimum version of iOS that your app requires. Unless you're using features only available in newer OS versions, iOS 3.0 is probably good, since it will allow anyone whose device is at least updated to iOS 3 to use your app.

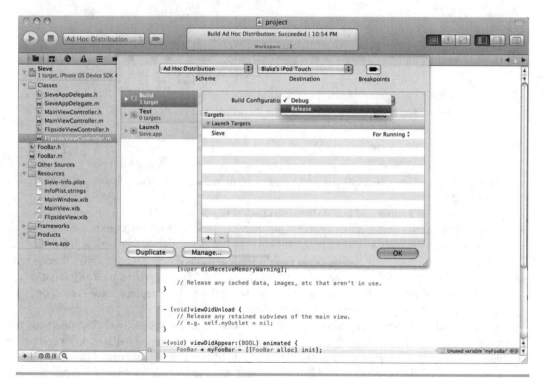

Figure 5-25   Setting the Build Configuration to Release

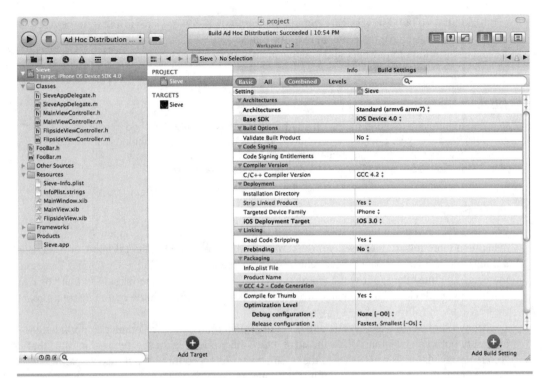

Figure 5-26 The Build Configuration's settings

Now we're ready to build the App file that you'll be sending to your ad hoc testers. Make sure that you're building for a device rather than the simulator by checking the pull-down menu. Then select Product | Clean Ad Hoc Distribution from the main menu followed by Product | Build Ad Hoc Distribution. You can check the Xcode Preferences to see where your App file was written, but it probably defaulted to Library/Developer/Xcode/DerivedData/*workspace-name*/Build/Products/Release-iphoneos/*app-name*. This is the file that you can send to your testers along with the Ad Hoc Distribution Profile that you created earlier. They can just drop both files onto iTunes and then sync their device to start testing.

Distributing Your App via the App Store

To really build the final version of your app for submission to the iTunes App Store, you should check Apple's current instructions for submitting apps. Complete instructions can be found on the iPhone Developer web site. You must have an iTunes Connect Account if you wish to sell your app on the App Store.

You will want to make another new scheme similar to the one we made in the preceding section, but this time, when creating the scheme, select Distribution Scheme rather than Launch Scheme. This will build an archived version of your app for uploading to iTunes Connect.

In addition to building a release version of your app, if you are submitting it to the App Store, you will also have to create an icon for it in several sizes, upload sample screenshots, write a description of your app, and pick a category for it. Complete instructions are available on Apple's web site.

NOTE

Remember, installing and debugging on your test devices that can be attached to your computer do not require anything other than what was covered in the beginning of this chapter. You are not required to create a different build configuration (scheme) or Ad Hoc Distribution Provisioning Profile to debug and test on your devices.

Summary

Effective debugging and testing of your application requires installing it on a test device. It is also much more rewarding to see your app run on a bona fide iPod Touch, iPhone, or iPad. But getting your application on a device requires you to become a paid iPhone Developer Program member. You must then follow the instructions to getting the proper credentials so that you can install on your device. Trust us when we say you can muddle through the online instructions, they are easy to follow.

Many iPhone errors are cryptic at best. Rather than running and rerunning an application aimlessly until you eventually find the error, take some time to learn the debugging tools that Xcode has available to you. Refer to the documents referenced throughout this chapter. Use the debugger to find errors. After debugging your application, test its memory usage on the iPhone Simulator. After testing on the iPhone Simulator, install the application on your device, and debug and test again. Pay careful attention to memory and resource use, as an iPhone's memory is limited. Also ensure your application runs quickly and is responsive. If you happen to only own a newer iOS device, be careful to also test on older-generation devices, since they have less memory and slower processors. Careful debugging and testing of your application can often be the difference between "just another mediocre app" and the "best app" in your category on the App Store. Chances are your application is not going to be the first of anything anymore, so try to make it the best.

Chapter 6

UIApplication and UIApplicationDelegate

Key Skills & Concepts

- Understanding the UIApplication class

- Understanding the UIApplicationDelegate protocol

- Handling application startup and termination

- Handling application interruptions

Every iOS application has one UIApplication. UIApplication is an iOS application's starting point and is responsible for initializing and displaying your application's UIWindow. It is also responsible for loading your application's first UIView into the UIWindow. Another responsibility UIApplication has is managing your application's life cycle. UIApplication fulfills this management responsibility using a delegate called UIApplicationDelegate. Although UIApplication receives events, it's the UIApplicationDelegate that handles how an application responds to those events. Events the UIApplicationDelegate might handle include application life cycle events, such as startup and shutdown, and system events like incoming phone calls and calendar alerts. In this chapter, after learning how to load an application's root view into the UIWindow, you explore handling system events using the UIApplicationDelegate protocol.

Try This Adding a UIView and UIViewController to a UIApplicationDelegate

Before continuing, create this chapter's project; this chapter uses the same project throughout. In this project, you start with the simplest iOS template, a Window-based application. You'll create the application from scratch by first creating a xib and a corresponding view controller. You'll then modify the application's delegate so that it loads the view.

1. Create a new Window-based Application in Xcode by selecting File | New | New Project and then selecting Application under iOS in the left column and Window-Based Application. Select iPhone in the Device Family pull-down. Name the project **AddViewProject**.

2. In the navigation pane, expand the Classes folder. This folder contains the AddViewProject AppDelegate.h and AddViewProjectAppDelegate.m files. These two files implement the project's custom class that adopts the UIApplicationDelegate protocol.

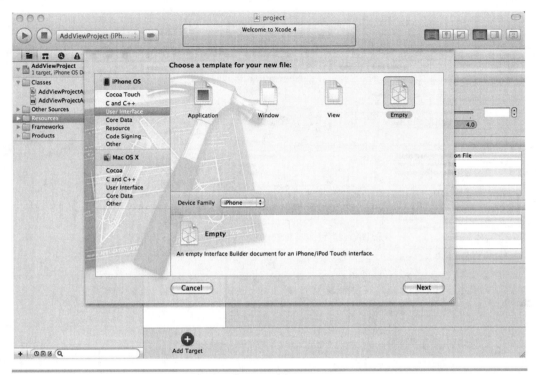

Figure 6-1   Creating an Empty XIB Interface Builder

3. Highlight the Resources folder. CTRL-click and select New File from the pop-up menu. Select User Interfaces from the New File dialog, and select Empty XIB (Figure 6-1). You may also have to select Resources as the group in the pull-down when naming the file.

4. Name the xib **FirstViewController** and click Finish.

5. Highlight the Classes folder. Select File | New File from the menu.

6. Select the UIViewController subclass from the Cocoa Touch Classes and click Next (Figure 6-2).

NOTE
You could have created the view controller first and then checked the "With XIB for user interface" check box; Xcode would then have generated the xib for you.

(continued)

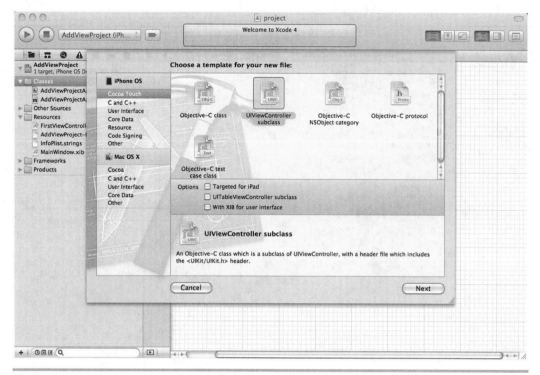

Figure 6-2 Creating a UIViewController

7. Name the file **FirstViewController.m**. Click Finish.

8. Click FirstViewController.xib to open it in Interface Builder. Select View | Utilities | Object Library from the main menu to display the object library in the lower-right Libraries pane.

9. Scroll down to the View object, and drag and drop it onto the FirstViewController.xib Document window.

10. Select File's Owner icon (the transparent cube to the left of the drawing area). Select View | Utilities | Identity from the main menu to switch the Inspector pane to display object identity. Now select FirstViewController as the class in the pull-down menu (Figure 6-3).

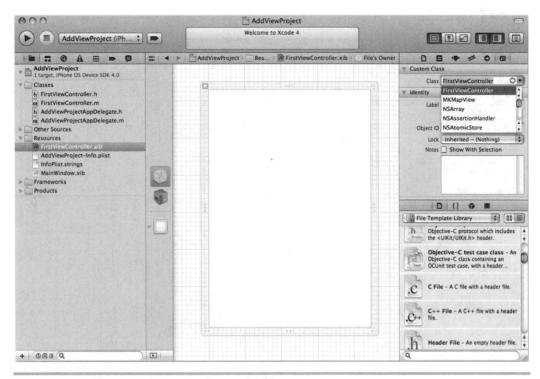

Figure 6-3   Select FirstViewController as the file's owner.

11. Select the File Owner icon again. Select View | Utilities | Connections from the main menu (or just click the connections button at the top of the Utilities Area). Drag from the circle next to View to the view in the drawing area to set the newly created view as FirstViewController's view outlet (Figure 6-4).

12. Select the view, select View | Utilities | Object Attributes from the main menu and then click in the background color box to change its color (Figure 6-5).

13. Save FirstViewController.xib.

14. Open AddViewProjectAppDelegate.h, import FirstViewController.h, and create a property referencing the FirstViewController class (Listing 6-1).

(continued)

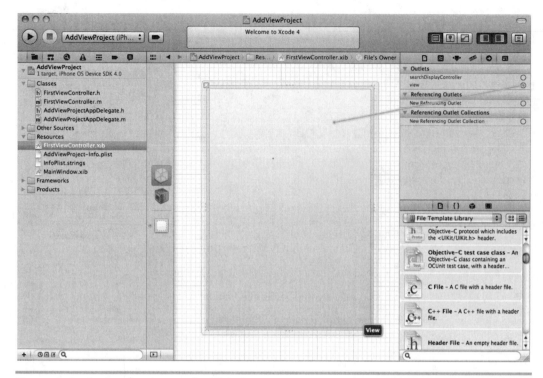

Figure 6-4 Setting the view as the File's Owner view

Listing 6-1 AddViewProjectAppDelegate.h interface

```
#import <UIKit/UIKit.h>
#import "FirstViewController.h"
@interface AddViewProjectAppDelegate : NSObject
<UIApplicationDelegate> {
  UIWindow *window;
  FirstViewController *first;
}
@property (nonatomic, retain) IBOutlet UIWindow *window;
@property (nonatomic, retain) FirstViewController *first;
@end
```

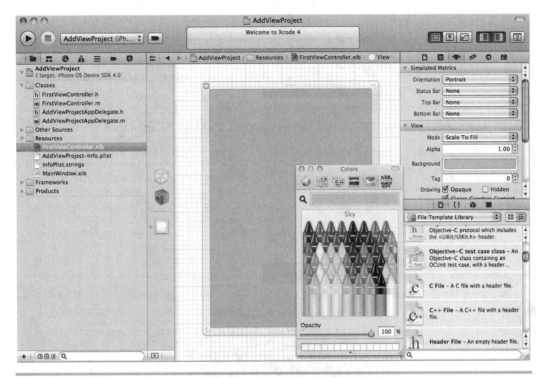

Figure 6-5 Changing the view's color

15. Open AddViewProjectAppDelegate.m, synthesize first, and modify applicationDidFinish
    Launching: so that it obtains a reference to FirstViewController from FirstViewController
    .xib and then adds its view as a subview to the window. FirstViewController.m should
    appear identical to Listing 6-2. Don't forget to deallocate the view in the delegate's dealloc
    method.

Listing 6-2   AddViewProjectAppDelegate.m implementation

```
#import "AddViewProjectAppDelegate.h"
@implementation AddViewProjectAppDelegate
@synthesize window;
@synthesize first;

- (BOOL)application:(UIApplication *)application
        didFinishLaunchingWithOptions:(NSDictionary *)launchOptions {
```
                                                        (continued)

```
    first = [[FirstViewController alloc]
        initWithNibName:@"FirstViewController" bundle:nil];
    [window addSubview: [first view]];
    [window makeKeyAndVisible];
    return YES;
}

- (void)applicationWillTerminate:(UIApplication *)application {

    // Save data if appropriate.
}
 -(void)dealloc {
    [window release];
    [first release];
    [super dealloc];
}
@end
```

16. Click the Run button. Your colored view should load into the iPhone Simulator (Figure 6-6).

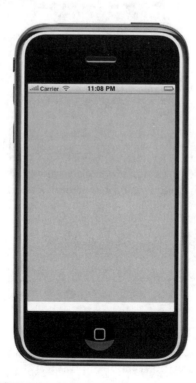

Figure 6-6 The application in iPhone Simulator

In Steps 10 and 11, you manually connected AddViewProjectAppDelegate to its UIView. Moreover, you placed that view in its own nib. Every nib has an owner. Recall that every application has one UIWindow. UIWindow is in a project's MainWindow.xib. That nib's owner is UIApplication. Also notice that Xcode added the AddViewProjectAppDelegate to MainWindow.xib and connected it to the UIWindow and set the UIApplication's delegate.

Nibs you create should have a class adopting the UIViewController protocol as an owner, which is what you did in Step 10. In Step 9, you tied the UIView created in the nib in Interface Builder to the UIViewController created in Xcode. This is how the two objects "know" about each other. You learn more about UIViewControllers and UIViews—and connecting them—in Chapter 7.

NOTE
Notice that you created FirstViewController's view in its own FirstViewController.xib file. You could have opened MainWindow.xib, dragged a view onto the window, and used this nib for your user interface. But this is not the preferred way of using views in nibs. Apple recommends one view per nib file. The reason for this recommendation is that an application must load all views and all controls that reside in the same nib. Using a new nib file for each view reduces your application's memory use because you only load views as needed.

Ask the Expert

Q: **What is that initWithNibName line in Listing 6-2?**

A: This method allows initializing a UIViewController's view from a nib file rather than from code. You use this method when you want to write code that initializes a view controller whose view resides in a nib. You should note that this is just one of several different ways you might load a view from a nib into a class. By the book's end, you will be familiar with most of them.

Connecting UIWindow, UIApplication, and UIApplicationDelegate

In the preceding section, I only briefly mentioned the connections in MainWindow.xib. But these connections warrant a closer look if you want to understand what the template actually did. Notice the UIWindow in Listing 6-1 is an IBOutlet. Your first experience with IBOutlets was in Chapter 1; you learn more on it in Chapter 7. But realize the window "lives" in the xib, not in the delegate. Although the window is released by the delegate in the dealloc method, it is neither allocated nor initialized by the delegate's code in Listing 6-2. Remember, all the dealloc method in Listing 6-2 is doing is releasing the class's reference to the window, not deallocating the window. Instead, MainWindow.xib handles allocating, initializing, and deallocating the UIWindow.

UIApplication knows to load MainWindow.xib by consulting the NSMainNibFile key in the Info.plist file. If you open the AddViewProject project's Info.plist, you will see that the "Main nib file base name" is set to MainWindow. While loading, the nib sets AddViewProjectApp Delegate as UIApplication's delegate and UIWindow as AddViewProjectAppDelegate's window. Both are outlets of their respective class in Interface Builder.

Try This   Exploring Main Window.xib

1. Open MainWindow.xib and display the document window.

2. Highlight the File's Owner and select the Object Identity tab in the Inspector. Notice its Custom Class is set to UIApplication (Figure 6-7). UIApplication loads MainWindow.xib.

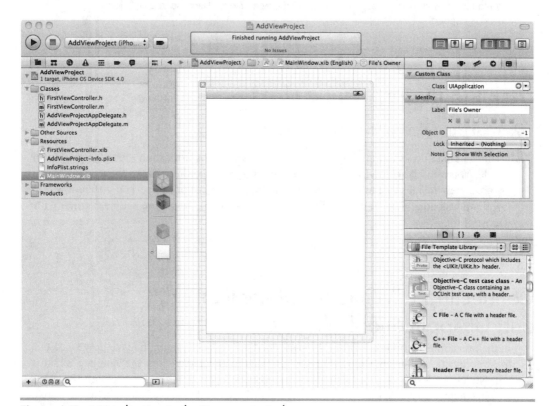

Figure 6-7 UIApplication in the Document window

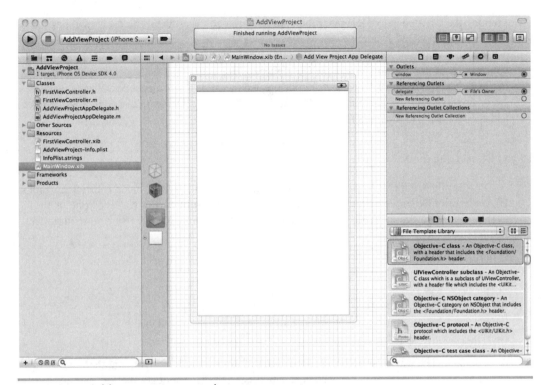

Figure 6-8 AddViewProjectAppDelegate's connections

3. Notice that the template automatically added the AddViewProjectAppDelegate object to the set of objects in the xib file (all of the objects are listed along the left side of the edit pane).

4. When you select the AddViewProjectAppDelete object and select the Connections pane, you will notice AddViewProjectAppDelegate's window IBOutlet is set to the UIWindow in the nib (Figure 6-8). Also notice that the UIApplication's delegate is set as AddViewProjectAppDelegate.

UIApplication and UIApplicationDelegate

Ignore UIApplication—you almost never modify it. Just know that UIApplication receives system events. It is your job to write code that handles those system events. You write that code in a class adopting the UIApplicationDelegate protocol. This protocol has several life cycle methods that handle application and system events. Table 6-1 lists UIApplicationDelegate's methods. If you begin with a template, Xcode creates the class adopting the UIApplicationDelegate protocol for you, but Xcode does not implement the UIApplicationDelegate's optional event-handling methods. For instance, in this chapter's project, Xcode created the AddViewProjectAppDelegate.h and AddViewProjectAppDelegate.m files. The AddViewProjectAppDelegate class extends NSObject and adopts the UIApplicationDelegate.

```
@interface AddViewProjectAppDelegate : NSObject
<UIApplicationDelegate>
```

The application's UIApplication, defined in MainWindow.xib, has a reference to its UIApplicationDelegate as an outlet (Figure 6-8). As UIApplication receives one of the events related to the methods in Table 6-1, it calls the appropriate method in its delegate if implemented.

Ask the Expert

Q: What is a delegate?

A: A delegate is a way to simplify the separation of processing logic from another class. It also avoids inheritance. For instance, subclassing the UIApplication object would be painful. Instead, Apple provides a UIApplicationDelegate. The UIApplication has a reference to the class implementing the UIApplicationDelegate. If implemented, the UIApplication delegates handling of an event to the appropriate method in the UIApplicationDelegate. It appears as if UIApplication is handling the event; in reality, its delegate, UIApplicationDelegate, handles the event. Delegates are a common object-oriented design pattern. For more information on delegates and object-oriented programming, refer to the "delegation pattern" on Wikipedia (www.wikipedia.org).

The main.m File

In the AddViewProject project, open main.m in the Other Sources folder in the Navigation pane. The file's code is listed in Listing 6-3.

Listing 6-3   File main.m in project

```
#import <UIKit/UIKit.h>
int main(int argc, char *argv[]) {
    NSAutoreleasePool * pool = [[NSAutoreleasePool alloc] init];
    int retVal = UIApplicationMain(argc, argv, nil, nil);
    [pool release];
    return retVal;
}
```

Main creates one UIApplication instance using the UIApplicationMain method. Every project has exactly one UIApplication object. You can obtain a reference to that object by calling UIApplication's sharedApplication class method. This method returns a singleton reference to your application's UIApplication object.

```
UIApplication * myApplication = [UIApplication
        sharedApplication];
```

You usually will not do much with the UIApplication object other than obtain a reference to its UIApplicationDelegate. You obtain a reference to the UIApplicationDelegate through the following code:

```
UIApplicationDelegate * myDelegate = [[UIApplication
sharedApplication] delegate];
```

Handling Application Life Cycle Events

UIApplication forwards several important events to its UIApplicationDelegate to handle. For instance, applicationSignificantTimeChange: handles a significant time change while your application is running. The method didChangeStatusBarOrientation: handles the event fired when the status bar's orientation is changed from portrait to landscape or landscape to portrait. The method didReceiveRemoteNotification: handles push notifications sent to your application. Table 6-1 lists UIApplicationDelegate's application life cycle event-handling methods.

With the exception of application:didFinishLaunchingWithOptions:, the methods in Table 6-1 are not required, but you'll need to implement many of them if you want to develop a robust, complete application. There are also four optional methods related to Apple's Push Notifications that are beyond the scope of this book because they also require extensive support on the server side.

Two of the more important application life cycle events are your application's startup and shutdown. The application:didFinishLaunchingWithOptions: method—a required method—is where you initialize your UIViewControllers, initialize your UIWindow, add a UIView to the window, and then launch your application's user interface. The method is also useful for restoring your application's state, and it is where you perform application initialization. The applicationWillTerminate: method is useful for saving your application's state. You might also use this method to perform cleanup.

UIApplicationDelegate Event-Handling Methods	Method Signature
application:didFinishLaunchingWithOptions:	- (BOOL) application: (UIApplication *) *application* didFinishLaunchingWithOptions: (NSDictionary *) *launchOptions*
applicationDidBecomeActive:	-(void) applicationDidBecomeActive: (UIApplication *) *application*
application:handleOpenURL:	- (BOOL) application: (UIApplication *) *application* handleOpenURL: (NSURL *) *url*
applicationDidBecomeActive:	- (void) applicationDidBecomeActive: (UIApplication *) *application*
applicationWillEnterForeground:	- (void) applicationWillEnterForeground: (UIApplication *) *application*
applicationWillResignActive:	- (void) applicationWillResignActive: (UIApplication *) *application*
applicationDidEnterBackground:	- (void) applicationDidEnterBackground: (UIApplication *) *application*
application:willChangeStatusBarFrame:	- (void) application: (UIApplication *) *application* willChangeStatusBarFrame: (CGRect) *newStatusBarFrame*
application:willChangeStatusBarOrientation:duration:	-(void) application: (UIApplication *) *application* willChangeStatusBarOrientation: (UIInterfaceOrientation) *newStatusBarOrientation* duration: (NSTimeInterval) *duration*
application:didChangeStatusBarFrame:	-(void) application:(UIApplication *) *application* didChangeStatusBarFrame: (CGRect) *oldStatusBarFrame*
application:didChangeStatusBarOrientation:	-(void) application: (UIApplication *) *application* didChangeStatusBarOrientation: (UIInterfaceOrientation) *oldStatusBarOrientation*
applicationDidReceiveMemoryWarning:	-(void) applicationDidReceiveMemoryWarning: (UIApplication *) *application*
applicationSignificantTimeChange:	-(void) applicationSignificantTimeChange: (UIApplication *) *application*
applicationWillTerminate:	-(void) applicationWillTerminate: (UIApplication *) *application*

Table 6-1 UIApplicationDelegate Event-Handling Methods

Xcode offers a feature called Code Sense. As you are typing, Xcode will suggest what it thinks you are typing. If it is correct, press the TAB key and Xcode finishes typing for you. You can ignore the suggestion by continuing to type. If you are not certain the suggestion is correct, press CTRL-SPACE and Xcode presents a drop-down list with possible completions (Figure 6-9). Xcode 4 also added a Fix-it feature so that Xcode will highlight coding errors the same way a word processor would highlight spelling mistakes. If you do not see this feature, ensure Xcode is configured correctly in Xcode Preferences (Figure 6-10).

Application Interruptions

As your application functions, it is likely to receive interruptions. An incoming phone call causes your application to become inactive. If you decide to answer the call, your application terminates. Other events that might cause your application to become inactive include calendar

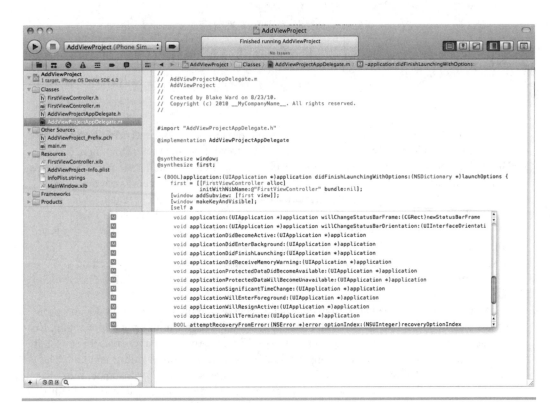

Figure 6-9 Code completion in Xcode

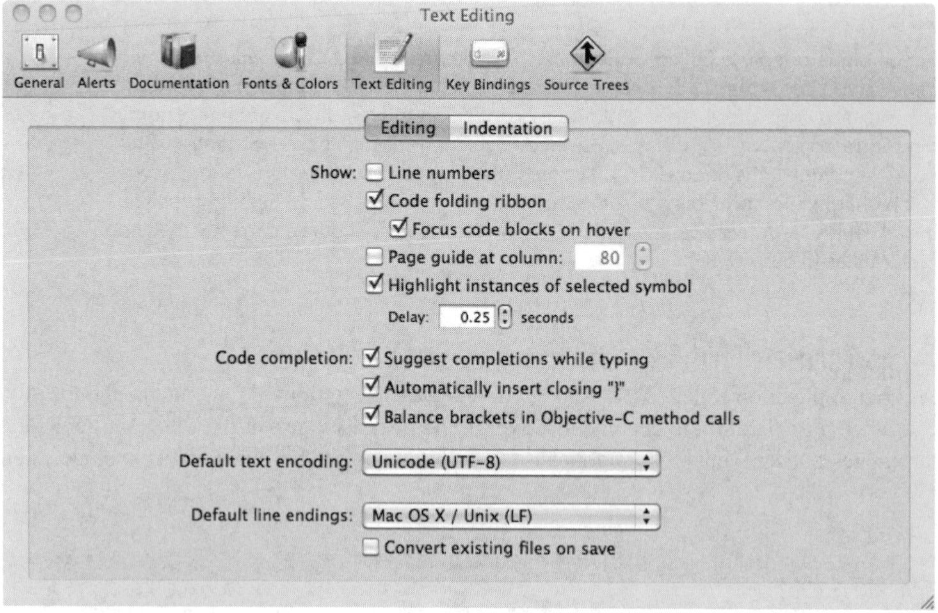

Figure 6-10 Xcode Preferences

alerts and putting your device to sleep (locking your device). The applicationWillResignActive: method in UIApplicationDelegate executes just prior to your application becoming inactive. The applicationDidBecomeActive: method executes just after your application becomes active again. For instance, if you are running your application and lock the screen, your application's delegate executes the applicationWillResignActive: method. When you later unlock the screen, your application's delegate executes the applicationDidBecomeActive: method.

The applicationDidEnterBackground and applicationWillEnterForeground methods are available in iOS 4.0 and later to support applications that use background execution. This is Apple's multitasking solution, and there are a number of requirements placed on your application if you want to do background processing. See the *iOS Application Programming Guide* for details.

Another important method is applicationDidReceiveMemoryWarning. iOS devices have limited memory—use too much and the operating system will terminate your application. But the operating system warns your application first. When UIApplication receives this event, it forwards the event to its delegate's applicationDidReceiveMemoryWarning: method. The delegate can then handle the application's response to the warning. For instance, it might release a shared data structure, empty and free image or data caches, or take other memory reclaiming actions.

CAUTION

Although this is not strictly required, your application should handle the events for becoming active/inactive and for low-memory situations in its UIApplicationDelegate. If it does not, Apple might reject your application when submitted for inclusion in the App Store.

Try This — Handling Application Interruptions

In this task, you explore the applicationDidReceiveMemoryWarning:, applicationWillResign Active:, and applicationDidBecomeActive: methods in UIApplicationDelegate.

1. Add the methods applicationDidReceiveMemoryWarning:, applicationDidBecomeActive:, and applicationWillResignActive: to AddViewProjectDelegate's implementation (Add ViewProjectAppDelegate.m). Add a single NSLog statement to each method. The methods should appear similar to Listing 6-4.

Listing 6-4   AddViewProjectAppDelegate's three additional methods

```
-(void)applicationDidReceiveMemoryWarning:(UIApplication *)
application { NSLog(@"hey got a memory warning....");
}
-(void)applicationWillResignActive:(UIApplication *) application {
NSLog(@"hey I'm about to resign active status....");
}
-(void)applicationDidBecomeActive:(UIApplication *) application {
NSLog(@"hey I'm active....");
}
```

2. Click Run, and execute the application in the iPhone Simulator.

3. Select Hardware | Simulate Memory Warning from the iPhone Simulator's menu.

4. Select Hardware | Lock from the iPhone Simulator's menu. Unlock and then quit your application.

5. Review the Debugger Console, which should appear similar to Listing 6-5.

Listing 6-5   Console output from running application

```
2010-08-25 11:24:24.147 AddViewProject[83787:207] hey I'm active....
2010-08-25 11:24:49.203 AddViewProject[83787:207] Received simulated
memory warning.
```

(continued)

```
2010-08-25 11:24:49.203 AddViewProject[83787:207] hey got a memory
warning....
2010-08-25 11:25:02.356 AddViewProject[83787:207] hey I'm about to
resign active status....
2010-08-25 11:25:14.290 AddViewProject[83787:207] hey I'm active....
2010-08-25 11:25:17.336 AddViewProject[83787:207] hey I'm about to
resign active status....
```

The application executed the applicationDidBecomeActive: method when you started it and then after you unlocked the Simulator. It called applicationDidReceiveMemoryWarning: when you selected the Simulate Memory Warning menu item. And when the application was about to become inactive after locking, the UIApplicationDelegate executed the applicationWillResignActive: method.

Summary

The UIApplication is your application's starting point. It is usually the first thing created by the main method in the main.m file. The application is always associated with a delegate. An application's delegate is a class that implements the UIApplicationDelegate protocol. The delegate is where you place code for handling your application's life cycle events.

A UIApplication has one UIApplicationDelegate. When using one of Xcode's templates, the connection between the UIWindow, UIApplication, and UIApplicationDelegate is done for you in the MainWindow.xib nib file. Moreover, you almost never have to manually create a UIApplication and UIApplicationDelegate, as every project template creates these objects for you. You also do not need to worry about having main.m create the application, nor do you need to worry about implementing the application:didFinishLaunchingWithOptions: method, as these methods are almost always generated for you too.

Chapter 7

UIView and UIViewController

Key Skills & Concepts

- Understanding the UIView and UIViewController

- Creating a single view application using the View-based Application template

- Creating a single view application using the Window-based Application template

- Understanding an application delegate's root view

- Setting an application's root view in Interface Builder

- Setting an application's root view using code

- Understanding UIView life cycle methods

UIViews are how the iOS displays information on the screen. The UIView class is responsible for displaying a rectangular area on the screen. The UIViewController manages the UIView and is responsible for handling the view's logic. The UIViewController is the glue between the view—the UIView—and your data classes—the model.

There are many UIView subclasses you might work with while developing an iOS application. In fact, every graphical component you use on an iOS graphical user interface (GUI) is a UIView subclass. Technically speaking, everything is a view. But typically, when documentation or some other material refers to a "view," it is referring to a content view. A *content* view is a view that has a view controller and is responsible for presenting a screen's worth of user interface.

The UIView Class

The UIView's responsibilities are drawing to the screen and handling events associated with a user's interaction with an application. A UIView has an associated UIViewController. The UIViewController manages the view. The view controller loads and unloads its associated views, manages views, and handles application life cycle events for its views.

Every graphical iOS control you use in Interface Builder is a UIView subclass. Table 7-1 lists the UIView subclasses. Notice that UIScrollView and UIControl both have further subclasses listed in the table's second column.

UIViews function as containers, controls, displays, alerts, action sheets, and navigation controls, and also as the application's window. In future chapters, we'll cover most of these UIView types. This chapter limits itself to a simple display view and associated view controller.

UIView Subclasses	Subclasses
UIWindow	
UILabel	
UIPickerView	
UIProgressView	
UIActivityIndicatorView	
UIImageView	
UITabBar	
UIToolBar	
UINavigationBar	
UITableViewCell	
UIActionSheet	
UIAlertView	
UIScrollView	UITableView
	UITextView
UIWebView	
UIControl	UIButton
	UIDatePicker
	UIPageControl
	UISegmentedControl
	UITextField
	UISlider
	UISwitch
UISearchBar	

Table 7-1 UIView Subclasses in UIKit

The UIViewController Class

The UIViewController manages UIViews. It is responsible for creating, displaying, hiding, and destroying a view. The UIViewControl is also responsible for responding to a view's life cycle events, handling orientation, and serving as a bridge between your application's view and model. The view controller is your application's controller in the model-view-controller design pattern.

View-Based Application Template

The easiest route to creating a single view application is using Xcode's View-based Application template. This template creates a single view and a view controller for managing the view. While the View-based application is not as useful as Xcode's other project templates, it is helpful here, as it generates the simplest iOS graphical application and provides a straightforward UIView and UIViewController example. In the next task, you will generate an application using this template. But, before continuing, first we will review IBOutlets and IBActions.

IBOutlet and IBAction

You have already used IBOutlets and IBActions in previous chapters. Without really knowing what they are, you probably already have a good idea of what they accomplish; outlets and actions are how you connect things in a nib with things outside a nib. An outlet connects an instance variable outside a nib to an object in a nib.

IBOutlet is a preprocessor directive, evaluates to void, and is ignored by the compiler, but all you really need to know is that IBOutlet is how Interface Builder knows the variable was created for its use. When you change the class of an object, Interface Builder scans the class for IBOutlets and knows those variables are intended as outlets. You can then easily connect your graphical component to the variable, as Interface Builder adds the outlets to the inspector automatically for you to select. Note, though, Interface Builder doesn't connect the outlets to anything; it just adds them. You are responsible for adding any connections.

Actions are messages sent from objects in the nib to methods outside the nib. You define an action in your code using the IBAction keyword. Like IBOutlet, it's a preprocessor directive and evaluates to void. You define an action in your code using the IBAction keyword. Also, like IBOutlet, when you assign a class to a control in Interface Builder, it scans the class for IBActions and adds them to the inspector for you to select. You can then connect user interface events to a specific method in your code. Note that a method designated as an action must not return a value, as the preprocessor replaces IBAction with void, and so all the compiler sees is void. An action also takes a single parameter, sender. The sender is the id of the control calling the action. So if a UIButton instance called an IBAction named changeLabelValue, the sender would be the pointer to the UIButton.

```
-(IBAction) changeLabelValue: (id) sender;
```

IBOutlet and IBAction don't require much explanation, as you use these two directives so frequently they become second nature. Any instance variable external to Interface Builder that must communicate with a control in Interface Builder must be an IBOutlet. Any method that must be called from a control in Interface Builder must be an IBAction.

Try This Using a View-Based Application Template

1. Create a new View-based Application using the template. Name the project **SimpleView**.

2. Expand the Classes group and notice XCode created the SimpleViewViewController class for you. Expand Resources and notice the template generated a separate nib, SimpleViewViewController.xib, for the SimpleViewViewController.

3. Open SimpleViewViewController.h and add a label and method for changing the label's value. Make the label an IBOutlet and the method an IBAction (Listing 7-1).

Listing 7-1 SimpleViewViewController.h

```
#import <UIKit/UIKit.h>
@interface SimpleViewViewController : UIViewController {
UILabel * theLabel;
}
@property (nonatomic, retain) IBOutlet UILabel *theLabel;
-(IBAction) changeLabelValue: (id) sender;
@end
```

4. Open SimpleViewViewController.m and add the IBOutlet and IBAction definitions (Listing 7-2).

Listing 7-2 SimpleViewViewController.m

```
#import "SimpleViewViewController.h"
@implementation SimpleViewViewController
@synthesize theLabel;
-(IBAction) changeLabelValue : (id) sender {
  [theLabel setText:@"Hello World."];
  UIButton *theBut = sender;
  NSLog(theBut.currentTitle);
  theBut.enabled = NO;
  [theBut setTitle:@"Pressed Already" forState:
UIControlStateDisabled];
}
-(void)dealloc {
  [theLabel release];
  [super dealloc];
}
@end
```

(continued)

5. Select SimpleViewViewController.xib to display it in Interface Builder and change the view's color. Add a UILabel and a UIButton to the UIView.

6. Notice that SimpleViewViewController is the File's Owner. Connect SimpleViewViewController's theLabel outlet to the label.

7. Connect SimpleViewViewController's changeTheLabel action to the button. Select Touch Up Inside.

8. Save your changes.

9. Click Build And Go to run the application.

Take a moment to examine what the View-based Application template did for you. It created the SimpleViewViewController.xib and it also created a UIViewController subclass, SimpleViewViewController, by creating the SimpleViewViewController.h and SimpleViewViewController.m files. Moreover, it added the controller to the delegate (Listing 7-3).

Listing 7-3   SimpleViewAppDelegate.h

```
#import <UIKit/UIKit.h>
@class SimpleViewViewController;
@interface SimpleViewAppDelegate : NSObject <UIApplicationDelegate> {
  UIWindow *window;
  SimpleViewViewController *viewController;
}
@property (nonatomic, retain) IBOutlet UIWindow *window;
@property (nonatomic, retain)    IBOutlet SimpleViewViewController
*viewController;
@end
```

In the delegate, the template created the application's window and view controller as outlets (Listings 7-3 and 7-4). In the delegate's applicationDidFinishLaunchingWithOptions: method, the template added the view controller's view to the window and then displayed the window. Notice that nowhere does the code allocate or initialize its window or view controller. Instead, Info.plist specifies that MainWindow.xib is the application's main nib, so it knows to load MainWindow.xib and the nib handles window and view controller initialization.

Listing 7-4   SimpleViewAppDelegate.m

```
#import "SimpleViewAppDelegate.h"
#import "SimpleViewViewController.h"
@implementation SimpleViewAppDelegate
@synthesize window;
```

```
@synthesize viewController;
- (BOOL)application:(UIApplication *)application
didFinishLaunchingWithOptions:(NSDictionary *)launchOptions {
  [window addSubview:viewController.view];
  [window makeKeyAndVisible];
  return YES;
}
-(void)dealloc {
  [viewController release];
  [window release]; [super dealloc];
}
@end
```

In the MainWindow nib, the template set the nib's file's owner to UIApplication. The template set SimpleViewAppDelegate as the application's delegate and set the delegate's window to the window in MainWindow.xib.

The template also added a view controller to MainWindow.xib and set it as the delegate's root view controller. Every delegate must have a root view controller. The root view controller in MainWindow.xib comes from the SimpleViewViewController.xib, also created by the template.

The template created the UIView in its own xib, SimpleViewViewController.xib. It set SimpleViewViewController.xib's file's owner to SimpleViewViewController. It also set the controller's view to the view in the xib.

Try This Using a Window-Based Application Template

The View-based Application template hides many development details. If new to iOS programming, chances are you will not find that the View-based Application template helps clarify a UIView, a UIViewController, and their relationship. To help make their relationship clearer, you should understand what the View-based Application template accomplishes automatically.

Unlike a View-based Application template, a Window-based Application template requires understanding UIViews and UIViewControllers. When using the Window-based Application template, you must manually create a view and a view controller and wire them together. In this project, you create a single view application starting with a Window-based Application template. Creating a Window-based Application should solidify your understanding of the steps used by Xcode when creating a View-based application.

1. Create a new Window-based Application and name it **SimpleWindow**.

2. CTRL-click the Resources folder and select New File. Select User Interface under iOS and select View to create a new xib. Name the xib **FirstViewController.xib**.

(continued)

3. Select File | New | New File. Add a UIViewController named **FirstViewController**. Xcode should create FirstViewController.h and FirstViewController.m. Be certain the check box to create a xib is not checked.

4. Open SimpleWindowAppDelegate.h and either import the FirstViewController or use an @class forward declaration. Add a UIViewController property to SimpleWindowAppDelegate.h so that it appears the same as Listing 7-5.

Listing 7-5　SimpleWindowAppDelegate.h

```
#import <UIKit/UIKit.h>
@class FirstViewController;
@interface SimpleWindowAppDelegate : NSObject <UIApplicationDelegate> {
 UIWindow *window;
 FirstViewController *rootViewController;
}
@property (nonatomic, retain) IBOutlet FirstViewController
*rootViewController;
@property (nonatomic, retain) IBOutlet UIWindow *window;
@end
```

5. Modify SimpleWindowAppDelegate.m so that it appears like Listing 7-6. Notice you must synthesize rootViewController and add its view to the window as a subview in the delegate's applicationDidFinishLaunching: method.

Listing 7-6　SimpleWindowAppDelegate.m

```
#import "SimpleWindowAppDelegate.h"
#import "FirstViewController.h"
@implementation SimpleWindowAppDelegate
@synthesize window;
@synthesize rootViewController;
-(void)applicationDidFinishLaunching:(UIApplication *)application {
  [window addSubview:rootViewController.view];
  [window makeKeyAndVisible];
}
-(void)dealloc {
  [window release];
  [rootViewController release];
  [super dealloc];
}
@end
```

6. Select FirstViewController.xib to display it in Interface Builder. Select the File's Owner and then select View | Utilities | Identity from the main menu. Notice that the class of the File's Owner isn't set.

7. Change its class to FirstViewController from the pull-down in the Object Identity Inspector pane.

8. Select the view, select Object Attributes in the Inspector pane, and change the view's color.

9. Select the File's Owner and click the Connections button in the Inspector pane, and then connect the view outlet to the view you added to the document window.

10. Save FirstViewController.xib and select MainWindow.xib to open it in Interface Builder.

11. Notice that there is no UIViewController or view set in the document window.

12. Scroll down in the list of objects and drag a view controller from the library to the editing pane. With the View Controller selected, go to the Object Identity Inspector pane and set its class to FirstViewController (Figure 7-1).

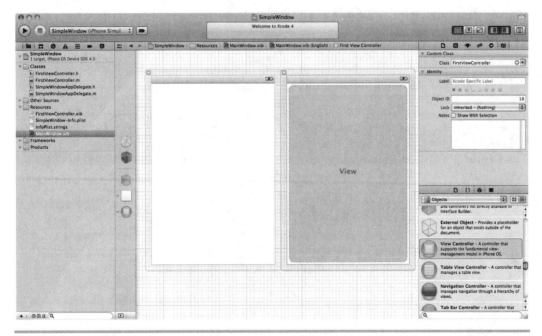

Figure 7-1 Adding FirstViewController to Mainwindow.xib

(continued)

13. In the Object Attributes Inspector pane, change its NIB Name to **FirstViewController**.

14. Select Simple Window App Delegate (one of the icons to the left of the editing pane). Select the Connections Inspector pane; notice the rootViewController outlet. Connect this to the view controller just added (Figure 7-2).

15. Save your changes.

16. Click Run to build and run your application. The view in FirstViewController.xib will be loaded into the window and displayed.

In Step 14, you connected the FirstViewController to the application's delegate. This was an important step; it allowed the nib to set the delegate's root view controller for you. The root view controller is the UIViewController that is first loaded by an application delegate. Remember, the application knew to load MainWindow.xib because it was in the application's Info.plist. The application loaded MainWindow.xib, saw the FirstViewController object that was added to the document window, and saw that the

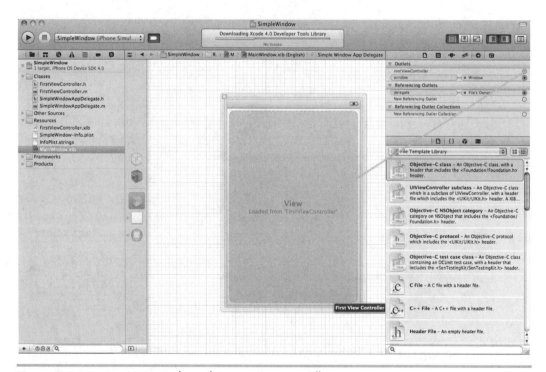

Figure 7-2 Setting Mainwindow.xib's root view controller

delegate's root view controller was set to FirstViewController. The application also knew the controller came from FirstViewController.xib. Because of the object, variable, and nib settings, the application knew to allocate and initialize a FirstViewController instance from FirstViewController.xib when loading MainWindow.xib. Because these relationships were established in Interface Builder, no manual code was necessary. This is how the View-based Application template builds a simple application, which you just duplicated manually using the Window-based application template.

NOTE

In this example, you manually created a xib and linked it to its associated view controller. Step 3 specifically instructed you not to check the check box that also created a xib; had you checked the check box, Xcode would have created a xib and automatically made most of these connections for you.

Ask the Expert

Q: Hey, wait a minute. What does the @class precompiler directive mean in Listing 7-3 and Listing 7-5, and why are you not importing the class's header?

A: The @class is a compiler directive that informs the compiler that a class of that type will exist. It is what's called a forward declaration, so named because it is informing the compiler before the class is actually declared. Using an @class directive in the header file and only importing the class's header in the implementation file is the preferred approach.

UIViewController and Application Life Cycle Events

UIViewController handles important life cycle events for its associated UIViews. Table 7-2 lists the UIViewController's view life cycle instance methods.

Note that several methods in Table 7-2 are similar to an application delegate's life cycle methods—for instance, the didReceiveMemoryWarning: method. Do not let this similarity confuse you; remember, life cycle methods in the view controller are for the controller's associated view and not the application as a whole. Conversely, life cycle methods in the delegate are designed to handle events for the application as a whole.

Instance Method for View Life Cycle Management	When Called
didReceiveMemoryWarning:	Called when a controller receives a memory warning
didRotateFromInterfaceOrientation:	Called after a view controller's view rotates
viewDidAppear:	Called after a controller's view appears
viewDidDisappear:	Called after a controller's view disappears
viewDidLoad:	Called after a controller's view loads into memory
viewDidUnload:	Called when a controller's view is released from memory
viewWillAppear:	Called just before a controller's view appears
viewWillDisappear:	Called just before a controller's view disappears
willRotateToInterfaceOrientation:duration:	Called when a controller begins rotating
willAnimateFirstHalfOfRotationToInterfaceOrientation:duration:	Called just before the first half of a view's rotation
willAnimateSecondHalfOfRotationFromInterfaceOrientation:duration:	Called just before the second half of a view's rotation

Table 7-2 UIViewController's Instance Methods for View Life Cycle Management

Try This Exploring Several Life Cycle Methods

1. Open the SimpleView project in Xcode.

2. Open SimpleViewController.m and note that Xcode generates many of the needed life cycle methods for you and then comments them. It even provides short descriptions of what each method does for you.

3. Add the life cycle methods in Listing 7-7 to the FirstViewController.m file. Because FirstViewController's parent class, UIViewController, declares all these methods, you are not required to add a declaration for the methods in FirstViewController's header file.

Listing 7-7   Life cycle methods added to FirstViewController.m

```
-(BOOL)shouldAutorotateToInterfaceOrientation:(UIInterfaceOrientation)
interfaceOrientation {
return YES;
}
```

```
-(void)didReceiveMemoryWarning {
  NSLog(@"received memory warning....");
  [super didReceiveMemoryWarning];
}
-(void)viewDidLoad {
  NSLog(@"view did load...");
  [super viewDidLoad];
}
-(void)viewWillAppear:(BOOL)animated {
  NSLog(@"view will appear...");
}
-(void)viewDidUnload {
  NSLog(@"view did unload...");
}
-(void)didRotateFromInterfaceOrientation:(UIInterfaceOrientation)
fromInterfaceOrientation {
  NSLog(@"view rotated....");
}
```

4. Click Run to run the application.

5. When the application is running, turn the simulator sideways by selecting Hardware |
   Rotate right from the simulator's menu (Figure 7-3).

6. Simulate a memory warning by selecting Hardware | Simulate Memory Warning.

7. Quit the application. The console's output should appear similar to Listing 7-8.

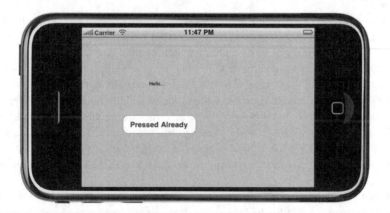

Figure 7-3 Running the application in landscape mode

(continued)

Listing 7-8 Console's logging

```
2010-08-26 23:47:10.931 SimpleView[42582:207] view did load...
2010-08-26 23:47:10.933 SimpleView[42582:207] view will appear...
2010-08-26 23:47:15.685 SimpleView[42582:207] view rotated....
2010-08-26 23:48:10.928 SimpleView[42582:207] Received simulated
memory warning.
2010-08-26 23:48:10.930 SimpleView[42582:207] received memory
warning....
```

Ask the Expert

Q: Hey, wait a minute. What does shouldAutoRotateToInterfaceOrientation: mean in Listing 7-7?

A: This method is for allowing or disallowing a view to rotate. To allow a view to rotate, return YES. To disallow, return NO. Most iPhone applications leave this set to the default NO, but when you create a universal application in Chapter 19, you'll need to handle rotation on the iPad and will be setting this to YES.

Summary

This chapter discussed the UIView and UIViewController classes. When developing an iOS application, every content view should have its own nib. Remember, placing views in their own nib conserves memory by only loading the components needed to render the current view. The development pattern for creating a view is straightforward: Subclass a UIViewController in Xcode. Create the UIView in its own nib. Then, in the nib, connect the view to the view controller. To make your code easier to test and debug, keep the name consistent between the view, view controller, and nib. Implement any view-related life cycle methods you wish to handle in the view's view controller. Keep your custom code to a minimum, though—remember, the controller's job is to serve as glue code between your view and your model. Consider placing more advanced code in helper classes, and then have your controller use these helpers.

Now that you understand how to build each screen's content, you can learn how to develop views that aggregate your individual views into a multiple-screen application. In the next chapter, you begin exploring multiview applications with the UITabBar and UITabBarController. After learning about tab bars, you move to the navigation controllers and then tables. These views let you aggregate content views into richer multiscreen applications.

Chapter 8

UITabBar and UITabBarController

Key Skills & Concepts

● Understanding tab bars

● Using the Tab Bar Application template

● Creating an application that uses a tab bar

● Adding tabs to a tab bar

● Customizing a tab bar

A tab bar consists of two or more tabs along a window's bottom. Each tab contains a view controller. As a user selects a tab, the tab loads its view controller, which in turn loads and displays its associated view. In this chapter, you explore creating tabbed applications. In the first task, you create a tabbed application using Xcode's Tab Bar Application template. After examining this template's results, you manually add a third tab to the tab bar. In the next task, you start with a Window-based Application template and create a two-tab application. In this task, you solidify your understanding by manually duplicating the steps taken by the Tab Bar Application template. The chapter's final task illustrates allowing users to customize a tab bar's tabs when it contains five or more tabs.

UITabBar, UITabBarController, UITabBarItem, and UITabBarControllerDelegate

The tab bar is useful for presenting different application subtasks or different views of the same data. If you own an iPhone, iPod touch, or iPad, you are certainly familiar with a tab bar controller, as several applications use tab bars. The Clock application, for instance, has a tab bar containing tabs with different subtasks (Figure 8-1). Each tab is a different subtask: World Clock, Alarm, Stopwatch, and Timer. The iPod application illustrates a tab bar containing different views of the same data (Figure 8-2). The Artists tab organizes your multimedia by artist; the Album tab organizes your media by album. Each tab is a different view of the same data, your iTunes multimedia. The iPod application illustrates another tab bar feature. When a tab bar has more than four tabs, it displays a More tab. When you press More, the tab bar presents the remaining tabs in a selectable list (Figure 8-3). You can also modify the iPod application's tab bar using the Edit button. Clicking the Edit button displays the tabs in a view that allows you to modify which tabs are displayed in the tab bar (see Figure 8-3). When presented with an application that contains a task with multiple subtasks or an application that requires different views of the same data, use a tab bar.

Figure 8-1   The Clock application has a tab for each subtask.

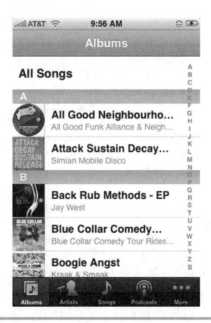

Figure 8-2   The iPod application has a tab for each data view.

Figure 8-3 The iPod application uses a More tab to display tabs.

NOTE

Do not use a tab bar for sequential navigation or data drill-down. The navigation control and tables (described in the next two chapters) are more appropriate choices for navigating sequential lists and data drill-down.

You create a tab bar using the UITabBar class. A UITabBar displays two or more tabs along a window's bottom edge. Individual tabs are UITabBarItem class instances. You tie these classes together using the UITabBarController and UITabBarControllerDelegate. Each UITabBarItem contains its own view controller. Click a tab, and the UITabBarItem loads its view controller. The view controller displays its view.

NOTE

A tab's view controller might be an advanced view, like a table or a navigation controller. Chapter 9 illustrates placing a navigation controller in a tab. Chapter 10 illustrates placing a navigation controller in a tab and then a table in the navigation controller.

A UITabBar has an associated UITabBarController and UITabBarDelegate. The UITabBarController manages the UIViewController objects in each tab. For instance, if a user wishes to add, remove, or rearrange tab bar items, the UITabBarController is responsible for implementing the behavior. You will see how to accomplish a rearrangeable tab bar later in this chapter. But first, consider the easiest tab bar implementation: the Tab Bar Application template.

Try This | Using the Tab Bar Application Template

The Tab Bar Application template is the easiest route to creating a tabbed application, and compared with last chapter's Single View Application template, this template is a more useful starting point for real-world projects. In this task, you create a simple tab bar application using the Tab Bar Application template. After examining the template's results, you manually add a third tab to the tab bar.

1. Create a new Tab Bar Application by selecting the template in the New Project dialog. Name the project **TabBarExOne**.

2. In the Navigation pane, expand Classes And Resources. At first glance, it appears the template created the same classes as it would for a View-based Application. However, the template added several tab bar–related classes for you, making this a slightly more complex application.

3. Open TabBarExOneAppDelegate.h and notice the application's delegate adopts the UITabBarControllerDelegate protocol. It also declares a UITabBarController property as an IBOutlet (Listing 8-1).

Listing 8-1   The TabBarExOneAppDelegate adopts the UITabBarControllerDelegate protocol

```
#import <UIKit/UIKit.h>
@interface TabBarExOneAppDelegate : NSObject <UIApplicationDelegate,
UITabBarControllerDelegate> {
 UIWindow *window;
 UITabBarController *tabBarController;
}
@property (nonatomic, retain) IBOutlet UIWindow *window;
@property (nonatomic, retain)
    IBOutlet UITabBarController *tabBarController;
@end
```

4. Open MainWindow.xib and review the objects in the xib (the icons to the left of the Editing pane). In particular, note that the template added a tab bar controller.

5. The template also added TabBarExOneAppDelegate as a proxy object to MainView .xib. Review TabBarExOneAppDelegate's connections in the View | Utilities | Connections pane. Notice Xcode added a tabBarController property as an IBOutlet. Interface Builder subsequently knew the application delegate had a tabBarController outlet and connected it to the tab bar controller in the document window.

6. In the Editing pane, select the tab labeled First and then select "First View Controller – First" in the hierarchy of objects across the top of the Edit pane and notice the "Tab Bar Item – First" object under it. The second tab view controller also has a tab bar item associated with it.

(continued)

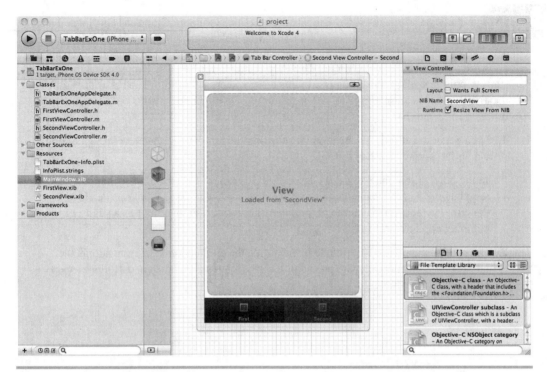

Figure 8-4   The second tab bar item's view controller is from another nib.

7. Highlight the second view controller in the document window. Notice in the controller's inspector that the UIViewController is from an external nib; the template specified the view controller's Nib name (Figure 8-4).

8. Build and run the application. A simple two-tab application runs in the simulator.

9. Open MainWindow.xib in Interface Builder.

10. On the tab bar controller's canvas, click the tab bar item labeled First. Be careful—only click once. Clicking the item once selects the tab bar item's view controller. You know you clicked once if the Object Identity Inspector pane lists the class as "FirstViewController".

11. Click the tab bar item twice, and you select the actual tab bar item. The Object Identity Inspector pane lists the class as "UITabBarItem".

The Tab Bar Application template generates a two-tabbed application. You will most certainly find situations where you need more tabs. Adding another tab to a tab bar is not difficult. In the next task, you add a third tab to the application.

Try This Adding a Tab Bar Item to a Tab Bar Application

1. Select File | New | New File to create another UIViewController subclass and name the controller **ThirdViewController**. Ensure the "With XIB for user interface" check box that creates an accompanying xib is also selected. Xcode should generate the ThirdViewController.h, ThirdViewController.m, and ThirdViewController.xib files.

2. Select ThirdViewController.xib to open it in Interface Builder. Change the view's color to something other than white and save your changes.

3. Open MainWindow.xib in Interface Builder and select the tab bar controller from the object icons on the left of the Editor pane.

4. Drag a new ViewController from the Object Library pane to the Editing pane and carefully drop it in the tab bar area. As you hover over the tab bar, the ViewController that you're dragging will shrink down and take on the appearance of a tab item.

5. Click the third tab bar item once. In the Inspector, change the class from UIViewController to **ThirdViewController**. Also type **ThirdViewController** for the nib name.

6. Click the third tab bar item two times. Change the tab's identifier to Search from the pull-down menu in the Tab Bar Item Attributes Inspector. A magnifying glass and Search appears in the tab (Figure 8-5).

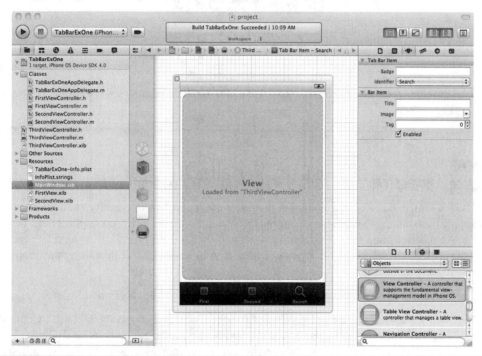

Figure 8-5 Changing a tab bar item's image to Search

(continued)

Figure 8-6 Running the three-tab application in iPhone Simulator

7. Save your changes and run the application. The application now has a third tab bar item (Figure 8-6).

Try This   Creating a Tab Bar Application from Scratch

Using a template is well and good, but it doesn't teach you how to actually build a tabbed application (unless you are able to use the template). So in this task, you duplicate the Tab Bar Application template's steps, but start with a Window-based Application template and manually add the tab bar items to your project. It is no more difficult than using the template—just slightly more tedious.

1. Create a new Window-based Application and name it **TabBarExTwo**.

2. Open TabBarExTwoAppDelegate.h and change it so that it adopts the UITabBarController Delegate protocol (Listing 8-2). Add a UITabBarController property as an IBOutlet. The UITabBarControllerDelegate.h should appear like Listing 8-2. Don't forget to synthesize the controller in UITabBarControllerDelegate.m. Save and build.

Listing 8-2   TabBarExTwoAppDelegate.h modified to use a UITabBarController

```
#import <UIKit/UIKit.h>
@interface TabBarExTwoAppDelegate : NSObject <UIApplicationDelegate,
UITabBarControllerDelegate> {
 UIWindow *window;
 UITabBarController *tabBarController;
}
@property (nonatomic, retain) IBOutlet UIWindow *window;
@property (nonatomic, retain) IBOutlet UITabBarController
*tabBarController;
@end
```

3. Create a new UIViewController class and name it **FirstViewController**. Be certain it also creates an associated xib. Xcode should generate the FirstViewController.h, FirstViewController.m, and FirstViewController.xib files.

4. Create another UIViewController and associated xib named **SecondViewController**.

5. Open FirstViewController.xib and change the view's color. Open SecondViewController .xib and change the view's color.

6. Save all of your changes.

7. Open MainWindow.xib and drag a new UITabBarController from the Object Library to the Editing pane. Interface Builder should show a tab bar controller with two tabs.

8. Select the TabBarExTwoAppDelegate's Connections Inspector and connect its tabBarController outlet to the tab bar controller in the document window.

9. Click once on the first tab of the TabBarController in the Editing pane, and change its class to FirstViewController in the Identity Inspector. Change its Nib Name to **FirstViewController**.

10. Change View Controller (Item 2) to the SecondViewController, using the same steps as the preceding step. Do not forget to set the NIB Name to **SecondViewController** in the Second View Controller Attributes Inspector.

11. Change the first tab's identifier to Recents and the second tab's identifier to Downloads (Figure 8-7).

12. Save your changes.

13. Open TabBarExTwoAppDelegate.m. Add the tab bar controller to the applicationDidFinishLaunching method (Listing 8-3).

(continued)

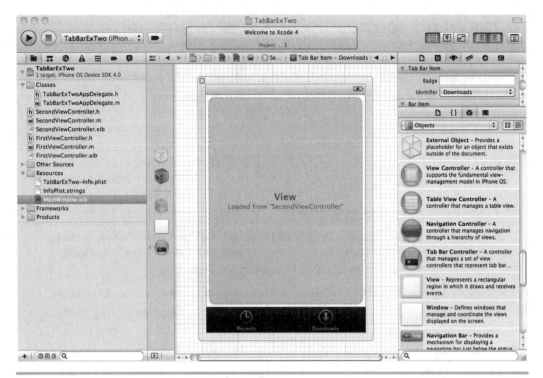

Figure 8-7 The first and second tab identifiers

Listing 8-3 TabBarExTwoAppDelegate.m modified to use a UITabBarController

```
#import "TabBarExTwoAppDelegate.h"
@implementation TabBarExTwoAppDelegate
@synthesize window;
@synthesize tabBarController;
-(void)applicationDidFinishLaunching:(UIApplication *)application {
    [window addSubview:tabBarController.view];
    [window makeKeyAndVisible];
}
-(void)dealloc {
    [window release];
    [tabBarController release];
    [super dealloc];
}
@end
```

14. Click Run, and a two-tab application runs in the iPhone Simulator (Figure 8-8).

Figure 8-8   Two-tabbed application running in iPhone Simulator

Try This Allowing Users to Customize a Tab Bar

Sometimes you might wish to add more than five tabs to your application. However, with six or more tabs, the iPhone tab bar will have to display four tabs and a More tab. When a user presses More, the excess tabs appear in a selectable list. By default, a navigation bar with an Edit button is displayed across the window's top. A user can then tap Edit and modify which tabs he or she wishes to see displayed on the tab bar.

The default behavior is to allow all tab bar items to be editable. If you wish to modify this default and limit which tabs are editable, you must modify the toolbar. In this task, you add more than four tabs to the first task's tab bar. You then make the tab bar non-editable, followed by making only some tabs editable.

1. Open TabBarExOne and add a new view controller. Name the class **FourthViewController**. Ensure it also creates an associated xib. Xcode should create the FourthViewController.h, FourthViewController.m, and FourthViewController.xib files.

(continued)

2. Open FourthViewController.xib in Interface Builder. Change the view's color.

3. Close FourthViewController.xib and open MainWindow.xib in Interface Builder.

4. Add three more tabs by dragging and dropping three new view controllers from the Object Library onto the tab bar. They should each shrink to a tab item as you hover over the tab bar before releasing the drag (Figure 8-9).

5. Change each view controller's class to **FourthViewController**. Also change each view controller's NIB name to **FourthViewController**.

NOTE

You would never use the same view controller for three different tabs in a real project, since each tab likely reveals a unique subtask or data view.

6. Save your changes and click Run. Notice it added the fourth tab and a More tab (Figure 8-10). When you click the More tab, it displays a UITableView with the other two tabs (Figure 8-11). When you click either tab, the tab's associated view controller's view is displayed.

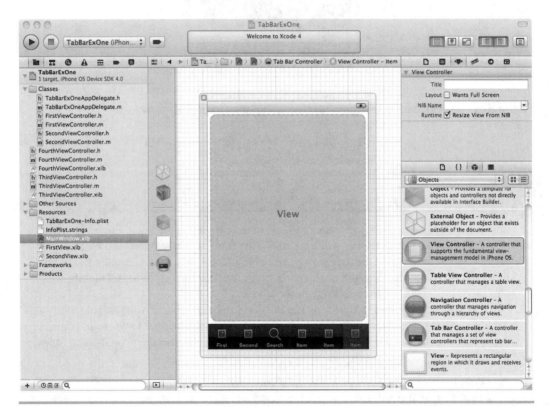

Figure 8-9 Adding three view controllers to the project

Figure 8-10   Application displaying four tabs and a More button

Figure 8-11   Clicking the More tab displays the remaining two tabs in a list.

(continued)

Figure 8-12 Clicking Edit displays a view for configuring the tab bar's tabs.

7. Click Edit, and a screen where you can configure the tab bar items is displayed (Figure 8-12).

8. Try dragging Two and Three to the tab bar and replacing a couple of the other tabs (Figure 8-13). Click Done to see the new tab order.

9. Open TabBarExOneAppDelegate.m and add the following line to the applicationDidFinish Launching method.

```
tabBarController.customizableViewControllers = nil;
```

10. Save changes and click Run. Notice the Edit button no longer appears after clicking More.

11. Now modify applicationDidFinishLaunching again. Change the code so it matches Listing 8-4.

Figure 8-13   Replacing a couple tabs with Two and Three

Listing 8-4   Setting the customizableViewControllers

```
-(void)applicationDidFinishLaunching:(UIApplication *)application {
    NSMutableArray * conts =
        [[[NSMutableArray alloc] init] autorelease];
    [conts addObject:[tabBarController.viewControllers
objectAtIndex:0]];
    [conts addObject:[tabBarController.viewControllers
objectAtIndex:1]];
    tabBarController.customizableViewControllers = conts;
    [window addSubview:tabBarController.view];
}
```

12. Save changes and click Run. Notice you can only edit First and Second (Figure 8-14).

(continued)

Figure 8-14 Only First and Second are editable.

A tab bar's default behavior is to allow users to rearrange, delete, and add tabs when a tab bar contains more than four tabs. To disable editing all tabs, set the tab bar controller's customizableViewControllers to nil. To disable only some tags, add the tabs that should be editable to the customizableViewControllers. Tabs not added to customizableViewControllers are automatically made non-editable.

Summary

As this chapter illustrated, creating a tabbed application is easy. First, ensure your application has a UITabBarControllerDelegate. Although you can create your own class to adopt the UITabBarControllerDelegate protocol, using the application's delegate is easier. But note, more complex applications that use tab bars should have a custom delegate associated with the tab bar and should not have the application's main delegate adopt the UITabBarController Delegate.

After changing your application's delegate to adopt the UITabBarController Delegate, add a UITabBarController property to the delegate. Then add a UITabBarController to MainWindow .xib and connect the controller to the application delegate's tabBarController property. After connecting the delegate and tab bar controller, connect the individual UITabBarItem objects to view controllers. Creating tabbed applications is that easy.

In this chapter, you learned how to create a tab bar, its associated controller, and its delegate. This chapter didn't have much in the way of explanation, as tab bars are best learned by doing. You created a tabbed application both using a template and manually. If you still do not understand tab bars, you should definitely reread this chapter, as tab bars are a navigation component you will use frequently for developing iOS applications. Think of all the situations where you use tabs in a desktop application—tabs are as ubiquitous on iOS applications. But remember conventional user interface (UI) wisdom: Use tab bars for subtasks and for different views on the same data set. Do not use tab bars for tasks involving sequential steps. A navigation bar and its associated controller are much more useful for this navigation. In the next chapter, you learn how to create and use a navigation bar and its associated controller. Moreover, you will place a navigation bar in a view controller as a tab bar item. After learning about the navigation bar, you then explore tables. After learning about a table's fundamentals, you will place a navigation item and a table in the same view controller in an individual tab. After learning about tables, you will then have the fundamentals for creating the navigation for virtually any iOS application.

Chapter 9

UINavigationBar and UINavigationController

Key Skills & Concepts

● Understanding UINavigationBar, UINavigationController, and UINavigationItem

● Understanding how to use a navigation bar in a simple application

● Understanding how to programmatically manipulate a navigation bar's items

● Adding a navigation bar to a tab in a tabbed application

A navigation bar is displayed along a window's top, just below the status bar. The navigation bar optionally contains a title for each view displayed and one or more buttons. Typically, the button on the bar's right, when clicked, takes the user to the next step in another view, although sometimes applications use the right button as a "done" button. The button on the bar's left is a Back button, returning to the previous view. Navigation bars are often used with tables, where a table is displayed with a navigation bar above it. When a user clicks a table's rows, the navigation bar's associated navigation controller takes the user to more detailed information about the selected item. For instance, the App Store application allows a user to refine his or her categories until the application of interest is found (Figure 9-1). For instance, if a user clicked Games, the navigation controller would take the user to a Games subcategory. If the user then clicked All Games, the navigation controller would take the user to a table of all games in the App Store. If a user wished to go back a step, he or she would press the button on the navigation bar's upper-left area. This button is the Back button. Note the navigation controller labeled the button's title with the previous view's title.

The navigation bar and navigation controller are useful for applications requiring hierarchical navigation, such as data drill-down. In the App Store application, you drill down to increasingly specific categories until reaching a list of items rather than further subcategories. When you select an item, it takes you to a more detailed view of your selection. Navigation bars are also useful for applications with multiple steps in a single task. In this chapter, you learn how to use a navigation bar and its associated classes. In the first task, you start with a Window-based application and manually create an application consisting of three views managed by a navigation controller. In the second task, you look at how the Utility Application template uses a navigation bar. This template uses a navigation bar on only one view and without using an associated navigation controller. Finally, this chapter presents a navigation controller embedded in a tab bar's tab. This is perhaps this chapter's most useful task and should not be skipped. You will find embedding a navigation controller in a tab a ubiquitous requirement when developing iOS applications.

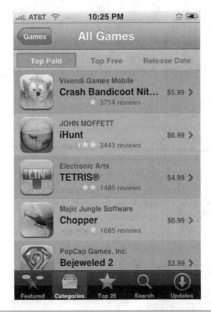

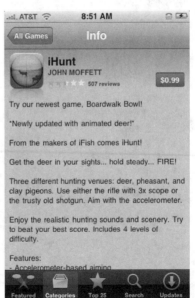

Figure 9-1 Using the App Store application

UINavigationBar, UINavigationController, and UINavigationItem

Below the status bar but above the application window's content, many applications have a navigation bar. Navigation bars display the current view's title and contain one or more buttons for navigating to other screens. In this chapter's introduction, you viewed the App Store application, a typical use for a navigation bar. The Notes application also uses a navigation bar (Figure 9-2). The navigation bar appears above the yellow notepad. Upon clicking the + key, the navigation bar displays a new note page. The navigation bar's title is New Note and contains a back button labeled "Notes" and a right button labeled "Done." When the user taps either button, the application returns the user to the application's primary page.

You add navigation bars to an application using the UINavigationBar class, but you almost never use a UINavigationBar class directly. Instead you'll use UINavigationBar's controller, UINavigationController. You control a UINavigationBar using a UINavigationController. A UINavigationController uses a stack data structure to manage one or more view controllers. The first view controller, or the root view controller, is the first item on the stack. To navigate to other views, you push the view's view controller onto the stack. To return to the previous view, you pop the current view from the stack.

Figure 9-2 The Notes App uses a navigation bar.

Ask the Expert

Q: **What is a stack?**

A: A stack is a data structure used to hold a collection of objects. You can only add or remove objects from the stack's top. Envision a stack of plates: You add plates to the top and remove plates from the top. Removing from the bottom would cause the plates to topple and break. The stack data structure has the same LIFO (last in first out) requirements. Placing a new item on the stack is called "pushing," while removing an item from the stack is called "popping."

Try This Building a Three-View Application Using a Navigation Bar

It is easiest to learn the UINavigationController by example. In this task, you create a simple application containing three views. You navigate between the three views using a navigation bar. The first view has a button on the navigation bar's right, which says "Next." When you click the button, the application takes you to the next view. This view has a Back button and a button in the view rather than on the navigation bar. When you click the button in the view, the application takes you to a third view. The third view has a navigation bar and a title.

1. Create a new Window-based Application. Name the application **ThreeViewNavCont**.

2. Create three UIViewController classes, naming them **FirstViewController**, **SecondViewController**, and **ThirdViewController**. Be certain to also generate xib files for each class.

3. Open each of the xibs and add a label object to each with the text "View One", "View Two", and "View Three" so that you can easily tell which view is visible when running your app.

4. Save each xib file after changing it.

5. Open MainWindow.xib and drag a navigation controller from the library to the Document window (Figure 9-3). Notice Interface Builder shows the navigation controller's canvas with a navigation bar and a view.

6. Select the navigation controller's view controller. You can do this by expanding the column of icons representing the objects in the xib, then clicking the disclosure arrow next to navigation controller, and then selecting the view controller. Change the controller's class to **FirstViewController** in the Inspector. Also change its NIB name to **FirstViewController** in the Inspector (Figure 9-4).

(continued)

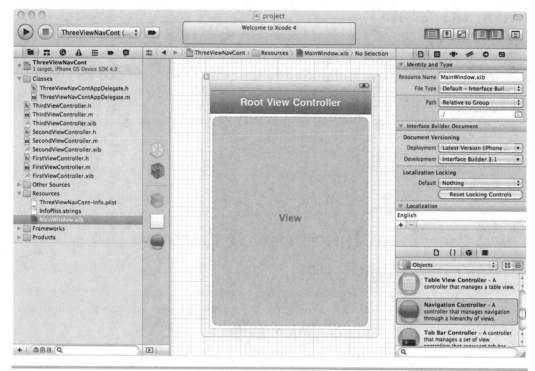

Figure 9-3 Adding a navigation controller to MainWindow.xib

7. Save your changes.

8. Open ThreeViewNavContAppDelegate.h in Xcode. Add a UINavigationControllerIBOutlet declaration to the header file (Listing 9-1).

Listing 9-1 ThreeViewNavContAppDelegate.h

```
#import<UIKit/UIKit.h>
@interface ThreeViewNavContAppDelegate :
NSObject<UIApplicationDelegate> {
    UIWindow *window;
    UINavigationController *navController;
}
@property (nonatomic, retain) IBOutlet UIWindow *window;
@property (nonatomic, retain) IBOutlet UINavigationController *
navController;
@end
```

Figure 9-4   Changing the view controller to FirstViewController

9. Add the UINavigationController to ThreeViewNavContAppDelegate.m and add the UINavigationController's view to the window (Listing 9-2). Save and build.

Listing 9-2   ThreeViewNavContAppDelegate.m

```
#import "ThreeViewNavContAppDelegate.h"
@implementation ThreeViewNavContAppDelegate
@synthesize window;
@synthesize navController;
- (BOOL)application:(UIApplication *)application
didFinishLaunchingWithOptions:(NSDictionary *)launchOptions {
    [window addSubview: navController.view];
    [window makeKeyAndVisible];
    return YES;
}
```

(continued)

```
- (void)applicationWillTerminate:(UIApplication *)application {
// Save data if appropriate.
}
- (void)dealloc {
    [navController release];
    [window release];
    [super dealloc];
}
@end
```

10. Switch back to MainWindow.xib in Interface Builder. Right-click ThreeViewNavContApp Delegate in the document window and connect the navController outlet to the UINavigationController (Figure 9-5).

11. Save your changes and click Run to run the application, and FirstViewController's view should appear (Figure 9-6).

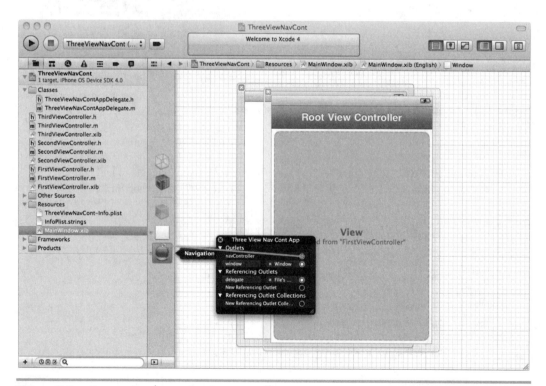

Figure 9-5 Connecting the navigation controller

Figure 9-6   The application running in iPhone Simulator

The first step to using a navigation bar is to add a navigation controller to a document window. Upon adding the navigation controller, Interface Builder also adds a root view controller, and you changed this view controller to your view controller. Making this connection in Interface Builder allows the nib to manage the property's life cycle. When you build and run the application, the application knows MainWindow.xib is the application's main nib and loads it. Upon loading, the nib initializes the objects it manages, which includes the navigation controller property, navController. The navigation controller loads its root view controller. Because the root view controller has an associated navigation item, the navigation controller adds a navigation bar above the view with the navigation item's title. Because MainWindow .xib handles all the application's initialization, all you do in the application:didFinish-LaunchingWithOptions method is add the view to the window. After adding the navigation controller, you must provide navigation controls so that a user can move from view to view. You can either add a button to the navigation bar itself or add a control to a view's canvas. The next few steps do both.

12. Open MainWindow.xib and select the navigation item in the document window (Figure 9-7). Change the navigation item's title to First View.

(continued)

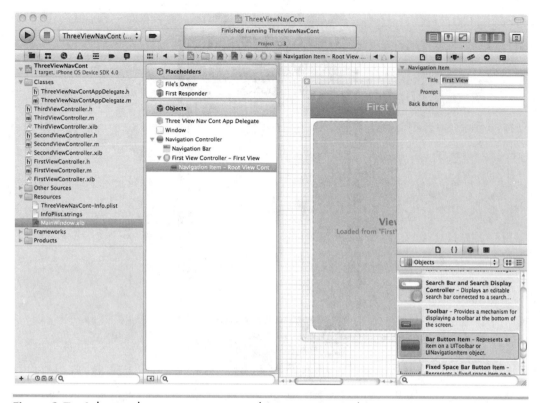

Figure 9-7 Selecting the navigation item in the Document window

13. Drag a bar button item from the library to the navigation bar and Interface Builder will highlight a rectangle where you can drop the button (Figure 9-8). Rename the button **Next**.

14. Save your changes and then open FirstViewController.h and add a new action called moveToNextView (Listing 9-3). Import SecondViewController and add SecondViewController as a property.

Listing 9-3 FirstViewController.h

```
#import <UIKit/UIKit.h>
@class SecondViewController;
@interface FirstViewController : UIViewController {
  SecondViewController * second;
}
@property (nonatomic, retain) SecondViewController * second;
-(IBAction) moveToNextView: (id) sender;
  @end
```

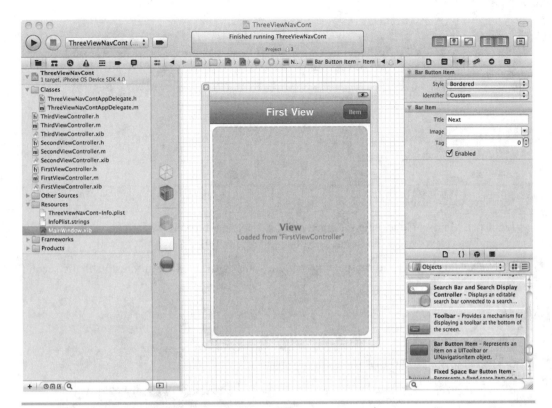

Figure 9-8   Adding a button to FirstViewController's navigation bar

15. Open FirstViewController.m and implement moveToNextView, as in Listing 9-4.

Listing 9-4   FirstViewController.m

```
#import "FirstViewController.h"
#import "SecondViewController.h"
@implementation FirstViewController
@synthesize second;
```

(continued)

```
-(IBAction) moveToNextView: (id) sender {
  self.second = [[[SecondViewController alloc]
     initWithNibName:@"SecondViewController" bundle:nil] autorelease];
  [self.navigationController pushViewController:self.second animated: YES];
}

-(void)dealloc {
  [second release];
  [super dealloc];
}
@end
```

16. Save your changes.

17. Open MainWindow.xib in Interface Builder, select the FirstViewController, and connect its moveToNextView action to the Next button (Figure 9-9).

18. Save and click Run to run the application. Tapping the Next button results in the second

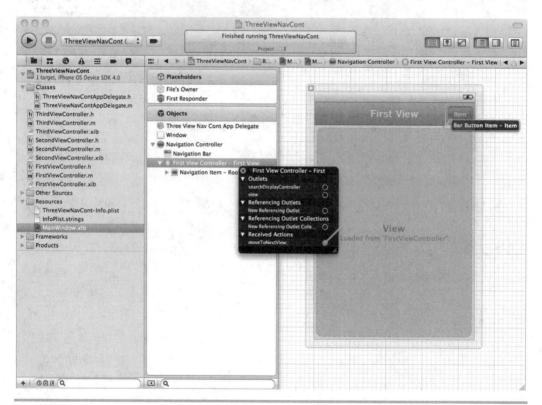

Figure 9-9 Connecting moveToNextView action to the navigation button

Figure 9-10 The application running in iPhone Simulator

view being displayed (Figure 9-10). Tap First View, and the application returns to the first view.

In Step 13, you changed the default title to your view's title. Actually, to be specific, you changed the default title to your view controller's navigation item's title. In Step 14, you added a bar button item to the navigation bar and set it as the navigation bar item's rightBarButtonItem. Establishing this connection ensures the application displays the button on the bar's right. You then created an action that, when clicked, pushes the second view controller onto the navigation controller's stack. The navigation controller displays this view and a navigation bar containing the new view's navigation bar element. Notice you must push view controllers onto the stack manually through code, as in Listing 9-4.

```
[self.navigationController pushViewController:self.second animated: YES];
```

If a view controller is in a navigation controller's stack, then the navigationController property automatically refers to the navigation controller managing the stack. So, the navigation controller in ThreeViewNavContAppDelegate pushes FirstViewController's SecondViewController onto the stack. Note that setting the animated parameter to YES causes the new view to slide in from the right or the old view from the left when navigating back.

As the task illustrates, creating an application using a navigation controller and associated navigation bar is not difficult. The Back button, and popping a view controller from the navigation controller, is implemented for you. You provide the control and action to push view controllers onto the navigation controller's stack.

Adding Another View

You are not limited to bar buttons if you wish to push views onto a navigation controller's stack. In the following steps, you first add a bar button item to SecondViewController. You then add an additional button to SecondViewController's view, but instead of it being a bar button, you use a regular button.

1. Open the ThreeViewNavCont project in Xcode.

2. Open SecondViewController and add an IBOutlet for a UIBarButtonItem to SecondViewController as a property. Name the property **navBut**; don't forget to synthesize the property in SecondViewController.m.

3. Open SecondViewController.m and implement the viewDidLoad method to set the navigationItem's right bar button item to navBut:

```
self.navigationItem.rightBarButtonItem = navBut;
```

4. Note that every UIViewController has a navigationItem and that it is a read-only property.

5. Open SecondViewController.xib in Interface Builder and add a new bar button item to the document window. Connect the newly added bar button item to the navBut outlet (Figure 9-11). Name the new bar button item **Next**.

6. Save and run the application, and the second view now displays its title in the navigation bar (Figure 9-12). But notice, clicking the Next button in the navigation bar has no effect because you haven't connected it to a method yet.

7. Open SecondViewController.h and add a new action called moveToNextView. Import ThirdViewController. Add a ThirdViewController as a property (Listing 9-5).

Listing 9-5   SecondViewController.h

```
#import <UIKit/UIKit.h>
@class ThirdViewController;
@interface SecondViewController : UIViewController {
```

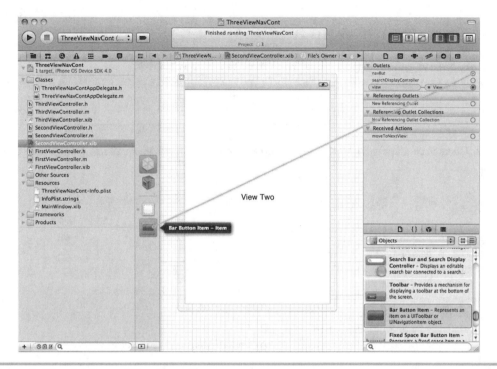

Figure 9-11 Adding a UIBarButtonItem

Figure 9-12 The application displaying the second view controller's navigation item's title

```
 ThirdViewController * third;
 UIBarButtonItem * navBut;
}
@property (nonatomic, retain) IBOutlet UIBarButtonItem * navBut;
@property (nonatomic, retain) ThirdViewController * third;
-(IBAction) moveToNextView: (id) sender;
@end
```

8. Open SecondViewController.m and implement moveToNextView, as in Listing 9-6. Save and build.

Listing 9-6   SecondViewController.m

```
#import "SecondViewController.h"
#import "ThirdViewController.h"
@implementation SecondViewController
@synthesize third;
@synthesize navBut;
-(void) viewDidLoad {
 self.navigationItem.title =
    @"SecondView"; self.navigationItem.rightBarButtonItem = navBut;
}

-(IBAction) moveToNextView: (id) sender {
 self.third = [[[ThirdViewController alloc]
    initWithNibName:@"ThirdViewController" bundle:nil] autorelease];
 [self.navigationController pushViewController: self.third animated: YES];
}

-(void)dealloc { [third release]; [super dealloc];
}
@end
```

9. Click SecondViewController.xib to edit it with Interface Builder. Connect the bar button's selector to the File's Owner moveToNextView action (Figure 9-13).

10. Save and run the application. The second view now has a Next button and tapping it moves to the next view (Figure 9-14). Now consider pushing a view onto the stack using a regular button.

11. Open SecondViewController.xib and add a button to the view. Connect the button to moveToNextView (Figure 9-15). Connect to the button's Touch Up Inside action.

12. Save and run the application. Click the button on the second view, and it, too, navigates to the third view.

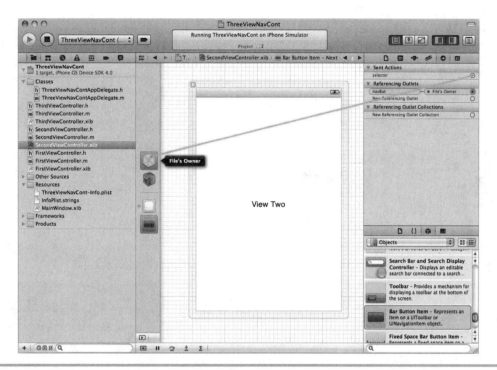

Figure 9-13 Connecting the bar button to the moveToNextView action

Figure 9-14 The third view, after clicking the Next button on the second view

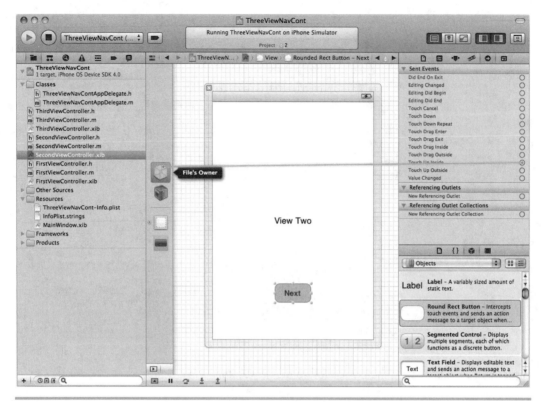

Figure 9-15 Connecting a button to the moveToNextView method

Using a button rather than a bar button item is that easy. Typically, though, in most iOS applications, you will see a table in the view rather than a button (see Figure 9-1). For instance, SecondViewController might have an embedded table listing categories. Upon clicking a table row, you would invoke the moveToNextView method, passing the specific table row's identifier as a parameter. The App Store application is an example of this type of navigation (see Figure 9-1).

Try This   See How a Utility Application Uses NavigationBar

Create a new Utility application using the Utility Application template, and then review the code. You will notice it uses a navigation bar in the FlipsideView to display a title and a Done button.

In our previous example, every view had a NavigationBar and we pushed each subsequent view onto a stack of views. With a Utility application, the show info button creates a new modal view and only that flipside view has a NavigationBar. Instead of defaulting to popping the view from the stack, the Done button invokes a done method that dismisses the modal view.

Remember that all of the application templates in Xcode are just generating code and xib files for you and you can experiment with creating any of them and then looking through the generated code to better understand how iOS applications work.

More on the UINavigationController

You are not limited to pushing items onto a stack. You can also pop items off the stack. You can also modify the navigation bar, hiding elements, adding new ones, and making other modifications.

Popping View Controllers

You pop view controllers from a stack using the method popViewControllerAnimated:. This method pops the top view controller off the navigation controller's stack and updates the displayed view to the stack's next view controller's view.

```
(UIViewController *) popViewControllerAnimated: (BOOL) animated
```

The method takes one parameter, which indicates if the transition should be animated. The method also returns the popped view controller, should you wish to retain it for future use.

Other methods you might use include popToRootViewControllerAnimated: and popToViewController:animated:. Refer to Apple's online reference, "UINavigationController Class Reference," for more information.

Configuring the Navigation Bar

You can also hide the navigation bar by calling the navigation controller's setNavigationBarHidden: method.

```
-(void) setNavigationBarHidden: (BOOL)hidden animated: (BOOL)animated
```

This method hides or displays the navigation bar, depending upon if you passed YES or NO as the initial parameter. You also specify if the navigation bar should slide in from the top by specifying YES for the animated parameter.

You might also change a navigation bar's style by changing its style property. You can use code to change the navigation bar's style, but the easiest way to do this is through Interface Builder. You can also change a navigation bar's color. You change the color using the tintColor property.

Try This ## Using a Navigation Controller in a Tab

Applications usually use a navigation bar with other navigation views, such as a tab bar or table view. You haven't learned about table views yet—you won't learn about using a table view with a navigation bar until Chapter 10. However, you learned about the tab bar in Chapter 8. A navigation bar might be placed within a tab bar. For instance, returning to the App Store application, notice the navigation screens are steps within the Categories tab (see Figure 9-1). The Featured, Categories, Top 25, and Updates tabs are different views on the same data. The Search tab is a subtask. Within the Categories tab, there is a navigation bar combined with a table view. This combination provides a way to drill down hierarchically to a specific application.

Although you don't learn about tables until Chapter 10, consider a navigation bar in a tab.

1. Create a new Window-based Application. Name the application **NavInTab**.

2. Create two new UIViewController classes. Name the first **FirstTabViewController** and the second **StepTwoViewController**; be certain to create nibs for both.

3. Open both newly created nibs and change the background color for each view.

4. Open MainWindow.xib and add a UITabBarController to the document.

5. Delete the first tab bar view controller. Drag a navigation controller to the document and drop it so that it is the first item below the tab bar. Change the navigation controller's root view controller to FirstTabViewController by changing its class and nib name in the Inspector. The canvas should indicate the view is from FirstTabViewController.nib (Figure 9-16).

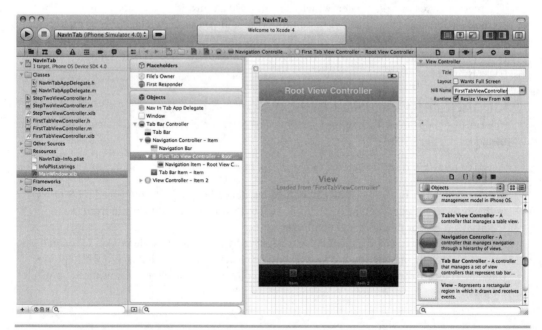

Figure 9-16 Canvas indicates view is from a different nib.

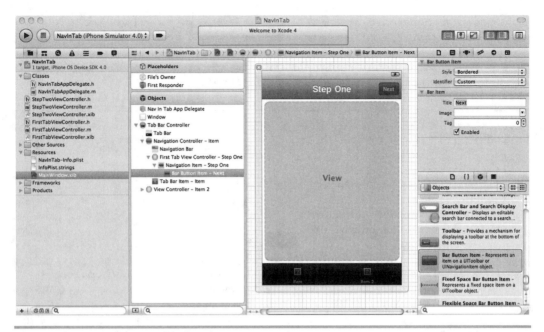

Figure 9-17   Bar button added to document window

6. Change the navigation item's title from "Root View Controller" to "step one."

7. Drag a bar button item from the library to the navigation bar in the editing window and drop it in the area for a right-hand button (Figure 9-17). Change the button's title to **Next**.

8. Save your changes.

9. Open NavInTabAppDelegate.h and NavInTabAppDelate.m and adopt the UITabBarController Delegate protocol. Also add a UITabBarController property and a UINavigationController property. Modify applicationDidFinishLaunching so that it loads the tabBarController property's root view. The files should match Listings 9-7 and 9-8. Save and build.

Listing 9-7   NavInTabAppDelegate.h

```
#import<UIKit/UIKit.h>
@interface NavInTabAppDelegate : NSObject<UIApplicationDelegate,
       UITabBarControllerDelegate> {
 UIWindow *window;
 UITabBarController *tabBarController;
 UINavigationController *navBarController;
}
```

(continued)

```
@property (nonatomic, retain) IBOutlet UIWindow *window;
@property (nonatomic, retain) IBOutlet
    UITabBarController*tabBarController;
@property (nonatomic, retain) IBOutlet
    UINavigationController *navBarController;
@end
```

Listing 9-8   NavInTabAppDelegate.m

```
#import "NavInTabAppDelegate.h"
@implementation NavInTabAppDelegate
@synthesize window;
@synthesize tabBarController;
@synthesize navBarController;

- (BOOL)application:(UIApplication *)application
    didFinishLaunchingWithOptions:(NSDictionary *)launchOptions {
 [window addSubview:tabBarController.view];
 [window makeKeyAndVisible];
 return YES;
}

-(void)dealloc {
 [tabBarController release];
 [navBarController release];
 [window release];
 [super dealloc];
}
@end
```

---

10. Open MainWindow.xib in Interface Builder and connect the NavInTabAppDelegate's navBarController to the newly added navigation controller (Figure 9-18). Connect the tabBarController to the newly added tab bar controller.

11. Save your changes.

12. Edit StepTwoViewController.m and implement the viewDidLoad method so that it sets the navigationItem's title to "step two" (Listing 9-9).

Listing 9-9   StepTwoViewController's viewDidLoad method

```
-(void)viewDidLoad {
[super viewDidLoad];
self.navigationItem.title = @"step two";
}
```

---

13. Open FirstTabViewController.h and import StepTwoViewController.h and NavInTabAppDelegate.h. Also add the method signature, takeNextStep (Listing 9-10).

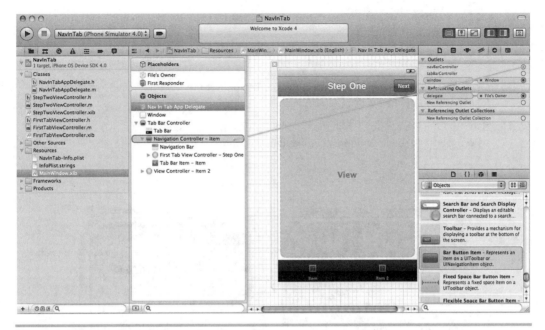

Figure 9-18 Connecting the navBarController

Listing 9-10 FirstTabViewController.h

```
#import<UIKit/UIKit.h>
#import "StepTwoViewController.h"
#import "NavInTabAppDelegate.h"
@interface FirstTabViewController : UIViewController {
}
-(IBAction) takeNextStep: (id) sender;
@end
```

---

14. Open FirstTabViewController.m and implement the newly added action. The file should match Listing 9-11. Note that you'll also want to call dealloc for third view when the second view is deallocated. Popping a view from the stack doesn't automatically deallocate it.

Listing 9-11 takeNextStep method added to FirstTabViewController.m

```
-(IBAction) takeNextStep : (id) sender {
  StepTwoViewController *varSecondViewController =
      [[StepTwoViewController alloc] initWithNibName:
      @"StepTwoViewController" bundle:nil];
```

(continued)

```
[self.navigationController pushViewController:varSecondViewController
    animated: YES];
}
```

15. Open MainWindow.xib and connect the bar button item to the FirstViewController's takeNextStep method.

16. Save and run the application in the iPhone Simulator. You should have a two-tab application, where the first tab has an embedded navigation control (Figure 9-19).

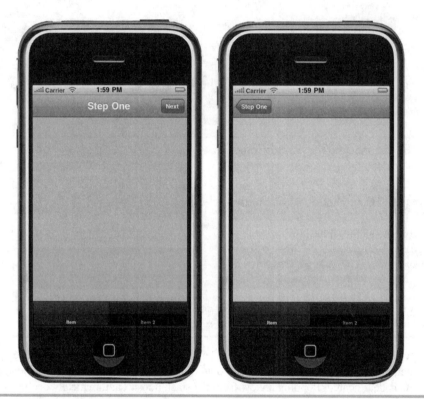

Figure 9-19 The finished application in iPhone Simulator

Summary

Creating an application with a navigation bar is straightforward. In the application's MainWindow.xib, add a UINavigationController. Set the navigation controller's root view controller, and create one or more other view controllers. Then add code that pushes the view controllers onto the navigation controller's stack. When a view controller is pushed onto the stack, it becomes the topmost view controller, and so the application displays the view controller's view. Popping a view controller off the stack is provided by default if you do not make the navigation bar's Back button invisible. If you do make the Back button invisible, or somehow disable the button, you must use one of the navigation controller's methods for popping view controllers.

In this chapter, you learned how to create an application containing a navigation controller with three views. You then looked at how the Utility Application template uses NavigationBar in a different manner. Finally, you embedded a navigation controller within a tab in a tab bar. But this chapter did omit the most common navigation controller use: a table combined with a navigation controller. In the next chapter, after learning about tables, we'll correct this omission by presenting a navigation controller combined with a table controller. After learning about this combination, you will have enough knowledge of view controllers that you should be able to tackle most iOS application navigation strategies.

Chapter 10

Tables Using UITableView and UITableViewController

Key Skills & Concepts

- Understanding table views
- Understanding table view delegates
- Understanding table view data sources
- Grouping and indexing table rows
- Selecting table rows
- Modifying a table's appearance
- Using a table in a navigation controller
- Editing a table's rows

Table views display content in a list. Tables have a single column and multiple rows. They can scroll vertically and display large data sets. For example, the Notes application is a good example of an application containing a table. Notes' first screen is a list consisting of zero or more notes. In Figure 10-1, the list contains three notes. Each row presents the note's text, its transcription time, and a disclosure arrow.

Figure 10-1 The Notes application consists of a UITableView and UINavigationBar.

Figure 10-2   Creating a new note using the Notes application

The disclosure arrow indicates that details are on the next screen. Upon tapping a row, the application takes the user to the detail view for that particular row's note (Figure 10-2).

Tables can be grouped and indexed. For instance, the Music application on an iPod touch uses an index (Figure 10-3). The Settings application's rows are grouped (Figure 10-4).

Figure 10-3   The Music application on an iPod touch uses a UITableView with an index.

Figure 10-4 The Settings application uses a grouped UITableView.

Table rows might also contain a picture and other customizations, as the YouTube and App Store applications illustrate (Figure 10-5).

As the applications in the first five figures illustrate, the table view is a powerful control for listing items. You can modify rows, add images, select rows, and edit them. In this chapter,

Figure 10-5 The YouTube and App Store applications use images and custom cells.

you learn how to use tables. You learn how to build a table, change its style to grouped, add an index to it, and accessorize it. You also learn how to place a table in a navigation controller and how to edit a table's rows. It is a long chapter, but the table view is a powerful control.

UITableView

The UITableView class represents a table view. This class is for displaying and editing information lists. It consists of a single column of multiple rows. Users can scroll vertically to navigate through a table's rows. Each row contains a cell. You can customize that cell's appearance considerably.

You can index tables and create tables with zero or more sections. When you create a table, you have a choice of two styles: UITableViewStylePlain or UITableViewStyleGrouped. A plain table style presents a table like that in Figure 10-3. A grouped table presents a table like that in Figure 10-4. You see examples implementing both styles later in this chapter.

UITableView classes have an associated UITableViewController, a UITableViewDelegate, and a UITableViewDataSource. The UITableViewController is the controller class for a table view. You create an instance of this class to manage the UITableView. The UITableViewDelegate is a protocol you adopt in a custom class you write. This protocol allows you to manage selections, configure headers and footers, and manage cells. The UITableViewDataSource is also a protocol you adopt in a custom class. This protocol allows you to manage a table's data source.

UITableViewDelegate and UITableViewDataSource

The UITableViewDelegate and UITableViewDataSource are protocols at least one class in your application must adopt if your application contains a UITableView. You can create your own custom classes to adopt these protocols, or create a UITableViewController that automatically adopts these protocols. If you choose to use a UITableViewController rather than custom classes, you simply connect the table view's dataSource and delegate outlets to the UITableViewController. You can then implement both protocols' methods in the UITableViewController.

UITableViewDelegate

A UITableView's delegate adopts the UITableViewDelegate protocol. This protocol manages selections, headers, footers, and other tasks. Table 10-1 lists the methods covered in this chapter.

UITableViewDataSource

A UITable's data source adopts the UITableViewDataSource protocol. A table's data source provides the table with its data. Table 10-2 lists the UITableViewDataSource protocol methods covered in this chapter.

Method	Description
tableView:heightForRowAtIndexPath:	Provides height to use in displaying a row.
tableView:accessoryButtonTappedForRowWithIndexPath:	Handles a row's detail disclosure button after it is tapped.
tableView:willSelectRowAtIndexPath:	Handles a row about to be selected.
tableView:didSelectRowAtIndexPath:	Handles a row once it is selected.
tableView:editingStyleForRowAtIndexPath:	Returns the editing style of a row. This determines if a cell displays an insertion accessory, deletion accessory, or no accessory.

Table 10-1 UITableViewDelegate Methods in This Chapter

The methods tableView:numberOfRowsInSection: and tableView:cellForRowAtIndexPath: are required methods that every table's data source must implement.

```
-(NSInteger)tableView:(UITableView *) tableView numberOfRowsInSection:
(NSInteger) section
-(UITableViewCell *)tableView:(UITableView *) tableView
cellForRowAtIndexPath: (NSIndexPath *) indexPath
```

The tableView:numberOfRowsInSection: method informs the data source how many rows a section contains. The tableView:cellForRowAtIndexPath: method provides a table view with its cells.

Method	Description
tableView:numberOfRowsInSection:	Provides the number of rows in a section.
tableView:cellForRowAtIndexPath:	Obtains cell from a data source to place at a particular row.
numberOfSectionsInTableView:	Obtains the number of sections in a table view from a data source.
sectionIndexTitlesForTableView:	Obtains titles for a table view from a data source.
tableView:commitEditingStyle:forRowAtIndexPath:	Commits a cell's editing.
tableView:canEditRowAtIndexPath:	Returns a Boolean value, informing a table view if a row can be edited.
tableView:canMoveRowAtIndexPath:	Returns a Boolean value, informing a table view if a row can be moved.
tableView:moveRowAtIndexPath:toIndexPath:	Allows a table cell to be moved.

Table 10-2 UITableViewDataSource Methods in This Chapter

Try This Adopting the UITableViewDelegate and UITableViewDataSource

In this first task, you create a UIViewController and have it manage the table view. You also implement a custom class that adopts the UITableViewDelegate and UITableViewDataSource.

Creating an Empty Table

1. Create a new Window-based application. Name the application **TableProjectOne**.

2. Create a new UIViewController subclass. Name the class **MyViewController**. Ensure that the check box is checked to create a xib file to go with it.

3. Open MyViewController.xib, click on the view icon to make it visible, and then drag a table view into the view (Figure 10-6). It will automatically resize to completely fill the view.

4. Save your changes.

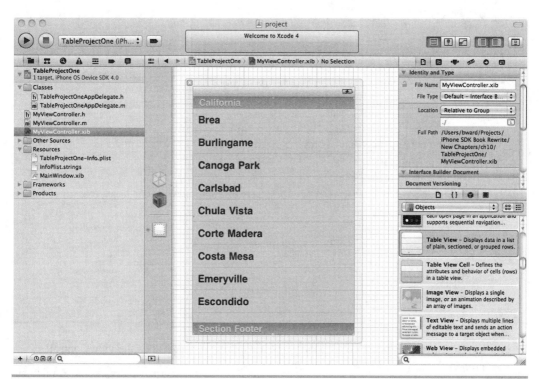

Figure 10-6 Adding a UITableView to a view

(continued)

5. Add a MyViewController as an IBOutlet to TableProjectOneAppDelegate (Listings 10-1 and 10-2).

Listing 10-1 TableProjectOneAppDelegate.h

```
#import <UIKit/UIKit.h>
@class MyViewController;
@interface TableProjectOneAppDelegate : NSObject
<UIApplicationDelegate> {
 UIWindow *window;
 MyViewController *viewController;
}
@property (nonatomic, retain) IBOutlet MyViewController
*viewController;
@property (nonatomic, retain) IBOutlet UIWindow *window;
@end
```

Listing 10-2 TableProjectOneAppDelegate.m

```
#import "TableProjectOneAppDelegate.h"
#import "MyViewController.h"
@implementation TableProjectOneAppDelegate
@synthesize window;
@synthesize viewController;
- (BOOL)application:(UIApplication *)application
didFinishLaunchingWithOptions:(NSDictionary *)launchOptions {
    [window addSubview:self.viewController.view];
    [window makeKeyAndVisible];
    return YES;
}

- (void)dealloc {
    [viewController release];
    [window release];
    [super dealloc];
}
@end
```

---

6. Modify application:didFinishLaunchingWithOptions so that it adds the viewController property's view. Build the application.

7. Open MainWindow.xib and drag a View Controller to the editing pane. Change its class and Nib Name to **MyViewController**.

Figure 10-7   An application with an empty UITableView

8. Connect the TableProjectOneAppDelegate's viewController outlet to the MyViewController you just added.

9. Save your changes and run the application. The application loads an empty table into the iPhone Simulator (Figure 10-7).

NOTE
In Steps 1–9, you added the table view as a subview to the view in the MyViewController nib. If you preferred, you could omit the extra view and just add the table view directly as the nib's view. But note, you would also change MyViewController from a UIViewController to a UITableViewController. Point is, you don't have to put the UITableView inside a UIView in order to use it. A UITableView can be added directly to the XIB and connected to a table view controller's view outlet, and it will work the same way. The next Try This example illustrates.

In this task's first step, you created a UITableView as a subview of a UIView. When the UIViewController loads and displays its view, the view automatically displays its subview, the table view. But all it loads is an empty table. To actually load data into the table, you must implement a delegate and a data source. Moreover, the data source must actually provide data for the table. In the next few steps, you create a delegate and data source for the table.

Try This Adding a Delegate and Data Source

1. Create a new class named TableHandler, derived from NSObject. Change TableHandler so that it adopts the UITableViewDelegate and UITableViewDataSource protocols (Listings 10-3 and 10-4).

Listing 10-3 TableHandler.h

```
#import <Foundation/Foundation.h>
@interface TableHandler : NSObject <UITableViewDelegate,
UITableViewDataSource> {
 NSArray * tableDataList;
}
@property (nonatomic, retain) NSArray * tableDataList;
-(void) fillList;
@end
```

Listing 10-4 TableHandler.m

```
#import "TableHandler.h"
@implementation TableHandler
@synthesize tableDataList;
-(void) fillList {
NSArray * tempArray = [[[NSArray alloc] initWithObjects:@"Item One",
@"Item Two", @"Item Three", @"Item Four", @"Item Five", @"Item Six",
@"Item Seven", @"Item Eight", @"Item Nine", @"Item Ten", @"Item Eleven",
@"Item Twelve", @"Item Thirteen", @"Item Fourteen", @"Item Fifteen",
@"Item Sixteen", @"Item Seventeen", @"Item Eighteen", @"Item Nineteen",
@"Item Twenty", nil] autorelease];
self.tableDataList = tempArray;
}
#pragma mark -
#pragma mark UITableViewDataSource Protocol Methods
-(NSInteger) tableView : (UITableView *) tableView
numberOfRowsInSection: (NSInteger) section
{
 return [self.tableDataList count];
}
```

```
-(UITableViewCell *) tableView : (UITableView *) tableView
    cellForRowAtIndexPath: (NSIndexPath *) indexPath {
 UITableViewCell *cell =
    [tableView dequeueReusableCellWithIdentifier: @"acell"];
 if(cell == nil) {
  cell = [[[UITableViewCell alloc]
        initWithStyle:UITableViewCellStyleDefault
        reuseIdentifier:@"acell"] autorelease];
 }
 cell.textLabel.text = [self.tableDataList
    objectAtIndex:[indexPath row]];
 return cell;
}

#pragma mark -
-(void)dealloc {
 [tableDataList release];
 [super dealloc];
}
@end
```

2. Add an NSArray property and a method named fillList for filling the array.

3. Implement the fillArray method so that the application has data to load into the table's cells.

4. Implement the tableView:numberOfRowsInSection: and tableView: cellForRowAtIndexPath: methods.

5. Modify MyViewController to have a TableHandler property (Listings 10-5 and 10-6). Ensure the property is an IBOutlet.

Listing 10-5   MyViewController.h

```
#import <UIKit/UIKit.h>
#import "TableHandler.h"
@interface MyViewController : UIViewController {
 TableHandler * myHandler;
}
@property (nonatomic, retain) IBOutlet TableHandler * myHandler;
@end
```

Listing 10-6   MyViewController.m

```
#import "MyViewController.h"
@implementation MyViewController
@synthesize myHandler;
```
(continued)

```
-(void) viewDidLoad {
  [self.myHandler fillList];
}
-(void)dealloc {
  [self.myHandler release];
  [super dealloc];
}
@end
```

6. Implement the viewDidLoad method in MyViewController so that it calls its TableHandler's fillList method to ensure that the table has data before it needs to draw.

7. Save your changes and build the project.

8. Open MyViewController.xib and drag an object to the editing pane. Change the object's class to TableHandler (Figure 10-8).

9. Connect the File's Owner myHandler outlet to the newly added TableHandler (Figure 10-9).

10. Connect the table view's dataSource and delegate outlets to the newly added TableHandler.

11. Save and click Run. The application displays 20 rows (Figure 10-10).

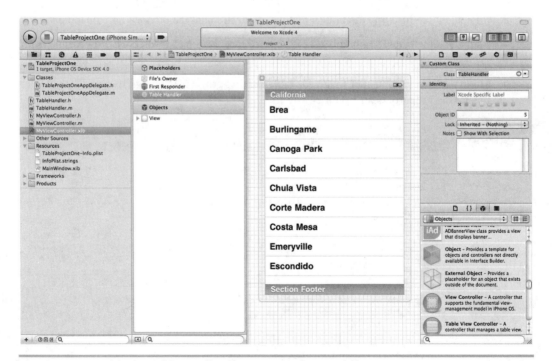

Figure 10-8 Adding a TableHandler object in Interface Builder

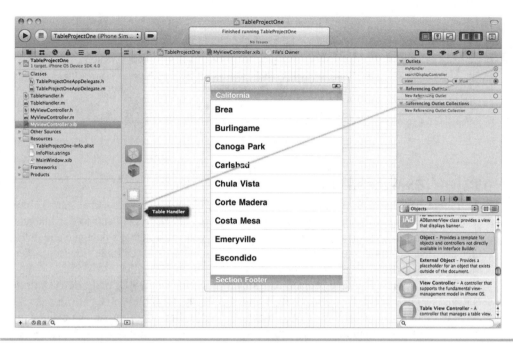

Figure 10-9   Connecting the controller to TableHandler

Figure 10-10   The project running in iPhone Simulator

(continued)

NOTE

The #pragma mark lines in the code listings for this example are a handy way to organize your code as your implementation files get larger. Click the file or function name displayed across the top of the editing pane and you'll see #pragma mark entries in the pull-down menu that appears. This lets you quickly jump around in a large file.

UITableViewController

The UITableViewController manages a table view. The UITableView can use objects defined in a table's nib to define a table's delegate and data source, or it can use itself as the delegate and data source. For instance, in the previous example, you set the table's delegate and data source properties to the TableHandler class. You could have added a UITableViewController, set it as the table's File's Owner, and then set its outlets to TableHandler.

If you do not provide a delegate and data source in a table's nib, a UITableViewController sets its data source and delegate to itself. By doing this, the UITableViewController saves you the work of having to create your own classes so that they adopt the delegate and data source. You still must implement any data source and delegate methods desired. However, rather than implementing these methods in separate custom classes, you implement them in a UITableViewController subclass. The UITableViewController then functions as the table's controller, delegate, and data source.

Try This Using a UITableViewController

In the last Try This task, you did things the hard way. However, the task's purpose was to illustrate adding a table view as a subview, with no controller. In this Try This task, you use a UITableViewController. Moreover, rather than adding a table view as a subview, you add it directly to the xib as the primary view.

1. Create a new Window-based Application. Name the application **TableProjectTwo**.

2. Create a new UITableViewController subclass (select the UIViewController subclass and then check the UITableViewController subclass check box). Name the class **MyTableViewController**. Make sure that it is also creating the XIB file.

3. Open MyTableViewController.xib. You'll notice that Xcode created a table view for you and connected it to the File's Owner. It also connected the table view's dataSource and delegate outlets to the File's Owner (Figure 10-11).

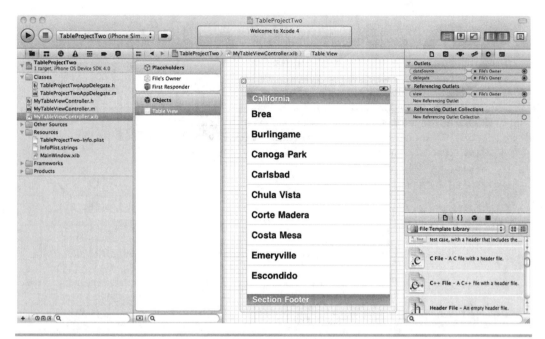

Figure 10-11 XIB automatically created for a UITableViewController subclass

4. Add a MyTableViewController as an IBOutlet to TableProjectTwoAppDelegate. Do not forget to import MyTableViewController. Modify application:didFinishLaunchingWithOptions so that it adds the viewController property's view (Listings 10-7 and 10-8).

Listing 10-7 TableProjectTwoAppDelegate.h

```
#import <UIKit/UIKit.h>
#import "MyTableViewController.h"
@interface TableProjectTwoAppDelegate : NSObject
<UIApplicationDelegate> {
 UIWindow *window;
 MyTableViewController *viewController;
}
@property (nonatomic, retain) IBOutlet MyTableViewController *
viewController;
@property (nonatomic, retain) IBOutlet UIWindow *window;
@end
```

(continued)

Listing 10-8 TableProjectTwoAppDelegate.m

```objc
#import "TableProjectTwoAppDelegate.h"
@implementation TableProjectTwoAppDelegate
@synthesize window;
@synthesize viewController;
- (BOOL)application:(UIApplication *)application
didFinishLaunchingWithOptions:(NSDictionary *)launchOptions {
    [window addSubview:self.viewController.view];
    [window makeKeyAndVisible];
    return YES;
}
-(void)dealloc {
 [window release];
 [viewController release];
 [super dealloc];
}
```

Listing 10-9 MyTableViewController.h

```objc
#import <Foundation/Foundation.h>
@interface MyTableViewController : UITableViewController {
 NSArray * tableDataList;
}
@property (nonatomic, retain) NSArray * tableDataList;
@end
```

5. Edit MyTableViewController.h and add the tableDataList value (Listing 10-9).

6. Edit MyTableViewController.m to replace the delegate methods required by the table with the methods in Listing 10-10.

Listing 10-10 MyTableViewController.m

```objc
#import "MyTableViewController.h"
@implementation MyTableViewController
@synthesize tableDataList;

-(void) viewDidLoad {
 NSArray * tempArray = [[[NSArray alloc] initWithObjects:@"Item One",
  @"Item Two", @"Item Three", @"Item Four", @"Item Five", @"Item Six",
  @"Item Seven", @"Item Eight", @"Item Nine", @"Item Ten", @"Item Eleven",
  @"Item Twelve", @"Item Thirteen", @"Item Fourteen", @"Item Fifteen",
  @"Item Sixteen", @"Item Seventeen", @"Item Eighteen", @"Item Nineteen",
  @"Item Twenty", nil] autorelease];
```

```
  self.tableDataList = tempArray;
}

-(NSInteger) tableView : (UITableView *) tableView
    numberOfRowsInSection: (NSInteger) section {
 return [self.tableDataList count];
}

-(UITableViewCell *) tableView : (UITableView *) tableView
    cellForRowAtIndexPath: (NSIndexPath *) indexPath {
UITableViewCell *cell =
    [tableView dequeueReusableCellWithIdentifier:@"acell"];
 if(cell == nil) {
  cell = [[[UITableViewCell alloc] initWithStyle:
       UITableViewCellStyleDefault reuseIdentifier:@"acell"] autorelease];
 }
 cell.textLabel.text = [self.tableDataList
                         objectAtIndex:[indexPath row]];
 return cell;
}

-(void)dealloc {
 [tableDataList release];
 [super dealloc];
}
@end
```

7. Open MainWindow.xib and drag a table view controller to the document window. Change its class and Nib Name to **MyTableViewController**. Since it will be loaded from the separate XIB file, you can delete the TableView that was automatically created under MyTableViewController when you dragged it to the editing pane.

8. Connect the TableProjectTwoAppDelegate's viewController outlet to the MyTableViewController added to the document window.

9. Save and run the application. The results should match the previous task's results (Figure 10-10).

Grouping and Indexing

Tables have two main styles: grouped and plain. Figure 10-3 illustrates a table with a plain style, while Figure 10-4 illustrates a table with a grouped style. Plain tables might also be indexed. An index sorts the rows and makes navigation quicker by letting a user jump to different locations in the index.

Grouped Table Style

Grouping is accomplished by changing a UITableView's style to grouped. You then tell a UITableView's data source how many sections belong in the table and how many rows belong in each section. The class adopting the UITableViewDataSource protocol informs the table how many sections via the numberOfSectionsInTableView: method. It informs the table how many rows are in each section via the tableView:numberOfRowsInSection: method.

```
-(NSInteger)numberOfSectionsInTableView:(UITableView *)tableView
-(NSInteger)tableView:(UITableView *) tableView numberOfRowsInSection:
(NSInteger)section
```

Each grouping might have a title. You add titles by having your UITableViewDataSource protocol adoption implement the tableView:titleForHeaderInSection method. This method provides a table view with a title for a section's header. You might also wish to add a footer to each grouping by implementing the tableView:titleForFooterInSection: method.

```
-(NSString *)tableView:(UITableView *)tableView titleForHeaderIn
Section:(NSInteger)section
-(NSString *)tableView:(UITableView *)tableView titleForFooterIn
Section:(NSInteger)section
```

Try This   Grouping

1. Copy TableProjectOne from the first task to a new location. Open the newly copied TableProjectOne in Xcode.

2. Modify the array in TableHandler so that tableDataList consists of an array of five arrays (Listing 10-11).

Listing 10-11   Table's list modified to an array of arrays

```
-(void) fillList {
NSArray * tempArrayA = [[[NSArray alloc] initWithObjects:@"AItem One",
@"AItem Two", nil] autorelease];
NSArray * tempArrayB = [[[NSArray alloc] initWithObjects:@"BItem Three",
@"BItem Four", nil] autorelease];
NSArray * tempArrayC = [[[NSArray alloc] initWithObjects:@"CItem Five",
@"CItem Six", nil] autorelease];
NSArray * tempArrayD = [[[NSArray alloc] initWithObjects:@"DItem Seven",
@"DItem Eight", nil] autorelease];
NSArray * tempArrayE = [[[NSArray alloc] initWithObjects:@"EItem Nine",
@"EItem Ten", nil] autorelease];
NSArray * tempArray = [[[NSArray alloc] initWithObjects:tempArrayA,
tempArrayB, tempArrayC, tempArrayD, tempArrayE, nil] autorelease];
 self.tableDataList = tempArray;
}
```

3. Add the numberOfSectionsInTableView and titleForHeaderInSection methods to
   TableHandler.m (Listing 10-12).

Listing 10-12   Modifications to TableHandler.m to support grouping

```
-(NSInteger) numberOfSectionsInTableView: (UITableView *) tableView {
 return [tableDataList count];
}
-(NSString *) tableView: (UITableView *) tableView
titleForHeaderInSection: (NSInteger) section {
 switch (section) {
 case 0: return @"A"; break;
 case 1: return @"B"; break;
 case 2: return @"C"; break;
 case 3: return @"D"; break;
 case 4: return @"E"; break;
 }
 return nil;
}
-(NSInteger) tableView : (UITableView *) tableView numberOfRowsInSection:
(NSInteger) section {
 return [[tableDataList objectAtIndex: section] count];
}
```

4. Modify numberOfRowsInSection to return [[tableDataList objectAtIndex: section] count]
   and modify numberOfSections to return [tableDataList count].

5. Modify cellForRowAtIndexPath so that it uses the section and the row (Listing 10-13).

Listing 10-13   The cellForRowAtIndexPath modified to use row and section

```
-(UITableViewCell *) tableView: (UITableView *) tableView
    cellForRowAtIndexPath: (NSIndexPath *) indexPath {
 UITableViewCell *cell =
    [tableView dequeueReusableCellWithIdentifier: @"acell"];
 if (cell == nil) {
  cell = [[[UITableViewCell alloc] initWithStyle:UITableViewCellStyleDefault
  reuseIdentifier: @"acell"] autorelease];
 }
 cell.textLabel.text = [[self.tableDataList objectAtIndex:indexPath.section]
 objectAtIndex:indexPath.row]; return cell;
}
```

6. Select MyViewController.xib to edit it. Change the table view's Style from Plain to
   Grouped (Figure 10-12).

7. Save and click Run. The table's rows are grouped (Figure 10-13).

(continued)

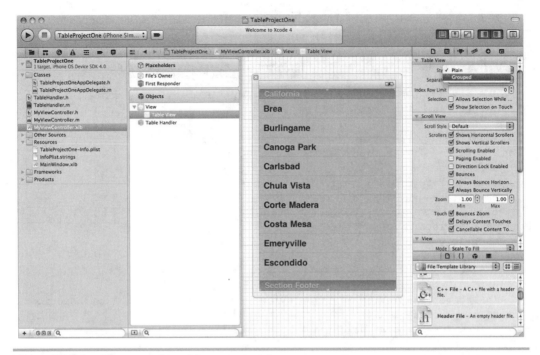

Figure 10-12 Changing the table to grouped

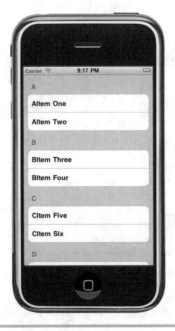

Figure 10-13 The application running in iPhone Simulator

The fillList method initializes an NSArray of five NSArrays. The tableView:titleForHeader InSection is hard-coded to return A, B, C, D, or E, depending upon the current section. When the table loads, five sections are created, each with a title from the titleForHeaderInSection method. Each row's content is determined from the cellForRowAtIndexPath method.

Indexing

Tables can be indexed. To index a table, a table's style should be plain. As with grouping, you implement the numberOfSectionsInTableView: and tableView:numberOfRowsInSection: methods, but you also implement a third method: sectionIndexTitlesForTableView:. This method, implemented in your UITableViewDataSource adoptee, creates the titles that appear along a table's right side. Upon clicking one of these values, a user is taken directly to the group with the corresponding title.

```
-(NSArray *) sectionIndexTitlesForTableView:(UITableView *) tableView
```

Try This Indexing

1. Open the TableProjectOne from the grouping Try This task you just completed.

2. Open MyViewController.xib and change the table view's style to Plain.

3. Save and click Run. Notice the application is still grouped, but the table's appearance is changed (Figure 10-14).

4. Implement the sectionIndexTitlesForTableView method, as in Listing 10-14, in TableHandler.m.

Listing 10-14   The sectionIndexTitlesForTableView method

```
-(NSArray *) sectionIndexTitlesForTableView:
    (UITableView *) tableView {
 NSArray * keys = [[[NSArray alloc] initWithObjects: @"A", @"B", @"C",
                        @"D", @"E",nil] autorelease];
 return keys;
}
```

5. Click Run. The application has an index (Figure 10-15).

(continued)

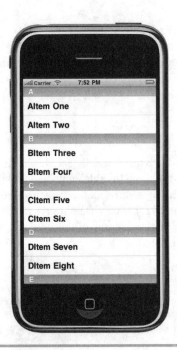

Figure 10-14 A plain table with groupings

Figure 10-15 The indexed table running in iPhone Simulator

NOTE

Don't let this chapter's reliance on simple NSArrays fool you into thinking you must use this collection class to hold a table's data. You can use any collection class, retrieve the data from a database, or use any other method you deem appropriate, provided you implement methods to obtain the data correctly.

Images in Tables

Adding an image to a table, provided you are happy with the image appearing in the row's upper-left corner, is not difficult. Simply add an image to the cell in the tableView:cellForRowAtIndexPath: method. Remember, this method loads a UITableViewCell into a row. You can use this method to initialize a table cell with an image using the UITableViewCell's imageView.image property. The image is then displayed in the table's row.

Try This Adding an Image

1. Open the last task's project. From the book's Resources folder, add the images power.png, icon.png, package.png, web.png, and colorize.png to the project's Resources folder.

2. Modify the tableView:cellForRowAtIndexPath: method to match Listing 10-15.

Listing 10-15   The tableView:cellForRowAtIndexPath: method added to TableHandler.m

```
-(UITableViewCell *) tableView : (UITableView *) tableView
    cellForRowAtIndexPath: (NSIndexPath *) indexPath {
UITableViewCell *cell =
    [tableView dequeueReusableCellWithIdentifier: @"acell"];
if(cell == nil) {
 cell = [[[UITableViewCell alloc] initWithStyle:
 UITableViewCellStyleDefault reuseIdentifier:@"acell"] autorelease];
}
cell.textLabel.text = [[self.tableDataList objectAtIndex:
    indexPath.section] objectAtIndex: indexPath.row];
UIImage * image;
switch (indexPath.section) {
 case 0: image = [UIImage imageNamed:@"power.png"]; break;
 case 1: image = [UIImage imageNamed:@"Icon.png"]; break;
```

(continued)

```
  case 2: image = [UIImage imageNamed:@"package_graphics.png"]; break;
  case 3: image = [UIImage imageNamed:@"colorize.png"]; break;
  case 4: image = [UIImage imageNamed:@"web.png"]; break;
}
cell.imageView.image = image;
return cell;
}
```

3. Click Run. Notice that iOS automatically scales any images that are too large so that they don't overrun the table cell bounds (Figure 10-16).

Figure 10-16 Images display on left side of each table row.

Selecting Rows

The UITableView allows you to select a row. Typically, a table presents rows to a user, where each row is an item in a hierarchical list. Upon selecting a row, the user is generally taken to another view presenting the item's details. You implement the tableView:willSelectRowAtIndex: and tableView:didSelectRowAtIndexPath: methods if you wish to allow a user to select a row.

```
-(NSIndexPath *) tableView:(UITableView *) tableView
willSelectRowAtIndexPath: (NSIndexPath *) indexPath
-(void) tableView:(UITableView *) tableView didSelectRowAtIndexPath:
(NSIndexPath *) indexPath
```

The tableView:willSelectRowAtIndexPath: method allows the delegate to react to a row about to be selected. The tableView:didSelectRowAtIndexPath: method allows a reaction to a row's selection. These methods are useful because they allow you to implement custom behavior in a table's delegate when a row is selected.

Try This Row Selection

1. Open the last task's project in Xcode.

2. Add the tableView:willSelectRowAtIndexPath: and the tableView:didSelectRowAtIndexPath: methods in Listing 10-16 to TableHandler.m.

Listing 10-16 The tableView:willSelectRowAtIndexPath: and tableView:didSelectRow AtIndexPath: methods

```
-(NSIndexPath *) tableView: (UITableView *) tableView
    willSelectRowAtIndexPath: (NSIndexPath *) indexPath {
 NSLog(@"Item at the %d array and %d item has value: %@",
    indexPath.section, indexPath.row,
    [[self.tableDataList objectAtIndex: indexPath.section]
       objectAtIndex: indexPath.row]);
 return indexPath;
}

-(void)tableView:(UITableView *) tableView didSelectRowAtIndexPath:
    (NSIndexPath *) index {
 NSLog(@"Yes I did....");
}
```

(continued)

3. Click Run. The application looks the same as the previous task's results. Clicking the items should result in logging similar to Listing 10-17.

Listing 10-17   Debugger Console logging

```
2010-08-31 20:27:54.220 TableProjectOne[53965:207] I selected the item
at the 0 array and 0 item, the value is: AItem One
2010-08-31 20:27:54.222 TableProjectOne[53965:207] Yes I did....
2010-08-31 20:27:56.900 TableProjectOne[53965:207] I selected the item
at the 1 array and 0 item, the value is: BItem Three
2010-08-31 20:27:56.901 TableProjectOne[53965:207] Yes I did....
```

Changing Row Height

A couple of sections ago, you added images that were too large to display in a table's row. iOS resized the images on the fly, so this wasn't a big issue. However, sometimes you want to display a larger image, text with a large font, or a custom cell. One way you can add space in a table's row is by increasing the row's height. You increase a row's height using the heightForRowAtIndexPath method.

Try This Changing Row Height

1. Open the previous task project in Xcode.

2. Add the heightForRowAtIndexPath: method in Listing 10-18 to TableHandler.m.

Listing 10-18   The heightForRowAtIndexPath method added to TableView

```
-(CGFloat) tableView : (UITableView *) tableView
heightForRowAtIndexPath: (NSIndexPath *) indexPath {
return 90;
}
```

3. Click Build And Go, and the rows are 90 pixels tall (Figure 10-17).

Figure 10-17   The application running with 90-pixel-high rows in iPhone Simulator

Accessorizing Table Cells

You can tell a cell to place a check mark, disclosure arrow, or detailed disclosure button in
the cell by setting the cell's accessoryView or accessoryType properties. Accessories are
visual user interface clues for users. For instance, the check mark might inform a user that
he or she has already selected a row. A disclosure arrow or a detailed disclosure button might
hint to a user that he or she can select the row to view the row's details in another view. The
check mark and disclosure button are visual clues for a user and do not provide events that
respond to a user tapping them. However, the detailed disclosure button can respond to a
user tapping it.

Try This   Accessorizing a Table Cell

1. Open the previous project in Xcode and comment out the sectionIndexTitlesForTableView method in TableHandler.m.

2. Add the tableView:accessoryButtonTappedForRowWithIndexPath: method to TableHandler.m (Listing 10-19). Also modify the tableView:cellForRowAtIndexPath: method to add the accessories to the table cells.

Listing 10-19   The tableView:cellForRowAtIndexPath: and tableView:accessoryButton TappedForRowWithIndexPath: methods

```
-(UITableViewCell *) tableView : (UITableView *) tableView
    cellForRowAtIndexPath: (NSIndexPath *) indexPath {
NSUInteger section = [indexPath section];
UITableViewCell *cell =
    [tableView dequeueReusableCellWithIdentifier: @"acell"];
if(cell == nil) {
 cell = [[[UITableViewCell alloc] initWithStyle:
 UITableViewCellStyleDefault reuseIdentifier:@"acell"] autorelease];
}
cell.textLabel.text = [[self.tableDataList objectAtIndex:section]
    objectAtIndex:[indexPath row]];
UIImage * image;
switch (indexPath.section) {
 case 0: image = [UIImage imageNamed:@"power.png"]; break;
 case 1: image = [UIImage imageNamed:@"Icon_resize.png"]; break;
 case 2: image = [UIImage imageNamed:@"package_graphics_resize.png"];
   break;
 case 3: image = [UIImage imageNamed:@"colorize.png"]; break;
 case 4: image = [UIImage imageNamed:@"web.png"]; break;
}
cell.imageView.image = image;
if(indexPath.section == 0) {
 cell.accessoryType = UITableViewCellAccessoryDisclosureIndicator;
} else if(indexPath.section == 1) {
   cell.accessoryType = UITableViewCellAccessoryDetailDisclosureButton;
 } else {
 cell.accessoryType = UITableViewCellAccessoryCheckmark;
 }
 return cell;
}

-(void) tableView:(UITableView *) tableView
    accessoryButtonTappedForRowWithIndexPath: (NSIndexPath *) indexPath {
NSLog(@"hey now....");
}
```

Figure 10-18   Accessorized table rows

3. Click Run. The rows contain accessories (Figure 10-18). When you tap the detailed
   disclosure button, the table calls the tableView:accessoryButtonTappedForRow
   WithIndexPath: method.

Customizing a Table Cell

Tables can be customized. Sometimes you might wish to format data differently than provided
by the default UITableViewCell. The most direct way to accomplish formatting a table cell is
by adding a view to the UITableViewCell. You do this in code, by adding a subview to a cell
when initializing it in the tableView:cellForRowAtIndexPath method. Another technique is
to create a subclass of a UITableViewCell and then create its graphical layout using Interface
Builder.

Try This Customizing a Cell Using Interface Builder

1. Create a new Navigation-based Application. Name the application **CustomizedCell**.

2. Create a new subclass of UITableViewCell. Note that Xcode provides a template for this class (select Objective-C class and then UITableViewCell from the pull-down). Name the class **MyCellView**.

3. In MyCellView, create a new UILabel outlet named theTextLabel (Listings 10-20 and 10-21).

Listing 10-20 MyCellView.h

```
#import <UIKit/UIKit.h>
@interface MyCellView : UITableViewCell {
 UILabel * theTextLabel;
}
@property (nonatomic, retain) IBOutlet UILabel * theTextLabel;
@end
```

Listing 10-21 MyCellView.m

```
#import "MyCellView.h"
@implementation MyCellView
@synthesize theTextLabel;
- (id)initWithStyle:(UITableViewCellStyle)style
      reuseIdentifier:(NSString *)reuseIdentifier {
 if ((self = [super initWithStyle:style reuseIdentifier:reuseIdentifier])) {
  // Initialization code
 }
 return self;
}

- (void)setSelected:(BOOL)selected animated:(BOOL)animated {
 [super setSelected:selected animated:animated];
}
- (void)dealloc {
 [theTextLabel release];
 [super dealloc];
}
@end
```

4. Drag the image money.png from this book's Resources folder to the Resources folder in the project. Save.

5. Create a new Empty XIB. Name the file MyCellView.xib and select it to view it in Interface Builder.

6. Add a table view cell from the library to the editing pane.

7. Change the cell's class from UITableViewCell to MyCellView.

8. Click My Cell View in the editing pane to select it.

9. In the Attributes Inspector, select money.png as the cell's image. Change the cell's background to yellow. Also, be certain to set the Identifier to MyCell (Figure 10-19).

CAUTION

If you do not set a cell's identifier, the cell can never be reused. This means every call to tableView:cellForRowAtIndexPath: results in a new table cell.

10. Drag a UIImageView and two UILabels to the canvas (Figure 10-20). Type some text in one label; delete the other label's text. Set the image view's image to money.png.

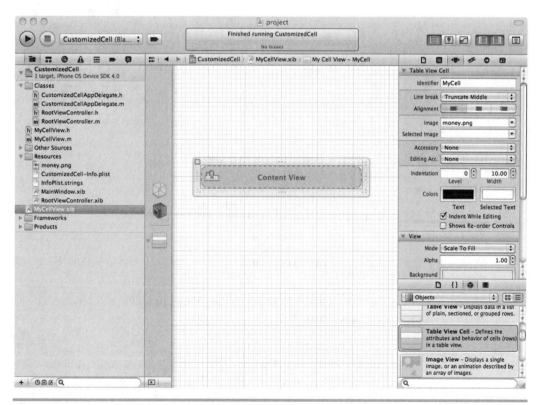

Figure 10-19   Setting the identifier to MyCell

(continued)

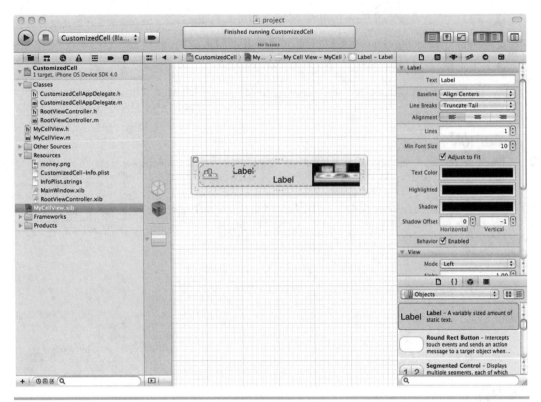

Figure 10-20 Adding UIImageView and UILabels to a view canvas

11. Connect the MyCellView's theTextLabel outlet to the newly added label.

12. Save your changes.

13. Open RootViewController.xib and change the table view's background to yellow. Save your changes.

14. Modify RootViewController to implement the UITableViewController methods needed so that they match Listings 10-22 and 10-23.

Listing 10-22 RootViewController.h

```
#import <UIKit/UIKit.h>
#import "MyCellView.h"
@interface RootViewController : UITableViewController { }
@end
```

Listing 10-23   RootViewController.m

```
#import "RootViewController.h"
#import "CustomizedCellAppDelegate.h"
@implementation RootViewController
-(NSInteger)numberOfSectionsInTableView:(UITableView *)tableView {
  return 1;
}

-(NSInteger)tableView: (UITableView *) tableView
      numberOfRowsInSection: (NSInteger) section {
  return 5;
}

-(CGFloat) tableView : (UITableView *) tableView
      heightForRowAtIndexPath: (NSIndexPath *) indexPath {
  return 110;
}

-(UITableViewCell *)tableView:(UITableView *) tableView
      cellForRowAtIndexPath: (NSIndexPath *) indexPath {
  MyCellView *cell = (MyCellView *) [tableView
      dequeueReusableCellWithIdentifier: @"MyCell"];
  if(cell == nil) {
    cell = [[[NSBundle mainBundle] loadNibNamed:
        @"MyCellView" owner:self options:nil] objectAtIndex:0];
  }
  [cell.theTextLabel setText:@"Just some static text."];
  NSString *imagePath = [[NSBundle mainBundle]
      pathForResource:@"money" ofType:@"png"];
  cell.imageView.image = [UIImage imageWithContentsOfFile:imagePath];
  [cell setAccessoryType:UITableViewCellAccessoryCheckmark];
  cell.contentView.backgroundColor = [UIColor yellowColor];
  cell.backgroundView.backgroundColor = [UIColor yellowColor];
  return cell;
}

-(void)dealloc {
  [super dealloc];
}
@end
```

15. Notice that the tableView:cellForRowAtIndexPath: method sets the cell's accessory, background color, and image.

16. Click Run. The table cells have the customized appearance (Figure 10-21).

Notice in the previous example that you initialize the cell every time it's called in the table View:CellForRowAtIndexPath: method. This initialization is per Apple's documentation, Table

(continued)

Figure 10-21 Application with background color

View Programming Guide for iOS. The "tableView:cellForRowAtIndexPath should always reset all content when reusing a cell." That is why in the tableView:cellForRowAtIndexPath: you set the cell's background color, image, and label text. In a more realistic example, you would probably vary a cell's content depending upon the row.

Implementing a UITableViewCell in its own nib does not require implementing a UITableViewCell class, as you did in the example. However, if you wish to override a UITableViewCell's methods, such as setSelected, you must implement your own custom class. You then set the UITableViewCell's type in Interface Builder to be your custom subclass. In this example, that class is MyCellView. Implementing a custom UITableViewCell subclass is also a convenient location to place IBOutlets and IBActions for the controls on your custom UITableViewCell control.

NOTE
For more information on table view cells, refer to "A Closer Look at Table-View Cells" in Apple's "Table View Programming Guide for iOS."

Using Tables with Navigation Bars and Tabs

Almost every application using a table associates that table with a navigation bar. Moreover, in applications of any complexity, the application also usually organizes its tasks into different tabs. For instance, the iPod application has different tabs for different views of its data. The Artists tab, for instance, shows a user's multimedia sorted by artist. At the iPod application's top is a navigation bar. When a user selects an artist row, the navigation controller pushes another view onto the navigation controller and displays it.

In the following Try This, we try to add some real-world credibility to this chapter by having you implement a table in a navigation controller that is in a Tab Bar tab. Although initially confusing, this is such a common user interface pattern that you should definitely understand the next task.

Try This Using a Table in a Navigation Controller in a Tab

This is a long but useful task. Much of it is repetition from previous chapters, but the combination of a table in a navigation controller in a tab is such a common application pattern that it is worth presenting here in detail, even if much of the task is repetitive.

Creating and Connecting the Views

1. Create a new Window-based Application. Name the application **TabNavTable**.

2. Add a UITabBarController as an IBOutlet to TabNavTableAppDelegate. Name the outlet myCont (Listing 10-24).

Listing 10-24   TabNavTableAppDelegate.h

```
#import <UIKit/UIKit.h>
@interface TabNavTableAppDelegate : NSObject <UIApplicationDelegate> {
UIWindow *window;
UITabBarController *myCont;
}
@property (nonatomic, retain) IBOutlet UIWindow *window;
@property (nonatomic, retain) IBOutlet UITabBarController *myCont;
@end
```

3. Change TabNavTableAppDelegate's application:didFinishLaunchingWithOptions method in TabNavTableAppDelegate to load the newly added tab bar controller's root view (Listing 10-25).

(continued)

Listing 10-25 TabNavTableAppDelegate.m

```
#import "TabNavTableAppDelegate.h"
@implementation TabNavTableAppDelegate
@synthesize window;
@synthesize myCont;
- (BOOL)application:(UIApplication *)application
    didFinishLaunchingWithOptions:(NSDictionary *) launchOptions {
 [window addSubview: myCont.view];
 [window makeKeyAndVisible];
}

- (void)dealloc {
 [myCont release];
 [window release];
 [super dealloc];
}
@end
```

4. Save your changes and open MainWindow.xib in Interface Builder.

5. Add a tab bar controller from the library to the document window.

6. Delete the tab bar controller's root view controller (View Controller - Item 1).

7. Add a navigation controller in the previously deleted root view controller's place (Figure 10-22).

8. Change the navigation controller's view controller, View Controller (Root View Controller), from a UIViewController to a UITableViewController. For now we'll leave its type as UITableViewController; then in a few steps, you change it to your own class, MyTableViewController.

9. Connect TabNavTableAppDelegate's myCont property to the tab bar controller (Figure 10-23).

10. Save your changes.

11. Create a new subclass of UITableViewController. Name the class MyTableViewController and add the table view controller methods in Listings 10-26 and 10-27.

Listing 10-26 MyTableViewController.h

```
#import <UIKit/UIKit.h>
@interface MyTableViewController : UITableViewController {
 NSMutableArray * tableDataList;
}
@property (nonatomic, retain) NSMutableArray * tableDataList;
@end
```

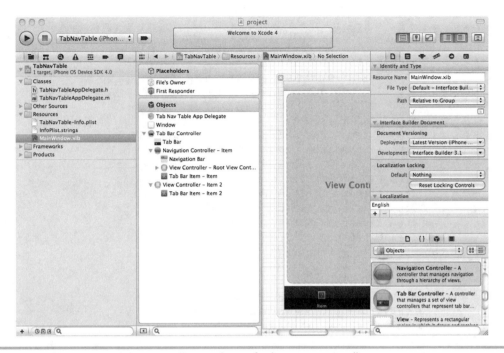

Figure 10-22   Navigation controller in place of tab's view controller

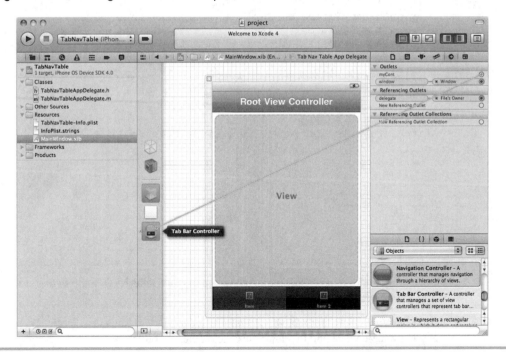

Figure 10-23   Application with a table, navigation bar, and tab bar   *(continued)*

Listing 10-27 MyTableViewController.m

```objc
#import "MyTableViewController.h"
@implementation MyTableViewController
@synthesize tableDataList;

-(void) viewDidLoad {
NSMutableArray * tempArray = [[[NSMutableArray alloc]
    initWithObjects:@"Item One", @"Item Two", @"Item Three",
        @"Item Four", @"Item Five", @"Item Six",@"Item Seven",
        @"Item Eight", @"Item Nine", @"Item Ten",
        @"Item Eleven", @"Item Twelve", @"Item Thirteen",
        @"Item Fourteen", @"Item Fifteen", @"Item Sixteen",
        @"Item Seventeen",@"Item Eighteen",
        @"Item Nineteen", @"Item Twenty", nil] autorelease];
 self.tableDataList = tempArray;
}

-(NSInteger) tableView : (UITableView *) tableView
    numberOfRowsInSection: (NSInteger) section {
 return [self.tableDataList count];
}

-(UITableViewCell *) tableView : (UITableView *) tableView
    cellForRowAtIndexPath:(NSIndexPath *) indexPath {
UITableViewCell *cell =
    [tableView dequeueReusableCellWithIdentifier:@"acell"];
 if(cell == nil) {
  cell = [[[UITableViewCell alloc] initWithStyle:
  UITableViewCellStyleDefault reuseIdentifier:@"acell"] autorelease];
 }
 cell.textLabel.text =
    [self.tableDataList objectAtIndex:[indexPath row]];
 return cell;
}

-(void)dealloc {
 [tableDataList release];
 [super dealloc];
}
@end
```

12. Notice that you're adding an NSMutableArray named tableDataList and populating it in MyTableViewController's viewDidLoad method.

13. Open MyTableViewController.xib, which was created along with the class. Notice that it already has a table view, and the dataSource and delegate outlets are already set up for you.

NOTE

In Step 14 you are adding the table directly to the nib as the main view. Contrast this with how you added the table view in this chapter's first Try This example. Both techniques work.

14. Open MainWindow.xib in Interface Builder.

15. In the document window, expand Tab Bar Controller, and then expand Navigation Controller (Item). Change the Table View Controller (Navigation Item) from a UITableViewController to MyTableViewController. Don't forget to change its NIB Name in the Attributes Inspector to MyTableViewController to show the table is loaded from another nib.

16. Save and click Run. The first tab contains a navigation bar and a table view (Figure 10-24).

Figure 10-24   Table in a tab bar

(continued)

Handling Row Selections

1. Add an IBOutlet to MyTableViewController that references a UINavigationController. Name the outlet navCont. Don't forget to synthesize it and to release it. Save and compile.

2. Open MainWindow.xib. In the editing pane, expand Tab Bar Controller and then Navigation Controller - Item. Connect MyTableViewController's navCont outlet to the Navigation Controller - Item.

3. Save and click Run. If you completed the steps correctly, there is no change in the application's appearance.

4. Create a new UIViewController subclass and name it TableViewDetailsViewController (Listings 10-28 and 10-29). Select the check box to also create an accompanying xib for the class. Although you leave this class empty in this task, in a real-world project, this class would contain logic.

Listing 10-28 TableViewDetailsViewController.h

```
#import <Foundation/Foundation.h>
@interface TableViewDetailsViewController : UIViewController {
}
@end
```

Listing 10-29 TableViewDetailsViewController.m

```
#import "TableViewDetailsViewController.h"
@implementation TableViewDetailsViewController
@end
```

5. Open TableViewDetailsViewController.xib in Interface Builder.

6. Change the view's background color.

7. Because you created the XIB at the same time as the class, the File's Owner class is already set to TableViewDetailsViewController and the File's Owner view outlet is already connected to the view in the document window.

8. Save your changes.

9. Open MyTableViewController and import TableViewDetailsViewController.h.

10. Implement the tableView:didSelectRowAtIndexPath method in MyTableViewController (Listing 10-30).

Listing 10-30 The tableView:didSelectRowAtIndexPath: method added to MyTableViewController

```
-(void)tableView:(UITableView *)tableView didSelectRowAtIndexPath:
(NSIndexPath *) indexPath {
NSLog(@"pushing...");
TableViewDetailsViewController * temp = [[
[TableViewDetailsViewController alloc] initWithNibName:
@"TableViewDetailsViewController" bundle:nil] autorelease];
[self.navCont pushViewController:temp animated:YES];
}
```

11. Build and run in iPhone Simulator. Upon clicking a row, you are taken to the details page (Figure 10-25).

Figure 10-25 Clicking the row takes the user to detail view.

Editing Table Cells

Table cells can be edited. You can add new rows, delete existing rows, and reorder rows. The way it works is like this: A user clicks a button that puts the table into edit mode. Edit mode displays insert or delete accessories used for adding and deleting rows. These accessories are displayed on a cell's left side. Editing mode displays reorder accessories on a table cell's right side.

Getting to Edit Mode

This chapter ends by discussing how to edit a table. Tables not only display data, they also allow adding rows, deleting rows, and changing the order of rows. A table has two modes: its normal display mode and edit mode. When a table is in edit mode, it can display accessories for inserting, deleting, and rearranging table cells. An application places a table in edit mode by sending a message to the table view's setEditing:animated: method. For instance, you might call a table's setEditing:animated: method by implementing an IBAction called by a button on a form.

```
-(IBAction) edit {
 [self.myTableView setEditing:YES animated:YES];
}
```

However, a self-created button is not how tables are usually placed into edit mode. Rather than specifically creating an action and manually calling a method, you usually use a navigation item and let it automatically activate a table view's edit mode. Remember, 90 percent of the time you will implement a table view in a navigation controller. That navigation controller's navigation bar can contain a right button. One choice you have when creating a navigation bar button is creating an Edit button.

```
self.navigationItem.rightBarButtonItem = myTableController
.editButtonItem;
```

When you set that button to a table controller's editButtonItem, the controller automatically knows to enter edit mode.

Edit Mode Methods

The methods tableView:canEditRowAtIndexPath:, tableView:canMoveRowAtIndexPath:, tableView:commitEditingStyle:forRowAtIndexPath:, and tableView:commitEditingStyle: forRowAtIndexPath: are four methods you should implement in your UITableViewDataSource protocol adoptee.

```
-(BOOL)tableView:(UITableView *)tableView canEditRowAtIndexPath:
(NSIndexPath *)indexPath
-(BOOL)tableView:(UITableView *)tableView canMoveRowAtIndexPath:
(NSIndexPath *)indexPath
-(void)tableView:(UITableView *)tableView commitEditingStyle:
(UITableViewCellEditingStyle) editingStyle forRowAtIndexPath:
(NSIndexPath *) indexPath
-(UITableViewCellEditingStyle)tableView:(UITableView *) tableView
editingStyleForRowAtIndexPath:(NSIndexPath *) indexPath
```

A table knows a row is editable by the tableView:canEditRowAtIndexPath: method. If you wish all rows to be editable, simply have the method return YES; otherwise, implement code to determine if a particular row is editable. If you omit this method, no rows are editable.

The tableView:editingStyleForRowAtIndexPath: method informs the table what style editing accessory the row should have. If this method returns a UITableViewCellEditingStyleNone, no accessory is displayed. If this method returns UITableViewCellEditingStyleDelete, the delete accessory is displayed. And if the method returns UITableViewCellEditingStyleInsert, the insert accessory is displayed. The example code in Listing 10-31 illustrates this.

Listing 10-31   The tableView:editingStyleForRowAtIndexPath method

```
-(UITableViewCellEditingStyle)tableView:(UITableView *)tableView
    editingStyleForRowAtIndexPath:(NSIndexPath *)indexPath {
 if(indexPath.row == 0 || indexPath.row == [self.tableDataList count]) {
  return UITableViewCellEditingStyleNone;
 }
 return UITableViewCellEditingStyleDelete;
}
```

A table knows a table row is movable by the tableView:canMoveRowAtIndexPath: method. Like the tableView:canEditRowAtIndexPath: method, simply have the method return YES if all rows are movable; otherwise, write your own custom code. If you omit this method, no rows are movable.

The tableView:canMoveRowAtIndexPath: method only prevents particular rows from being directly moved by a user. A user can still move another row to the position held by the unmovable row, thus moving the unmovable row indirectly. To prevent this behavior, you can implement the tableView:targetIndexPathForMoveFromRowAtIndexPath:toProposedIndexPath: method in your table view's delegate. If a proposed move is acceptable, return the proposedDestinationIndexPath; otherwise, return the sourceIndexPath. The method's signature follows.

```
 -(NSIndexPath *)tableView:(UITableView *)tableView
targetIndexPathForMoveFromRowAtIndexPath:(NSIndexPath *)sourceIndexPath
toProposedIndexPath:(NSIndexPath *)proposedDestinationIndexPath
```

The tableView:commitEditingStyle:forRowAtIndexPath: commits a row insertion or deletion. Notice the editingStyle parameter. If a row is deleted, the table view sends a UITableViewCellEditingStyleDelete style as the editingStyle parameter. If a row is inserted, the table view sends a UITableViewCellEditingStyleInsert style. It uses the editingStyle parameter to tell it which action resulted in the method being called.

This method is for implementing code that handles a row insertion or deletion. For instance, in this chapter, data comes from an NSArray or NSMutableArray. When using an NSMutableArray as a data source for a table, deleting a row means you must delete the corresponding item from the array. If inserting, you must add an item at the index where the row was inserted and remove the item from its old location in the array.

Editing Rows

1. Copy the TabNavTable project to a new location and open it in Xcode.

2. Edit MyTableViewController to add the editing functionality (Listings 10-32 and 10-33)

3. Create a new view controller class called AddItemViewController. Be sure to select the "With XIB for user interface" check box to create an associated xib.

Listing 10-32 MyTableViewController.h

```
#import <UIKit/UIKit.h>
#import "TableViewDetailsViewController.h"
#import "AddItemViewController.h"
@interface MyTableViewController : UITableViewController {
 NSMutableArray * tableDataList;
UINavigationController * navCont;
AddItemViewController * addItemController;
UIBarButtonItem * addButton;
}
@property (nonatomic, retain) IBOutlet UINavigationController *
navCont;
@property (nonatomic, retain) NSMutableArray * tableDataList;
@property (nonatomic, retain) AddItemViewController *
addItemController;
@property (nonatomic, retain) IBOutlet UIBarButtonItem * addButton;
-(IBAction) exitAndSave: (NSString *) newValue;
-(IBAction) enterAddMode: (id) sender;
@end
```

Listing 10-33 MyTableViewController.m

```
#import "MyTableViewController.h"
@implementation MyTableViewController
@synthesize tableDataList;
@synthesize navCont;
@synthesize addItemController;
@synthesize addButton;

-(IBAction) enterAddMode: (id) sender {
 self.addItemController = [[[AddItemViewController alloc]
    initWithNibName: @"AddItemViewController" bundle:nil] autorelease];
 [self.navCont pushViewController:self.addItemController
    animated:YES]; self.addItemController.parentTable = self;
}
```

```objc
-(void) exitAndSave : (NSString *) newValue {
 [self.tableDataList addObject: newValue];
 [self.navCont popToRootViewControllerAnimated:YES];
 [self.tableView reloadData];
}


-(void) viewDidLoad {
 NSMutableArray * tempArray = [[[NSMutableArray alloc]
    initWithObjects: @"Item One", @"Item Two", @"Item Three",
         @"Item Four", @"Item Five", @"Item Six",
         @"Item Seven", @"Item Eight", @"Item Nine",
         @"Item Ten", @"Item Eleven", @"Item Twelve",
         @"Item Thirteen", @"Item Fourteen", @"Item Fifteen",
         @"Item Sixteen", @"Item Seventeen",
         @"Item Eighteen", @"Item Nineteen", @"Item Twenty",
         nil] autorelease];
 self.tableDataList = tempArray;
 self.navigationItem.rightBarButtonItem = self.editButtonItem;
 self.navigationItem.leftBarButtonItem = self.addButton;
}


-(NSInteger) tableView : (UITableView *) tableView
 numberOfRowsInSection: (NSInteger) section {
 return [self.tableDataList count];
}


-(UITableViewCell *) tableView : (UITableView *) tableView
    cellForRowAtIndexPath: (NSIndexPath *) indexPath {
 UITableViewCell *cell = [tableView
     dequeueReusableCellWithIdentifier: @"acell"];
 if(cell == nil) {
  cell = [[[UITableViewCell alloc] initWithStyle:
         UITableViewCellStyleDefault reuseIdentifier:@"acell"]
         autorelease];
 }
 cell.textLabel.text =
     [self.tableDataList objectAtIndex:[indexPath row]];
 return cell;
}


-(void)tableView:(UITableView *)tableView didSelectRowAtIndexPath:
    (NSIndexPath *) indexPath {
 TableViewDetailsViewController * temp =
     [[[TableViewDetailsViewController alloc] initWithNibName:
     @"TableViewDetailsViewController" bundle:nil] autorelease];
 [self.navCont pushViewController:temp animated:YES];
}
```

(continued)

```objc
-(void)tableView:(UITableView *)tableView commitEditingStyle:
  (UITableViewCellEditingStyle)editingStyle forRowAtIndexPath:
 (NSIndexPath *) indexPath {
 if (editingStyle == UITableViewCellEditingStyleDelete) {
  [self.tableDataList removeObjectAtIndex:indexPath.row];
  [tableView deleteRowsAtIndexPaths:[NSArray
     arrayWithObject:indexPath] withRowAnimation:YES];
  } else if (editingStyle == UITableViewCellEditingStyleInsert) {
    [self.tableDataList insertObject:@"Uninitialized"
          atIndex:indexPath.row];
    [tableView insertRowsAtIndexPaths:[NSArray
          arrayWithObject:indexPath] withRowAnimation:YES];
  }
}

-(void)tableView:(UITableView *)tableView moveRowAtIndexPath:
    (NSIndexPath *) fromIndexPath toIndexPath:
    (NSIndexPath *) toIndexPath {
 id object =
  [[self.tableDataList objectAtIndex:fromIndexPath.row] retain];
 [self.tableDataList removeObjectAtIndex:fromIndexPath.row];
 [self.tableDataList insertObject:object atIndex: toIndexPath.row];
 [object release];
}

-(UITableViewCellEditingStyle) tableView: (UITableView *)
    tableView editingStyleForRowAtIndexPath:
    (NSIndexPath *) indexPath {
 return UITableViewCellEditingStyleDelete;
}

-(BOOL)tableView:(UITableView *)tableView canMoveRowAtIndexPath:
    (NSIndexPath *) indexPath {
 return YES;
}

-(BOOL)tableView:(UITableView *)tableView canEditRowAtIndexPath:
    (NSIndexPath *) indexPath {
 return YES;
}

-(void)dealloc {
 [tableDataList release];
 [navCont release];
 [addItemController release];
 [addButton release];
 [super dealloc];
}
@end
```

4. Add a reference to MyTableViewController in AddItemViewController; however, instead of importing MyTableViewController, use the @class macro (Listings 10-34 and 10-35). Name the property parentTable.

Listing 10-34   AddItemViewController.h

```
#import <UIKit/UIKit.h>
@class MyTableViewController;
@interface AddItemViewController : UIViewController {
 MyTableViewController * parentTable;
 UITextField * addedName;
 UIBarButtonItem * doneButton;
}
@property (nonatomic, retain) IBOutlet UITextField * addedName;
@property (nonatomic, retain) MyTableViewController * parentTable;
@property (nonatomic, retain) IBOutlet UIBarButtonItem * doneButton;
-(IBAction) exitAndSave: (id) sender;
@end
```

Listing 10-35   AddItemViewController.m

```
#import "AddItemViewController.h"
@implementation AddItemViewController
@synthesize addedName;
@synthesize parentTable;
@synthesize doneButton;
@synthesize addedName;

-(void) viewDidLoad {
 self.navigationItem.title = @"Add Item";
 self.navigationItem.rightBarButtonItem = self.doneButton;
}

-(void)dealloc {
 [parentTable release];
 [doneButton release];
 [addedName release];
 [super dealloc];
}

-(IBAction) exitAndSave: (id) sender {
 [self.parentTable exitAndSave:self.addedName.text];
}
@end
```

5. Add an IBOutlet for a UITextField. Name the text field addedName. Add an IBOutlet for a bar button item. Name the button doneButton. Do not forget to synthesize the outlets/ properties. Add an IBAction called exitAndSave (Listings 10-34 and 10-35).

(continued)

6. Open MyTableViewController and import AddItemViewController. Add a property referencing the AddItemViewController. Name the reference addItemController. Also, add a method named exitAndSave and an IBAction named enterAddMode. Note that exitAndSave takes an NSString as a parameter and is not an IBAction (see Listings 10-32 and 10-33).

7. Add an IBOutlet for a bar button item named addButton (see Listing 10-32).

8. Change the viewDidLoad method so that it sets its navigation item's rightBarButtonItem to its editButtonItem and its navigation item's leftBarButtonItem to addButton (see Listing 10-33).

9. Implement the UITableViewDataSource protocol methods: tableView:canEditRowAtIndex path:, tableView:commitEditingStyle:forRowAtIndex:, tableView:moveRowAtIndexPath: toIndexPath:, tableView: editingStyleForRowAtIndexPath:, and tableView:canMoveRowA tIndexPath: (see Listing 10-33).

10. Open AddItemViewController.xib and add a bar button item to the editing pane. Change the newly added bar button's identifier to Done.

11. Connect the File's Owner doneButton outlet to the newly created Done button.

12. Add a UITextField to the canvas. Attach it to the File's Owner addedName outlet.

13. Connect the File's Owner exitAndSave action to the newly added Done bar button item.

14. Save your changes.

15. Open AddItemViewController and implement the viewDidLoadMethod so that it initializes its navigationItem's title to "Add Item" and its rightBarButtonItem to its doneButton (Listing 10-35).

16. Open MyTableViewController.xib in Interface Builder and add a bar button item to the document window. Change the button's identifier to Add.

17. Connect the File's Owner enterAddMode property to the newly added bar button item. Also connect the File's Owner addButton to the newly added bar button item.

18. Return to MyTableViewController and implement the exitAndSave and the enterAddMode methods like Listing 10-33.

19. Return to AddItemViewController and implement the exitAndSave method like Listing 10-35.

20. Ensure all your properties are being properly released in each class dealloc method.

21. Save all of your changes and click Run.

When the application starts, it presents the user with the table view. Upon tapping the Edit button, the application presents the table in edit mode (Figure 10-26). If the user clicks one of the table's delete accessories, the accessory rotates 90 degrees and presents a Delete button (Figure 10-27). Upon clicking Delete, the row is deleted. When a user clicks and drags the move accessory on the right, he or she can move the row to the new location desired (Figure 10-28).

Figure 10-26   The table view in edit mode

Figure 10-27   Deleting a row

(continued)

Figure 10-28 Moving a row

If a user decides to add a row, he or she taps the Add button, which presents the user with a view to enter the new object's details (Figure 10-29). If the user decides to cancel this action, he or she simply taps the Back button. If the user decides to save the record, he or she taps the Done button, which saves the record and returns the user to the table with the newly added table row (Figure 10-30).

To support moving rows, you implemented the tableView:moveRowAtIndexPath:toIndex Path: method. In that method, you obtained the object from its old position in the tableDataList, removed it, and then added it to its new location. You also implemented the tableView:canMove RowAtIndexPath: and tableView:canEditRowAtIndexPath: methods. If you needed to only allow certain rows to be editable, you would add that code to the tableView:canEditRowAt IndexPath: method. If you needed to only allow certain rows to be movable, you would add code to the tableView:canMoveRowAtIndexPath: method. Here, both methods simply return YES.

Supporting delete functionality requires a little more code than moving rows, but not much. You implemented the tableView:commitEditingStyle:forRowAtIndexPath: method. In the example, this method removes an object from the index and deletes the row from the table.

Notice you disallowed inserting rows by implementing the tableView:editingStyleForRow AtIndexPath: and having it return UITableViewCellEditingStyleDelete. This method informs a table what accessory, if any, it should display in a row when the table enters edit mode. Here, it displays the delete accessory.

Figure 10-29 Adding an item

Figure 10-30 The table view with the newly added item

(continued)

You did not implement insert functionality at all. Inserting uses similar logic to deleting a row, only the style is UITableViewCellEditingStyleInsert. You would also implement code to initialize an object and then insert it in the data source at the proper location. For instance, in the previous example, you could change it to support inserting rows if you changed tableView: editingStyleForRowAtIndexPath: to return UITableViewCellEditingStyleInsert and added the following lines to the tableView:commitEditingStyle:forRowAtIndex: method:

```
else if (editingStyle == UITableViewCellEditingStyleInsert) {
    [self.tableDataList insertObject:@"Uninitialized" atIndex:indexPath.row];
    [tableView insertRowsAtIndexPaths:[NSArray arrayWithObject:indexPath]
        withRowAnimation:YES];
}
```

In this example, however, adding a row does not use a table's edit mode. Although it is possible to insert a row using a table's edit mode, it is often not practical. Usually, a table lists items, where each row represents an individual item. Because each item has details associated with it, adding is often accomplished using a separate view controller. Here, you added a left bar button with an addition symbol. When a user clicks the button, it calls MyTableViewController's enterAddMode method. This method presents the AddItemViewController's view. Note that AddItemViewController and MyTableViewController both have references to each other. Upon finishing entering the new item, a user clicks Done, and the Done button fires AddItemViewController's exitAndSave method. This method calls MyTableViewController's exitAndSave method and the row is added as the table's last row.

Summary

This was a long and difficult chapter. But the UITableView is arguably iOS's most difficult, yet most important, view. If you do not understand the UITableView and its associated classes, you do not understand iOS programming. In this chapter, you learned how to use a UITableView and implement a table view's delegate and data source in a custom class. You also learned how to group a table and how to index it. And you learned how to customize a table cell's appearance.

After learning how to implement a table and customize it, you then learned a technique for adding a table to a navigation controller contained in a tab. This was a long task, but as it is such a ubiquitous layout pattern, it is a necessary task. After learning this technique, you then learned how to add, move, and delete rows from a table.

NOTE

There are many more methods and properties you can use to customize a table cell's behavior and appearance than presented in this chapter. For more information, refer to the online class references for each of the classes covered in this chapter and also reference Apple's "Table View Programming Guide for iOS."

Chapter 11

Activity Progress and Alerting Users

Key Skills & Concepts

● Using a UIActivityIndicatorView to indicate processing

● Using a UIProgressView to indicate processing

● Using a UIAlertView to warn users

● Using a UIActionSheet to inform users

● Using application badges to remind users of items needing their attention

While processing, many times an application must inform users that they must wait. A poorly constructed application provides no graphical clue that the application is busy processing; a well-constructed application does provide a graphical clue. The iOS SDK provides the UIActivityIndicatorView and UIProgressView classes to tell a user to "please wait, I'm working." The UIActivityIndicatorView uses a spinning "gear" to tell a user an application is processing and that it will eventually complete. The UIProgressView control also tells a user to "please wait," but it provides a visual clue as to how much processing remains. The two controls' names highlight their difference: The activity indicator shows activity, while the progress view shows progress.

A user-friendly application also informs a user when something unexpected occurs, and it informs a user when his or her decision might be potentially damaging. Moreover, the application informs the user in a way that highlights the importance of the problem. Sometimes unexpected events occur or a user makes a potentially destructive decision. For these situations, an application presents an alert dialog. Alerts provide information in a box separate from the underlying interface. This separation reinforces the alert's message that the situation is important and unusual, separate from an application's typical functionality. Alerts are also modal, meaning a user can do nothing else until clicking one of the alert's buttons to release it. Action sheets are similar to alerts but provide alternatives to actions and slide in from an application's top (desktop OS X applications) or from an application's bottom (iOS applications). You use action sheets for similar situations to an alert, but action sheets are more appropriate for actions that are a planned part of application activity.

Showing Activity—the UIActivityIndicatorView

A UIActivityIndicatorView class creates an animated indeterminate progress indicator. This control tells the user to "please wait, I'm processing." The control does not tell the user how long he or she must wait. Apple's reference for this class, which refers to the visual element as an animated "gear," illustrates an activity indicator in use (Figure 11-1). When I start the Amazon.com application, it fetches my content from its web server. Fetching this content takes time—how much time, the application doesn't know—and so the application uses a UIActivityIndicatorView.

Using a UIActivityIndicatorView in an application is easy. Begin the indicator's animation by calling its startAnimating method, and stop the indicator's animation by calling the stopAnimating method. If you wish to hide the indicator when not animated, set the property hidesWhenStopped to YES. You can also specify the activity indicator's size and style using its activityIndicatorViewStyle property. The indicator types are large white (UIActivityIndicatorViewStyleWhiteLarge), white (UIActivityIndicatorViewStyleWhite), and gray (UIActivityViewStyleGray). Figure 11-2 illustrates setting this property in Interface Builder. Figure 11-3 shows the three styles in iPhone Simulator.

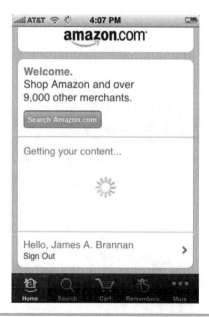

Figure 11-1   An activity indicator on Amazon.com's application

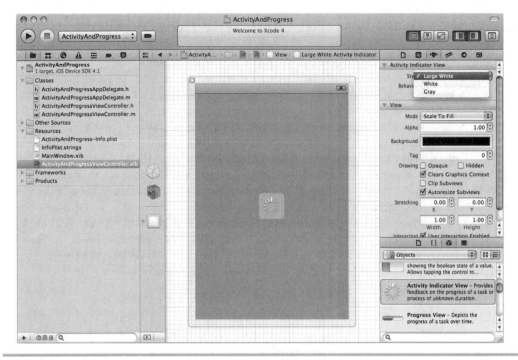

Figure 11-2 Setting a UIActivityIndicatorView's style

Figure 11-3 Three different UIActivityIndicatorView styles

Try This Using a UIActivityIndicatorView

1. Create a new View-based Application. Name the application **ActivityAndProgress**.

2. Open ActivityAndProgressViewController, add an IBOutlet for a UIActivityIndicatorView, and add an IBAction called doIt (Listings 11-1 and 11-2). Save and build.

Listing 11-1 ActivityAndProgressViewController.h

```
@interface ActivityAndProgressViewController : UIViewController {
 IBOutlet UIActivityIndicatorView * myActivityView;
}
@property (nonatomic, retain) IBOutlet
            UIActivityIndicatorView *myActivityView;
-(IBAction) doIt: (id) sender;
@end
```

Listing 11-2 ActivityAndProgressViewController.m

```
#import "ActivityAndProgressViewController.h"
@implementation ActivityAndProgressViewController
@synthesize myActivityView;
-(IBAction) doIt: (id) sender {
 if( [myActivityView isAnimating])
   [myActivityView stopAnimating];
 else
   [myActivityView startAnimating];
}
-(void)dealloc {
 [myActivityView release];
 [super dealloc];
}
@end
```

3. Open ActivityAndProgressViewController.xib.

4. Drag a button and activity indicator view from the library to the view's canvas (Figure 11-4).

5. Connect the File's Owner doIt action to the button's Touch Up Inside event. Connect the myActivityView outlet to the activity indicator view added to the canvas (Figure 11-5).

6. Select the activity indicator view, and open its view attributes in the Inspector. Ensure the indicator's Hides When Stopped and Hidden check boxes are checked (Figure 11-6).

7. Click Run to view the application in the iPhone Simulator.

8. Click the button two times (Figure 11-7).

(continued)

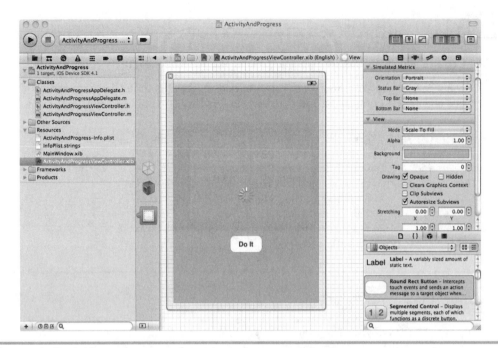

Figure 11-4 Adding a button and activity indicator to a view's canvas

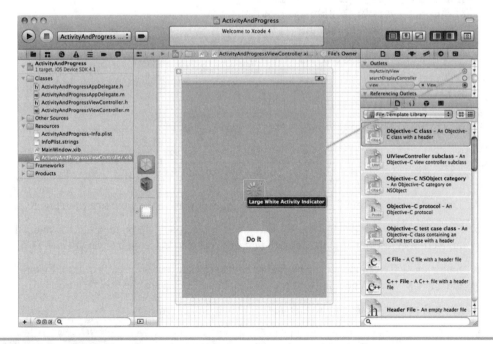

Figure 11-5 Connecting the myActivityView outlet to the activity indicator

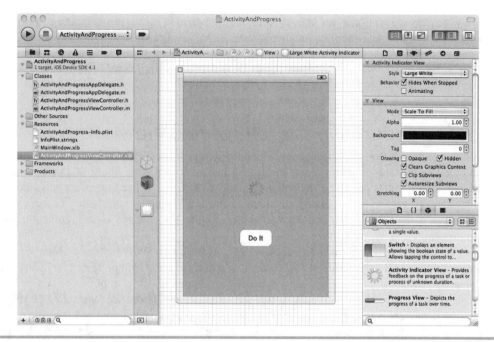

Figure 11-6   Ensuring the indicator's Hides When Stopped and Hidden check boxes are checked

Figure 11-7   The application running in iPhone Simulator   *(continued)*

When the application loads, it hides the activity indicator, as it is not animating. When you first click the button, the application displays the activity indicator and begins animating it. The next time you click the button, the application stops animating the indicator and hides it.

Showing Progress—the UIProgressView

A progress bar shows a task's progress. It is intended as a "please wait, I'm processing and I have this much processing remaining" for tasks with a known duration. For instance, an application might process a file's content, and as the file is processing, the application calculates the percentage remaining and displays it using a progress bar. As the file's content is processed, the progress bar updates its display to reflect the new percentage remaining until completion.

Creating a progress bar is more involved than creating an activity indicator. However, it is still not difficult. Before beginning this task, note that a common technique in many books and online tutorials is to set a progress view in an alert. Although it's easy, as of this book's writing, Apple neither supports nor recommends this technique. The recommended way of displaying a UIProgressView is by creating a new view with a transparent background and showing the progress bar in the new view. Because the view overlays the content view, the progress bar is modal. That is the strategy taken here.

Try This Using a UIProgress View

1. Open the ActivityAndProgress project from the previous task.

2. Create a new UIViewController named **PleaseWaitViewController**. Ensure that it also creates an associated xib.

3. Add an IBOutlet for a UIProgressView to PleaseWaitViewController (Listings 11-3 and 11-4).

Listing 11-3 PleaseWaitViewController.h

```
#import <UIKit/UIKit.h>
@interface PleaseWaitViewController : UIViewController {
 IBOutlet UIProgressView * myProgress;
}
@property (nonatomic, retain) IBOutlet UIProgressView * myProgress;
@end
```

Listing 11-4   PleaseWaitViewController.m

```
#import "PleaseWaitViewController.h"
@implementation PleaseWaitViewController
@synthesize myProgress;
-(void)dealloc {
 [myProgress release];
 [super dealloc];
}
@end
```

4. Drag starcopy.png from the book's Resources folder to the Resources folder in Xcode.

5. Build and then open PleaseWaitViewController.xib in Interface Builder.

6. Add an image view from the library to the view's canvas. Select starcopy.png as the image and set the mode to Scale To Fill if it didn't default to that.

7. Add a label and a progress view from the library to the view's canvas (Figure 11-8). Set the current value of the progress bar to 0.

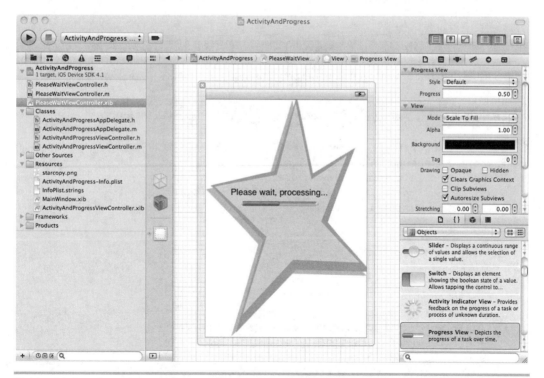

Figure 11-8   PleaseWaitViewController's view in Interface Builder

(continued)

8. Connect the UIProgressView on the canvas to the myProgress outlet in PleaseWaitView Controller.

9. Save your changes.

10. Open ActivityAndProgressController.h, add a forward reference to the PleaseWaitView Controller class, and change the myActivityView IBOutlet to use the new class. Add a method called moveBar. Listing 11-5 contains the completed ActivityAndProgressController.h.

Listing 11-5   ActivityAndProgressViewController.h modified for this task

```
#import <UIKit/UIKit.h>
@class PleaseWaitViewController;
@interface ActivityAndProgressViewController : UIViewController {
    PleaseWaitViewController * myActivityView;
}
@property (nonatomic, retain) IBOutlet PleaseWaitViewController *
myActivityView;

-(void) moveBar: (id) object;
-(IBAction) doIt: (id) sender;
@end
```

11. Open ActivityAndProgressController.m and implement the methods to match Listing 11-6. Note that doIt has changed from the previous task.

Listing 11-6   ActivityAndProgressViewController.m modified for this task

```
#import "ActivityAndProgressViewController.h"
#import "PleaseWaitViewController.h"
#import "ActivityAndProgressAppDelegate.h"
@implementation ActivityAndProgressViewController
@synthesize myActivityView;

int completed = 0;
-(void) moveBar: (id) object {
 completed ++;
 myActivityView.myProgress.progress = completed/20.0f;
 if(completed > 20) {
   [object invalidate];
   [self.myActivityView.view removeFromSuperview];
   [self.view setAlpha:1.0f];
   completed = 0;
   self.myActivityView.myProgress.progress = 0;
 }
}
```

```
-(IBAction) doIt: (id) sender {
myActivityView.view.backgroundColor = [UIColor clearColor];
[self.view setAlpha:0.7f];
[((ActivityAndProgressAppDelegate *)
    [UIApplication sharedApplication].delegate).window
    insertSubview:myActivityView.view aboveSubview: self.view];
[NSTimer scheduledTimerWithTimeInterval: 0.5 target: self
    selector: @selector(moveBar:) userInfo: nil repeats: YES];
}
-(void)dealloc {
[myActivityView release];
[super dealloc];
}
@end
```

12. Open ActivityAndProgressController.xib in Interface Builder and add several controls
    (Figure 11-9). The selection is not important, as they are not used.

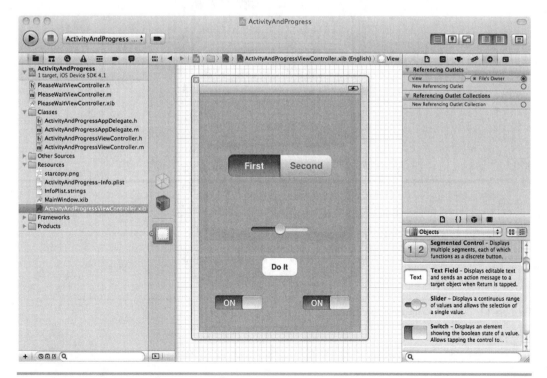

Figure 11-9 ActivityAndProgressViewController's canvas

(continued)

13. Add a view controller from the library to the document window. Change the controller's class to **PleaseWaitViewController**. Also, change the controller's NIB name to **PleaseWaitViewController**.

14. Connect the File's Owner myActivityView outlet to the newly added controller.

15. Save your changes and click Run. After the application loads in the iPhone Simulator (Figure 11-10), click the button. The PleaseWaitViewController's view is displayed and the progress view updates (Figure 11-11). Upon completion, the application removes the view and displays the original view once again.

Figure 11-10 The application running in iPhone Simulator

Figure 11-11   The application displaying the UIProgressView you added to the project

This task is pretty cool. You first created a separate view controller and view to contain the UIProgressView. Not happy with just a normal view, you added an image and placed the controls over the image. Later, because the view's background color is set to clear, this created the impression of a non-rectangular view (see Figure 11-8).

Ask the Expert

Q: So you create a non-rectangular view by using a UIImageView on a clear view?

A: Yes, this is one technique. A more robust technique is drawing the user interface yourself, but drawing a user interface from scratch is hard. Using a UIImageView on a view with a clear background is easy. Make your application's window clear, make the views clear, and then place any controls so that they overlay the image. For instance, Figure 11-12 illustrates a simple non-rectangular view.

Figure 11-12 A simple non-rectangular view

You also added a UIProgressView to the PleaseWaitViewController (Listing 11-3) as an outlet. You then added a PleaseWaitViewController (Listing 11-5) as an outlet of ActivityAndProgress ViewController. This allows you to reference both the PleaseWaitViewController and its UIProgressView from code in ActivityAndProgressViewController.

In ActivityAndProgressViewController, you created a method called moveBar and modified the doIt method. The doIt method is called when a user clicks the button on the ActivityAndProgressViewController. The method first sets its myActivity view's background color to clear, making the view transparent.

```
myActivityView.view.backgroundColor = [UIColor clearColor];
```

The method then sets the view's alpha level, giving it a faded, semitransparent appearance.

```
[self.view setAlpha:0.7f];
```

The doIt method also then gets a reference to the application's window and adds myActivity's view above the ActivityAndProgressViewController's view.

```
[((ActivityAndProgressAppDelegate *)
   [UIApplication sharedApplication] .delegate).window insertSubview:
   myActivityView.view aboveSubview: self.view];
```

To simulate a long-standing task, you use an NSTimer, which every half a second calls ActivityAndProgressViewController's moveBar method.

```
[NSTimer scheduledTimerWithTimeInterval: 0.5 target: self selector:
    @selector(moveBar:) userInfo: nil repeats: YES];
```

The moveBar method updates the progress bar until it reaches 20. It then invalidates the timer, removes PleaseWaitViewController's view, and sets the original view's alpha back to full strength. It also reinitializes the UIProgressView's progress value to zero.

```
[NSTimer scheduledTimerWithTimeInterval: 0.5 target: self selector:
    @selector(moveBar:) userInfo: nil repeats: YES];
```

Ask the Expert

Q: What is an NSTimer?

A: The NSTimer is a timer. Timers fire events at a specified interval. For instance, you set the interval to 0.5 seconds. You specified the target, self, and the message, moveBar. Every 0.5 seconds, the timer fires, executing the moveBar method in ActivityAnd ProgressViewController. The moveBar method gets called with a single argument, id, which is a pointer to the timer itself. To make a timer repeat, you specify YES for the repeats parameter. To remove a time, you invalidate the timer. For more information, refer to the NSTimer Class Reference.

Alerting Users

You should use alerts to inform users of impending actions that might be destructive, "are you sure" types of messages. Usually these are a result of some unexpected action. Alerts should have two buttons: an "okay" button and a "cancel" button. Alerts can also be used to notify the user that something very important just happened that wouldn't otherwise be obvious in the user interface. In general, you should try to use alerts sparingly to avoid annoying users.

Use action sheets to inform users of alternatives to an action. As Apple points out in their documentation, the Photos application contains a good example of using an action sheet (Figure 11-13). The user has a choice: use the photo as wallpaper, e-mail the photo, assign it to a contact, or do nothing (cancel). Action sheets are also appropriate when informing a user he or she is performing a potentially destructive task.

Figure 11-13 An action sheet in the Photo application

UIAlertView and UIAlertViewDelegate

A UIAlertView presents a modal alert to users. The alert appears and floats above the underlying view. Displaying a UIAlertView is easy: Create the class and display it. As the alert is modal, a user can do nothing else until she clicks one of the alert's buttons. The UIAlertViewDelegate handles the alert's button actions. If you add buttons to an alert, implement the clickedButtonAtIndex: method in your delegate. Other methods you might implement include the alertViewCancel: or didPresentAlertView: method. For a complete listing, refer to Apple's UIAlertViewDelegate Protocol Reference.

Alerts should not be misused. Present too many alerts, and you have an annoying application. Also, place buttons according to Apple's recommendation. When alerting a user to a potentially destructive outcome, place the Cancel button on the right (Figure 11-14). When alerting a user to a harmless action, place the Cancel button on the left (Figure 11-15).

Figure 11-14 Alert warning of a potentially destructive action

Figure 11-15 Alert warning of a benign action

Try This Creating a Simple UIAlertView

1. Create a new View-based Application. Name the application **AlertsProgress**.

2. Change AlertsProgressViewController to adopt the UIAlertViewDelegate protocol (Listing 11-7).

Listing 11-7 AlertsProgressViewController.h

```
#import <UIKit/UIKit.h>
@interface AlertsProgressViewController : UIViewController
<UIAlertViewDelegate> {
}
@end
```

3. Open AlertsProgressViewController.m and add an alert in the viewDidLoad method (Listing 11-8). Also, implement the didDismissWithButtonIndex: delegate method.

Listing 11-8 AlertsProgressViewController.m

```
#import "AlertsProgressViewController.h"
@implementation AlertsProgressViewController
-(void)viewDidLoad {
 [super viewDidLoad];
 UIAlertView * myAlert = [[[UIAlertView alloc]
    initWithTitle:@"View Loaded" message:@"View loaded successfully."
    delegate:self cancelButtonTitle:@"OK" otherButtonTitles:nil] autorelease];
 [myAlert show];
}
-(void)alertView:(UIAlertView *)alertView
    didDismissWithButtonIndex: (NSInteger) buttonIndex {
 NSLog(@"buttonIndex: %i", buttonIndex);
}
-(void)dealloc {
 [super dealloc];
}
@end
```

4. Click Run to try the application in the iPhone Simulator (Figure 11-16). Tap the button, and the button's index is logged to the Debugger Console.

In this simple application, the view's controller implements a UIAlertViewDelegate. Upon clicking the button, the delegate's didDismissWithButtonAtIndex method executes. This method

Figure 11-16 A simple alert

determines which button a user clicked and routes the user accordingly. The didDismissWith ButtonAtIndex method is an instance method declared in UIAlertViewDelegateProtocol and has the following signature:

```
-(void)alertView:(UIAlertView *) alertView didDismissWithButtonAtIndex:
(NSInteger) buttonIndex
```

The method takes the clicked button's index as an NSInteger via the buttonIndex parameter. After processing, this method dismisses the alert.

You created a UIAlertView instance through the following code:

```
UIAlertView * myAlert = [[[UIAlertView alloc] initWithTitle:@"View
Loaded" message:@"View loaded successfully." delegate:self
cancelButtonTitle:nil otherButtonTitles:nil] autorelease];
```

This method is convenient for initializing the alert view. If you wish, you can add more buttons to an alert using the otherButtonTitles parameter in the initWithTitle method. The next task illustrates an alert with two buttons.

Try This Using an Alert with Multiple Buttons

1. Open AlertsProgress in Xcode.

2. Modify AlertsProgressViewController's viewDidLoad method so it matches Listing 11-9.

Listing 11-9 Code to display an alert with two buttons

```
-(void)viewDidLoad {
  [super viewDidLoad];
  UIAlertView * myAlert = [[[UIAlertView alloc] initWithTitle:
     @"View Loaded" message:@"View loaded successfully."
     delegate:self cancelButtonTitle:@"OK"
     otherButtonTitles:@"Cancel",nil] autorelease];
  [myAlert show];
}
```

3. Click Run. The alert shows two buttons (Figure 11-17). Click either button, and the button's index is logged to the debugger console. You use this index to determine which button is clicked and route processing accordingly.

Figure 11-17 An alert with two buttons

UIActionSheet and UIActionSheetDelegate

While an alert displays as a pop-up box, the UIActionSheet slides in from a view's bottom, a view's toolbar, or a view's tab bar. You set where a toolbar slides in from when you display the action sheet. For instance, the following code slides the action sheet from the view's bottom.

```
[myActionSheet showInView:self.view];
```

The action sheet's bottom is aligned with the view's bottom. Note that if you use this setting when using a tab bar or toolbar, the action sheet's bottom is hidden by the bar. To prevent this, you display the action sheet using the showFromTabBar: or showFromToolBar: method. For instance, the following code slides the action sheet from the tab bar's top and aligns the action sheet's bottom with the bottom of the tab bar.

```
[myActionSheet showFromTabBar:self.view];
```

UIActionSheets are otherwise very similar to UIAlertViews. You specify an action sheet's delegate by creating a class adopting the UIActionSheetDelegate. You use this delegate to implement button actions. Methods are similar to UIAlertViewDelegate's. For instance, the following code handles a button click.

```
-(void)actionSheet:(UIActionSheet *)actionSheet clickedButtonAtIndex:
(NSInteger) buttonIndex
```

Try This Using a UIActionSheet

1. Open AlertsProgress in Xcode.

2. Open AlertsProgressViewController.h and change the class so that it adopts the UIActionSheetDelegate protocol (Listing 11-10).

Listing 11-10   AlertsProgressViewController.h

```
#import <UIKit/UIKit.h>
@interface AlertsProgressViewController : UIViewController
<UIActionSheetDelegate> {
}
-(IBAction) removeAll: (id) sender;
@end
```

3. Add an IBAction called removeAll. In the method's implementation, add a UIActionSheet that asks the user for confirmation (Listing 11-11). Remove the viewDidLoad method.

(continued)

Listing 11-11 AlertsProgressViewController.m

```
#import "AlertsProgressViewController.h"
@implementation AlertsProgressViewController
-(IBAction) removeAll: (id) sender {
 UIActionSheet * myActionSheet = [[[UIActionSheet alloc]
       initWithTitle: @"Remove all?" delegate:self cancelButtonTitle:
       @"No" destructiveButtonTitle: @"Yes"
       otherButtonTitles:@"Not Sure",nil] autorelease];
 [myActionSheet showInView:self.view];
}
-(void) actionSheet: (UIActionSheet *) actionSheet
       didDismissWithButtonIndex: (NSInteger) buttonIndex {
 NSLog(@"buttons index: %i", buttonIndex);
 if(buttonIndex == [actionSheet cancelButtonIndex]) {
   NSLog(@"cancelled...");
 }
}
-(void)dealloc {
 [super dealloc];
}
@end
```

4. Open AlertsProgressViewController.xib, add a button to the view, and connect the removeAll action in the File's Owner to the button's Touch Up Inside event (Figure 11-18). Save your changes.

5. Open AlertsProgressViewController.m and implement the didDismissWithButtonIndex: method (Listing 11-11).

6. Click Run (Figure 11-19). Click each button in the action sheet, and the debugger console should produce logging results similar to Listing 11-12.

Listing 11-12 Debugger console output

```
Attaching to process 11451.
2010-09-08 10:06:34.529 AlertsProgress[11451:207] buttons index: 0
2010-09-08 10:06:37.186 AlertsProgress[11451:207] buttons index: 1
2010-09-08 10:06:39.511 AlertsProgress[11451:207] buttons index: 2
2010-09-08 10:06:39.512 AlertsProgress[11451:207] cancelled...
```

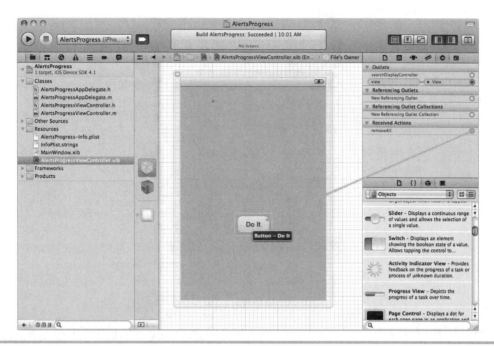

Figure 11-18 Connecting File's Owner removeAll action to a button

Figure 11-19 A UIActionSheet in action

Figure 11-20   An application badge tells me I have 39 e-mails in my inbox.

Application Badges

The iPhone's Mail application illustrates using a badge. For instance, in Figure 11-20, I have 39 e-mails in my inbox. Using this functionality is easy. Simply access your application's applicationBadgeNumber property and set it. A user's iPhone will remember the value between uses of your program. To clear a badge, simply set its value to zero.

Try This   Adding an Application Badge

1. Open the previous task in Xcode.

2. Modify the didDismissWithButtonIndex method to match Listing 11-13.

Listing 11-13   The didDismissWithButtonIndex method modified to use an application badge

```
-(void) actionSheet: (UIActionSheet *) actionSheet
     didDismissWithButtonIndex: (NSInteger) buttonIndex {
 if(buttonIndex == [actionSheet cancelButtonIndex])
  [UIApplication sharedApplication].applicationIconBadgeNumber -= 1;
 else if (buttonIndex == [actionSheet destructiveButtonIndex])
  [UIApplication sharedApplication].applicationIconBadgeNumber += 1;
}
```

Figure 11-21   The application has an application badge.

3. Click Build And Go to run the application.

4. Click the "Yes" button four or five times. Quit the application, but keep the simulator running. The application's icon is adorned with an application badge (Figure 11-21).

5. Start the application again; click the "No" button a few times. Quit the application, but keep the simulator running and notice the application's badge was decremented.

Summary

In this chapter you learned techniques for alerting users. Tasks that take time to complete should provide feedback to a user. When an application can estimate how long a task will take to complete, provide a UIProgressView. When an application cannot estimate how long a task will take to complete, provide a UIActivityView. When an unusual situation arises that requires a user decision, present a UIAlertView. When a user is making a decision that is potentially destructive, present a UIAlertView or a UIActionSheet, depending upon the uniqueness of the situation. If the situation is something commonly occurring while using an application, use a UIActionSheet. If it is an unusual situation, use a UIAlertView. But be careful not to overuse these two controls, as they interrupt an application's flow.

This chapter ended by presenting application badges. Application badges are useful to alert a user of unprocessed items or items needing a user's attention. Application badges are easy to incorporate into your application, but like alerts and action sheets, they should not be misused. For instance, you should not use an application badge to tell a user how many notes he or she has written in the Notes application. These notes do not require some action. Informing a user how many unread e-mails are in his or her inbox is an appropriate application badge use. Use your best judgment.

Chapter 12

Controls—Part One: Using Buttons, Sliders, Switches, and Text Fields

Key Skills & Concepts

- Modifying buttons

- Understanding the UIToolbar

- Understanding the UISlider and UISwitch

- Understanding UITextField and UITextArea

- Understanding using a UIWebView

In this chapter you learn how to use several of the iOS SDK's available controls. You also learn about the toolbar and the web view. Although this chapter is not comprehensive, it will help you get started understanding the many controls you might use when creating an iOS application. Several of the screenshots come directly from Apple's UICatalog example application (Figure 12-1). You can download this application at Apple's web site. But note, the controls it illustrates are largely created programmatically, and not using Interface Builder.

Figure 12-1 Apple's UICatalog sample application

Buttons

The most rudimentary control is arguably the button. What can you say about buttons? You click them, or on an iPhone, you tap them, and something happens. iOS has several different button styles (Figure 12-2). Implementing a button is not hard. In the next few sections you examine the buttons available when programming for an iOS device.

UIButton with a Background Image and Image

Although Apple's stock button, the rounded rectangular button, is sometimes appropriate (Figure 12-3), it is usually rather ugly.

You are not limited to plain buttons, though; you can make your buttons appear nicer. For instance, you can add a background image or an image. Creating custom buttons by adding an image or background image is not hard, but the artistic effort making the images appear correctly is time consuming. However, the results are usually worth the extra effort.

Figure 12-2 Apple's UICatalog's buttons screen

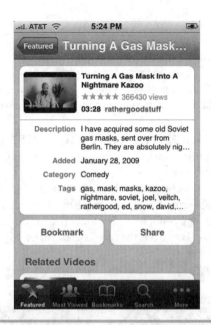

Figure 12-3 The YouTube App uses plain buttons.

Try This Using a Custom Button Background Image and Image

1. Create a new View-based Application. Name it **ButtonsBackground**.

2. Add outlets for two UIButtons to ButtonsBackgroundViewController (Listings 12-1 and 12-2).

Listing 12-1 ButtonsBackgroundViewController.h

```
#import <UIKit/UIKit.h>
@interface ButtonsBackgroundViewController : UIViewController {
 UIButton * clearButton;
 UIButton * smallButton;
}
@property (nonatomic, retain) IBOutlet UIButton * clearButton;
@property (nonatomic, retain) IBOutlet UIButton * smallButton;
- (IBAction) disableBut: (id) sender;
@end
```

Listing 12-2 ButtonsBackgroundViewController.m

```
#import "ButtonsBackgroundViewController.h"
@implementation ButtonsBackgroundViewController
@synthesize clearButton;
@synthesize smallButton;
- (IBAction) disableBut: (id) sender {
  if(clearButton.enabled == YES) {
  clearButton.enabled = NO;
  smallButton.enabled = NO;
  [((UIButton *) sender) setTitle:@"Enable"
forState: UIControlStateNormal];
  }
  else {
  clearButton.enabled = YES;
  smallButton.enabled = YES;
  [((UIButton *) sender) setTitle:@"Disable"
forState: UIControlStateNormal];
  }
}
- (void)dealloc {      [clearButton release];
  [smallButton release];
  [super dealloc];
}
@end
```

3. Add an action called disableBut and add the code in Listing 12-2 to the method.

4. Add butbackgray.png, butbackbluegray.png, butbackgraydisabled.png, power.png, and powerdisable.png to the Resources folder in Groups & Files. You will find these images in this book's resources folder.

5. Open ButtonsBackgroundViewController.xib.

6. Drag three buttons vertically aligned onto the view's canvas. Connect the second button to one of the outlets and connect the third button to one of the outlets.

7. Connect the disableBut action to the top button's Touch Up Inside.

8. Add the text Disable to the top button.

9. For the second button, open the inspector to Buttons Attributes. Ensure Shows Touch On Highlight is checked (Figure 12-4).

10. Notice the drop-down (Figure 12-5). Here you select the button's state, and the related field's values will only apply to that state. Ensure Default State Configuration is selected.

11. Change Background to butbackgray.png and change Image to power.png.

(continued)

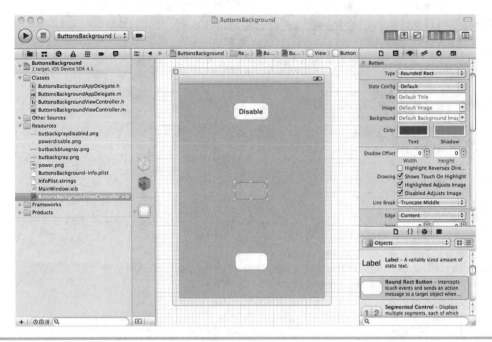

Figure 12-4 Ensure *Shows Touch on Highlight* is checked.

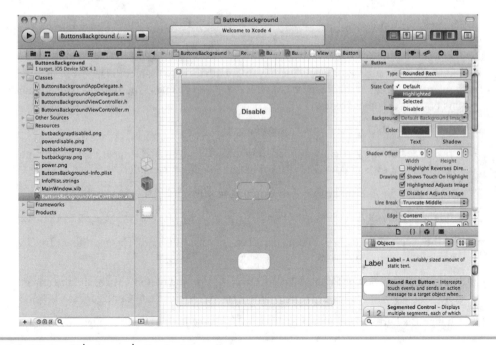

Figure 12-5 Selecting a button's state

12. Select Highlighted State Configuration and change Background to butbackbluegray.png. Once an image is set for the default state, it is the default image for the other states as well. Since the image isn't changing for the highlighted state, we can leave it blank.

13. Select Disabled State Configuration and change Background to butbackgraydisabled.png and Image to powerdisabled.png.

14. For the third button, ensure Default State Configuration is selected and add the text "Shock" to Title. Select the butbackgray.png for Background.

15. Select Highlighted State Configuration and add the text "Shocking" to Title. Select butbackbluegray.png as the Background. Note: do not make any changes to the Disable setting.

16. Resize the buttons as necessary so that they appear nice.

17. Click Run to build and run the application.

Notice the results upon tapping the buttons. The buttons change the background image from gray to bluish-gray (Figure 12-6). The bottom button also changes its title. Click Disable, and the buttons are grayed out (Figure 12-7). The button with the image changes its background image and image to the choices you've made. The button with the title text has

Figure 12-6   The buttons' background image changes.

Figure 12-7 The buttons are grayed-out when disabled.

this functionality built in. Making the button appear disabled was done automatically for you without your specifying images for the disabled state. iOS will also manage the disabled state for buttons with images, so it isn't actually necessary to specify a different background image unless you want a specific look and feel for a disabled image button.

TIP
Another way to create a custom button is by setting a button's type to custom. That technique is not shown here. It is not hard, though. First, add an image to a button. Second, change the button's type to custom and only the image is visible. Note that you can use different images for different button states, exactly as you did in the previous example application.

Button Types
There are buttons types other than Round Rect and custom that you might use. Figure 12-8 illustrates creating a Detail Disclosure button. To create a Detail Disclosure button, select a Round Rect Button from the library in Interface Builder and then change its type to Detail Disclosure button.

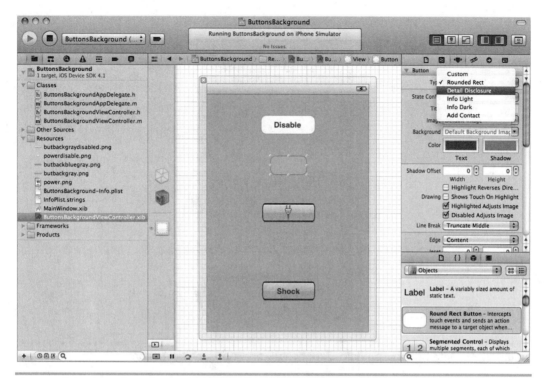

Figure 12-8   Detail Disclosure button

You create the Info Light and Info Dark buttons, like the Detail Disclosure button, by selecting a Round Rect button and changing its type to Info Light or Info Dark (Figure 12-9). You create a Contact button the same way you created the other button styles, by selecting a Round Rect button and changing its type (Figure 12-9).

UIToolBar

Toolbars are for adding buttons of type UIBarButtonItem in a bar, usually along a view's bottom. With a little ingenuity, you can place just about anything on a toolbar, although some items you are not really adding to a toolbar, but rather you are placing over the toolbar (Figure 12-10). You can add the following controls to a toolbar: Bar Button Item, Fixed Space Bar Button Item, Flexible Space, Bar Button Item, Text Field, Switch, Slider, and Button. Placing other items above a toolbar require using a fixed or flexible spacer (Figure 12-11). Place a spacer on the toolbar at the location on the toolbar you wish to overlay with a control, and then place the control over the spacer.

Figure 12-9   Info Light button, Info Dark button, and Add Contact button

Figure 12-10   You can go crazy with a toolbar.

Figure 12-11 Using spacers to place controls, such as labels on a toolbar

NOTE

For the sanity of your users, Apple may not approve your application if you get too crazy with a toolbar. When in doubt, refer to Apple's user interface guidelines. If you use controls in a predictable way, your users will know how to use your application without instructions.

Try This Creating a UIToolbar

1. Create a new View-based Application. Name the application **ToolBarProject**.

2. Open ToolBarProjectViewController.xib in Interface Builder.

3. Drag a Toolbar from the library window to the view's canvas. Notice it placed one button on the toolbar for you (Figure 12-12).

4. Drag a Fixed Space Bar Button Item from the library window to the view's canvas. Enlarge the spacer's size. Add another Bar Button Item to the spacer's right (Figure 12-13).

5. Select the toolbar and open its Inspector window. Change the toolbar's style to Black Translucent (Figure 12-14).

6. Save and click Run. The application displays the toolbar (Figure 12-15).

(continued)

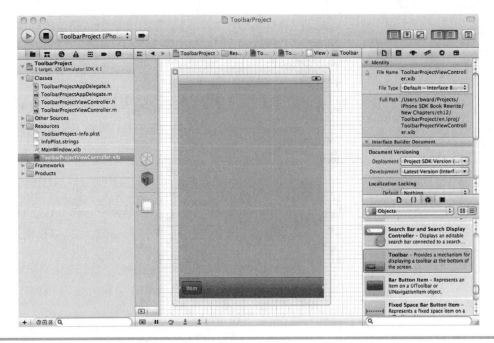

Figure 12-12 A toolbar on a view's canvas

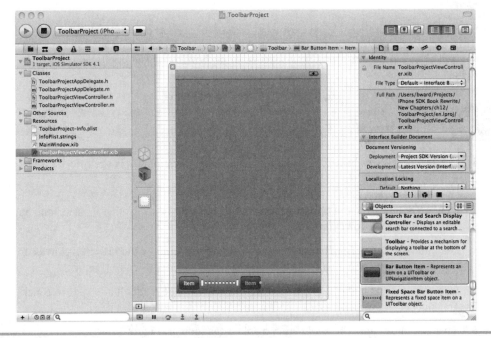

Figure 12-13 Adding a spacer to a toolbar

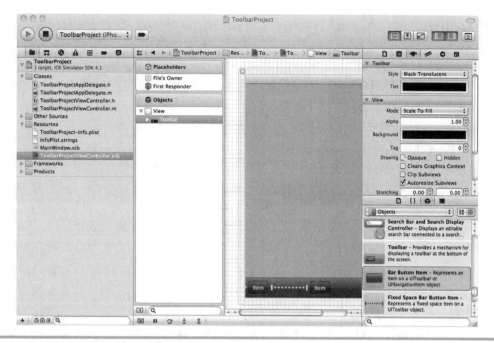

Figure 12-14   Making the toolbar translucent

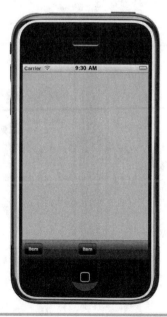

Figure 12-15   The sample application displaying a toolbar

UISwitch

A UISwitch, similar to a toggle button, is on or off. Figure 12-16 illustrates a UISwitch's appearance. A UISwitch has a property and method for changing its state. The switch is on when the Boolean property is YES. The switch is off when NO. The following is the declaration for the on property.

```
@property(nonatomic, getter=isOn) BOOL on
```

Notice that the getter is entitled isOn, you can use this getter to obtain the on property's value or the property itself. For instance, the following two statements are equivalent:

```
if( ((UISwitch *) sender).on == YES)
if( [((UISwitch *) sender) isOn] == YES)
```

You can change the switch's value programmatically using the setOn method. This method's signature follows.

```
-(void) setOn: (BOOL) on animated: (BOOL) animated
```

UISlider

Sliders are a horizontal bar with a small round indicator that a user can move to the right or left to change the slider's value. Figure 12-16 contains a slider example.

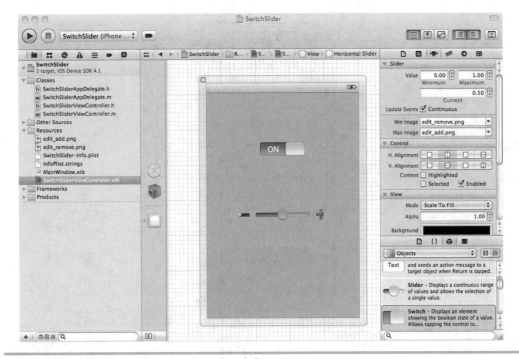

Figure 12-16 A view with a switch and a slider

Appearance

The UISlider class has several properties and methods you might use to modify a slider's appearance. You can modify the indicator using the setThumbImage method.

```
- (void) setThumbImage:(UIImage *)image forState: (UIControlState) state
```

This method allows you to provide the slider an image in place of the round indicator. Interface Builder does not provide a means to set this value, so you must do so programmatically when first loading the view containing the slider.

You can also specify minimum and maximum images that appear directly to the slider's left and right. Set a slider's image appearing to the right using the maximumValueImage property.

```
@property(nonatomic, retain) UIImage *maximumValueImage
```

Set a slider's image appearing to the left using the minimumValueImage property.

```
@property(nonatomic, retain) UIImage *minimumValueImage
```

The next Try This example sets both properties using the Inspector pane in Interface Builder. There are more modifications you might make to a UISlider; refer to the UISlider Class Reference for a complete listing.

Values

By default, a UISlider's values begin with minimum of 0, a maximum of 1.00, and a .50 initial value. The slider's values are floats, and you can set the value programmatically using the setValue method or the value property.

```
- (void) setValue:(float) value animated:(BOOL) animated
```

The minimum, maximum, and initial values are all properties that you can set programmatically or through Interface Builder.

Continuous Property

A slider changes its values continuously as a user adjusts the indicator. For instance, as a user moves the indicator from left to right, the slider is continuously firing value-changed events. You can change this behavior by changing the continuous property to NO. If the value is NO, the slider fires the event only when a user lifts his or her finger from the indicator. You can set this property programmatically, or through Interface Builder.

Try This Using a Switch and a Slider

1. Create a new View-based Application. Name the application **SwitchSlider**.

2. Drag the edit_add.png and edit_remove.png images from the resources folder to the Resources folder in Groups & Files.

3. Open SwitchSliderViewController.xib in Interface Builder.

(continued)

4. Add a Slider and a Switch from the library. Resize the slider to be larger and set the edit_ remove .png as the minimum image and edit_add.png as the maximum image (Figure 12-16).

5. Notice that the Slider's minimum value is zero and maximum is one. Leave the values unchanged.

6. Save your changes.

7. Open SwitchSliderViewController and implement a method named handleSwitch and a method named handleSlider (Listings 12-3 and 12-4). Also implement a property for the UISwitch named mySwitch.

Listing 12-3   SwitchSliderViewController.h

```
#import <UIKit/UIKit.h>
@interface SwitchSliderViewController : UIViewController {
  UISwitch * mySwitch;
}
@property(nonatomic, retain) IBOutlet UISwitch * mySwitch;
- (IBAction) handleSwitch: (id) sender;
- (IBAction) handleSlider: (id) sender;
@end
```

Listing 12-4   SwitchSliderViewController.m

```
#import "SwitchSliderViewController.h"
@implementation SwitchSliderViewController
@synthesize mySwitch;
- (IBAction) handleSwitch: (id) sender {
  if( [((UISwitch *) sender) isOn] == YES) {
    NSLog(@"It's on");
  } else {
    NSLog(@"It's off");
  }
}
- (IBAction) handleSlider: (id) sender {
  NSLog(@"value: %f", ((UISlider *)sender).value);
  [mySwitch setOn: ([((UISlider *) sender) value] == ((UISlider *)
sender).maximumValue)];
}
- (void)dealloc {
  [mySwitch release];
  [super dealloc];
}
@end
```

8. Save and open SwitchSliderViewController.xib.

9. Connect the mySwitch outlet to the switch on the canvas.

10. Connect the handleSlider action to the slider's Value Changed event.

11. Connect the handleSwitch action to the switch's Value Changed event.

12. Save and exit Interface Builder.

13. Save and click Run (Figure 12-17). Click the switch and it logs to the Debugger Console. Change the slider's value to the far right. The switch's value changes to ON (Figure 12-18).

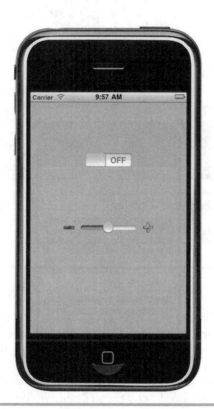

Figure 12-17   The application running in the iPhone Simulator

(continued)

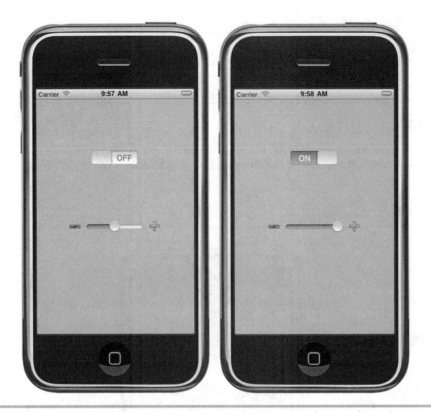

Figure 12-18 Moving the slider to the maximum value changes the switch's value.

UITextField

iOS uses the UITextField class to render text fields. A text field is associated with a keyboard that appears when a user taps in the text field. Keyboard styles include Number Pad, Phone Pad, URL, and several others. You can set the keyboard style programmatically or using Interface Builder (Figure 12-19).

Figure 12-20 illustrates several other text field properties you might set. You can specify how text should be capitalized. Valid choices are None, Words, Sentences, and All Characters. You can also specify if the text field should attempt to correct spelling errors by setting the correction property to YES. If you want the text field to behave like a password, then check the Secure check box in Interface Builder. Other properties you might want to change are the text field's border, background, font, and return key for the keyboard. Figure 12-20 shows the valid choices for a keyboard's return key. For a complete listing of properties and methods available to you, refer to the UITextField Class Reference.

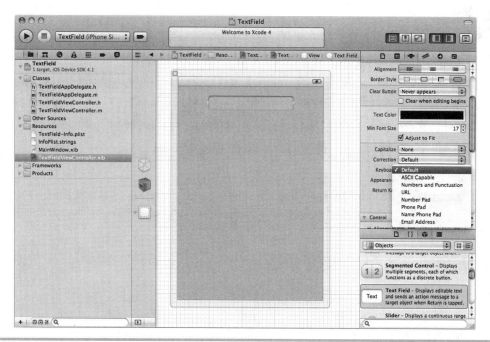

Figure 12-19　Setting a text field's keyboard type

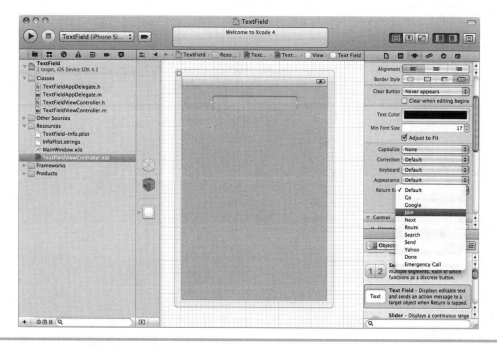

Figure 12-20　Valid choices for a keyboard's return key

Try This Using UITextField (with a Number Pad)

1. Create a new View-based Application named **TextField**.

2. Open TextViewController.xib in Interface Builder. Drag two UITextField controls from the library to the view's canvas and resize the text fields.

3. Select the second text field and in its inspector, change its Keyboard to Number Pad.

4. Select the first text field and change its Return Key to Done.

5. Save your changes.

6. Open TextFieldViewController and implement the textFieldDone action (Listings 12-5 and 12-6). Also, add an IBOutlet for the second text field and implement the numberFieldDone method.

Listing 12-5 TextFieldViewController.h

```
#import <UIKit/UIKit.h>
@interface TextFieldViewController : UIViewController {
 UITextField * numberField;
}
@property(nonatomic, retain) IBOutlet UITextField * numberField;
- (IBAction) textFieldDone: (id) sender;
- (IBAction) numberFieldDone: (id) sender;
@end
```

Listing 12-6 TextFieldViewController.m

```
#import "TextFieldViewController.h"
@implementation TextFieldViewController
@synthesize numberField;
- (IBAction) textFieldDone: (id) sender {
    [sender resignFirstResponder];
}
- (IBAction) numberFieldDone: (id) sender {
    [numberField resignFirstResponder];
}
- (void)dealloc {
    [numberField release];
    [super dealloc];
}
@end
```

Figure 12-21 The number pad has no Done key.

7. Save and then open TextFieldViewController.xib. Connect the textFieldDone action to the first text field's Did End on Exit event.

8. Save and click Run. Notice that when finished editing the first text field, upon clicking Done, the text pad disappears. The number pad, though, has no Done key (Figure 12-21).

9. Reopen TextFieldViewController.xib and drag a button onto the view's canvas. Resize the button to cover the entire canvas.

10. In the Document window, expand the View and ensure the newly added button is behind the two text fields (Figure 12-22).

11. In the Inspector's Button Attributes pane, change the button's Type to custom and uncheck any checked drawing check boxes (Figure 12-23).

12. Connect the numberField outlet to the second text field. Connect the numberFieldDone action to the Touch Up Inside event for the button added to the canvas (Figure 12-24).

13. Save and then click Run. Click the second text field and the number pad appears. Tap anywhere outside the two text fields to close the number pad. Tapping in the first text field causes the number pad to switch to the keyboard (Figure 12-25).

Note that in textFieldDone and numberFieldDone we are calling the resignFirstResponder method. This is an essential step that actually dismisses the keyboard.

(continued)

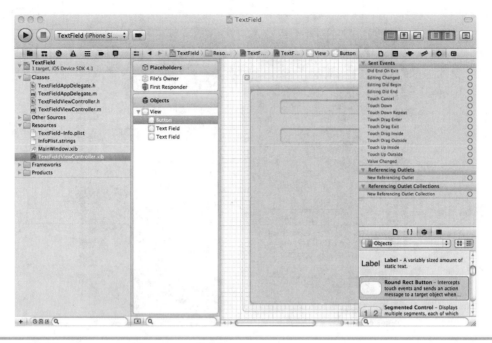

Figure 12-22 Button is under two textfields.

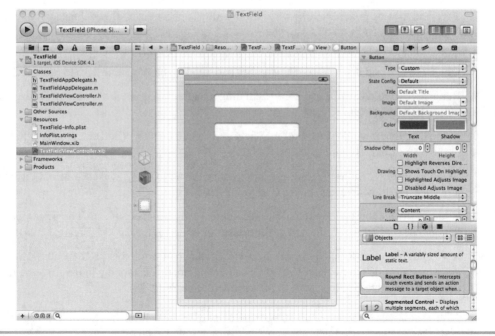

Figure 12-23 Changing button's type to Custom

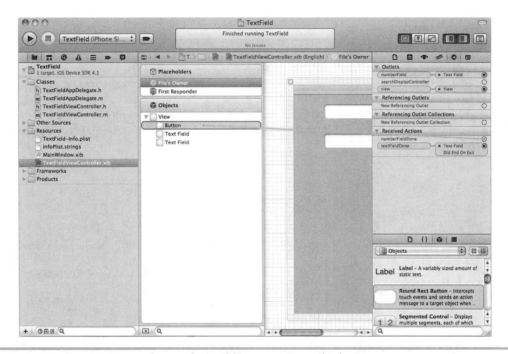

Figure 12-24 Connecting the numberFieldDone action to the button

Figure 12-25 The number pad appears and disappears from the application.

UITextView

Use a UITextView to capture multiple lines of text in a scrollable, multiline text area. It's generally used for entering paragraphs of text rather than a single line. There are several properties you can set to customize the control's appearance, including the font, textColor, editable, and textAlignment properties. You can also check if it has text using the hasText method. Figure 12-26 illustrates several properties you might want to set for a UITextView in Interface Builder. For more information on the UITextView, refer to the UITextView Class Reference.

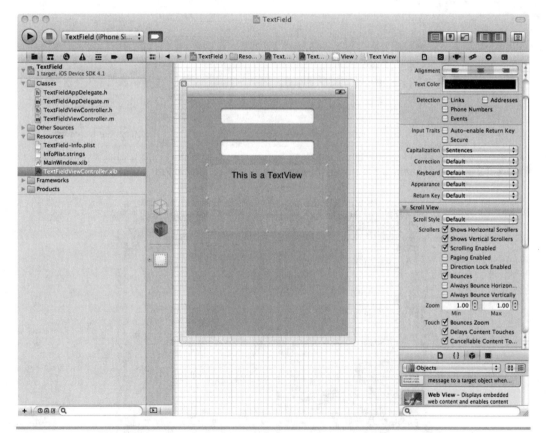

Figure 12-26 UITextView properties you might want to set in Interface Builder

UISegmentedControl

A segmented control groups together two or more segments, where each segment acts as an independent button. The next task illustrates a segmented control.

Try This   Using a UISegmentedControl

1. Create a new View-based Application named **Segment**.

2. Add the images colorize.png and wizard.png from the resources folder to the Resources folder in Groups & Files.

3. Open SegmentViewController.xib and add a Segmented Control to the view's canvas.

4. Change the control so that it has three segments. Change the Segment 0's name to Kids, the first segment's image to colorize.png, and the second segment's image to wizard.png (Figure 12-27). Change the control's style to Bordered.

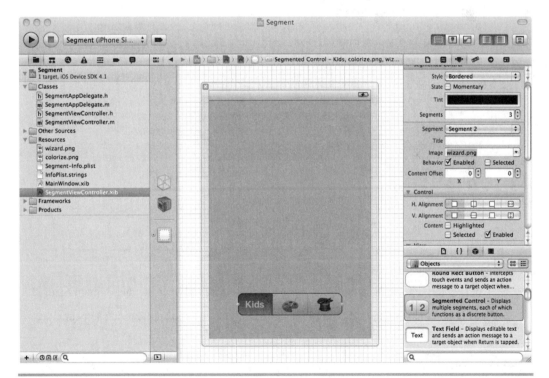

Figure 12-27   Modifying the segmented control in Interface builder

(continued)

5. Save your changes.

6. Open SegmentViewController and add an IBAction called handleSegment to SegmentViewController (Listings 12-7 and 12-8).

Listing 12-7   SegmentViewController.h

```
#import <UIKit/UIKit.h>
@interface SegmentViewController : UIViewController {
}
- (IBAction) handleSegment: (id) sender;
@end
```

Listing 12-8   SegmentViewController.m

```
#import "SegmentViewController.h"
@implementation SegmentViewController
- (IBAction) handleSegment: (id) sender {
  UISegmentedControl * myseg = (UISegmentedControl *) sender;
  if(myseg.selectedSegmentIndex == 0) {
    NSLog(@"selected zero index...");
  }
  else if(myseg.selectedSegmentIndex == 1) {
    NSLog(@"selected one index...");
  }
  else {
    NSLog(@"selected two index...");
  }
}
- (void)dealloc {
  [super dealloc];
}
@end
```

---

7. Save and then switch to SegmentViewController.xib.

8. Connect the segment's Value Changed event to the File's Owner handleSegment method.

9. Save your changes and click Run. Figure 12-28 illustrates the application's appearance, and Listing 12-9 contains the Debugger Console's logging.

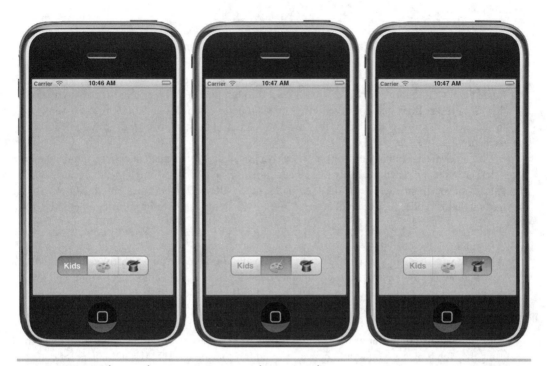

Figure 12-28   The application running in iPhone Simulator

Listing 12-9   The Debugger Console's logging for application

```
2010-09-09 10:47:03.535 Segment[19281:207] selected one index...
2010-09-09 10:47:19.737 Segment[19281:207] selected two index...
```

The Web View

This chapter wraps up its discussion of controls by discussing the web view. The UIWebView is the class you use to add a web browser to your application. It's based upon the same code foundation as Safari, and so you can use CSS and JavaScript. Using the web view can be easy or more difficult, depending upon how much you want your application to interact with the browser. In this chapter we keep it simple.

UIWebView

The UIWebView is responsible for the web view's display. It is an easy means of embedding web content in your application. The loadRequest: method is how you load web content. You can check on the control's progress loading a resource using the loading property. You might also want to move forward or backward through the user's browsing history—you do this using the goBack and goForward methods. Of course, you should check first to see if the control can move backward or forward by examining the canGoBack or canGoForward properties.

If you own an iPhone, then you've probably noticed that you can tap telephone numbers in the Safari browser and it automatically dials the number. The UIWebView implements this behavior unless you specifically tell it not to by setting the detectsPhoneNumbers property to NO. Another method that is subtle, yet powerful is the stringByEvaluatingJavaScriptFromString: method.

```
- (NSString *)stringByEvaluatingJavaScriptFromString:(NSString *)script
```

Why is this method so powerful? The stringByEvaluatingJavaScriptFromString: method lets you evaluate *any* JavaScript string. You can access a page's Document Object Model (DOM) through JavaScript, and thereby manipulate an HTML page's content.

The HTML DOM is a W3C standard for manipulating HTML documents. HTML DOM is outside this book's scope, but for more information refer to the W3C School's HTML DOM Tutorial, available online at www.w3schools.com. If you want to do sophisticated programming using the web browser, you would be well served by learning the HTML DOM. The following Try This example, illustrates using the stringByEvaluatingJavaScriptFromString: method to print a page's HTML content.

You navigate to a specific page by using the UIWebView's loadRequest method.

```
- (void) loadRequest: (NSURLRequest *) request
```

The loadRequest method takes a URL request as a parameter and navigates to the resource represented by the underlying URL. A NSURL class wraps the NSURLRequest's underlying URL. Both NSURLRequest and NSURL are part of the Foundation framework. You use both in the next Try This example application.

UIWebViewDelegate

UIWebViews can also have a delegate. You create a delegate for a UIWebView by creating a class that adopts the UIWebViewDelegate protocol and then assigning the UIWebView's delegate property to the custom class. The UIWebViewDelegate handles key events when loading a web page. When an event occurs, the web view calls the appropriate delegate method. For instance, when a web view is about to load a page, it calls the webView:should StartLoadWithRequest:navigationType: method.

```
- (BOOL)webView:(UIWebView *)webView
     shouldStartLoadWithRequest:
     (NSURLRequest *) request
     navigationType:(UIWebViewNavigationType)navigationType
```

When a web view starts loading a page, it calls the webViewDidStartLoad: method.

```
- (void)webViewDidStartLoad:(UIWebView *)webView
```

When a web view finishes loading a page, it calls the webViewDidFinishLoad: method, unless an error occurs, when instead it calls the webView:didFailLoadWithError: method.

```
- (void)webViewDidFinishLoad:(UIWebView *)webView
- (void)webView:(UIWebView *)webView didFailLoadWithError:(NSError *)
error
```

Try This   Creating a Simple Web Browser

1. Create a new View-based Application named **MyWeb**.

2. Create a new class called MyWebViewDelegate and have it adopt the UIWebViewDelegate protocol (Listings 12-10 and 12-11).

Listing 12-10   MyWebViewDelegate.h

```
#import <Foundation/Foundation.h>
@interface MyWebViewDelegate : NSObject <UIWebViewDelegate> {
}
@end
```

Listing 12-11   MyWebViewDelegate.m

```
#import "MyWebViewDelegate.h"
@implementation MyWebViewDelegate
- (void)webViewDidFinishLoad: (UIWebView *) webView {
  NSLog(@"%@", [webView stringByEvaluatingJavaScriptFromString:
       @"document.documentElement.textContent"]);
}
@end
```

3. Open MyWebViewController.xib in Interface Builder.

4. Add a Web View from the Library to the canvas. Also add a text field and a button (Figure 12-29).

(continued)

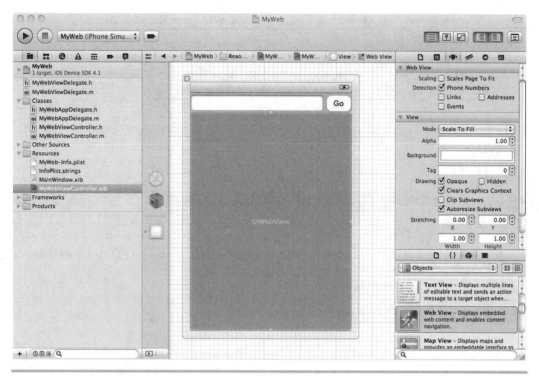

Figure 12-29 A simple web browser in Interface Builder

5. Change the text field's keyboard type to URL.

6. Save your changes.

7. Open MyWebViewController and add IBOutlets for the text field and the web view (Listings 12-12 and 12-13). Add an IBAction called changeLocation. Add the MyWebViewDelegate as a property and implement the viewDidLoad method.

Listing 12-12 MyWebViewController.h

```
#import <UIKit/UIKit.h>
@class MyWebViewDelegate;
@interface MyWebViewController : UIViewController {
  UITextField * myTextField;
  UIWebView * myWebView;
  MyWebViewDelegate * myWebViewDelegate;
}
```

```
@property(nonatomic, retain) IBOutlet UIWebView * myWebView;
@property(nonatomic, retain) IBOutlet UITextField * myTextField;
@property(nonatomic, retain) MyWebViewDelegate * myWebViewDelegate;
- (IBAction) changeLocation: (id) sender;
@end
```

Listing 12-13   MyWebViewController.m

```
#import "MyWebViewController.h"
#import "MyWebViewDelegate.h"
@implementation MyWebViewController
@synthesize myWebView;
@synthesize myTextField;
@synthesize myWebViewDelegate;
- (void) viewDidLoad {
  myWebViewDelegate = [[MyWebViewDelegate alloc] init];
   myWebView.delegate = myWebViewDelegate;
}
- (void)dealloc {
  myWebView.delegate = nil;
  [myWebViewDelegate release];
  [myTextField release];
  [myWebView release];
  [super dealloc];
}
- (IBAction) changeLocation: (id) sender {
  [myTextField resignFirstResponder];
  NSURL * url = [NSURL URLWithString: myTextField.text];
  NSURLRequest * request = [NSURLRequest requestWithURL:url];
  [myWebView loadRequest:request];
}
@end
```

8. Save your changes and switch back to MyWebViewController.xib.

9. Connect the button's Touch Up Inside action to the changeLocation action. Connect the text field and web view to their respective outlets.

10. Save your changes and click Run.

11. Type **http://www.apple.com** in the text field and tap GO and the web page loads in the web view (Figure 12-30). The web page's HTML is also logged to the Debugger Console (not provided as a listing due to its length).

(continued)

Figure 12-30 A simple web browser displaying Apple's home page

Summary

This chapter discussed some of the controls available to you in the iOS SDK. First you reviewed buttons. After buttons, you learned about the toolbar, followed by switches, sliders, and text fields. Note the subtleties of using the keyboard; you must explicitly release the keyboard using the resignFirstResponder method. Moreover, when using a number pad, if you want to release the keyboard you need to resort to an "invisible button" trick. You then learned about using the text view and segmented control and then finished up with the UIWebView.

Chapter 13

Controls—Part Two: Using Pickers and Using the Camera

Key Skills & Concepts

- Using a UIDatePicker to select dates

- Using a UIPickerView to select values

- Using a UIPickerView with multiple components

- Using a UIPickerView with UIImageView

- Using the UIImagePickerController to control the camera and access the photo library

- Using simple NSNotifications

What do the UIPickerView and the UIImagePicker classes have in common? Nothing, really, other than they are both ultimately UIViews. But they are both controls you might use in an iOS application, and so they are covered together in this second chapter on iOS controls. This chapter's first half covers using the UIDatePicker and UIPickerView classes. These classes create visual controls that appear similar to Las Vegas slot machines. This chapter's second half covers using the UIImagePickerController. This class gives you a way to programmatically access the photo library on any iOS device and the camera roll and camera on an iPhone or new iPod Touch that includes a camera.

Using Pickers: Date Pickers and Pickers

You use pickers to select one of several values. There are two types of pickers: *date pickers* and *pickers*. As you would expect, date pickers are used for selecting a date, time, or countdown interval. Pickers are used for selecting one of many values.

Date Pickers

Date pickers pick dates and times, placing the selected values in an NSDate class, and are implemented using the UIDatePicker class. If using Interface Builder to develop an iOS application, you drag a date picker onto your view's canvas from the library and modify the picker's properties in the Inspector. You then create an IBOutlet for the picker in your view's associated view controller and connect it to the picker on your view's canvas. The view controller uses this outlet to obtain the UIDatePicker object's selected date. The example later in this section illustrates this process.

UIDatePicker

A UIDatePicker has rotating wheels, allowing a user to select the date and time. If using a date picker to pick a date and time, valid modes are Date & Time, Time, and Date. If using a date

Figure 13-1   UIDatePicker has four modes: Date & Time, Time, Date, and Timer.

picker to pick a countdown time, the valid mode is Timer. Figure 13-1 illustrates the picker's visual appearance for the different modes.

There are several attributes you might change from the default when using a UIDatePicker. Figure 13-2 illustrates the mode, locale, timeZone, date, minimumDate, maximumDate, and interval properties, as viewed in the Inspector.

The locale is an NSLocale. This class encapsulates how the date should be formatted for a different date or culture. The timeZone is an NSTimeZone; its default value is the operating system's time zone. The minuteInterval is the minute intervals displayed by the picker. For instance, Figure 13-3 illustrates a UIDatePicker using 30-minute intervals and a UIDatePicker using 1-minute intervals.

NSDate

UIDatePickers return values as an NSDate. You access a date picker's value through its date property. For instance, the following sets an NSDate from a UIDatePicker's date property.

```
NSDate * theDate = self.datePicker.date;
```

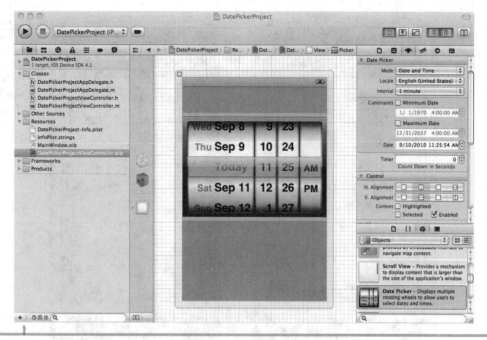

Figure 13-2 Several UIDatePicker properties you might change in the Inspector

Figure 13-3 A UIDatePicker showing 30-minute intervals and a UIDatePicker showing 1-minute intervals

An NSDate is a date and time. Several NSDate methods you might use include isEqualToDate:, earlierDate:, compare:, and laterDate:. For a more complete understanding of date and time programming, refer to Apple's "Date and Time Programming Guide for Cocoa," available online.

NSDateFormatter

When you wish to display a date, you use an NSDateFormatter. An NSDateFormatter allows a date to be displayed as a formatted NSString. There are many formats you might use. For instance, consider the two formatters.

```
NSDateFormatter * dateFormatter =
     [[[NSDateFormatter alloc] init] autorelease];
[dateFormatter setDateFormat:@"MM/dd/yyyy"];
```

The "MM/dd/yyyy" format outputs August 26, 2008, as "08/26/2008."

```
[dateFormatter setDateFormat:@"EEEE MMMM d',' yyyy"];
```

The "EEEE MMMM d',' yyyy" format outputs "Tuesday August 26, 2008," as the date. These are only two of many choices you might select to format dates and times. For more formats, refer to Apple's "Data Formatting Programming Guide for Cocoa," available online.

Try This   Using a Date Picker

1. Create a new View-based Application. Name the application **DatePickerProject**.

2. Open DatePickerProjectViewController.xib in Interface Builder.

3. Add a date picker to the canvas and add a label (Figure 13-4).

4. Change the date picker's mode to Date (Figure 13-5).

5. Save your changes.

6. Open DatePickerProjectViewController and add an IBOutlet for the UIDatePicker and an IBOutlet for the UILabel (Listings 13-1 and 13-2). Also add an IBAction called changeValue. Don't forget to release the two outlets in the dealloc method.

Listing 13-1   DatePickerProjectViewController.h

```
#import <UIKit/UIKit.h>
@interface DatePickerProjectViewController : UIViewController {
 UIDatePicker * datePicker;
 UILabel * theLabel;
}
```

(continued)

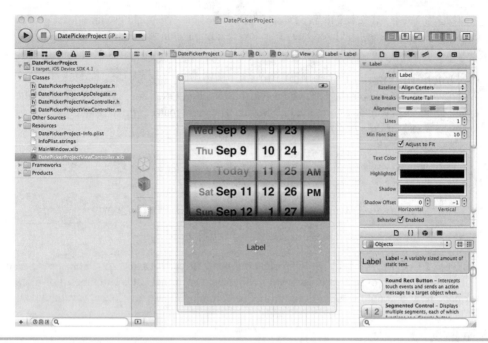

Figure 13-4 Adding a UIDatePicker and UILabel to the view

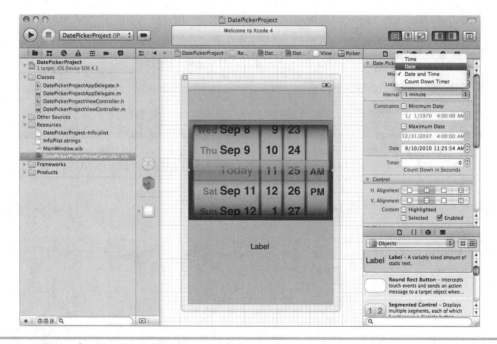

Figure 13-5 Change a UIDatePicker's mode to Date

```
@property (nonatomic, retain) IBOutlet UIDatePicker * datePicker;
@property (nonatomic, retain) IBOutlet UILabel * theLabel;
- (IBAction) changeValue: (id) sender;
@end
```

Listing 13-2   DatePickerProjectViewController.m

```
#import "DatePickerProjectViewController.h"
@implementation DatePickerProjectViewController
@synthesize datePicker;
@synthesize theLabel;
- (IBAction) changeValue: (id) sender {
  NSDate * theDate = self.datePicker.date;
  NSLog(@"the date picked is: %@", [theDate description]);
  NSDateFormatter * dateFormatter = [[[NSDateFormatter alloc] init]
autorelease];
  [dateFormatter setDateFormat:@"MM/dd/yyyy"];
  NSLog(@"formatted: %@", [dateFormatter stringFromDate:theDate]);
  [dateFormatter setDateFormat:@"EEEE MMMM d',' yyyy"];
  NSLog(@"formatted: %@", [dateFormatter stringFromDate:theDate]);
  [theLabel setText:[theDate description]];
}
- (void)dealloc {
  [datePicker release];
  [theLabel release];
  [super dealloc];
}
@end
```

7. Save your changes and open DatePickerProjectViewController.xib in Interface Builder.

8. Connect the File's Owner datePicker outlet to the UIDatePicker on the canvas. Connect the File's Owner theLabel to the UILabel on the canvas.

9. Connect the File's Owner changeValue action to the UIDatePicker's Value Changed event (Figure 13-6).

10. Save your changes and click Run to run the application in iPhone Simulator (Figure 13-7). The Debugger Console should have logging similar to Listing 13-3.

Listing 13-3   Debugger Console output

```
2010-09-10 11:38:36.445 DatePickerProject[7095:207] the date picked is:
2010-09-11 17:25:54 GMT
```

(continued)

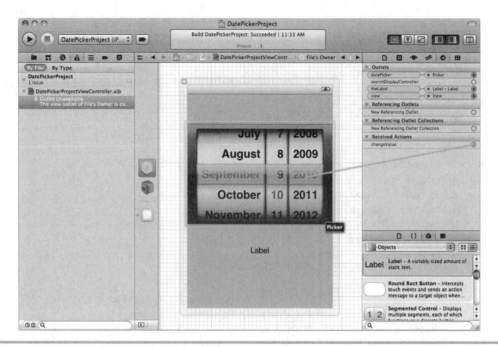

Figure 13-6 Connecting to the UIDatePicker's value changed event

Figure 13-7 The application running in iPhone Simulator

```
2010-09-10 11:38:36.455 DatePickerProject[7095:207] formatted: 09/11/2010
2010-09-10 11:38:36.455 DatePickerProject[7095:207] formatted: Saturday
September 11, 2010
2010-09-10 11:38:58.838 DatePickerProject[7095:207] the date picked is:
2010-10-11 17:25:54 GMT
2010-09-10 11:38:58.840 DatePickerProject[7095:207] formatted: 10/11/2010
2010-09-10 11:38:58.841 DatePickerProject[7095:207] formatted: Monday
October 11, 2010
```

Try This   Using a UIDatePicker in Timer Mode

UIDatePicker classes are also useful for selecting a duration for an NSTimer. A UIDatePicker selects an NSDate, which consists of a date and a time; therefore, you can create a timer using an NSDate's time. But a UIDatePicker does not implement a timer; it only provides a visual way to pick duration. You must then use this duration with an NSTimer. This task illustrates using a UIDatePicker to select a duration for an NSTimer and, in the process, illustrates using the NSCalendar, NSDateFormatter, and NSDateComponents classes.

1. Create a new View-based Application in Xcode named **ATimer**.

2. Create a new IBOutlet named timePicker for a UIDateTime and an IBAction called echoTime (Listing 13-4).

Listing 13-4   ATimerViewController.h

```
#import <UIKit/UIKit.h>
@interface ATimerViewController : UIViewController {
 UIDatePicker * timePicker;
}
@property (nonatomic, retain) IBOutlet UIDatePicker * timePicker;
- (IBAction) echoTime: (id) sender;
- (void) echoIt: (NSTimer *) timer;
@end
```

3. Implement the echoTime method so that it implements an NSTimer that fires a timer every second (Listing 13-5).

Listing 13-5   ATimerViewController.m

```
#import "ATimerViewController.h"
@implementation ATimerViewController
@synthesize timePicker;
```

(continued)

```
NSInteger seconds = 0;
- (IBAction) echoTime: (id) sender {
  NSDate * time = timePicker.date;
  NSDateFormatter * dateFormatter =
      [[[NSDateFormatter alloc] init] autorelease];
  [dateFormatter setDateFormat:@"HH:MM:SS"];
  NSLog(@"date: %@",[dateFormatter stringFromDate:time]);
  NSCalendar *gregorian =
      [[NSCalendar alloc] initWithCalendarIdentifier: NSGregorianCalendar];
  NSDateComponents * comps = [gregorian components:(NSHourCalendarUnit |
  NSMinuteCalendarUnit) fromDate:time];
  NSInteger hour = [comps hour];
  NSInteger minute = [comps minute];
  NSLog(@"Hour: %i", hour);
  NSLog(@"minute: %i", minute);
  NSInteger secs = hour * 60 * 60 + minute * 60;
  NSNumber * elapsedSeconds = [[NSNumber alloc] initWithInt:secs];
  NSDictionary * myDict = [NSDictionary dictionaryWithObject:
      elapsedSeconds forKey:@"TotalSeconds"];
  [NSTimer scheduledTimerWithTimeInterval:1 target: self selector: @
  selector(echoIt:) userInfo: myDict repeats: YES];
}
- (void) echoIt: (NSTimer *) timer {
  NSNumber * num =
      (NSNumber *) [[timer userInfo] valueForKey:@"TotalSeconds"];
  seconds++;
  NSInteger secs = [num integerValue] - seconds;
  NSLog(@"elapsed: %i, remaining: %i", seconds, secs);
}
- (void)dealloc {
  [timePicker release];
  [super dealloc];
}
@end
```

4. Add a method called echoIt for the timer to call when firing.

5. Open ATimerViewController.xib in Interface Builder and place a UIDatePicker on the canvas. Change the picker's mode to Timer in the Inspector and set the interval to one minute. Also place a button on the canvas (Figure 13-8).

6. Connect the File's Owner timePicker property to the picker.

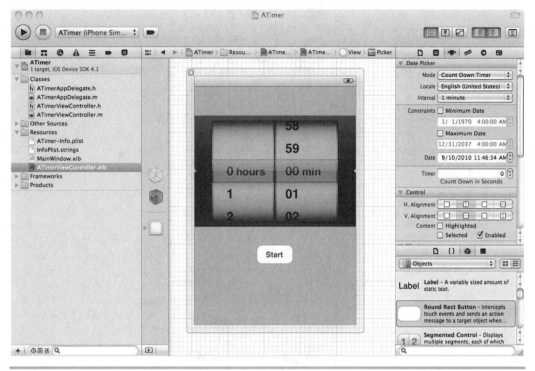

Figure 13-8   Adding a button to the canvas

7. Connect the File's Owner echoTime action to the button's Touch Up Inside event.

8. Save your changes and click Run (Figure 13-9). The output to the Debugger Console should appear like Listing 13-6.

Listing 13-6   The ATimer application logging to Debugger Console

```
2010-09-10 11:52:22.658 ATimer[7271:207] date: 01:12:00
2010-09-10 11:52:22.658 ATimer[7271:207] Hour: 1
2010-09-10 11:52:22.659 ATimer[7271:207] minute: 0
2010-09-10 11:52:26.028 ATimer[7271:207] elapsed: 1, remaining: 3599
2010-09-10 11:52:34.723 ATimer[7271:207] elapsed: 2, remaining: 3598
2010-09-10 11:52:43.023 ATimer[7271:207] elapsed: 3, remaining: 3597
2010-09-10 11:52:44.032 ATimer[7271:207] elapsed: 4, remaining: 3596
```

(continued)

Figure 13-9 Running the application in iPhone Simulator

This example code involves several concepts not covered elsewhere in this book. Notice the NSDictionary, NSCalendar, and NSDateComponents classes. The UIDatePicker picks the hours and minutes for the timer. When the button is clicked, the echoTime method creates an NSCalendar and obtains date components from the time. After obtaining the total seconds, echoTime adds the seconds to an NSDictionary and creates a timer that fires every second. When firing, the timer calls the echoIt method, passing itself as the parameter. The echoIt method obtains the seconds from the userInfo stored in the timer. The echoIt method then determines the elapsed seconds and logs it to the Debugger Console.

UIPickerView

A UIPickerView allows the selection of a value or values from one or more value sets. A UIPickerView consists of rows and components. Think of the component as the column in a table of values and the row as the row. If you have a three-wheel UIPickerView, the third wheel is the third component. A UIPickerView must have an associated class that adopts the

UIPickerViewDelegate and a class that adopts the UIPickerViewDataSource. The same class can adopt both protocols.

UIPickerViewDelegate

The UIPickerViewDelegate protocol dictates how a UIPickerView is to construct itself. This protocol contains five methods a class might implement when adopting this protocol: the picker View:rowHeightForComponent:, pickerView:widthForComponent:, pickerView:titleForRow: forComponent:, pickerView:viewForRow:forComponent:reusingView:, and pickerView:did SelectRow:inComponent: methods.

Width and Height   The pickerView:rowHeightForComponent: and pickerView:widthFor Component: methods set a picker's component dimensions. Remember, a picker's component can contain rows of strings or view controls, like a UIImageView. These methods accommodate controls by allowing you to set a component's height and width. Each method's signature follows.

```
- (CGFloat)pickerView:(UIPickerView *) pickerView rowHeightForComponent:
(NSInteger) component
- (CGFloat)pickerView:(UIPickerView *) pickerView widthForComponent:
(NSInteger) component
```

Content   The pickerView:titleForRow:forComponent: and pickerView:viewForRow:for Component: methods provide a component's title or view. The title or the view is what is displayed as the rows in a picker. You must implement one of the two methods. If you need to pick from several strings, implement the pickerView:titleForRow:forComponent: method; if your choices are more complex, use a view for each and implement the pickerView:viewFor Row:forComponent: method. Each method's signature follows.

```
- (NSString *)pickerView:(UIPickerView *)pickerView titleForRow:
(NSInteger) row forComponent: (NSInteger) component
- (UIView *)pickerView:(UIPickerView *)pickerView
viewForRow:(NSInteger) row forComponent:(NSInteger) component
reusingView:(UIView *)view
```

Selecting   The UIPickerView calls the pickerView:didSelectRow:inComponent: method when a user selects a component's row. It takes the component's index number and the row's index number as parameters, so you can determine the component selected and the component's row. The method's signature follows.

```
- (void)pickerView:(UIPickerView *)pickerView didSelectRow:(NSInteger)row
inComponent:(NSInteger)component
```

UIPickerViewDatasource

A UIPickerViewDatasource handles a UIPickerView's data. It contains two methods you should define when adopting this protocol: the numberOfComponentsInPickerView: and pickerView:numberOfRowsInComponent: methods. The numberOfComponentsInPickerView: method returns how many components, or columns, a picker must display.

```
- (NSInteger)pickerView:(UIPickerView *)pickerView
numberOfRowsInComponent: (NSInteger) component
```

The pickerView:numberOfRowsInComponent: method returns a component's row count.

```
- (NSInteger)pickerView:(UIPickerView *)pickerView
numberOfRowsInComponent: (NSInteger) component
```

Try This   Using a Picker

1. Create a new View-based Application named **APicker**.

2. Open APickerViewController.xib in Interface Builder.

3. Drag a picker view from the library to the canvas. Right-click and notice that the control doesn't have the choices a UIDatePicker has (Figure 13-10).

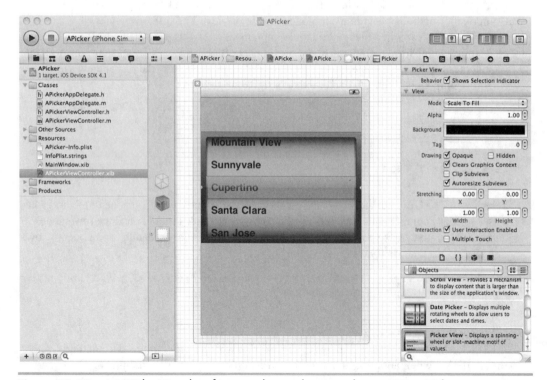

Figure 13-10   A UIPickerView has fewer outlets and actions than a UIDatePicker.

4. Add a button to the canvas.

5. Save your changes.

6. Create a new NSObject named MyPickerDelegate and change it to adopt the UIPickerViewDelegate and UIPickerViewDataSource protocols. Have MyPickerDelegate implement the needed methods (Listings 13-7 and 13-8).

Listing 13-7 MyPickerDelegate.h

```
#import <Foundation/Foundation.h>
@interface MyPickerDelegate : NSObject <UIPickerViewDelegate,
UIPickerViewDataSource> {
  NSArray * myData;
}
@property (nonatomic, retain) NSArray * myData;
@end
```

Listing 13-8 MyPickerDelegate.m

```
#import "MyPickerDelegate.h"
@implementation MyPickerDelegate
@synthesize myData;
- (id) init {
  if([super init] == nil) return nil;
  myData = [[NSArray alloc] initWithObjects:
      @"Red",@"Yellow",@"Green",@"Blue", @"Purple", @"Orange",
      @"Black", @"Gray", @"Tan", @"Pink", @"Coral", nil];
  return self;
}
- (void)pickerView:(UIPickerView *)pickerView didSelectRow:(NSInteger)row
            inComponent:(NSInteger)component {
  NSLog(@"picked row: %i, component: %i", row, component);
  NSLog(@"the value: %@", [self.myData objectAtIndex:row]);
}
- (NSInteger) numberOfComponentsInPickerView: (UIPickerView *) pickerView {
  return 1;
}
- (NSInteger) pickerView: (UIPickerView *) pickerView
  numberOfRowsInComponent: (NSInteger) component {
  return [self.myData count];
}
```

(continued)

```
- (NSString *) pickerView: (UIPickerView *) pickerView titleForRow:
        (NSInteger) row forComponent: (NSInteger) component {
  return [self.myData objectAtIndex:row];
}
- (void)dealloc {
  [myData release];
  [super dealloc];
}
@end
```

7. Open APickerViewController and add IBOutlets for UIPickerView and MyPickerDelegate (Listing 13-9). Add an IBAction called changeColor.

Listing 13-9 APickerViewController.h

```
#import <UIKit/UIKit.h>
#import "MyPickerDelegate.h"
@class MyPickerDelegate;
@interface APickerViewController : UIViewController {
 UIPickerView * myPicker;
 MyPickerDelegate * myPickerDelegate;
}
@property (nonatomic, retain) IBOutlet UIPickerView * myPicker;
@property (nonatomic, retain) IBOutlet MyPickerDelegate *
myPickerDelegate;
- (IBAction) changeColor: (id) sender;
@end
```

8. Implement the changeColor action (Listing 13-10).

Listing 13-10 APickerViewController.m

```
#import "APickerViewController.h"
#import "MyPickerDelegate.h"
@implementation APickerViewController
@synthesize myPicker;
@synthesize myPickerDelegate;
- (IBAction) changeColor: (id) sender {
  NSLog(@"the color is: %@", (NSString *)[myPickerDelegate.myData
objectAtIndex: [myPicker selectedRowInComponent:0]]);
}
- (void)dealloc {
  [myPickerDelegate release];
```

```
    [myPicker release];
    [super dealloc];
}
@end
```

9. Save and open APickerViewController.xib in Interface Builder.

10. Connect the File's Owner changeColor action to the button's Touch Up Inside event.

11. Connect the File's Owner myPicker outlet to the UIPickerView.

12. Drag an object from the library to the editing pane. Change the object's type to MyPickerDelegate.

13. Connect the File's Owner myPickerDelegate outlet to the object just added.

14. Connect the UIPickerView's dataSource and delegate outlets to the newly added MyPickerDelegate object.

15. Save your changes and click Run to run the application in iPhone Simulator. When the button is pushed, the Debugger Console logs the picker's chosen color (Figure 13-11 and Listing 13-11).

Figure 13-11   Running the application in iPhone Simulator

(continued)

Listing 13-11   Debug Console output from running APicker application

```
2010-09-10 12:13:43.184 APicker[7497:207] picked row: 1, component: 0
2010-09-10 12:13:43.188 APicker[7497:207] the value: Yellow
2010-09-10 12:13:45.123 APicker[7497:207] the color is: Yellow
2010-09-10 12:13:54.053 APicker[7497:207] picked row: 2, component: 0
2010-09-10 12:13:54.054 APicker[7497:207] the value: Green
2010-09-10 12:13:55.037 APicker[7497:207] the color is: Green
```

A UIPickerView must have helper classes adopting the UIPickerViewDelegate and UIPickerViewDataSource protocols. In this example you had one class, MyPickerDelegate, adopt both protocols. The delegate uses a simple NSArray to hold NSString objects. Because the data is simple strings, the delegate implements the titleForRow method. When a user selects a row, the didSelectRow method logs the row, component, and value to the Debugger Console.

Try This Using a UIPickerView with Two Components

1. Make a copy of the APicker project you just finished and then open it in Xcode.

2. Modify MyPickerDelegate's numberOfComponentsInPickerView to return the number 2 (Listing 13-13).

3. Click Build And Go. Notice the picker now shows two independent spinning wheels (Figure 13-12).

4. Add a second value array. Call the array myData2 and initialize it in the init method, as you did before with myData (Listings 13-12 and 13-13).

Listing 13-12   MyPickerDelegate.h modified to reflect two wheels

```
#import <Foundation/Foundation.h>
#define COLOR_WHEEL 0
#define SHADE_WHEEL 1
@interface MyPickerDelegate : NSObject <UIPickerViewDelegate,
UIPickerViewDataSource> {
  NSArray * myData;
  NSArray * myData2;
}
@property (nonatomic, retain) NSArray * myData;
@property (nonatomic, retain) NSArray * myData2;
@end
```

Figure 13-12   A UIPickerView with two components

Listing 13-13   MyPickerDelegate.m modified to reflect two wheels

```
#import "MyPickerDelegate.h"
@implementation MyPickerDelegate
@synthesize myData;
@synthesize myData2;
- (id) init {
  if([super init] == nil)
   return nil;
  myData = [[NSArray alloc]initWithObjects:
     @"Red", @"Yellow", @"Green", @"Blue",
     @"Purple", @"Orange", @"Black", @"Gray", @"Tan", @"Pink", @"Coral", nil];
  myData2 = [[NSArray alloc] initWithObjects:
     @"Very Dark", @"Dark", @"Normal", @"Light", @"Very Light", nil];
  return self;
}
```

(continued)

```objc
- (NSInteger) numberOfComponentsInPickerView: (UIPickerView *) pickerView {
  return 2;
}
- (void)pickerView:(UIPickerView *)pickerView didSelectRow:
      (NSInteger)row inComponent:(NSInteger)component {
  NSLog(@"picked row: %i, component: %i", row, component);
  if(component == COLOR_WHEEL)
    NSLog(@"the value: %@", [self.myData objectAtIndex:row]);
  else
    NSLog(@"the value: %@", [self.myData2 objectAtIndex:row]);
  }
- (NSInteger) pickerView: (UIPickerView *)pickerView
      numberOfRowsInComponent (NSInteger) component {
  if(component == COLOR_WHEEL)
    return [self.myData count];
  else
    return [self.myData2 count];
}
- (NSString *) pickerView: (UIPickerView *) pickerView
      titleForRow: (NSInteger) row forComponent: (NSInteger) component {
  if(component == COLOR_WHEEL)
    return [self.myData objectAtIndex:row];
  else
    return [self.myData2 objectAtIndex:row];
}
- (void)dealloc {
  [myData release];
  [myData2 release];
  [super dealloc];
}
@end
```

5. Create two constants representing the different wheels: COLOR_WHEEL for the wheel containing the myData values and SHADE_WHEEL for the wheel containing the myData2 values (Listing 13-12).

6. Modify the numberOfRowsInComponent method and titleForRow method to reflect the newly added wheel.

7. Open APickerViewController.m and modify the changeColor method to reflect the second wheel (Listing 13-14).

Listing 13-14   The changeColor method modified to reflect two wheels

```
- (IBAction) changeColor: (id) sender {
  NSLog(@"the color is: %@ and the shade is: %@",
     (NSString *)[myPickerDelegate.myData objectAtIndex:
           [myPicker selectedRowInComponent: COLOR_WHEEL]],
     (NSString *)[myPickerDelegate.myData2 objectAtIndex:
           [myPicker selectedRowInComponent:SHADE_WHEEL]]);
}
```

---

8. Save your changes and click Run. The application shows two wheels. Upon clicking the button, the Debugger Console logs the first wheel's color and the second wheel's shade (Figure 13-13 and Listing 13-15).

Figure 13-13   Running the application in iPhone Simulator

(continued)

Listing 13-15   Debugger Console logging from running APicker application

```
2010-09-10 12:26:48.705 APicker[7655:207] picked row: 1, component: 0
2010-09-10 12:26:48.715 APicker[7655:207] the value: Yellow
2010-09-10 12:26:49.658 APicker[7655:207] picked row: 2, component: 1
2010-09-10 12:26:49.660 APicker[7655:207] the value: Normal
2010-09-10 12:26:50.964 APicker[7655:207] the color is: Yellow and the
shade is: Normal
```

Using more components involves adding code to check which component was selected. Note that rather than use the raw integers, you created constants for both components, producing more readable code. Each delegate's method then checks which component the user selected.

```
if(component == COLOR_WHEEL)
  return [self.myData objectAtIndex:row];
else
  return [self.myData2 objectAtIndex:row];
```

Try This   Loading UIImageViews into a UIPickerView

1. Make a copy of the original APicker project created earlier—not the project with two components, but the earlier project with only one component. Open it in Xcode.

2. Replace the pickerView:titleForRow:forComponent: method in MyPickerDelegate with pickerView:viewForRow:forComponent: (Listing 13-16).

Listing 13-16   MyPickerDelegate.m modified to load images into the UIPickerView

```
#import "MyPickerDelegate.h"
@implementation MyPickerDelegate
@synthesize myData;
- (id) init {
  if([super init] == nil)
    return nil;
  UIImageView * one = [[UIImageView alloc] initWithImage:
        [[UIImage alloc] initWithContentsOfFile:
            [[[NSBundle mainBundle] resourcePath]
                stringByAppendingPathComponent:@"wizard.png"]]];
  UIImageView * two =[[UIImageView alloc] initWithImage:
        [[UIImage alloc] initWithContentsOfFile:
            [[[NSBundle mainBundle] resourcePath]
                stringByAppendingPathComponent: @"tux.png"]]];
```

```
UIImageView * three =[[UIImageView alloc] initWithImage:
        [[UIImage alloc] initWithContentsOfFile:
            [[[NSBundle mainBundle] resourcePath]
                    stringByAppendingPathComponent:@"money.png"]]];
    myData = [[NSArray alloc] initWithObjects:one,two,three,nil];
    return self;
}
- (void)pickerView:(UIPickerView *)pickerView didSelectRow:
            (NSInteger) row inComponent: (NSInteger)component {
    NSLog(@"picked row: %i, component: %i", row, component);
}
- (NSInteger) numberOfComponentsInPickerView:
                (UIPickerView *)pickerView {
    return 1;
}
- (NSInteger) pickerView:
        (UIPickerView *) pickerView
        numberOfRowsInComponent: (NSInteger) component {
    return [self.myData count];
}
- (UIView *)pickerView:(UIPickerView *)pickerView
        viewForRow:(NSInteger) row
        forComponent:(NSInteger)component
        reusingView:(UIView *)view {
    return [self.myData objectAtIndex:row];
}
- (void)dealloc {
    [myData release];
    [super dealloc];
}
@end
```

3. Add the images money.png, wizard.png, and tux.png to the project. You can find these images in the book's resources folder.

4. Modify the MyPickerDelegate's init: method to load UIImageViews rather than strings into myData (Listing 13-16).

5. Modify the pickerView:didSelectRow:inComponent: to only log the row and component to the Debugger Console (Listing 13-16).

6. Save your changes and open APickerViewController.xib and remove the button.

7. Save your changes, and click Run. The application loads the images into the UIPickerView (Figure 13-14).

(continued)

Figure 13-14 A UIPickerView that uses UIImageView objects as its components

Using the Camera: UIImagePickerController

Rather than working directly with an iPhone's camera, you use the UIImagePickerController to manipulate an iPhone's camera and photo library. Using the UIImagePickerController, you take, or select, a photo, optionally edit the photo, and then dismiss the UIImagePickerController, returning control back to your application.

UIImagePickerController

The UIImagePickerController is different from other view controllers. Rather than developers creating the controller's view and adding components to the view's canvas, the UIImage PickerController's views are already created and are part of the UIKit library. Developers simply determine the controller's source type and implement a delegate for the controller. The controller creates and manages the views, while the delegate responds to the view being dismissed by a user.

Source

Earlier models of the iPod touch, the original iPad, and the iPhone Simulator all lack a camera. If you attempt to use a device's nonexistent camera, you will get an exception, and if that exception isn't caught, the application will terminate unexpectedly. If you're attempting to use the camera on an iPhone Simulator, it will also log a message to the Debugger Console.

```
2010-09-10 13:53:16.010 CameraProject[8418:207] *** Terminating app
due to uncaught exception 'NSInvalidArgumentException', reason:
'Source type 1 not available'
```

To avoid an exception or an application that unexpectedly quits, the UIImagePickerController provides the isSourceTypeAvailable: method.

```
+ (BOOL)isSourceTypeAvailable:(UIImagePickerControllerSourceType)
sourceType
```

This method returns YES if a source type is available and NO if unavailable. Valid source types are UIImagePickerControllerSourceTypePhotoLibrary, for selecting images from the photo library; UIImagePickerControllerSourceTypeCamera, for selecting images from the camera; and UIImagePickerControllerSourceTypeSavedPhotosAlbum, for selecting images from a camera roll, or from the photo library if the device doesn't have a camera.

After ensuring a device has a source type, you set the UIImagePickerController's sourceType property. This property determines what controls the UIImagePickerController displays. Allowable source types are the same as with the isSourceTypeAvailable: method.

Editing and Delegating

The controller also has an allowsEditing property and delegate property (note that prior to iOS 3.1 this property was called allowsImageEditing). The allowsEditing property determines if a user should be allowed to edit an image after taking or selecting the image. The delegate property specifies the class's UIImagePickerControllerDelegate.

UIImagePickerControllerDelegate

The UIImagePickerControllerDelegate's protocol has two methods your delegate should implement for the image picker. The imagePickerController:didFinishPickingMediaWithInfo :info: method is called after a user selects an image. This could be selecting an image from a camera roll or photo library, or after taking a photo using the camera. The method's signature follows.

```
- (void)imagePickerController:(UIImagePickerController *) picker
didFinishPickingMediaWithInfo: (NSDictionary *) info;
```

If you cancel a photo selected, the imagePickerControllerDidCancel: method is called. The method's signature follows:

```
- (void)imagePickerControllerDidCancel:(UIImagePickerController *)picker
```

The imagePickerController:didFinishPickingMediaWithInfo:info: has three parameters. The first parameter holds a reference to the image picker, the second to the image picked, and the third to an NSDictionary containing editing information. If editing is disabled, the third parameter holds nil. If editing is enabled, the parameter holds the unedited image and the cropped rectangle. For more information on the imagePickerController:didFinish PickingMediaWithInfo:info method, refer to Apple's online "UIImagePickerControllerDelegate Reference."

Try This Using the UIImagePickerController

NOTE
Using the camera or camera roll requires having an iPhone or iPod with a camera and running the application on the device, which will require a paid developer's membership, and a provision profile for this example application. Even if you can't try the camera part of this example, you can still select a photo from a photo album.

1. Create a new View-based Application. Name the project **CameraProject**.

2. Open CameraProjectViewController.xib in Interface Builder.

3. Drag a toolbar from the library onto the view's canvas.

4. Rename the first button **Take Photo**. Add another button to the toolbar and call it **Select Photo**. Add a UIImageView to the canvas (Figure 13-15).

5. Save your changes.

6. Create a new class called MyImagePickerDelegate derived from NSObject. Modify the class so that it adopts the UINavigationControllerDelegate and UIImagePickerControllerDelegate protocols (Listing 13-17). Add a property that contains the UIImage that the image picker will select.

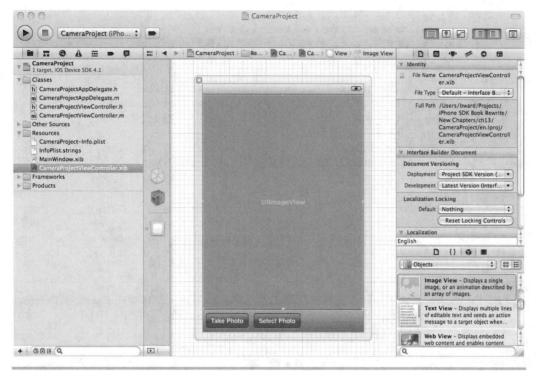

Figure 13-15 The application's canvas

Listing 13-17 MyImagePickerDelegate.h

```
#import <Foundation/Foundation.h>
@interface MyImagePickerDelegate : NSObject
<UINavigationControllerDelegate, UIImagePickerControllerDelegate> {
  UIImage * selectedImage;
}
@property (nonatomic, retain) UIImage * selectedImage;
@end
```

7. Implement the imagePickerController methods (Listing 13-18).

Listing 13-18 MyImagePickerDelegate.m

```
#import "MyImagePickerDelegate.h"
@implementation MyImagePickerDelegate
@synthesize selectedImage;
```

(continued)

```
- (void) imagePickerControllerDidCancel:
            (UIImagePickerController *) picker {
    [picker.parentViewController dismissModalViewControllerAnimated:YES];
    [picker release];
}
- (void)imagePickerController:(UIImagePickerController *) picker
            didFinishPickingMediaWithInfo:(NSDictionary *) info {
    self.selectedImage = (UIImage*)[info objectForKey:
            UIImagePickerControllerOriginalImage];
    [picker.parentViewController
            dismissModalViewControllerAnimated: YES];
    [picker release];
}
- (void) dealloc {
    [selectedImage release];
    [super dealloc];
}
@end
```

8. Open CameraProjectViewController.h and add a forward reference to MyImagePickerDelegate.
Add an IBOutlet for MyImagePickerDelegate, the UIImageView and the takePhoto
UIBarButtonItem (Listing 13-19).

Listing 13-19   CameraProjectViewController.h

```
#import <UIKit/UIKit.h>
@class MyImagePickerDelegate;
@interface CameraProjectViewController : UIViewController {
    MyImagePickerDelegate * imgPickerDelegate;
    UIImageView * theImageView;
    UIBarButtonItem * theTakePhotoButton;
}
@property (nonatomic, retain) IBOutlet
    MyImagePickerDelegate *imgPickerDelegate;
@property (nonatomic, retain) IBOutlet UIImageView * theImageView;
@property (nonatomic, retain) IBOutlet
    UIBarButtonItem *theTakePhotoButton;
- (IBAction) takePicture: (id) sender;
- (IBAction) selectPicture: (id) sender;
@end
```

---

9. Add two IBActions to CameraProjectViewController. Name one action takePicture and the
other selectPicture (Listing 13-19). Implement both methods as shown in Listing 13-20.

Listing 13-20   CameraProjectViewController.m

```objc
#import "CameraProjectViewController.h"
#import "MyImagePickerDelegate.h"
@implementation CameraProjectViewController
@synthesize imgPickerDelegate;
@synthesize theImageView;
@synthesize theTakePhotoButton;
- (void) viewDidLoad {
  [super viewDidLoad];
  // Only enable the button if a camera is actually available
  theTakePhotoButton.enabled = ([UIImagePickerController
        isSourceTypeAvailable:
        UIImagePickerControllerSourceTypeCamera]);
}
- (IBAction) takePicture: (id) sender {
  UIImagePickerController * pickCont =
      [[UIImagePickerController alloc] init];
  pickCont.delegate = imgPickerDelegate;
  pickCont.allowsEditing = YES;
  pickCont.sourceType = UIImagePickerControllerSourceTypeCamera;
  [self presentModalViewController:pickCont animated:YES];
  NSLog(@"heynow");
  if(self.imgPickerDelegate.selectedImage != nil)
    self.theImageView.image = self.imgPickerDelegate.selectedImage;
}

- (IBAction) selectPicture: (id) sender {
  UIImagePickerController * pickCont =
      [[UIImagePickerController alloc] init];
  pickCont.delegate = imgPickerDelegate;
  pickCont.allowsEditing = YES;
  pickCont.sourceType = UIImagePickerControllerSourceTypePhotoLibrary;
  [self presentModalViewController:pickCont animated:YES];
  NSLog(@"heynow");
  if(self.imgPickerDelegate.selectedImage != nil)
    self.theImageView.image = self.imgPickerDelegate.selectedImage;
  }

- (void)dealloc {
  [theImageView release];
  [imgPickerDelegate release];
  [super dealloc];
}
@end
```

(continued)

10. Implement the viewDidLoad method in CameraProjectViewController so that we enable the Take Photo button only when the camera is available (Listing 13-20).

11. Save your changes.

12. Open CameraProjectViewController.xib in Interface Builder.

13. Connect the File's Owner theImageView outlet to the UIImageView on the canvas. Connect the File's Owner theTakePhotoButton IBOutlet to the Take Photo bar item.

14. Connect the selectPicture action to the Select Photo button and the takePicture action to the Take Photo button.

15. Drag an object from the library to the Document window. Change its type to **MyImagePickerDelegate**.

16. Connect the File's Owner imgPickerDelegate outlet to the newly created object.

17. Save your changes.

18. If you want to use the camera, follow the necessary steps to register and provision the application so that you can install it on your iPhone. Otherwise, you can use the Select Photo button and select a photo from the simulator's photo albums.

19. Run the application. Everything works as expected, *except* notice that the view's image is not set to the image selected by the image picker.

Nothing happens after selecting or taking a photo, unless you click one of the application's buttons a second time. The photo previously selected is then displayed (Figure 13-16). What is supposed to happen is that the theImageView in CameraProjectViewController should display the newly taken photo. You might have thought that placing the following lines in the selectPicture method would have worked, but they didn't.

```
if(self.imgPickerDelegate.selectedImage != nil)
   self.theImageView.image = self.imgPickerDelegate.selectedImage;
```

Notice the "heynow" logging added to the delegate's methods. Immediately after displaying the image picker, the Debugger Console logs "heynow." If the logging does not wait for the image picker to finish, the two lines setting the image don't wait either, and so the image isn't set correctly until the next time you push one of the application's two buttons.

CameraProjectController must be changed to be notified when a picture is taken so that it can update its view. There are two ways you might fix the image not displaying. First, you could add a reference to the CameraProjectViewController in MyImagePickerDelegate, but that isn't an ideal solution. Why? Adding a CameraProjectViewController to MyImagePickerDelegate as a property introduces close coupling between the two classes. You can never again reuse MyImagePickerDelegate, unless you reuse CameraProjectViewController. Using a notification would be a better solution.

Figure 13-16 Running the application in iPhone Simulator and using the provided photo library

Notifications

If you have ever used Java listeners, you already know the general idea behind notifications. Cocoa's notifications are similar to Java's listeners, only easier and more flexible. Every Cocoa application has a notification center, NSNotificationCenter. Classes in your application can post notifications, NSNotification, to the notification center. Other classes can register with the notification center to listen for notifications. Through notifications, classes can communicate with each other without even knowing about one another's existence. Although this book doesn't present notifications in any detail, in the next few steps, you add a notification to the CameraProjectViewController.

NOTE

Refer to Apple's *Introduction to Notification Programming Topics* for more information on using notifications.

Try This Using Notifications

1. Reopen CameraProject in Xcode.

2. Modify the imagePickerController:didFinishPickingMediaWithInfo:info: method to post a notification (Listing 13-21).

Listing 13-21   The didFinishPickingMediaWithInfo modified to post a notification

```
- (void)imagePickerController:(UIImagePickerController *) picker
        didFinishPickingMediaWithInfo:(NSDictionary *) info {
  self.selectedImage = (UIImage*)[info
  objectForKey:UIImagePickerControllerOriginalImage];
  [[NSNotificationCenter defaultCenter] postNotificationName:
        @"Image Picked" object:nil];
  [picker.parentViewController dismissModalViewControllerAnimated:YES];
  [picker release];
}
```

3. Add a method called changeImage to CameraProjectViewController (Listing 13-22).

Listing 13-22   The changeImage method

```
- (void) changeImage {
  NSLog(@"IMAGE CHANGED");
  self.theImageView.image = self.imgPickerDelegate.selectedImage;
}
```

4. Modify viewDidLoad to observe the notification (Listing 13-23). Also, modify dealloc to unregister the controller as a notification listener.

Listing 13-23   The viewDidLoad method modified to have CameraViewController observe the notification

```
-(void) viewDidLoad {
 [super viewDidLoad];
 theTakePhotoButton.enabled =([UIImagePickerController
       isSourceTypeAvailable:
UIImagePickerControllerSourceTypeCamera]);
 [[NSNotificationCenter defaultCenter] addObserver:self selector:
       @selector(changeImage) name:@"ImagePicked" object:nil];
}
-(void) dealloc {
 [super dealloc];
 [theImageView release];
 [imgPickerDelegate release];
 [[NSNotificationCenter defaultCenter] removeObserver:self];
}
```

5. Save your changes and click Run. Now the application sets the UIImageView's image as expected.

NOTE

Notifications worked well in the preceding Try This example, but another way of achieving the same result would be to use an observer. Refer to Apple's *Introduction to Notification Programming Topics* for more information on using observers.

In the last two tasks, you created an application that uses the UIImagePickerController to control an iPhone's camera. You created two buttons, one for taking a photo using the camera and one for selecting an image from the photo library. If you obtained provisioning for the application and installed the provisioning on your iPhone, you could install the application on your iPhone and use the camera (Figure 13-17). Alternatively, you selected photos from the photo library while running the application on the iPhone Simulator. You used isSourceTypeAvailable to only enable the Take Photo button when a camera is available. Depending on the design of your application, rather than disabling a button, it could make more sense to only display a button for taking a picture if the camera is present.

Figure 13-17 Using the camera on an iPhone

Summary

In this chapter, you used a UIDatePicker, a UIPickerView, and a UIImagePickerController. A UIDatePicker is for selecting a date and time. You used a UIDatePicker to select a date and to select a time interval. After the UIDatePicker, you learned about UIPickerViews. A UIPickerView is for selecting a string value or an object descending from UIView. You used a UIPickerView with one component and then used one with two components. You then modified the one-component UIPickerView to display images rather than strings. After examining the UIDatePicker and UIPickerView controls, you learned about the UIImagePickerController. This class allows you to select images from an iPhone's camera, camera roll, or photo album. Only the third option, selecting from a photo album, works on the iPhone Simulator or earlier iPod Touch models, as neither has a camera. In this chapter's final task, you used a UIImagePickerController to select a photo from the iPhone Simulator's photo album.

Chapter 14

Application Settings

Key Skills & Concepts

● Creating a settings bundle

● Understanding settings field types

● Initializing an application with a settings bundle's values

You adjust the settings for your iOS device through the Settings application (Figure 14-1). For instance, you can set your device's brightness, Wi-Fi settings, and wallpaper settings using the Settings application. Different applications can also use the Settings application for setting their own configuration preferences. In this chapter, you learn how to add an application's settings to the Settings application.

Figure 14-1 The iOS Settings application

The Settings Application

The Settings application is used for setting both a device's preferences and preferences for different applications. When using the Settings application for an application's preferences, use it only for an application's configuration settings and not for settings that change frequently. It will be much more convenient for your users if they change volatile preferences through the application's interface rather than the Settings application.

The Settings Bundle

An application's preferences are stored in an Extended Markup Language (XML) file called Root.plist. Root.plist is stored in a bundle called Settings.bundle. A settings bundle is not automatically added to your project, and so you must add it to your application if you want to use the Settings application (Figure 14-2). In addition to Root.plist, a settings bundle can

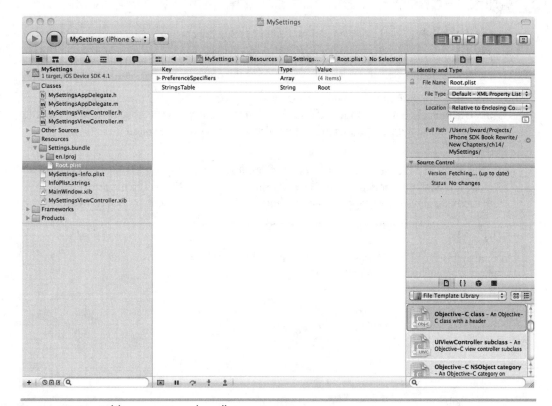

Figure 14-2 Adding a settings bundle

contain any additional .plist files, any images used for sliders, and one or more .lproj files. Additional .plist files are for any child preference panes your application might require. The .lproj files are for localized string resources (not covered in this chapter). You can also store 16 × 16 pixel images you might want to use as the minimumImage and maximumImage on a slider pane in your preference panes.

NOTE

You can also specify an icon for your application in the Settings application. Create a 29 × 29 pixel Portable Network Graphics (PNG) image and name it **Icon-Settings .png**. This file should be placed in your Xcode project's Resources folder in Groups & Files.

Try This   Creating a Settings Bundle

1. Create a new View-based Application named **MySettings**.

2. Expand the Resources folder and add a new resource file of type Settings Bundle. Accept the default name. Select the Resources group as the place to add the Settings.bundle.

3. Expand Settings.bundle and click Root.plist (Figure 14-2). (You may need to display the Utilities pane and change the type of Settings.bundle to Directory instead of Bundle in order to see a disclosure triangle next to it so that you can expand it and select Root .plist.)

4. Click Run. Tap the Home button to end the application, and tap the Settings application's icon. The Settings application includes MySettings (Figure 14-3). Tap the arrow, and Settings displays the MySettings application's default settings screen (Figure 14-4).

NOTE

To change this example's title displayed in Settings, change the application's Bundle Display Name in the MySettings-Info.plist file (Figure 14-5).

Figure 14-3   Settings application with MySettings

Figure 14-4   MySettings application's settings   *(continued)*

Figure 14-5 Changing the application's name

Settings Field Types

You add preferences to the settings bundle through Root.plist. The different settings display differently in the Settings application. Possible values for settings are PSTextFieldSpecifier, PSTitleValueSpecifier, PSToggleSwitchSpecifier, PSMultiValueSpecifier, PSGroupSpecifier, and PSChildPaneSpecifier. This section considers each setting in turn.

TIP

We use the word "expand" rather than "disclose" throughout this book. In this chapter, you will notice you "expand" rows; you don't "disclose" them. The little arrows, called Disclosure buttons, when clicked, are said to "disclose" their content.

PSGroupSpecifier

The PSGroupSpecifier groups settings into a group. If you have many settings, consider using this specifier to group your settings into logical groupings. Table 14-1 summarizes the PSGroupSpecifier's settings.

PSTextFieldSpecifier

The PSTextFieldSpecifier is for a preference whose value is a string. Table 14-2 summarizes a PSTextFieldSpecifier's settings.

Key	Purpose	Type	Valid Values	Required
Type	Specifies preference type.	String	PSGroupSpecifier	Yes
Title	Specifies the title displayed by Settings application.	String	Any string value	Yes

Table 14-1   PSGroupSpecifier Settings

Key	Purpose	Type	Valid Values	Required
Type	Specifies preference type.	String	PSTextFieldSpecifier	Yes
Title	Specifies the title displayed by the Settings application.	String	Any string value	Yes
Key	Specifies the preference's key used for storage and retrieval.	String	Any string value	Yes
Default Value	Specifies a default value for the preference.	String	Any string value	No
IsSecure	Specifies if preference should be treated as password.	Boolean	Yes or No	No
KeyboardType	Specifies type of keyboard to display when tapped.	String	Alphabet, NumbersAndPunctuation, NumberPad, URL, EmailAddress: default is Alphabet	No
AutoCapitalization Type	Specifies if autocapitalization should occur.	String	None, Sentences, Words, AllCharacters; default is None	No
AutoCorrection Type	Specifies if spelling should be automatically corrected.	String	Default, Yes, No	Default

Table 14-2   PSTextFieldSpecifier Settings

Try This   Adding a PSTextFieldSpecifier

1. Open MySettings in Xcode. Open Root.plist in the Editor window.

2. Expand PreferenceSpecifiers and delete Item 1, Item 2, and Item 3, leaving just Item 0.

3. Select Item 0 and click the plus sign to its right. It adds a new row (Item 1). Note that this row is a child of PreferenceSpecifiers.

4. Select Item 1 and change its type to Dictionary.

5. Control-click Item 1, expand it, and select Add Row. A new child row should be added. Note that this row is a child of Item 1. Add two more new child rows; ensure that they are children of Item 1. Change each row to match Figure 14-6.

6. Save the .plist file.

7. Click Run. Navigate to Settings and MySettings settings. Click the text field, and your Simulator should match Figure 14-7.

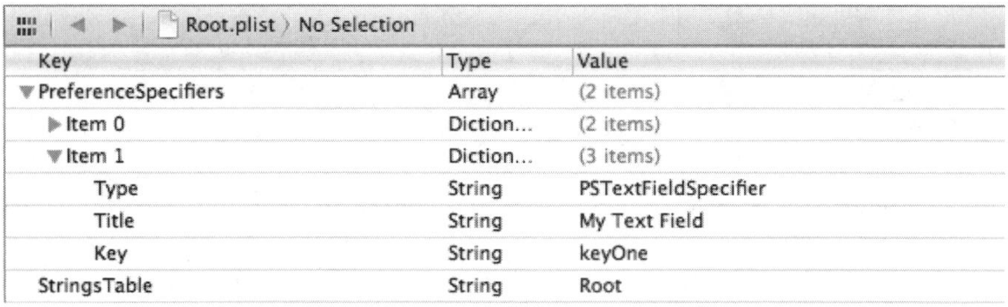

Key	Type	Value
▼ PreferenceSpecifiers	Array	(2 items)
▶ Item 0	Diction...	(2 items)
▼ Item 1	Diction...	(3 items)
Type	String	PSTextFieldSpecifier
Title	String	My Text Field
Key	String	keyOne
StringsTable	String	Root

Root.plist ⟩ No Selection

Figure 14-6   Root.plist with PSTextFieldSpecifier

Figure 14-7   Settings reflecting the new setting

Key	Purpose	Type	Valid Values	Required
Type	Specifies preference type.	String	PSMultiValueSpecifier	Yes
Title	Specifies the title displayed by the Settings application.	String	Any string value	Yes
Key	Specifies the preference's key used for storage and retrieval.	String	Any string value	Yes
Values	Specifies an array of values.	Array	Array of Key-Value entries	Yes
Titles	Specifies titles for array of values.	Array	Array of Key-Value entries	Yes
Default Value	Specifies a default value for the preference.	Any	Any value from the Values array	Yes

Table 14-3   PSMultiValueSpecifier Settings

PSMultiValueSpecifier

The PSMultiValueSpecifier is for selecting one of many alternative choices. Table 14-3 summarizes the PSMultiValueSpecifier's settings. Note that you create entries below the Values and Titles settings for each value and for each title.

Try This   Adding a PSMultiValueSpecifier

1. Return to MySettings in Xcode. Open the Root.plist in the editor.

2. Create an Item 2 below PreferenceSpecifiers and ensure its type is Dictionary.

3. Expand Item 2 and add six new child rows.

4. Change the first child row to have Type for the key, String for the type, and PSMultiValueSpecifier for the value (Figure 14-8).

5. Change the next child row to have Title for the key, String for the type, and Colors for the value.

6. Change the next child row to have DefaultValue for the key, String for the type, and blue for the value.

7. Change the next child row to have Key for the key, String for the type, and keyTwo for the value.

8. Change the next two child rows to have Titles and then Values for the key and Array for the type.

9. Expand Titles and then add three child rows to it. Do the same for Values (see Figure 14-8). Assign the three child Titles the values Red, Blue, and Orange. Assign the three child Values the values red, blue, and orange.

10. Save the .plist file.

11. Click Run. Navigate to the Settings application, and the new setting appears (Figure 14-9).

Root.plist 〉 No Selection

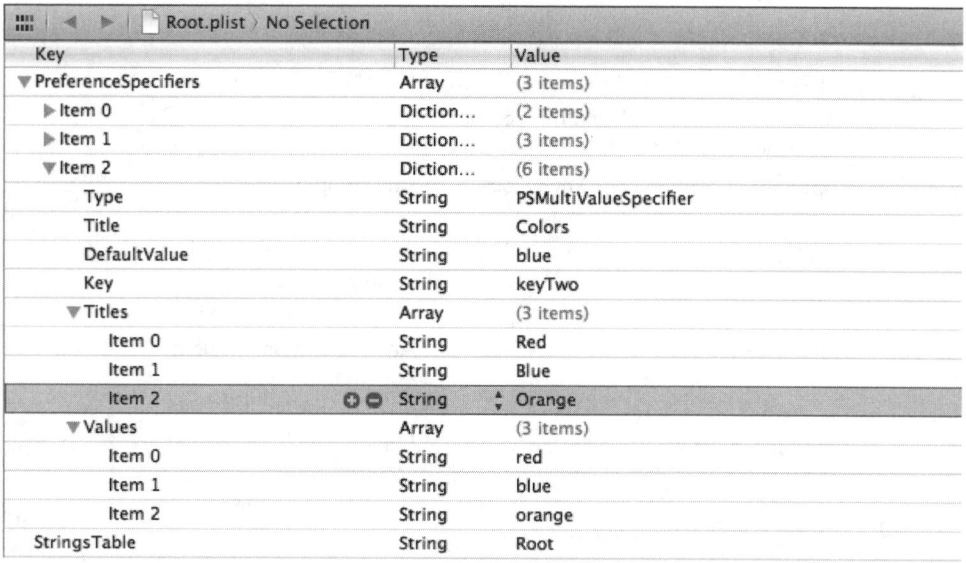

Key	Type	Value
▼PreferenceSpecifiers	Array	(3 items)
▶Item 0	Diction...	(2 items)
▶Item 1	Diction...	(3 items)
▼Item 2	Diction...	(6 items)
Type	String	PSMultiValueSpecifier
Title	String	Colors
DefaultValue	String	blue
Key	String	keyTwo
▼Titles	Array	(3 items)
Item 0	String	Red
Item 1	String	Blue
Item 2	String	Orange
▼Values	Array	(3 items)
Item 0	String	red
Item 1	String	blue
Item 2	String	orange
StringsTable	String	Root

Figure 14-8 Root.plist with the PSMultiValueSpecifier added

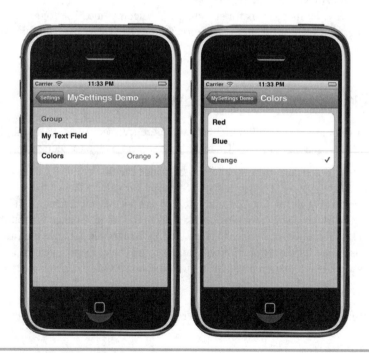

Figure 14-9 Settings reflecting the new setting

Key	Purpose	Type	Valid Values	Required
Type	Specifies preference type.	String	PSToggleSwitchSpecifier	Yes
Title	Specifies the title displayed by the Settings application.	String	Any string value	Yes
Key	Specifies the preference's key used for storage and retrieval.	String	Any string value	Yes
TrueValue	The value for on.	Any	Any scaler type, including Boolean, String, Number, or Data. Default is Boolean	No
FalseValue	The value for off.	Any	Any scaler type, including Boolean, String, Number, or Data. Default is Boolean	No
DefaultValue	Specifies a default value for the preference.	Any	String value from TrueValue or FalseValue	Yes

Table 14-4   PSToggleSwitchSpecifier Settings

PSToggleSwitchSpecifier

The PSToggleSwitchSpecifier is for selecting a Boolean value. The toggle switch displayed in the Settings application for this specifier is On or Off. Table 14-4 summarizes the PSToggleSwitchSpecifier's settings.

Try This   Adding a PSToggleSwitchSpecifier

1. Return to Root.plist and add Item 3 below PreferenceSpecifiers (i.e., highlight Item 2 and click the plus sign on the right). Change the new item's type to Dictionary.

2. Expand Item 3 and add six new child rows. Change the first child row to have a Type for key, String for type, and PSToggleSwitchSpecifier for value. Change the second child row to have Title for key, String for type, and Use Colors? for the value. Change the third child row to have Key for key, String for type, and keyThree for value. Change the fourth child row to have TrueValue for key, String for type, and YES for value. Change the fifth child row to have FalseValue for key, String for type, and NO for value. Finally, change the sixth child row to have DefaultValue for key, String for type, and NO for value (Figure 14-10).

3. Save the .plist file.

4. Click Run. Navigate to Settings, and the new value appears (Figure 14-11).

NOTE

Notice we keep stating to "save the .plist file" as its own step. The reason for this is that Run does not automatically save the .plist file.

Key	Type	Value
▦ ◀ ▶ 🗋 Root.plist › No Selection		
Key	Type	Value
▼ PreferenceSpecifiers	Array	(4 items)
▶ Item 0	Diction...	(2 items)
▶ Item 1	Diction...	(3 items)
▼ Item 2	Diction...	(6 items)
Type	String	PSMultiValueSpecifier
Title	String	Colors
DefaultValue	String	blue
Key	String	keyTwo
▶ Titles	Array	(3 items)
▶ Values	Array	(3 items)
▼ Item 3	Diction...	(6 items)
Type	String	PSToggleSwitchSpecifier
Title	String	Use Colors?
Key	String	keyThree
TrueValue	String	YES
FalseValue	String	NO
DefaultValue	String	NO
StringsTable	String	Root

Figure 14-10   Root.plist with the PSToggleSwitchSpecifier added

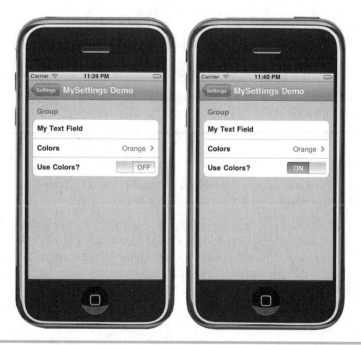

Figure 14-11   Settings reflecting the new setting

Key	Purpose	Type	Valid Values	Required
Type	Specifies preference type	String	PSSliderSpecifier	Yes
Key	Specifies the preference's key used for storage and retrieval	String	Any string value	Yes
DefaultValue	Specifies a default value for the preference	Real	Any number between minimum and maximum values	Yes
MinimumValue	Minimum value for slider	Real	Any number	Yes
MaximumValue	Maximum value for slider	Real	Any number	Yes
MinimumValueImage	Path to image (21 × 21 pixels)	String	Valid path	No
MaximumValueImage	Path to image (21 × 21) pixels	String	Valid path	No

Table 14-5   PSSliderSpecifier Settings

PSSliderSpecifier

The PSSliderSpecifier is for selecting a value from a range of values. Table 14-5 summarizes PSSliderSpecifier's settings.

Try This Adding a PSSliderSpecifier

1. Return to Root.plist and add a new item below Item 3.

2. Change the newly added item to a Dictionary type. Expand the new Item 4 and add two child rows below it.

3. Assign the first child item's key to Type, type to String, and value to PSGroupSpecifier.

4. Assign the second child item's key to Title, type to String, and value to Intensity.

5. Close Item 4 and add another item after it. Change the new Item 5's type to Dictionary. Expand the newly added item and add six child rows.

6. Change the first child row's key to Type, type to String, and value to PSSliderSpecifier. Change the third child row's key to Key, type to String, and value to keyFour. Change the fourth child row's key to DefaultValue, type to Number, and value to 5. Change the fifth child row's key to MinimumValue, type to Number, and value to 0. Change the sixth child row's key to MaximumValue, type to Number, and value to 10. Figure 14-12 shows Root. plist after making the changes.

7. Save the .plist file.

8. Click Run, and the changes appear in the Settings application (Figure 14-13).

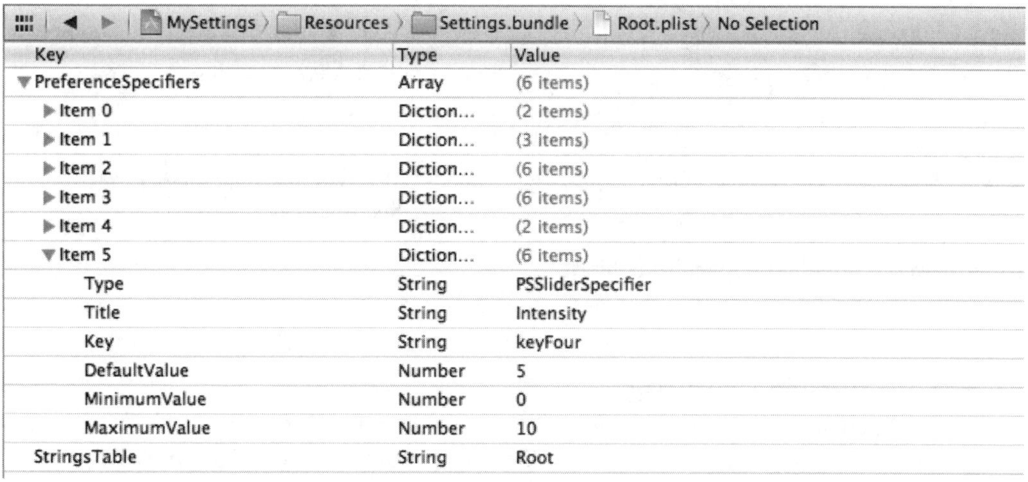

Key	Type	Value
▼ PreferenceSpecifiers	Array	(6 items)
▶ Item 0	Diction...	(2 items)
▶ Item 1	Diction...	(3 items)
▶ Item 2	Diction...	(6 items)
▶ Item 3	Diction...	(6 items)
▶ Item 4	Diction...	(2 items)
▼ Item 5	Diction...	(6 items)
Type	String	PSSliderSpecifier
Title	String	Intensity
Key	String	keyFour
DefaultValue	Number	5
MinimumValue	Number	0
MaximumValue	Number	10
StringsTable	String	Root

Toolbar: MySettings ⟩ Resources ⟩ Settings.bundle ⟩ Root.plist ⟩ No Selection

Figure 14-12   Root.plist with the PSSliderSpecifier added

Figure 14-13   Settings reflects the new setting

Key	Purpose	Type	Valid Values	Required
Type	Specifies preference type.	String	PSChildPaneSpecifier	Yes
Title	Specifies the title displayed by the Settings application.	String	Any string value	Yes
File	Specifies the file used for the child pane.	String	The .plist file name without the extension	Yes

Table 14-6 PSChildPaneSpecifier Settings

PSChildPaneSpecifier

The PSChildPaneSpecifier is for specifying a child pane in the Settings application. You define the settings in this pane in a separate .plist file. Table 14-6 summarizes PSChildSpecifier's settings.

Try This Adding a PSChildPaneSpecifier

1. Return to Root.plist and add Item 6. Change its type to Dictionary. Expand and add three child rows.

2. Change the first child row's key to Type, type to String, and value to PSChildPaneSpecifier. Change the second child row's key to Title, type to String, and value to Shade. Change the third child row's key to File, type to String, and value to Shades (Figure 14-14).

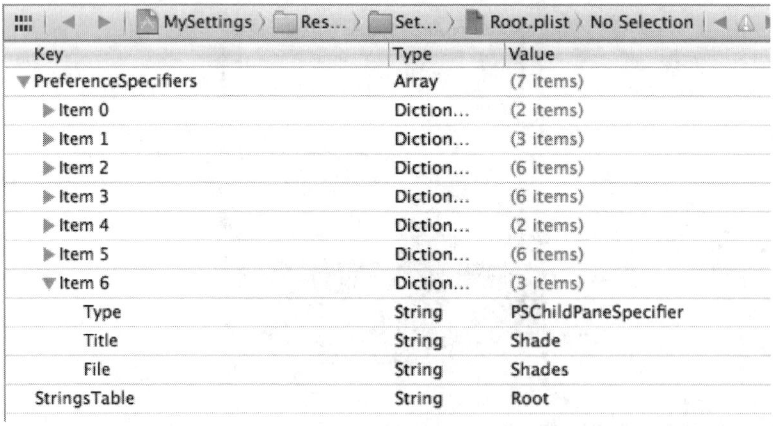

Key	Type	Value
▼ PreferenceSpecifiers	Array	(7 items)
▶ Item 0	Diction...	(2 items)
▶ Item 1	Diction...	(3 items)
▶ Item 2	Diction...	(6 items)
▶ Item 3	Diction...	(6 items)
▶ Item 4	Diction...	(2 items)
▶ Item 5	Diction...	(6 items)
▼ Item 6	Diction...	(3 items)
Type	String	PSChildPaneSpecifier
Title	String	Shade
File	String	Shades
StringsTable	String	Root

Figure 14-14 Root.plist with the PSChildPaneSpecifier added

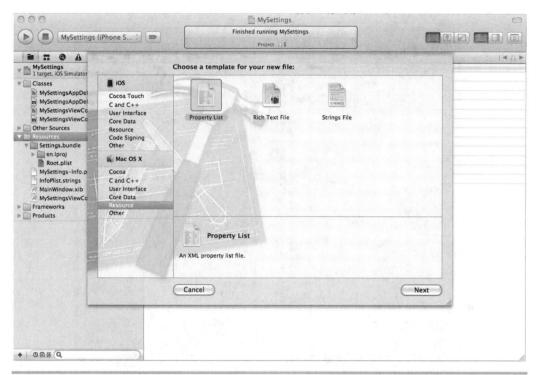

Figure 14-15 Creating a new property list

3. Save.

4. Create a new property list (Figure 14-15). Name the file **Shades**.

5. Open Shades.plist in the editor and add one row. Change the row's key to Title, type to String, and value to Shades (Figure 14-16).

6. Save.

7. Click Build And Go. The change is reflected in the Settings application (Figure 14-17).

Key	Type	Value
Title	String	Shades

MySettings ⟩ Resources ⟩ Shades.plist ⟩ No Selection

Figure 14-16 The Shades.plist settings

(continued)

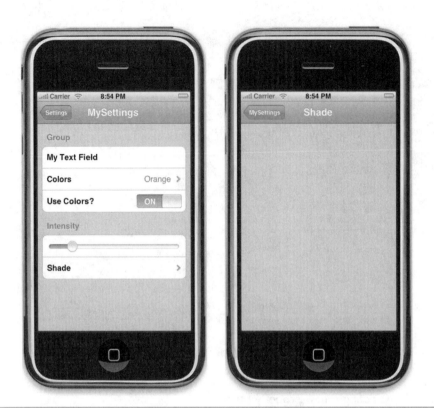

Figure 14-17 Application's settings pane shows the new subpane

Reading Settings Using NSUserDefaults

You use the NSUserDefaults class to access the defaults system. The defaults for an application are loaded at startup time and cached. You access these values using the NSUserDefaults class's methods. Methods for obtaining values include arrayForKey:, boolForKey:, dataForKey:, dictionaryForKey:, floatForKey:, integerForKey:, objectForKey:, stringArrayForKey:, and stringForKey:. For instance, to obtain a string value from a key holding a string, you use the stringForKey: method.

```
NSString* value = [[[NSUserDefaults standardUserDefaults]
stringForKey:@"myKey"] retain];
```

Try This Reading the Settings Bundle

1. Open MySettingsAppDelegate.m and modify applicationDidFinishLaunchingWithOptions: to log the application's settings (Listing 14-1). Notice that you also initialize the application's settings.

Listing 14-1 The applicationDidFinishLaunchingWithOptions method in MySettingsAppDelegate

```
(BOOL)application:(UIApplication *)application
         didFinishLaunchingWithOptions:(NSDictionary *)launchOptions {
  NSString *testValue = [[NSUserDefaults standardUserDefaults]
                            stringForKey:@"keyOne"];
  if (testValue == nil) {
    NSDictionary *appDefaults =
              [NSDictionary dictionaryWithObjectsAndKeys:
                     @"keyOneValue", @"keyOne",@"keyTwoValue",
                     @"keyTwo",@"0", @"keyThree", @"keyFourValue",
                     @"keyFour", nil];
    [[NSUserDefaults standardUserDefaults]
          registerDefaults: appDefaults];
    [[NSUserDefaults standardUserDefaults] synchronize];
  }
  NSUserDefaults * defaults = [NSUserDefaults standardUserDefaults];
  NSLog(@"%@",[defaults stringForKey:@"keyOne"]);
  NSLog(@"%@",[defaults stringForKey:@"keyTwo"]);
  NSLog(@"%@",[defaults stringForKey:@"keyThree"]);
  NSLog(@"%@",[defaults stringForKey:@"keyFour"]);
  [window addSubview:viewController.view];
  [window makeKeyAndVisible];
  return YES;
}
```

2. Click Run. The Debugger Console logs the default values (Listing 14-2).

Listing 14-2 Debugger Console logging settings

```
2010-09-11 00:53:00.407 MySettings[12014:207] keyOneValue
2010-09-11 00:53:00.409 MySettings[12014:207] keyTwoValue
2010-09-11 00:53:00.410 MySettings[12014:207] 0
2010-09-11 00:53:00.410 MySettings[12014:207] keyFourValue
```

(continued)

3. Tap the Home button and navigate to the Settings application. Change MySetting's values. Exit the Settings application. Terminate the iPhone Simulator.

4. Click Run again, and this time, the values you changed in the Settings application should appear in the Debugger Console.

Notice the console does not log the text value represented by keyOne. This is because you did not specify a default value. If you navigate to the Settings application, add a value for the text field, and then exit Settings, the next time you start the application, keyOne will log a value.

Although not well documented, in Apple's AppSettings sample application, code is provided that handles uninitialized preferences. Listing 14-1 uses the sample application's logic to first check if the first setting was set. If not, it creates default settings for the user settings values. Note that it doesn't save these values, though. Until a user actually goes into the Settings application and changes the settings, the MySettings application's user preferences will always default to the values set in the applicationDidFinishLaunching: method.

Changed Settings While Suspended

Prior to iOS 4, when the user pressed the Home button to leave your application, your application was terminated and unloaded from memory. If that user went to the Settings and changed your application's settings, you would notice the change when loading settings NSUserDefaults in applicationDidFinishLaunchingWithOptions the next time your application launched. However, any new applications that are built for iOS 4 now default to supporting a limited version of multitasking. When the user presses the Home button, your application is initially only suspended. If they launch your application again, iOS just resumes it where it left off. If the user changed your settings while it was suspended, you will need to notice the change.

Fortunately, there is an easy way to watch for new settings. When your settings are changed, iOS will send your application a NSUserDefaultsDidChangeNotification. Register for this notification when your application initially launches and you'll be able to react to any settings changes that might occur while your application is running.

```
[[NSNotificationCenter defaultCenter] addObserver:self
    selector:selector(settingsHaveChanged)
    name: NSUserDefaultsDidChangeNotification object:nil]
```

When your settingsHaveChanged method is called, call [notification object] to get the NSUserDefaults object.

Summary

It is important to remember that application settings are for preferences that will not change often. For instance, a user's username, password, and e-mail address are not likely to change often. An application's preferences are set up using the Root.plist and zero or more plists for child panes. Users modify an application's preferences through the Settings application. The application can access its preferences through the NSUserDefault class.

Chapter 15

Property Lists and Archiving

Key Skills & Concepts

● Understanding the iOS directory structure

● Persisting a collection as a property list

● Archiving an object hierarchy

In this chapter, you learn how to persist your data to a file using properties and then how to persist your data using archiving. However, before learning about these two topics, you briefly explore the iOS's file system.

An iOS Application's Directory Structure

Persisting and archiving require writing data to a file, but an iOS application can only read and write to files in the application's sandbox. When installed, an application is placed in its own home directory. This directory is the application's root directory and should be left untouched, lest you risk corrupting your application. Under the application's home directory are the directories you may write to. These directories are the Documents, Preferences, Caches, and tmp directories.

```
<application home directory>/Documents
<application home directory>/Library/Preferences
<application home directory>/Library/Caches
<application home directory>/tmp
```

The Documents directory is where you should write your application's data files. The Preferences directory is where your application's preferences are stored. These are the preferences set through the iOS's Settings application, using the NSUserDefaults class, not preferences you might create programmatically. The Caches directory, like the Documents directory, is another location you can persist files to, although, as the name implies, this directory should be reserved for caching data rather than storing an application's files. The tmp directory is a temporary directory for writing files that do not need to be persisted between application launches. Your application should remove files from this directory when not needed and iOS also removes files from this folder when an application is not running.

Directories

You will mostly read and write from two directories: the Documents directory and the tmp directory. Files you want to persist between application launches should go in the Documents directory. These files are also backed up by iTunes when an iPhone, iPod touch, or iPad is synchronized with a user's computer. Files placed in the tmp folder are temporary and should be deleted when an application terminates. If the application does not clean the folder, iOS might delete them depending on when space is needed on your device. You should never hard-code a path in your code to either folder. When using the Documents folder, you should use the NSHomeDirectory method combined with the NSSearchPathForDirectoriesInDomain method. When obtaining the tmp directory, you should use the NSTemporaryDirectory method.

NSHomeDirectory

The NSHomeDirectory is how you should obtain an application's root directory.

```
NSString * NSHomeDirectory (void);
```

Obtain the path to your Documents directory using the NSHomeDirectory. By itself, this method isn't very useful, as you usually want to obtain the Documents directory.

NSSearchPathForDirectoriesInDomains

Obtain the path to your application's Documents directory using the NSSearchPathFor DirectoriesInDomains.

```
NSArray * NSSearchPathForDirectoriesInDomains (
    NSSearchPathDirectory directory,
NSSearchPathDomainMask domainMask, BOOL expandTilde );
```

The method takes three parameters: the directory to begin the search, the search path domain mask, and a flag indicating if tildes should be converted to actual paths. The method returns an array of paths. Although on a desktop or laptop there might be multiple elements in the array, on an iOS device, there will only be one result in the array. The following code illustrates how to obtain an application's Documents directory on an iOS device:

```
NSArray * myPaths = NSSearchPathForDirectoriesInDomains(
    NSDocumentDirectory, NSUserDomainMask, YES);
NSString * myDocPath = [myPaths objectAtIndex:0];
```

Values you might use for the directory parameter on an iOS device include NSDocumentDirectory, NSApplicationDirectory, NSCachesDirectory, and NSApplicationSupportDirectory.

NSTemporaryDirectory

The NSTemporaryDirectory method returns the path to your application's tmp directory.

```
NSString * NSTemporaryDirectory (void);
```

Unlike the NSHomeDirectory method, the NSTemporaryDirectory method is useful by itself, as it is the most direct way to obtain a path to your application's tmp directory.

Property Lists

The easiest way to save your application's preferences if you're managing them within your application is using a property list. If an object can be serialized, you can persist it to a file using a path or URL. You can also reconstitute the object by reading it from the file.

It is worth noting that only objects can be serialized. A common source of frustration is trying to serialize a primitive int. Since primitive data types are not serializable, they need to be converted to NSObjects (e.g., int to NSNumber).

Simple Serialization

The NSDictionary, NSArray, NSString, NSNumber, and NSData classes, and their mutable equivalents, can all be saved as a property list using the writeToFile: or writeToURL: method.

```
- (BOOL) writeToFile: (NSString *) path atomically: (BOOL) flag
- (BOOL) writeToURL: (NSURL *) aURL atomically: (BOOL) flag
```

The first parameter is the path, or URL, to save the file as. The second parameter is a flag indicating if the file should first be saved to an auxiliary file. If the flag is YES, the data is written to an auxiliary file that is then renamed to the file indicated by the path or URL. Writing to an auxiliary file prevents the file system from becoming corrupt should writing the file fail midstream.

NOTE
You can refer to the NSDictionary, NSArray, NSString, NSNumber, or NSData classes, or one of their mutable equivalents, as a property list object. So you could say "the property list objects all contain . . ." rather than naming each property list object individually.

Reading a property list back into the object uses the initWithContentsOfFile: or initWithContentsOfURL: method.

```
- (id) initWithContentsOfFile: (NSString *) path
- (id) initWithContentsOfURL: (NSURL *) aURL
```

The initWithContentsOfFile: method takes a path to the property file, while the initWithContentsOfURL: takes a URL. Both return an id.

Try This Preserving an NSArray

1. Create a new View-based Application named **SimpleArray**.

2. Open SimpleArrayAppDelegate.m and modify applicationDidFinishLaunching WithOptions to match Listing 15-1.

3. Click Run (Listing 15-2).

4. After running the application, navigate to properties.plist in the file system and open it using TextEdit (Listing 15-3).

Listing 15-1 The applicationDidFinishLaunching method in SimpleArrayAppDelegate.m

```
(BOOL)application:(UIApplication *)application
        didFinishLaunchingWithOptions:(NSDictionary *)launchOptions {
  NSMutableArray * dataArray = [[NSMutableArray alloc]
        initWithObjects: @"First", @"Second", @"Third", nil];
  NSString * path = [(NSString *) [NSSearchPathForDirectoriesInDomains
        (NSDocumentDirectory, NSUserDomainMask, YES) objectAtIndex:0]
      stringByAppendingPathComponent:@"properties.plist"];
  [dataArray writeToFile:path atomically:YES];
  NSArray * dataArray2 = [[NSArray alloc] initWithContentsOfFile:path];
  NSLog(@"objects: %@, %@, %@",
        [dataArray2 objectAtIndex:0], [dataArray2 objectAtIndex:1],
        [dataArray2 objectAtIndex:2]);
  [window addSubview:viewController.view];
  [window makeKeyAndVisible];
  [dataArray release];
  [dataArray2 release];
}
```

Listing 15-2 Logging to the Debugger Console

```
2010-09-11 11:17:41.591 SimpleArray[14500:207] objects: First, Second,
Third
```

Listing 15-3 The properties.plist file is saved as XML.

```
<?xml version="1.0" encoding="UTF-8"?>
<!DOCTYPE plist PUBLIC "-//Apple//DTD PLIST 1.0//EN"
"http://www.apple.com/DTDs/PropertyList-1.0.dtd">
<plist version="1.0">
<array>
<string>First</string>
<string>Second</string>
<string>Third</string>
</array>
</plist>
```

The application first gets a path to its Documents directory and adds the filename to the path. After creating the path, the application persists the array to a file. Immediately after persisting the file, it creates a new array from the file's content and logs the array's values to the Debugger Console.

One thing interesting to note is that the application persists the array in an XML format. If you wished, you could easily modify the data in any text editor. You could also persist the application to a URL, and since it is XML with a published document type definition (DTD), you could process the file with almost any back-end programming language that had libraries for parsing XML and DTD files. However, note that the writeToURL:atomically: method is synchronous and your application will halt processing until the data is successfully written to the URL, so you are better off using the NSURLConnection class so that your application doesn't appear to freeze up until all of the data has been written.

NSPropertyListSerialization

Using the writeToFile: method to save a property list object as a simple property list is usually sufficient, but another way you can persist a property list object to a property list is by using the NSPropertyListSerialization class.

Serializing

To serialize a property list object, use the dataFromPropertyList:format:errorDescription: method.

```
+(NSData *)dataFromPropertyList:(id)plist format:
(NSPropertyListFormat *)format
errorDescription:(NSString **) errorString
```

This method's first parameter is an id that references the property list data and must be a property list object. Note that the dataFromPropertyList:format:errorDescription: method doesn't open and read a file's content; you must first obtain the data using the initWithContentsOfFile: or initWithContentsOfURL: method. The method's second parameter is the property list's desired format. This parameter is one of the valid NSPropertyListFormat types: NSPropertyListOpenStepFormat, NSPropertyListXMLFormat_v1_0, or NSPropertyListBinaryFormat_v1_0. The method's final parameter is a string to place an error description should something fail. Note, you must release this string should an error occur. The method returns an NSData object. You can then write this object to disk, using the writeToFile: or writeToURL: method.

Deserializing

To deserialize a property list, use the propertyListFromData:mutabilityOption:format: errorDescription: method.

```
+ (id)propertyListFromData:(NSData *)data
    mutabilityOption: (NSPropertyListMutabilityOptions) opt
    format: (NSPropertyListFormat *)format
    errorDescription:(NSString **) errorString
```

This method's first parameter is the data to deserialize. The method's second parameter indicates if the properties should be immutable or mutable. The method's third parameter indicates the format to make the property list, and the fourth parameter is the error description. Valid values for the second parameter are NSPropertyListImmutable, NSPropertyListMutableContainers, and NSPropertyListMutableContainersAndLeaves. Valid values for the third parameter are NSPropertyListOpenStepFormat, NSPropertyListXMLFormat_v1_0, and NSPropertyListBinary Format_v1_0. Note that as with the dataFromPropertyList: method, should something fail, you must release the NSString holding the error description.

NOTE

Do not take this task's more complex data structure as implying you cannot use a property list object's writeToFile: or writeToURL: method to persist complex data structures. You can, provided all items in a data structure are a property list object. For instance, if an NSArray's elements each contained an NSDictionary, you could serialize the entire data structure at once by writing the NSArray to a file.

Try This Preserving to an XML Property List

1. Create a new View-based Application named **Properties**.

2. Open PropertiesAppDelegate.m and modify the applicationDidFinishLaunching WithOptions method (Listing 15-4).

3. Click Build And Go.

Listing 15-4 The PropertiesAppDelegate's applicationDidFinishLaunchingWithOptions method

```
- (BOOL)application:(UIApplication *)application
        didFinishLaunchingWithOptions:(NSDictionary *)launchOptions {
  NSString * errorDescription;
  NSString *pathToFile = [[NSSearchPathForDirectoriesInDomains
        (NSDocumentDirectory, NSUserDomainMask,YES) objectAtIndex:0]
        stringByAppendingPathComponent:@"properties.plist"];
  NSData * myData;
  NSLog(@"%@", pathToFile);
  if ([[NSFileManager defaultManager] fileExistsAtPath:pathToFile] == NO) {
    NSMutableDictionary * dict2Serialize =
            [[[NSMutableDictionary alloc] init] autorelease];
```

```
        NSString * name = @"James";
        NSArray * kids = [NSArray arrayWithObjects:
                            @"Nicolas", @"Juliana", nil];
        NSNumber * age = [NSNumber numberWithInt:40];
        [dict2Serialize setObject:name forKey:@"name"];
        [dict2Serialize setObject:kids forKey:@"kids"];
        [dict2Serialize setObject:age forKey:@"age"];
        myData = [NSPropertyListSerialization dataFromPropertyList:(id)
            dict2Serialize format:NSPropertyListXMLFormat_v1_0
            errorDescription:&errorDescription];
        if (myData)
            [myData writeToFile:pathToFile atomically:YES];
        else {
            NSLog(@"Error writing to myData, error: %@", errorDescription);
            [errorDescription release];
        }
    }
    else {
        NSLog(@"property file exists....");
        NSPropertyListFormat format;
        NSData * plistData = [NSData dataWithContentsOfFile:pathToFile];
        NSDictionary * props = (NSDictionary *)[NSPropertyListSerialization
                    propertyListFromData:plistData
                    mutabilityOption:NSPropertyListImmutable
                    format: &format errorDescription: &errorDescription];
        if (props) {
            NSLog(@"name: %@", [props objectForKey:@"name"]);
            NSLog(@"age: %i",
                [(NSNumber *)[props objectForKey:@"age"] intValue]);
            NSLog(@"kid: %@", (NSString *)[(NSArray *)
                        [props objectForKey:@"kids"] objectAtIndex:0]);
            NSLog(@"kid: %@", (NSString *)[(NSArray *)
                        [props objectForKey:@"kids"] objectAtIndex:1]);
        } else {
            NSLog(@"Error reading properties, error: %@", errorDescription);
            [errorDescription release];
        }
    }
    [window addSubview:viewController.view];
    [window makeKeyAndVisible];
    return YES;
}
```

The first time you run the application, the debugger output will contain only a path. The second time, however, the application logs the property list contents to the Debugger Console. Notice that rather than writing the NSDictionary directly to disk, you first transformed it into an NSData object representing the property list. Had this first step of converting to XML gone awry, you would have the error description informing you (hopefully) where the problem occurred. This error handling is not provided using the NSMutableDictionary's writeToFile: method. After converting to a property list, you then persisted it using the NSData's writeToFile method. Listing 15-5 lists the file's XML content. Upon running the application a second time, you read the property list as an NSData object and converted it to an NSDictionary. To prove that the data was in fact reconstituted correctly, you logged the output to the Debugger Console (Listing 15-6).

Listing 15-5   The application's plist saved as XML

```
<?xml version="1.0" encoding="UTF-8"?>
<!DOCTYPE plist PUBLIC "-//Apple//DTD PLIST 1.0//EN" "http://www
.apple.com/DTDs/PropertyList-1.0.dtd">
<plist version="1.0">
<dict>
 <key>age</key>
<integer>40</integer>
<key>kids</key>
<array>
<string>Nicolas</string>
<string>Juliana</string>
</array>
<key>name</key>
<string>James</string>
</dict> </plist>
```

Listing 15-6   The application's Debugger Console logging

```
2010-09-11 11:35:07.918 Properties[14672:207] /Users/bward/Library/
Application Support/iPhone Simulator/4.1/Applications/3D6D7BC3-8957-
4F2A-977B-6016E86F28C4/Documents/properties.plist
2010-09-11 11:35:07.920 Properties[14672:207] property file exists....
2010-09-11 11:35:07.922 Properties[14672:207] name: James
2010-09-11 11:35:07.922 Properties[14672:207] age: 40
2010-09-11 11:35:07.924 Properties[14672:207] kid: Nicolas
2010-09-11 11:35:07.925 Properties[14672:207] kid: Juliana
```

Archiving

You can only serialize and deserialize property list objects. Moreover, all of a property list object's constituent objects must also be property list objects. This limitation hinders the usefulness of property lists. Therefore, rather than using a property list, you can use archiving. Archiving is a more flexible approach to persisting an object than a property list.

You create an archive using an NSKeyedArchiver. This class persists any object that adopts the NSCoding protocol. You reconstitute an object by using NSKeyedArchiver's complement, the NSKeyedUnarchiver class. In this section, you learn how to create a class that adopts the NSCoding protocol. You then learn how to archive and unarchive this class.

Protocols to Adopt

Archiving a class requires that a class adopt the NSCoding protocol. The class should also adopt the NSCopying protocol if you're creating a class that adopts the NSCoding protocol.

NSCoding

Classes that adopt this protocol must implement the encodeWithCoder: and initWithCoder: methods. The encodeWithCoder: method encodes the object and the object's instance variables so that they can be archived.

```
-(void)encodeWithCoder:(NSCoder *)encoder
```

The initWithCoder: method decodes the object and the object's instance variables.

```
-(id)initWithCoder:(NSCoder *)decoder
```

You use both methods in the example task that follows.

NSCopying

When implementing the NSCoding protocol, best practices dictate that you also implement the NSCopying protocol. Classes that implement the NSCopying protocol must implement the copyWithZone method. Remember, when you set one object to another, you are merely creating another reference to the same underlying physical object. For instance, in the following code, both A and B are pointing to the same Foo that was originally allocated and initialized by A.

```
Foo * A = [[Foo alloc] init];
Foo * B = A;
```

When you copy an object, you obtain a distinct physical object, as if the object obtaining the copy actually allocated and initialized the object.

```
Foo * A = [[Foo alloc] init];
Foo * B = [A copy];
```

The method that allows copying is the copyWithZone: method.

```
-(id)copyWithZone:(NSZone *)zone
```

You can use either this method or NSObject's copy method to obtain what is called a "deep copy" of an object. For more information, refer to Apple's "Memory Management Programming Guide for Cocoa," available online.

NOTE

This chapter only discusses NSCopying briefly, as it is not used in this chapter. It is included because best practices dictate that if a class implements the NSCoding protocol for archiving, it must also implement the NSCopying protocol.

NSKeyedArchiver and NSKeyedUnarchiver

The NSKeyedArchiver class archives objects, while the NSKeyedUnarchiver class unarchives objects.

NSKeyedArchiver

NSKeyedArchiver stores one or more objects to an archive using the initForWritingWith MutableData method. To be archived, an object must implement the NSCoding protocol.

```
-(id)initForWritingWithMutableData:(NSMutableData *)data
```

This method takes a writable data object and returns the archived object as an id. You can then write the archive to disk.

The steps for creating and writing an archive to disk are as follows. First, create an NSMutableData object.

```
NSMutableData * theData = [NSMutableData data];
```

After creating the data object, create an NSKeyedArchiver, passing the newly created data object as a parameter.

```
NSKeyedArchiver * archiver = [[NSKeyedArchiver alloc]
        initForWritingWithMutableData:theData];
```

After initializing the NSKeyedArchiver, encode the objects to archive. If you wish, you can encode multiple objects using the same archiver, provided all archived objects adopt the NSCoding protocol. The following code snippet illustrates:

```
[archiver encodeObject:objectA forKey:@"a"];
[archiver encodeObject:objectB forKey:@"b"];
[archiver encodeObject:objectC forKey:@"c"];
[archiver finishEncoding];
```

After archiving, write the data object, which now contains the archived objects, to a file.

```
[theData writeToFile:"myfile.archive" atomically:YES]
```

NSKeyedUnarchiver

You use NSKeyedUnarchiver to unarchive an archive. NSKeyedUnarchiver reconstitutes one or more objects from a data object that was initialized with an archive. To be unarchived, an object must implement the NSCoding protocol. When programming for iOS, you use the initForReadingWithData: method.

```
-(id)initForReadingWithData:(NSData *)data
```

The steps to unarchive are similar to archiving. First, create an NSData object from the previously archived file.

```
NSData * theData =[NSData dataWithContentsOfFile:"myfile.archive"];
```

After creating the data object, create and initialize an NSKeyedUnarchiver instance.

```
NSKeyedUnarchiver * uarchiver = [[NSKeyedUnarchiver alloc] initForRead
ingWithData:theData];
```

After initializing the NSKeyedUnarchiver, unarchive the objects previously archived.

```
A * objA = [[unarchiver decodeObjectForKey:@"a"] retain];
B * objB = [[unarchiver decodeObjectForKey:@"b"] retain];
C * objC = [[unarchiver decodeObjectForKey:@"c"] retain];
[unarchiver finishDecoding];
[unarchiver release];
```

Try This Archiving and Unarchiving an Object

1. Create a new View-based Application called **Encoding**.

2. Create a new Objective-C class called Foo.

3. Add two properties to Foo. Make one property an NSString and name it "name" and make the other property an NSNumber and name it "age."

4. Have Foo adopt the NSCopying and NSCoding protocols (Listings 15-7 and 15-8). Remember, Foo must get deep copies of name and age.

5. Modify Foo so that it implements the encodeWithCoder:, initWithCoder:, and copyWithZone: methods.

6. Add Foo as a property to EncodingAppDelegate (Listings 15-9 and 15-10).

7. Implement the applicationWillTerminate: method and modify the applicationDidFinish LaunchingWithOptions: method to decode and encode Foo.

8. If you're building for SDK 4.0 or later, then iOS will suspend rather than terminate your application, so the applicationWillTerminate will never be called. Edit Encoding-Info.plist in Resources and add another value to the end of the plist with key UIApplicationExitsOnSuspend, type Boolean and value YES. (Later we'll talk about using archiving to save your application's state on suspension, so that it can resume where it left off whether iOS terminates it or only suspends it.)

9. Click Run and the debugging log will indicate that it's the first pass through. Stop execution and then Run again and the debugging log will indicate that you've unarchived the Foo object.

Listing 15-7   Foo.h

```
#import <Foundation/Foundation.h>
@interface Foo : NSObject <NSCoding, NSCopying> {
 NSString * name;
 NSNumber * age;
}
@property (nonatomic, retain) NSString * name;
@property (nonatomic, retain) NSNumber * age;
@end
```

Listing 15-8   Foo.m

```
#import "Foo.h"
@implementation Foo
@synthesize name;
@synthesize age;
-(id) copyWithZone: (NSZone *) zone {
  Foo * aFoo = [[Foo allocWithZone:zone] init];
  aFoo.name = [NSString stringWithString: self.name];
  aFoo.age = [NSNumber numberWithInt:[self.age intValue]];
  return aFoo;
}
-(void) encodeWithCoder: (NSCoder *) coder {
  [coder encodeObject: name forKey: @"name"];
  [coder encodeObject:age forKey: @"age"];
}
```

```
-(id) initWithCoder: (NSCoder *) coder {
  self = [super init];
  name = [[coder decodeObjectForKey:@"name"] retain];
  age = [[coder decodeObjectForKey:@"age"] retain];
  return self;
}
-(void) dealloc {
  [name release];
  [age release];
  [super dealloc];
}
@end
```

Listing 15-9   EncodingAppDelegate.h

```
#import <UIKit/UIKit.h>
@class Foo;
@class EncodingViewController;
@interface EncodingAppDelegate : NSObject <UIApplicationDelegate> {
  UIWindow *window;
  EncodingViewController *viewController;
  Foo * myFoo;
}
@property (nonatomic, retain) Foo * myFoo;
@property (nonatomic, retain) IBOutlet UIWindow *window;
@property (nonatomic, retain) IBOutlet EncodingViewController
*viewController;
@end
```

Listing 15-10   EncodingAppDelegate.m

```
#import "EncodingAppDelegate.h"
#import "EncodingViewController.h"
#import "Foo.h"
@implementation EncodingAppDelegate
@synthesize window;
@synthesize viewController;
@synthesize myFoo;
- (BOOL)application:(UIApplication *)application
        didFinishLaunchingWithOptions:(NSDictionary *)launchOptions {
```

```objc
    NSString *pathToFile = [[NSSearchPathForDirectoriesInDomains(
        NSDocumentDirectory, NSUserDomainMask,YES) objectAtIndex:0]
        stringByAppendingPathComponent:@"foo.archive"];
    NSLog(@"%@",pathToFile);
    NSData * theData =[NSData dataWithContentsOfFile:pathToFile];
    if([theData length] > 0) {
        NSKeyedUnarchiver * archiver = [[[NSKeyedUnarchiver alloc]
            initForReadingWithData:theData] autorelease];
        myFoo = [archiver decodeObjectForKey:@"myfoo"];
        [archiver finishDecoding];
        NSLog(@"nth run - name: %@ age: %i", myFoo.name,
            [myFoo.age intValue]);
    }
    else {
        NSLog(@"first run: no name or age");
        myFoo =[[Foo alloc] init];
        myFoo.name = @"James";
        myFoo.age = [NSNumber numberWithInt:40];
    }
    [window addSubview:viewController.view];
    [window makeKeyAndVisible];
    return YES;
}
-(void) applicationWillTerminate: (UIApplication *) application {
  NSString *pathToFile = [[NSSearchPathForDirectoriesInDomains(
      NSDocumentDirectory, NSUserDomainMask,YES) objectAtIndex:0]
      stringByAppendingPathComponent:@"foo.archive"];
  NSMutableData * theData = [NSMutableData data];
  NSKeyedArchiver * archiver = [[[NSKeyedArchiver alloc]
      initForWritingWithMutableData:theData] autorelease];
  [archiver encodeObject:self.myFoo forKey:@"myfoo"];
  [archiver finishEncoding];
  if([theData writeToFile:pathToFile atomically:YES] == NO)
    NSLog(@"writing failed....");
}
-(void)dealloc {
    [myFoo release];
    [viewController release];
    [foo release];
    [window release];
    [super dealloc];
}
  @end
```

Try This Archiving and Unarchiving an Object Hierarchy

1. Open the previous application, Encoding, in Xcode.

2. Create a new Objective-C class and name it Bar. Have it adopt the NSCoding and NSCopying protocols (Listings 15-11 and 15-12).

3. Add an NSMutableArray as a property in Bar.

4. Override init to add a couple of Foo objects to the array (Listing 15-13).

5. Implement the initWithCoder:, encodeWithCoder:, and copyWithZone: methods (Listing 15-14).

6. Add Bar as a property to EncodingAppDelegate. Remember, you must have a forward reference to the class, since you are adding it as a property to the header, and then import the Bar class and synthesize the property in the implementation.

7. Modify EncodingAppDelegate's applicationDidFinishLaunchingWithOptions: and applicationWillTerminate: methods to include the newly created Bar property.

8. Note that we changed the name of the archive file to foo2.archive to avoid conflicting with the previous task.

9. Click Run.

Listing 15-11   Bar.h

```
#import <Foundation/Foundation.h>
#import "Foo.h"
@interface Bar : NSObject <NSCoding, NSCopying> {
 NSMutableArray * foos;
}
@property (nonatomic, retain) NSMutableArray * foos;
@end
```

Listing 15-12   Bar.m

```
#import "Bar.h"
@implementation Bar
@synthesize foos;
```

```objc
-(id) init {
  if([super init] == nil)
    return nil;
  Foo * foo1 = [[Foo alloc] init];
  foo1.name = @"Juliana";
  foo1.age = [NSNumber numberWithInt:7];
  Foo * foo2 = [[Foo alloc] init];
  foo2.name = @"Nicolas";
  foo2.age = [NSNumber numberWithInt:3];
  foos = [[NSMutableArray alloc] initWithObjects:foo1, foo2, nil];
  return self;
}
-(void) encodeWithCoder: (NSCoder *) coder {
  [coder encodeObject: foos forKey:@"foos"];
}
-(id) initWithCoder: (NSCoder *) coder {
  self = [super init];
  foos = [[coder decodeObjectForKey:@"foos"] retain];
  return self;
}
-(id) copyWithZone: (NSZone *) zone {
  Bar * aBar = [[Bar allocWithZone:zone] init];
  NSMutableArray *newArray = [[[NSMutableArray alloc] initWithArray:
      self.foos copyItems:YES] autorelease];
  aBar.foos = newArray;
  return aBar;
}
- (void) dealloc {
  [foos release];
  [super dealloc];
}
@end
```

Listing 15-13   EncodingAppDelegate.h

```objc
#import <UIKit/UIKit.h>
@class Bar
@class Foo;
@class EncodingViewController;
@interface EncodingAppDelegate : NSObject <UIApplicationDelegate> {
  UIWindow *window;
  EncodingViewController *viewController;
  Foo * myFoo;
  Bar * myBar;
}
```

```objc
@property (nonatomic, retain) Foo * myFoo;
@property (nonatomic, retain) Bar * myBar;
@property (nonatomic, retain) IBOutlet UIWindow *window;
@property (nonatomic, retain) IBOutlet EncodingViewController
*viewController;
@end
```

Listing 15-14 EncodingAppDelegate.m

```objc
#import "EncodingAppDelegate.h"
#import "EncodingViewController.h"
#import "Foo.h"
#import "Bar.h"
@implementation EncodingAppDelegate
@synthesize window;
@synthesize viewController;
@synthesize myFoo;
@synthesize myBar;
-(void)applicationDidFinishLaunching:(UIApplication *)application {
  NSString *pathToFile = [[NSSearchPathForDirectoriesInDomains(
      NSDocumentDirectory, NSUserDomainMask,YES) objectAtIndex:0]
      stringByAppendingPathComponent:@"foo2.archive"];
  NSLog(@"%@", pathToFile);
  NSData * theData =[NSData dataWithContentsOfFile:pathToFile];
  if([theData length] > 0) {
    NSKeyedUnarchiver * archiver = [[[NSKeyedUnarchiver alloc]
        initForReadingWithData:theData] autorelease];
    myFoo = [archiver decodeObjectForKey:@"myfoo"];
    myBar = [archiver decodeObjectForKey:@"mybar"];
    [archiver finishDecoding];
    NSLog(@"nth run - name: %@ age: %i", myFoo.name,
      [myFoo.age intValue]);
    NSArray * array = myBar.foos;
    for(Foo * aFoo in array) {
      NSLog(@"Foo: name: %@, age: %i", aFoo.name, [aFoo.age intValue]);
    }
  }
  else {
    NSLog(@"first run: no name or age");
    myFoo =[[Foo alloc] init];
    myFoo.name = @"James";
    myFoo.age = [NSNumber numberWithInt:40];
    myBar = [[Bar alloc] init];
  }
```

```
    [window addSubview:viewController.view];
    [window makeKeyAndVisible];
}
-(void) applicationWillTerminate: (UIApplication *) application {
    NSString *pathToFile = [[NSSearchPathForDirectoriesInDomains(
        NSDocumentDirectory, NSUserDomainMask,YES) objectAtIndex:0]
        stringByAppendingPathComponent:@"foo2.archive"];
    NSMutableData * theData = [NSMutableData data];
    NSKeyedArchiver * archiver = [[[NSKeyedArchiver alloc]
    initForWritingWithMutableData:theData] autorelease];
    [archiver encodeObject:myFoo forKey:@"myfoo"];
    [archiver encodeObject:myBar forKey:@"mybar"];
    [archiver finishEncoding];
    if( [theData writeToFile:pathToFile atomically:YES] == NO)
      NSLog(@"writing failed....");
}
-(void)dealloc {
    [myFoo release];
    [myBar release];
    [viewController release];
    [window release];
    [super dealloc];
}
@end
```

When the application starts, it loads the archive file into a data object. If the data object is null, the file doesn't exist. If the file does exist, the data is unarchived. When the application terminates, it archives Foo. Because Bar contains constituent Foo objects in an array, it also archives those objects. The key for the archived Foo is "myfoo," and "mybar" for the archived Bar object. Both Foo and Bar implement the NSCoding protocol. This allows them to be archived. Notice that Bar contains an NSMutableArray of Foo objects. Because NSMutableArray adopts the NSCoding protocol, NSMutableArray can be encoded and decoded. Moreover, the NSMutableArray knows to encode or decode its constituent elements.

Now examine Bar's copyWithZone method. Because Bar contains an NSMutableArray of Foo objects, when copying a Bar you must also copy the Bar's Foo array. But you cannot just set the new Bar's array to the old Bar's array, as the new Bar's array will simply be a pointer to the old Bar's array. Instead you must create a new NSMutableArray and initialize the new array with the old array, being certain to specify copyItems as YES. By taking this step, the new Bar obtains a deep copy of the old Bar's array of Foo objects.

NOTE

For more information on archiving, refer to "Apple's Archives and Serializations Programming Guide for Cocoa."

Multitasking and Saving Application State

In versions of the iOS prior to 4, when the user pressed the Home button, your application was terminated. Now the default behavior is to leave your application in memory and just suspend it. Then if the user wants to return to it later, it can launch instantly and they're exactly where they left off. We actually had to turn this behavior off in the encoding task so that it would terminate and save our test data. For simple apps that launch quickly and aren't likely to be returned to over and over, it makes sense to set that flag and not worry about coding for application suspension. However, for more complex applications your users will really appreciate being able to switch to another app and then instantly return to yours, continuing right where they left off.

So, what does this have to do with archiving? If all the iOS ever did was temporarily freeze your app in memory and then continue it later, there wouldn't be any need for persistence. But, if iOS runs low on memory or the user doesn't return to your application for a while, then it can be purged from memory without warning. This creates unpredictable behavior for your users. Sometimes when they switch to another app and then return to yours, everything is exactly as they left it (e.g., they're in the middle of a gaming level or tunneled deeply down into some nested UITableViews). Other times, when they return to your app it seems to be starting up fresh (because it is—iOS had to purge it from memory). The recommended way to deal with this inconsistency is to always save away enough state information when your application is suspended so that you can restore it to the exact same context if your application is purged from memory before the user can return to it. That's where archiving comes in.

The state information you'll need to save is going to be different for every application, but the easiest way to save that information is going to be a set of objects serialized and archived to a file in the application's Documents directory. For a game you might need to serialize a number indicating the level they were on along with a hierarchy of objects that encode the state of enemies, puzzles, etc., on that level. For a reference application that browses hierarchical data, it might be saving a trail of which item they chose at each level and where they were scrolled to on the current view. In either case, you will likely want to implement the NSCoding protocol for a selection of objects, so that you can archive them when your application is suspended. Implement the applicationDidEnterBackground method in your AppDelegate class and save your state information there as well as freeing up any resources you don't need.

```
- (void)applicationDidEnterBackground:(UIApplication *)application
```

Implement the applicationWillEnterForeground method in your AppDelegate class to restore your state information.

```
- (void)applicationWillEnterForeground:(UIApplication *)application
```

Summary

In this chapter, you learned how to persist an application's data using property lists and archiving. These techniques are really only practical for persisting a few reasonably small objects to a file. Large object hierarchies are much better persisted using SQLite or better yet, the Core Data framework. But for state information, user preferences, etc., persisting to a property list or archiving is fine. In this chapter, you learned methods for doing both. As a rule of thumb, if persisting variables not tied to particular objects, simply place them in a collection and persist the collection as a property list. But if persisting variables that are object properties, have the objects adopt the NSCoding protocol and archive the objects. If persisting a moderate to large amount of data, use SQLite or use the Core Data framework. If you want to use the data outside of an iOS or Cocoa application, you should use SQLite. Both SQLite and Core Data will be discussed in upcoming chapters.

Chapter 16

Data Persistence Using SQLite

Key Skills & Concepts

- Creating a database and adding data to it

- Including the database in Xcode

- Reading from a database

- Making a database writable

- Inserting a record

- Updating a record

- Deleting a record

The SQLite database is a popular open-source database written in C. The database is small and designed for embedding in an application, unlike a database such as Oracle that was designed to run on a separate, large server. SQLite is part of the standard open-source Linux/BSD server stack, and as OS X is essentially FreeBSD, it was only natural Apple chose SQLite as the iOS's embedded database.

Adding a SQLite Database

Adding a SQLite database to your project involves two steps. First, you must create the database. In this chapter's first task, you create a database using the Firefox SQLite Manager plug-in. Second, you must add the SQLite library to your Xcode project. The first task also illustrates adding the SQLite library to your Xcode project. After creating the database and loading it, you can then use the database programmatically via its C programming interface.

Try This Creating a Simple Database Using FireFox SQLite Manager

1. If you don't already have Firefox, download and install it.

2. Select Add-ons from the Tools menu (Figure 16-1).

3. Select Get Add-ons, type **SQLite** in the search box, and install SQLite Manager.

4. Once installed and you have restarted Firefox, select Tools | SQLite Manager.

Figure 16-1 Adding SQLite Manager to Firefox

5. Select the New icon (the blank paper graphic), and create a new database named **myDatabase**. Save the database file some place where you can easily find it later. Note SQLite Manager automatically adds the .sqlite extension.

6. Click Create Table and create a new table named **photos**.

7. Add three columns: **id**, **name**, and **photo**. Make id an INTEGER and check Primary Key and Autoinc check boxes.

8. Make name a VARCHAR and check only Allow Null.

9. Make photo a BLOB and check only Allow Null.

10. Your screen should resemble Figure 16-2.

11. Click OK and the SQLite Manager generates the database table.

(continued)

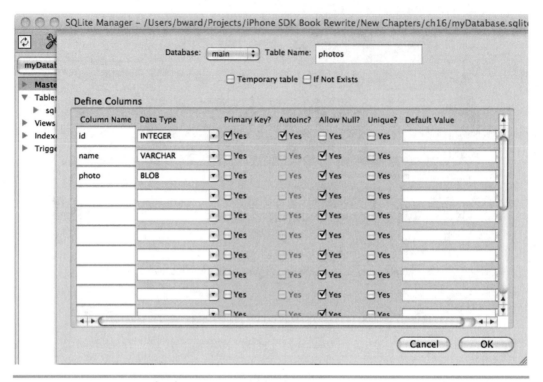

Figure 16-2 Creating a database using SQLite Manager

NOTE

SQLite does not enforce foreign key relationships. You must instead write triggers manually to enforce foreign key relationships. SQLite does not support right outer joins or full outer joins. SQLite views are read-only.

12. Click the Browse & Search tab, and then click the Add Record button.

13. In the action sheet, leave id blank. Type **Icon One** for the name. Notice the small paper clip beside photo. Move your mouse over the paper clip, and the tooltip should say "Add File as a Blob" (Figure 16-3). Click the paper clip and add any photo from your computer. If the photo column doesn't say something like BLOB (Size: 65984), the file was not correctly added as a blob.

14. Click OK, and the record will be added. Add another record, selecting any other image from your computer.

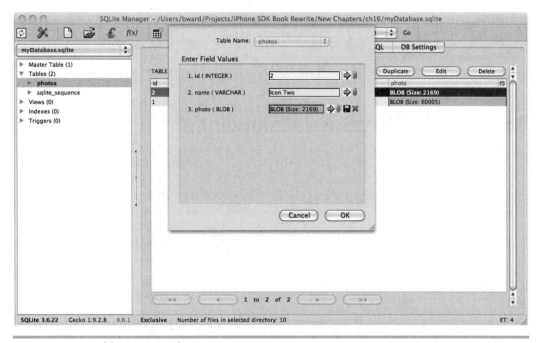

Figure 16-3 Adding a record using SQLite Manager

15. From the menu, select Database | Close Database from the main menus to close the database. You can now exit SQLite Manager and quit Firefox.

16. Open Xcode and create a new View-based Application. Name the application **MyDBProject**.

17. Expand Frameworks in the Navigator and right-click on any one of the frameworks (e.g., UIKit) and select Show in Finder from the pop-up menu. This will get you to the folder with all of your frameworks on your computer. Move up two folder levels from there to the SDK folder and then open user/lib.

18. Drag and drop the libsqlite3.0.dylib framework from that folder to Frameworks in the Navigator in Xcode. In the dialog that pops up, be sure to uncheck "Copy items into destination group's folder" and click Finish.

19. Add the database file that you created earlier to the Resources folder. Be sure to check the Copy Items check box so that the database file gets copied into MyDBProject.

20. This task is now complete with the SQLite library added to the project and the database file copied into the project's resources. Do not delete the project or database, as you will use them for the remainder of this chapter.

NOTE

Adding binary data using SQLite Manager in Firefox seems to be buggy. Sometimes it works, sometimes not. If after adding a record the photo column is blank, just edit the row and add the photo file's content again. Updating the blob seems to be more stable in SQLite Manager.

Basic SQLite Database Manipulation

If you have ever used a database from within a programming language, SQLite database manipulation using C should seem intuitive. You open the database. You create a prepared statement containing a SQL string. That statement might have one or more parameters you bind values to. After binding, you execute the statement. If the statement returns results, you loop through each record and load the record's column values into your program's variables. After looping through all records, you finalize the statement, and, if you are finished with the database, you close the database. The steps are similar for most languages and databases.

Opening the Database

You open a database using the sqlite3_open, sqlite_open16, or sqlite3_open_v2 commands. This chapter uses the sqlite3_open command exclusively. The sqlite3_open command takes a database filename as a UTF-8 string and opens the database. Listing 16-1, taken from the SQLite's online documentation, lists the sqlite_open3 method signature.

Listing 16-1   The sqlite3_open method signature (from SQLite online documentation)

```
int sqlite3_open(
  const char *filename, /* Database filename (UTF-8) */
  sqlite3 **ppDb /* OUT: SQLite db handle */
);
```

The method returns an integer as the method's success or failure code. Listing 16-2, from the SQLite online documentation, lists several common result codes.

Listing 16-2   SQLite return codes (taken from SQLite online documentation)

```
#define SQLITE_OK           0   /* Successful result */
#define SQLITE_ERROR        1   /* SQL error or missing database */
#define SQLITE_READONLY     8   /* Attempt to write a readonly database */
#define SQLITE_INTERRUPT    9   /* Operation terminated by */
#define SQLITE_IOERR       10   /* Some kind of disk I/O error occurred */
#define SQLITE_CANTOPEN    14   /* Unable to open the database file */
#define SQLITE_MISMATCH    20   /* Data type mismatch */
#define SQLITE_ROW        100   /* sqlite3_step() has another row ready */
#define SQLITE_DONE       101   /* sqlite3_step() has finished executing */
```

Statements, Preparing Statements, and Executing Statements

There are two primary ways of executing SQL statements using SQLite's C interface. One method is the sqlite3_exec method. Although a powerful method, it is more advanced C programming, and so this chapter uses the sqlite3_stmt structure and the sqlite3_prepare_v2 and sqlite3_step statements instead of the sqlite3_exec function.

The SQLite sqlite3_stmt

The sqlite3_stmt encapsulates a SQL statement. For instance, "select * from photos" is a SQL statement. In your program, you encapsulate this SQL string using a statement. For instance, the following code snippet illustrates creating a SQL string, initializing a statement, and loading the statement (Listing 16-3).

Listing 16-3   Using a sqlite3_stmt in a C program

```
const char *sqlselect = "SELECT id,name,photo FROM photos";
static sqlite3_stmt *statement = nil;
sqlite3_prepare_v2(database, sqlselect, -1, &statement, NULL);
```

The SQLite sqlite3_prepare_v2 Method

You load a SQL string into a statement using sqlite3_prepare methods. The prepare methods are sqlite3_prepare, sqlite3_prepare_v2, sqlite3_prepare_16, and sqlite3_prepare16_v2. This chapter uses only the sqlite3_prepare_v2 method. Notice the prepare statement takes a C string, not an NString, but getting the C string from an NString is not difficult—simply call the NSString's UTF8String method. The sqlite3_prepare_v2 method's signature is in Listing 16-4. Notice, like the open statements, the prepare statement returns an integer result code you should check when calling the method.

Listing 16-4   The sqlite3_prepare_v2 method signature (taken from the SQLite online documentation)

```
int sqlite3_prepare_v2(
  sqlite3 *db,  /* Database handle */
  const char *zSql,  /* SQL statement, UTF-8 encoded */
  int nByte,  /* Maximum length of zSql in bytes. */
  sqlite3_stmt **ppStmt,  /* OUT: Statement handle */
  const char **pzTail  /* OUT: Pointer to unused portion of zSql */
);
```

After preparing the statement, you execute it and step through the results.

The SQLite sqlite3_step Method

The sqlite3_step method executes a prepared statement. You must call this method at least once. For instance, when calling insert or update, you call sqlite3_step once. You only call it once because these statements do not result in a record set being returned from the database. When selecting data, you typically call this method multiple times until you receive no more results. The following is the method's signature.

```
int sqlite3_step(sqlite3_stmt*);
```

Like the other SQLite methods, this method returns a response code you should check after calling the method.

Select

You select one or more records from a SQL database using a select statement. Because a select statement usually returns multiple rows, you must loop through the row set if you wish to obtain all records.

```
while (sqlite3_step(statement) == SQLITE_ROW){
  //process row here
}
```

Obtaining SQLite Column Values

You obtain column values through a method in Listing 16-5. Using these methods will become more apparent after the next task.

Listing 16-5   Methods for obtaining column data (from SQLite online documentation)

```
const void *sqlite3_column_blob(sqlite3_stmt*, int iCol);
int sqlite3_column_bytes(sqlite3_stmt*, int iCol);
int sqlite3_column_bytes16(sqlite3_stmt*, int iCol);
double sqlite3_column_double(sqlite3_stmt*, int iCol);
int sqlite3_column_int(sqlite3_stmt*, int iCol);
sqlite3_int64 sqlite3_column_int64(sqlite3_stmt*, int iCol);
const unsigned char *sqlite3_column_text(sqlite3_stmt*, int iCol);
const void *sqlite3_column_text16(sqlite3_stmt*, int iCol);
int sqlite3_column_type(sqlite3_stmt*, int iCol);
sqlite3_value *sqlite3_column_value(sqlite3_stmt*, int iCol);
```

NOTE

The int iCol arguments in the methods in Listing 16-5 are a zero-based index into the columns in the results of the sqlite3_stmt, not an index into the columns of a SQLite database table.

Try This Opening and Querying a Database

1. Return to your MyDBProject in Xcode.

2. In Classes, create a new group called Model.

3. Create a new Objective-C class in the Model group called PhotosDAO. Create another Objective-C class in the same group called PhotoDAO.

4. Add a name, photoID, and photo property to PhotoDAO.h and PhotoDAO.m (Listings 16-6 and 16-7).

Listing 16-6 PhotoDAO.h

```
#import <Foundation/Foundation.h>
@interface PhotoDAO : NSObject {
  NSString * name;
  NSInteger photoID;
  UIImage * photo;
}
@property (nonatomic, retain) NSString * name;
@property (nonatomic, assign) NSInteger photoID;
@property (nonatomic, retain) UIImage * photo;
@end
```

Listing 16-7 PhotoDAO.m

```
#import "PhotoDAO.h"
@implementation PhotoDAO
@synthesize name;
@synthesize photoID;
@synthesize photo;
- (void) dealloc {
  [name release];
  [photo release];
  [super dealloc];
}
@end
```

5. Open PhotosDAO.h and import SQLite3. Add a reference to the database you will use (Listing 16-8).

(continued)

Listing 16-8   PhotosDAO.h

```
#import <Foundation/Foundation.h>
#import <sqlite3.h>
@interface PhotosDAO : NSObject {
  sqlite3 *database;
}
- (NSMutableArray *) getAllPhotos;
@end
```

---

6. Add a getAllPhotos method to PhotosDAO and implement the method (Listing 16-9).

Listing 16-9   PhotosDAO.m

```
#import "PhotosDAO.h"
#import "PhotoDAO.h"
@implementation PhotosDAO
- (NSMutableArray *) getAllPhotos {
  NSMutableArray * photosArray = [[NSMutableArray alloc] init];
  @try {
  NSFileManager *fileManager = [NSFileManager defaultManager];
  NSString *theDBPath = [[[NSBundle mainBundle] resourcePath]
stringByAppendingPathComponent:@"myDatabase.sqlite"];
  BOOL success = [fileManager fileExistsAtPath:theDBPath];
  if (!success) {
    NSLog(@"Failed to find database file '%@'.", theDBPath);
  }
  if (!(sqlite3_open([theDBPath UTF8String], &database) == SQLITE_OK)) {
      NSLog(@"An error opening database, normally handle error here.");
  }
  const char *sql = "SELECT id,name,photo FROM photos";
  sqlite3_stmt *statement;
  if (sqlite3_prepare_v2(database, sql, -1, &statement, NULL) !=
                       SQLITE_OK) {
    NSLog(@"Error, failed to prepare statement, handle error here.");
  }
  while (sqlite3_step(statement) == SQLITE_ROW) {
    PhotoDAO * aPhoto = [[PhotoDAO alloc] init];
    aPhoto.photoID = sqlite3_column_int(statement, 0);
    aPhoto.name = [NSString stringWithUTF8String:(char *)
    sqlite3_column_text(statement, 1)];
```

```
      const char * rawData = sqlite3_column_blob(statement, 2);
      int rawDataLength = sqlite3_column_bytes(statement, 2);
      NSData *data = [NSData dataWithBytes:rawData length: rawDataLength];
      aPhoto.photo = [[UIImage alloc] initWithData:data];
      [photosArray addObject:aPhoto];
      [aPhoto release];
    }
    if(sqlite3_finalize(statement) != SQLITE_OK){
      NSLog(@"Failed to finalize data statement, error handling here.");
    }
    if (sqlite3_close(database) != SQLITE_OK) {
      NSLog(@"Failed to close database, normally error handling here.");
    }
  } @catch (NSException *e) {
    NSLog(@"An exception occurred: %@", [e reason]);
    return nil;
  }
  return photosArray;
}
@end
```

7. Open MyDBProjectViewController.h and add an NSMutableArray property to hold the photos. Add an IBOutlet for a UIImageView. Add a UILabel named theLabel, add an IBAction, and name the method changeImage (Listing 16-10).

Listing 16-10   MyDBProjectViewController.h

```
#import <UIKit/UIKit.h>
@interface MyDBProjectViewController : UIViewController {
  NSMutableArray * photos;
  UIImageView * theImageView;
  UILabel * theLabel;
}
@property (nonatomic, retain) NSMutableArray * photos;
@property (nonatomic, retain) IBOutlet UIImageView * theImageView;
@property (nonatomic, retain) IBOutlet UILabel * theLabel;
- (IBAction) changeImage: (id) sender;
@end
```

8. Open MyDBProjectViewController.m and synthesize photos and theImageView (Listing 16-11).

(continued)

Listing 16-11 MyDBProjectViewController.m

```objc
#import "MyDBProjectViewController.h"
#import "PhotoDAO.h";
#import "PhotosDAO.h";
@implementation MyDBProjectViewController
@synthesize photos;
@synthesize theImageView;
@synthesize theLabel;
- (void)viewDidLoad {
  PhotosDAO * myPhotos = [[PhotosDAO alloc] init];
  self.photos = [myPhotos getAllPhotos];
  [self.theImageView setImage:((PhotoDAO *)[self.photos
objectAtIndex:0]).photo];
  [self.theLabel setText:((PhotoDAO *)
        [self.photos objectAtIndex:0]).name];
  [myPhotos release];
  [super viewDidLoad];
}
- (IBAction) changeImage: (id) sender {
  static NSInteger currentElement = 0;
  if(++currentElement == [self.photos count]) currentElement = 0;
  PhotoDAO * aPhoto =
      (PhotoDAO *) [self.photos objectAtIndex: currentElement];
  [self.theLabel setText:aPhoto.name];
  [self.theImageView setImage:aPhoto.photo];
}
- (void)dealloc {
  [photos release];
  [theImageView release];
  [theLabel release];
  [super dealloc];
}
@end
```

---

9. Implement the viewDidLoad and changeImage methods so that they match Listing 16-11.

10. Save your changes and open MyDBProjectViewController.xib. Add a toolbar, a label, and a UIImageView (Figure 16-4). Change the button's title to Next. Remove the text from the label.

11. Connect the File's Owner theLabel outlet to the label added to the toolbar. Connect the theImageView outlet to the UIImageView. Connect the changeImage action to the Next button. Save your changes.

12. Run the application in iPhone Simulator, as shown in Figures 16-5 and 16-6.

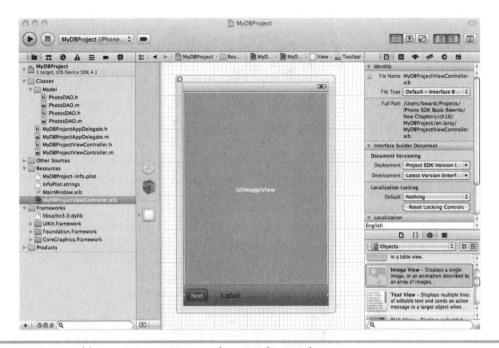

Figure 16-4   Adding a UIImageView and a UIToolBar to the view's canvas

Figure 16-5   Running the application (first image)   *(continued)*

Figure 16-6 Running the application (second image)

NOTE
You would normally never load an entire database at once in a real application, especially when using large blobs, like this example. Memory is limited in an iOS device—only load what you need when you need it.

The Model-View-Controller
When writing a program for any platform, you should adhere to the MVC design pattern as closely as possible. Rather than placing the database logic in a view or view controller, you created separate classes, insulating the view and controller layers from the database layer. The MyDBProjectViewController knows nothing about the underlying SQLite3 library; the view controller only knows about PhotosDAO and PhotoDAO. Notice you further separated the code by placing it in its own group, Model, under Classes. All this separation makes debugging and maintaining the program easier. It also makes reading and understanding this chapter's example code easier.

Opening the Database

To keep the task's length manageable and focused, rather than creating several data access methods in PhotosDAO, you only created one.

```
- (NSMutableArray *) getAllPhotos;
```

This method returns an array of PhotoDAO objects. The getAllPhotos method first finds the database and opens it. Because the database is in the resources folder, you can access it directly using the bundle's resourcePath. (When you want to create an application that uses canned [predefined] data, this task illustrated how to create that data in advance [using SQLite Manager in Firefox] and then embed it in your application.)

```
NSFileManager *fileManager = [NSFileManager defaultManager];
NSString *theDBPath = [[[NSBundle mainBundle] resourcePath]
stringByAppendingPathComponent: @"myDatabase.sqlite"];
```

After obtaining the database's path, you open it.

```
if (!(sqlite3_open([theDBPath UTF8String], &database) == SQLITE_OK))
```

Notice that you obtain the UTF8String from the NSString before passing the sqlite3_open method the path. Since opening the database is a common activity, you might want to move that portion of the code into its own method for easy reuse.

Querying the Data

After opening the database, you query it for the photo records. If you have ever worked with a database using code, for instance, Java Database Connectivity (JDBC), then this code should look familiar. The getAllPhotos method first creates the SQL select string. Next, the method places the string in a statement and then queries the database. After obtaining the data, getAllPhotos loops through each record.

For each new record, getAllPhotos creates a new PhotoDAO. The newly created PhotoDAO object's values are then set to the appropriate values from the current record. After initializing the PhotoDAO object, getAllPhotos places the object into PhotosDAO's photosArray.

Loading a Blob into NSData

This code snippet is useful. It shows you a quick, easy way to load a blob, any blob, into an NSData object. First, load the blob into a C string.

```
const char * rawData = sqlite3_column_blob(statement, 2);
```

Second, obtain the blob's byte size.

```
int rawDataLength = sqlite3_column_bytes(statement, 2);
```

Third, create an NSData class using the C string and size variables.

```
NSData *data = [NSData dataWithBytes:rawData length:rawDataLength];
```

As you already know the database blob is an image, you initialize the PhotoDAO's photo property using the UIImage's initWithData method.

```
aPhoto.photo = [[UIImage alloc] initWithData:data];
```

This same technique works for other binary data as well (replacing UIImage with the appropriate class).

Closing the Database

When finished using a statement, you release its resources by finalizing the statement.

```
if(sqlite3_finalize(statement) != SQLITE_OK)
```

After you no longer need the database, you close it.

```
if (sqlite3_close(database) != SQLITE_OK)
```

Selecting all records only has limited value. Rarely will you use SQL statements where you do not wish to limit the results returned. For this, you typically add parameters to your SQL statements and then replace the parameters with values in your program. This is called binding your program's values to the statements' parameters. Programs usually also allow more than simply selecting data; most applications allow users to add, edit, and delete records. In the next section, you learn about binding, inserting, updating, and deleting records.

SQLite Binding, Inserting, Updating, and Deleting

SQL allows limiting data to only the data needed via the where clause. For instance, the following statement only selects records whose age column is greater than 30.

```
select * from mytable where age > 30
```

When placing SQL statements like this into a SQLite statement, you can parameterize the where clause's value. For instance, to parameterize age's value, write the following code.

```
select * from mytable where age > ?
```

You then bind your program's value to the SQL statement's parameter.

Binding

You bind one of your program's values to a SQL statement's parameter using a bind method (Listing 16-12). Different data types have different bind methods.

Listing 16-12 SQLite bind methods (from the SQLite online documentation)

```
int sqlite3_bind_blob(sqlite3_stmt*, int, const void*, int n,
void(*)(void*));
int sqlite3_bind_double(sqlite3_stmt*, int, double);
```

```
int sqlite3_bind_int(sqlite3_stmt*, int, int);
int sqlite3_bind_int64(sqlite3_stmt*, int, sqlite3_int64);
int sqlite3_bind_null(sqlite3_stmt*, int);
int sqlite3_bind_text(sqlite3_stmt*, int, const char*, int n,
     void(*)(void*));
int sqlite3_bind_text16(sqlite3_stmt*, int, const void*, int,
     void(*)(void*));
int sqlite3_bind_value(sqlite3_stmt*, int, const sqlite3_value*);
int sqlite3_bind_zeroblob(sqlite3_stmt*, int, int n);
```

NOTE
Bindings start with 1 rather than 0.

For instance, the following code snippet shows a SQL statement and its subsequent binding (without the error checking shown).

```
const char * select = "Select * from photos where name = ?";
sqlite3_stmt *select_statement;
sqlite3_prepare_v2(database, select, -1, &select_statement, NULL);
sqlite3_bind_text(&select_statement, 1, [photo.name UTF8String], -1,
SQLITE_TRANSIENT);
```

The first argument is a pointer to the prepared statement. The second argument is the SQL statement's parameter number. The third argument is the value that should be bound to the SQL statement's parameter. The fourth argument is the number of bytes in the value—if negative, the length is automatically determined from the C string.

Insert, Update, and Delete
There is little difference between the steps for inserting, updating, or deleting records using the SQLite C library. The primary difference is you only call the sqlite3_step method once. Usually, you use insert, update, or delete with bindings. For instance,

```
insert into customers (name, age, company, location) values (?, ?, ?, ?);
```

or

```
update customers set location = ? where company = ?;
```

or

```
delete customers where company = ?;
```

In the following task, you insert, update, and delete a record.

Try This Inserting, Updating, and Deleting Records

1. Open the MyDBProject project in Xcode.

2. Add a class method named moveDatabase to PhotosDAO. Remember, a class method uses a plus rather than a minus.

3. Implement the method in PhotosDAO.m as in Listing 16-13.

Listing 16-13   The moveDatabase and getAllPhotos methods

```
+ (void) moveDatabase {
  NSFileManager *fileManager = [NSFileManager defaultManager];
  NSString *theDBPath = [[[NSBundle mainBundle] resourcePath]
        stringByAppendingPathComponent:@"myDatabase.sqlite"];
  NSError *error;
  BOOL success;
  NSArray * paths =
        NSSearchPathForDirectoriesInDomains(NSDocumentDirectory,
                          NSUserDomainMask, YES);
  NSString * docsDir = [paths objectAtIndex:0];
  NSString * newPath =
        [docsDir stringByAppendingPathComponent:@"myDatabase.sqlite"];
  [fileManager removeItemAtPath:newPath error: &error];
  success = [fileManager copyItemAtPath:theDBPath
                      toPath:newPath error: &error];
  if (!success) {
    NSLog(@"Failed to copy database...error handling here %@.",
                  [error localizedDescription]);
  }
}

- (NSMutableArray *) getAllPhotos {
  NSMutableArray * photosArray = [[NSMutableArray alloc] init];
  @try {
    NSFileManager *fileManager = [NSFileManager defaultManager];
    NSArray * paths = NSSearchPathForDirectoriesInDomains
    (NSDocumentDirectory, NSUserDomainMask, YES);
    NSString * docsDir = [paths objectAtIndex:0];
    NSString * theDBPath = [docsDir stringByAppendingPathComponent:
                        @"myDatabase.sqlite"];
    BOOL success = [fileManager fileExistsAtPath:theDBPath];
    if (!success) {
      NSLog(@"Failed to find database file '%@'.");
    }
```

```
    if (!(sqlite3_open([theDBPath UTF8String], &database) ==
                            SQLITE_OK)) {
      NSLog(@"An error opening database, handle error here.");
    }
    const char *sql = "SELECT id,name,photo FROM photos";
    sqlite3_stmt *statement;
    if (sqlite3_prepare_v2(database, sql, -1, &statement, NULL) !=
                            SQLITE_OK) {
      NSLog(@"Error, failed to prepare statement, handle error here.");
    }
    while (sqlite3_step(statement) == SQLITE_ROW) {
      PhotoDAO * aPhoto = [[PhotoDAO alloc] init];
      aPhoto.photoID = sqlite3_column_int(statement, 0);
      aPhoto.name = [NSString stringWithUTF8String:(char *)
                                sqlite3_column_text(statement, 1)];
      const char * rawData = sqlite3_column_blob(statement, 2);
      int rawDataLength = sqlite3_column_bytes(statement, 2);
      NSData *data = [NSData dataWithBytes:rawData length:
                        rawDataLength];
      aPhoto.photo = [[UIImage alloc] initWithData:data];
      [photosArray addObject:aPhoto];
    }
    if(sqlite3_finalize(statement) != SQLITE_OK){
      NSLog(@"Failed to finalize data statement, error handling here.");
    }
    if (sqlite3_close(database) != SQLITE_OK) {
      NSLog(@"Failed to close database, error handling here.");
    }
  } @catch (NSException *e) {
    NSLog(@"An exception occurred: %@", [e reason]);
    return nil;
  }
  return photosArray;
}
```

4. Modify the getAllPhotos method in PhotosDAO to obtain the records from the documents directory (Listing 16-13).

5. Open MYDBProjectViewController.m and add a call to the moveDatabase method to the first line of viewDidLoad (Listing 16-14).

(continued)

Listing 16-14 The viewDidLoad method

```
- (void)viewDidLoad {
  [PhotosDAO moveDatabase];
  PhotosDAO * myPhotos = [[PhotosDAO alloc] init];
  self.photos = [myPhotos getAllPhotos];
  [self.theImageView setImage:((PhotoDAO *)[self.photos
objectAtIndex:0]).photo];
  [self.theLabel setText:((PhotoDAO *)
      [self.photos objectAtIndex:0]).name];
  [myPhotos release];
  [super viewDidLoad];
}
```

The first thing you did was make the database writable. The Resources folder is read-only. Saving changes requires the database to be writable, so you copied the database to your documents directory. You also modified the getAllPhotos method so that it obtained the database from the application's document directory rather than the resources directory.

Try This Inserting Records

1. Add any photo from your computer to the project's Resources group and remember the photo's name so that you can use it later in the addThirdPhoto method.

2. Add a new method to PhotosDAO called addPhoto. Implement the method (Listing 16-15).

Listing 16-15 The addPhoto method

```
- (void) addPhoto : (PhotoDAO *) photo {
  const char * sql = "insert into photos (name, photo) values (?, ?)";
  sqlite3_stmt *insert_statement = nil;
  NSArray * paths = NSSearchPathForDirectoriesInDomains
      (NSDocumentDirectory, NSUserDomainMask, YES);
  NSString * docsDir = [paths objectAtIndex:0];
  NSString * thePath = [docsDir stringByAppendingPathComponent:
      @"myDatabase.sqlite"];
  sqlite3_open([thePath UTF8String], &database);
  sqlite3_prepare_v2(database, sql, -1, &insert_statement, NULL);
  sqlite3_bind_text(insert_statement, 1, [photo.name UTF8String], -1,
```

```
        SQLITE_TRANSIENT);
    NSData * binData = UIImagePNGRepresentation(photo.photo);
    sqlite3_bind_blob(insert_statement, 2, [binData bytes],
            [binData length], SQLITE_TRANSIENT);
    sqlite3_step(insert_statement);
    sqlite3_finalize(insert_statement);
    sqlite3_close(database);
}
```

3. Create a new IBAction in MyDBProjectViewController called addThirdPhoto (Listing 16-16).

Listing 16-16   The addThirdPhoto IBAction

```
- (IBAction) addThirdPhoto: (id) sender {
    static BOOL wasAdded;
    if (!wasAdded) {
      PhotosDAO * myPhotos = [[PhotosDAO alloc] init];
      PhotoDAO * aPhoto = [[PhotoDAO alloc] init];
      // Use the name of your photo in the next line
      NSString * imgPath = [[[NSBundle mainBundle] resourcePath]
            stringByAppendingPathComponent:@"photo3.png"];
      aPhoto.name = @"Another Photo";
      aPhoto.photo = [[UIImage alloc] initWithContentsOfFile:imgPath];
      [myPhotos addPhoto:aPhoto];
      [self.photos release];
      self.photos = [myPhotos getAllPhotos];
      [myPhotos release];
      wasAdded = YES;
    }
}
```

4. Save your changes and open MyDBProjectViewController.xib and add a new Bar Button item to the toolbar. Change the bar button's title to Add.

5. Connect the addThirdPhoto action to the Add button.

6. Save your changes and click Run to view the application in the iPhone Simulator (Figure 16-7).

(continued)

Figure 16-7   Running the application with an add button

The addPhoto method (Listing 16-15) allows new photos to be inserted. To keep this example simple, the add button invokes the addThirdPhoto method that merely gets the photo from your resources group. The addPhoto method first creates a SQL string with parameters. The method then replaces the question marks by binding them to the appropriate value. For instance, the name column is text, so addPhoto binds it to a C string. The UIImage is binary, so it is bound to a blob. After binding, addPhoto then inserts the record by calling the sqlite3_step method. This method is called only once, as no data is returned from the insert statement. Notice, for brevity, an examination of the return code is omitted, as is other error handling from Listing 16-6 forward.

Try This   Updating Records

1. Return to the Xcode project.

2. Add another photo to your Resources folder and remember its name to use in the changePhotosImage method added in Step 5.

3. Add a new NSInteger called currentID to MyDBProjectViewController.m. Change the changeImage method to update this new variable with the current photo's id from the database (Listing 16-17).

Listing 16-17 The currentID variable, and modified changeImage

```
NSInteger currentID = 0;
- (IBAction) changeImage: (id) sender {
  static NSInteger currentElement = 0;
  if(++currentElement == [self.photos count])
    currentElement = 0;
  PhotoDAO * aPhoto = (PhotoDAO *)
          [self.photos objectAtIndex: currentElement];
  currentID = aPhoto.photoID;
  [self.theLabel setText:aPhoto.name];
  [self.theImageView setImage:aPhoto.photo];
}
```

4. Add a new method called changeAPhotoImage to PhotosDAO (Listing 16-18).

Listing 16-18 The changeAPhotoImage method

```
- (void) changeAPhotoImage: (UIImage *) image theID: (NSInteger) photoID {
  const char * sql = "update photos set photo = ? where id = ?";
  sqlite3_stmt *update_statement = nil;
  NSArray * paths = NSSearchPathForDirectoriesInDomains(NSDocumentDirectory,
                    NSUserDomainMask, YES);
  NSString * docsDir = [paths objectAtIndex:0];
  NSString * thePath =
      [docsDir stringByAppendingPathComponent:@"myDatabase.sqlite"];
  sqlite3_open([thePath UTF8String], &database);
  sqlite3_prepare_v2(database, sql, -1, &update_statement, NULL);
  NSData * binData = UIImagePNGRepresentation(image);
  sqlite3_bind_blob(update_statement, 1, [binData bytes],
        [binData length],SQLITE_TRANSIENT);
  sqlite3_bind_int(update_statement, 2, photoID);
  sqlite3_step(update_statement);
  sqlite3_finalize(update_statement);
  sqlite3_close(database);
}
```

5. Add a new IBAction called changePhotosImage to MyDBProjectViewController
   (Listing 16-19). Save your changes.

(continued)

Listing 16-19 The changePhotosImage method

```
-(IBAction) changePhotosImage: (id) sender {
  PhotosDAO * myPhotos = [[PhotosDAO alloc] init];
  NSString * imgPath = [[[NSBundle mainBundle] resourcePath]
      stringByAppendingPathComponent:@"photo4.png"];
  [myPhotos changeAPhotoImage:[[UIImage alloc] initWithContentsOfFile:
      imgPath] theID: currentID];
  [self.photos release];
  self.photos = [myPhotos getAllPhotos];
  [myPhotos release];
}
```

6. Open MyDBProjectViewController.xib and add another bar button to the toolbar. Change the button's title to Change.

7. Connect the changePhotosImage action to the Change button.

8. Save and exit Interface Builder. Click Build And Go to run the application in the iPhone Simulator (Figure 16-8).

Figure 16-8 Changing the image

Updating a record is as straightforward as inserting it. The changeAPhotoImage first creates a SQL string with parameters. It then binds a file's binary data to photo and an integer to id. After binding, it then calls the step function once, finalizes the statement, and closes the database. Notice that updating requires the record's id, as SQLite uses the id to update the correct record. To accommodate this requirement, you added a currentID variable and changed the changeImage method to set the currentID with the currently selected photo record.

Try This Deleting Records

1. Quit the application and return to Xcode.

2. Add a new method called deletePhoto to PhotosDAO (Listing 16-20).

Listing 16-20   The deletePhoto method in PhotosDAO

```
- (void) deletePhoto: (NSInteger) photoID {
  const char * sql = "delete from photos where id = ?";
  sqlite3_stmt *delete_statement = nil;
  NSArray * paths = NSSearchPathForDirectoriesInDomains(NSDocumentDirectory,
      NSUserDomainMask, YES);
  NSString * docsDir = [paths objectAtIndex:0];

  NSString * thePath = [docsDir stringByAppendingPathComponent:
      @"myDatabase.sqlite"];
  sqlite3_open([thePath UTF8String], &database);
  sqlite3_prepare_v2(database, sql, -1, &delete_statement, NULL);
  sqlite3_bind_int(delete_statement, 1, photoID);
  sqlite3_step(delete_statement);
  sqlite3_finalize(delete_statement);
  sqlite3_close(database);
}
```

3. Create a new IBAction called deletePhoto to MyDBProjectViewController (Listing 16-21).

Listing 16-21   The deletePhoto IBAction in MyDBProjectViewController

```
- (IBAction) deletePhoto : (id) sender {
  PhotosDAO * myPhotos = [[PhotosDAO alloc] init];
  [myPhotos deletePhoto:currentID];
  [self.photos release];
  self.photos = [myPhotos getAllPhotos];
  currentElement = 0;
  [myPhotos release];
}
```

(continued)

4. Move the static NSInteger currentElement from the changeImage method in Listing 16-11 to just below the currentID variable (Listing 16-22). Remove the static qualifier.

Listing 16-22 Placing currentElement at the class's top so it's shared in the class

```
@implementation MyDBProjectViewController
@synthesize photos;
@synthesize theImageView;
@synthesize theLabel;
NSInteger currentID = 0;
NSInteger currentElement = 0;
```

5. Save your changes and open MyDBProjectViewController.xib.

6. Add another button to the toolbar and change its title to Delete.

7. Resize the image and move the label to above the toolbar, as you are running out of space on the toolbar (Figure 16-9).

8. Connect the button to the deletePhoto action.

9. Click Run and try deleting a photo.

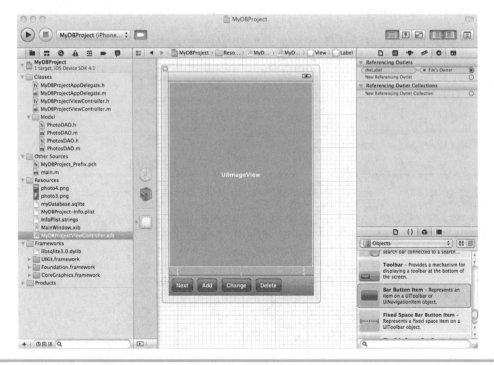

Figure 16-9 The MyDBProjectViewController view's canvas

The delete statement follows the same pattern as insert and update. The only real difference is the SQL string.

```
const char * sql = "delete from photos where id = ?";
```

Summary

If your application needs to store and retrieve complex object hierarchies, you'll want to consider using CoreData, which we'll be covering in the next chapter. However, for simple data storage needs, or for a database that you can use in a non-iOS application, SQLite is an efficient, powerful solution.

This chapter covered all of the basics for adding a database to your application. You learned how to create a new database, embed it in your application and retrieve values from the database. Then you learned how to make the database writable and implement insert, update, and delete operations.

If you do much programming for iOS, you will quickly find that all but the simplest applications need to store data. For that reason, the techniques that you learned in this chapter are very important. You will need to understand and master the techniques of this chapter or the next one on CoreData if you're going to do any significant iOS development.

Chapter 17

Core Data

Key Skills & Concepts

● Understanding Core Data's basics

● Creating a Core Data model

● Understanding how to load, fetch, and save a model's data

● Building a complex navigation-based application using Core Data

● Knowing where to obtain more Core Data information

With its addition to the iOS SDK, Core Data is arguably the best choice for persisting an application's data. It is more robust than using properties and is easier than using SQLite. You can visually lay out your application's data model, much as you would when using a database-modeling tool. Moreover, it provides the infrastructure for managing the objects you create, freeing you from writing the typical object management code. As this chapter will demonstrate, using Core Data is a natural choice for persisting an application's data. Core Data allows you to focus on the application rather than on the code persisting the application's data.

In previous chapters, the Try This examples were generally very small applications that illustrated a single concept but would never be mistaken for a full iOS application that you might find in the App Store. In this chapter, we're going to build a more complex reference application. By the end of this chapter, you'll have a fairly useful application that, while not quite ready for the App Store, just needs a little more data and some polish. In Chapter 19 we'll take the result of this chapter and turn it into a universal application that will also run native on the iPad with its larger screen.

Since the application we are building will have several views and build on skills that you learned in earlier chapters, in the interest of readability, we will only provide complete in-line code listings where we are illustrating new functionality. Before getting started on this chapter, it will be helpful to download the DogBreeds-Final sample code for this chapter. With the completed sample application code handy, you can reference it when you're not sure how to do a particular step.

Core Data in Brief

Core Data is a framework used to easily manage an application's data objects. Core Data consists of managed object models, managed object contexts, and persistent data stores.

A managed object model contains an object graph. The object graph is a collection of objects and their relationships with one another. You create a graph using Xcode's data modeler. The data modeler is where you visually add entities and create relationships between them.

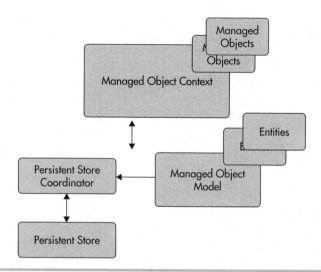

Figure 17-1 Core Data's architecture (simplified)

A managed object context contains the objects created from the entities in the managed object model. A managed object context has a persistent store coordinator that manages one or more persistent stores. A persistent data store persists objects created by the managed object context. Although an application can have multiple persistent stores, in this chapter, you restrict yourself to one persistent store. Figure 17-1 illustrates Core Data's architecture.

Creating a Model

A model contains entities. Entities contain attributes. Relationships model how one or more entities relate to one another. You model these concepts using Xcode's data modeler. You add a model to your application by creating a file with an .xcdatamodel extension through Xcode's New File dialog (Figure 17-2). It is best to place the model file in a new Models folder. After creating the model, when you select the file, Xcode should automatically display the data modeler in the Editor window.

Entities

Entities, represented by the NSEntityDescription class, are patterns describing NSManagedObject instances. NSManagedObjects are what you persist. For Core Data to know how to instantiate new object instances and persist the instances, it needs a pattern. Entities in the model provide those patterns. For instance, you might want to create a handy reference application that lists all of the American Kennel Club (AKC) dog breeds. The AKC divides all of the dog breeds into categories like "herding group" and "sporting group," so we'll need an AKCGroup class to represent these groups. Within each group there are a number of dog breeds, so we also have

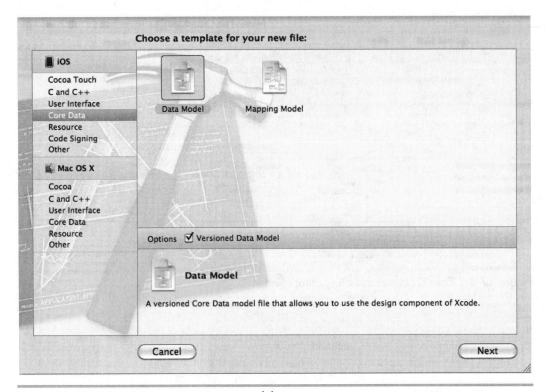

Figure 17-2 Creating a new Core Data model

a Breed class to represent the breeds. These straightforward Objective-C classes will be subclasses of NSManagedObject, and you tell Core Data how to persist them using entities.

Attributes
Entities tell Core Data which classes we will need to persist. In order to actually save objects in a persistent store and reconstitute them later, Core Data also needs to know what information must be saved for each object. Therefore, in our data model, entities have *attributes* that describe each of the properties that will need to be persisted.

Relationships
In all but the simplest of applications, there will also be relationships between the classes you define. For instance, each AKCGroup will contain one or more Breed objects and every Breed will be in exactly one group. The objects were modeled with entities, and how they are interrelated is modeled with relationships. Entities can have relationships with other entities. For instance, an apple and an orange are both types of fruit, a crate might hold one or more apples and oranges, and a fruit stand might contain one or more crates.

Try This Adding Entities and Relationships to a Core Data Model

Reference applications are particularly popular in the App Store. They typically contain hierarchical information that is easily viewed with a navigation-based iOS application. In fact, this pattern is so common that Xcode provides a template that creates a navigation-based application that is tied to a Core Data model. In this first task, you will first create a new navigation-based application and tell Xcode that it uses Core Data. Then you create the entities needed for a dog breeds reference application and add attributes and relationships. Later tasks will generate Objective-C classes that correspond to those entities, and then write the code to create, delete, and navigate those objects.

1. Create a new Navigation-based Application named **DogBreeds**. Be certain to select the Use Core Data check box (Figure 17-3). Xcode will create an almost functional Navigation-based Application with Core Data support, including a default xcdatamodel file.

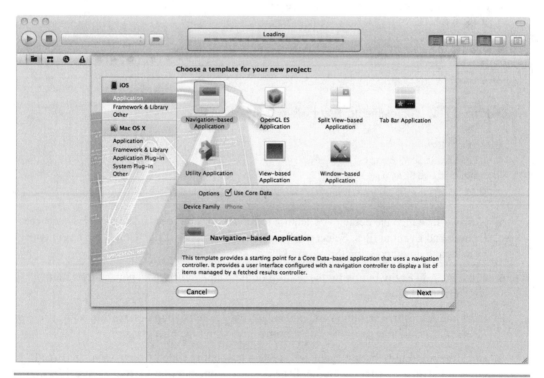

Figure 17-3 Creating a new Navigation-based Application

(continued)

2. The default xcdatamodel contains a single Event entity. If there were corresponding Event.h and Event.m class files for the Event entity, you would be able to run the new application that was just created. Fortunately, Xcode will create the class definition for you based on the attributes defined in the xcdatamodel. Select the Entity and then select Create NSManagedObject Subclass from the Editor menu.

3. Event.h and Event.m will be generated (Listings 17-1 and 17-2). Run the application. You will notice that you can create new "events" in the list, and edit the list to delete events. If you quit the application and later relaunch it, the events have all been persisted.

4. Take a few minutes to look at the generated source code for the AppDelegate and RootViewController and familiarize yourself with the methods that were automatically generated for you.

Listing 17-1 Definition of a simple Event class

```
#import <Cocoa/Cocoa.h>
@interface Event : NSManagedObject {
@private
}
@property (nonatomic, retain) NSDate * timeStamp;
@end
```

Listing 17-2 Implementation of a simple Event class

```
#import "Event.h"
@implementation Event
@dynamic timeStamp;
@end
```

---

5. Now we'll change the default application to reflect our dog breeds data model. Delete the Event.h and Event.m files. Select the DogBreeds.xcdatamodel file. Delete the Event entity by selecting it and pressing the DELETE key.

6. Click the Add Entity button (at the bottom of the pane) and create a new entity called **AKCGroup** (Figure 17-4).

7. Click the Add Attribute button and add an attribute called **groupDescription** with type String. Create another attribute called **name**, also with type String.

8. Click the Add Entity button again and create a new entity called **Breed**. Give the Breed entity three String attributes: **name**, **breedDescription**, and **photoURL** (Figure 17-5).

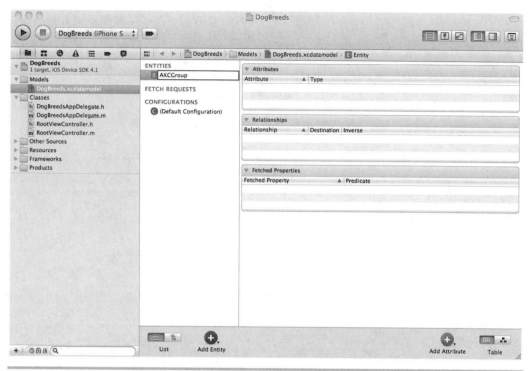

Figure 17-4   Adding the AKCGroup entity

9. With the Breed entity selected, click and hold on the Add Attribute button and select Add Relationship. Name the new relationship group and select AKCGroup from the Destination pull-down menu.

10. Select View I Utilities I Core Data Model to display the relationship details. Uncheck the Optional check box.

11. Select the AKCGroup entity and add a new relationship to it called **breeds**. Set its destination to Breed and Inverse to group. Select the To-Many Relationship check box and set the delete rule to Cascade (Figure 17-6).

12. Save the model. You are finished describing the objects we need to persist and how they relate to each other. Core Data will use this information to determine how and when to save your objects in an underlying SQLite database.

13. Now you need to create the underlying classes for the AKCGroup and Breed entities. Highlight AKCGroup and Breed and then select Editor I Create NSManagedObject Subclass from the main menu.

(continued)

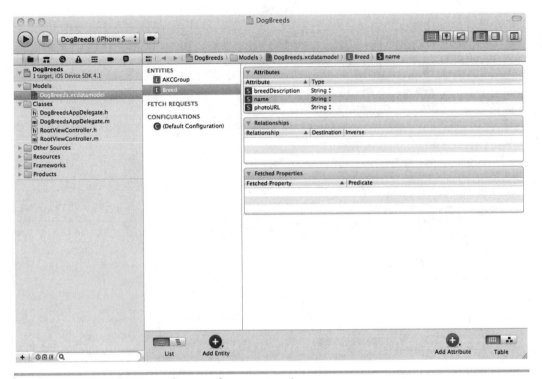

Figure 17-5 Breed entity with its attributes

14. Xcode will generate four files for you, Breed.h, Breed.m, AKCGroup.h, and AKCGroup.m, based on the entity descriptions we created earlier.

15. Select Breed.h and take a look at what was generated for you. You will notice that the Breed class has properties defined for each of the attributes in the entity. You will also notice that the Breed class doesn't contain instance variables for the properties. Instead, for Core Data managed classes, they are defined with the @dynamic directive in the implementation file.

NOTE

NSManagedObjects have no dealloc methods, as the Core Data framework manages their life cycle. Core Data is also responsible for generating NSManagedObjects' accessor methods at runtime.

16. Select the AKCGroup.h file and take a look at what was generated for you. There are properties for the two attributes and the relationship that we defined in the xcdatamodel file.

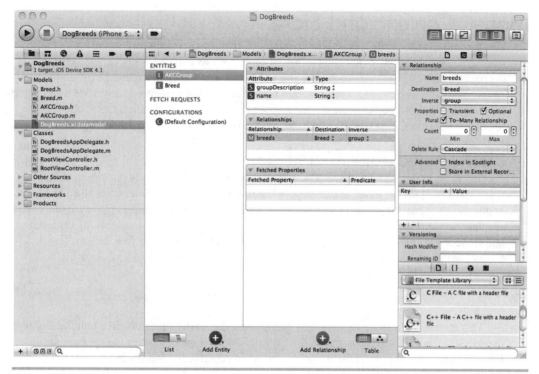

Figure 17-6 Relationship between AKCGroup and Breeds

17. We have changed the object model since you ran the default application in Step 2, so you need to completely delete the application from the iPhone Simulator so that the database containing the Event data will also be deleted. Otherwise, when you run the modified application in the next task, you will get an error because the model changed from Event entities to Breeds and AKCGroups.

Notice you specified that the relationship between AKCGroup and Breed has a Cascade Delete Rule. This rule informs the model that when an AKCGroup object is deleted, then any Breed objects that it references should also be deleted. Other delete rules you might specify include Nullify, Deny, and No Action.

NOTE
For more information on creating models using Xcode, refer to Apple's "Creating a Managed Object Model with Xcode."

Model, Context, and Store

The preceding task created the model used to create entities and their relationships in a managed object context. When an application runs, it needs a model instance, the context, and the persistent store. The persistent store and the model are largely transparent to you when coding your application. You simply obtain both these items and then set properties referencing them in the managed object context. Because we started from a navigation-based application template set to use Core Data, Xcode added code to create and manage these for us.

NSManagedObjectModel

As discussed earlier, an application's managed object model contains entities and their relationships. It serves as an application's schema by describing the entities used in an application's managed object context. Take a look at DogBreedsAppDelegate and you will see that Xcode added a property to the AppDelegate to hold the NSManagedObjectModel and an accessor method that creates the managedObjectModel on the first access. The easiest way to obtain the model is through the mergedModelFromBundles: class method.

```
managedObjectModel =
        [[NSManagedObjectModel mergedModelFromBundles: nil] retain];
```

This method creates a data model by merging all the models it finds into a bundle. Because the previous code specifies nil, the method simply finds all the models in the application's Resources folder and merges them into one NSManagedObjectModel instance.

NSPersistentStoreCoordinator

A persistent store coordinator coordinates one or more persistent stores and associates them with a managed object model. While the managed object model defines what gets persisted, the persistent store takes care of the low-level details of how and where the data is actually saved. Although advanced applications might have more than one persistent store, this chapter limits consideration to single-store applications. Core Data can persist data in several different ways. Store types you might use to persist data include NSSQLiteStoreType, NSBinaryStoreType, or NSInMemoryStoreType. For most purposes, you'll want to use a SQLite database for the Persistent Store and that is what Xcode created in the persistentStoreCoordinator accessor in DogBreedsAppDelegate.

```
NSURL *storeUrl =
        [NSURL fileURLWithPath:
        [[self applicationDocumentsDirectory]
        stringByAppendingPathComponent: @"DogBreeds.sqlite"]];
```

After obtaining the URL to the store, it creates an NSPersistentStoreCoordinator instance using the managed object model instance. The persistent store contains the data, while the model defines how to interpret that data.

```
persistentStoreCoordinator = [[NSPersistentStoreCoordinator alloc]
        initWithManagedObjectModel: [self managedObjectModel]];
```

```
NSError *error = nil;
[persistentStoreCoordinator
        addPersistentStoreWithType: NSSQLiteStoreType
        configuration: nil
        URL: storeUrl options:nil error:&error]
```

NSManagedObjectContext

The NSManagedObjectContext represents an application's managed object context, or the object instances (NSManagedObject classes) that your application is manipulating. Managed objects are fetched from the persistent store into the NSManagedObjectContext, and it is where you modify the objects. Apple describes the context as a big "scratch-pad" because no manipulations to a context are persisted until code explicitly tells the context to persist the changes.

Xcode added a managedObjectContext property to DogBreedsAppDelegate and an accessor that creates the context on first access. Obtain an application's managed context by allocating and initializing a new NSManagedObjectContext instance. You then set its persistent store coordinator.

```
managedObjectContext = [[NSManagedObjectContext alloc] init];
[managedObjectContext setPersistentStoreCoordinator: coordinator];
```

NSManagedObject

The NSManagedObjectContext manages NSManagedObject instances. NSManagedObjects are not entities, but rather, created from entities. An application obtains data from the persistent store and uses the entities in the model to create the NSManagedObjects placed in the context. Consider NSEntityDescriptions as the classes and NSManagedObjects as the objects.

The previous Try This task created entities in the xcdatamodel file. Although the NSManagedObjectModel uses these entities, the NSManagedObjectContext does not; it manages NSManagedObjects. Our AKCGroup and Breed classes are therefore subclasses of NSManagedObject.

NSFetchedResultsController

As a navigation-based application, the DogBreeds application will use a hierarchy of UITableViews to display our AKC groups and breeds. Displaying objects from Core Data in UITableViews is such a common task that iOS provides support for easily connecting fetched results to a table view. The NSFetchedResultsController object and NSFetchedResultsControllerDelegate protocol make it relatively easy to retrieve a set of objects from Core Data and modify the set as the user adds, deletes, and updates them via a table view.

NSFetchRequest

The NSFetchRequest class is how you query a persistent object store for its data. It uses an NSEntityDescription to know which entity to fetch. Listing 17-3 illustrates creation of an NSFetchRequest and an NSEntityDescription, and assigns the description to the request. The NSManagedObjectContext then executes the request and returns the matching objects in an NSArray.

Listing 17-3   NSFetchRequest example

```
NSFetchRequest * myRequest = [[NSFetchRequest alloc] init];
NSEntityDescription * entDesc = [NSEntityDescription
        entityForName:@"AKCGroup" inManagedObjectContext:myContext];
[myRequest setEntity:entDesc];
NSError * error;
NSArray * fetchResults = [self.managedObjectContext
executeFetchRequest:myRequest
error:&error];
if(fetchResults == nil) {
  NSLog(@"an error occurred");
  [error release];
}
```

Notice Listing 17-3 selects all the AKCGroups in myContext. Unless you know there will always be a reasonable number of results, you will want to limit the results returned. One way you could do this is through the NSFetchRequest's fetchLimit property. This property limits the objects returned by a fetch request. However, this property does not distinguish which objects to exclude. Often, you will want to limit results to only objects meeting certain criteria. For instance, you might want all Breeds in a particular AKCGroup. The way you limit results based upon given criteria is through the NSPredicate class.

NSPredicate

The NSPredicate class restricts the data returned by an NSFetchRequest. It is similar to a SQL statement's WHERE clause. The easiest way to create a predicate is by using the predicateWithFormat class method.

```
+ (NSPredicate *)predicateWithFormat:(NSString *)format,
```

The code is similar to initializing an NSString with a format. You write the expression and include a substitution parameter, followed by one or more substitution values. For instance, you might create a predicate limiting Breeds to those with a particular group.

```
NSPredicate *groupFilter =
        [NSPredicate predicateWithFormat:
            @"group = %@", self.selectedGroup];
```

Notice the preceding predicate does not tell you which entity the predicate is associated with; to make the association, you set the entity and predicate in the same fetch request.

```
[myRequest setEntity:entDesc];
[myRequest setPredicate: groupFilter];
```

Predicates can have more than one item in the substitution list. For instance, you might create the following predicate:

```
NSPredicate * predicate = [NSPredicate predicateWithFormat:
@"group = %@ and hairLength like %@", self.selectedGroup, @"short"];
```

This predicate assigns a specific AKCGroup to the group value and short to the hairLength value. Notice the "like" keyword; there are many similarities between Apple's predicate syntax and SQL.

NOTE

Apple's predicate syntax is quite detailed. For more information on predicate syntax, see Apple's "Predicate Programming Guide."

NSSortDescriptor

By default, fetched objects are unsorted; sorting the objects requires an NSSortDescriptor instance. This class represents the sort order for a fetched object collection. The following statement creates and initializes an NSSortDescriptor that sorts AKCGroups in ascending order based upon their name:

```
NSSortDescriptor * myDesc = [[NSSortDescriptor alloc]
initWithKey:@"name" ascending:YES];
```

A request can have more than one sort descriptor, so you add your NSSortDescriptors to an NSArray and then add the array to the NSFetchRequest using its setSortDescriptors method if you want to sort by multiple values.

NOTE

Although the topic is not covered in this chapter, you can predefine fetch requests, predicates, and sort descriptors in an application's xcdatamodel file. Then at runtime, you can fetch those predefined objects from the data model and use them in your code.

If you take a look at the RootViewController class that Xcode automatically generated for us, you'll see a property to store the NSFetchedResultsController and an accessor that instantiates the controller the first time it's accessed. In the default template the accessor fetches Event objects, so our next task is to change it to retrieve and manipulate the AKCGroup objects at the top of our hierarchy.

Try This Fetching All AKCGroup Entities

1. Open DogBreeds in Xcode.

2. Open RootViewController.m and modify the NSEntityDescription to change it from Event to AKCGroup. Change the NSSortDescriptor to sort on name in ascending order and comment out the limit on the fetch, since we know there will never be more than a few AKC groups (Listing 17-4).

Listing 17-4 fetchedResultsController Accessor in RootViewController

```
- (NSFetchedResultsController *)fetchedResultsController {
  if (fetchedResultsController != nil) {
    return fetchedResultsController;
  }
  // Create the fetch request for the entity.
  NSFetchRequest *fetchRequest = [[NSFetchRequest alloc] init];
  // Edit the entity name as appropriate.
  NSEntityDescription *entity = [NSEntityDescription
          entityForName:@"AKCGroup"
          inManagedObjectContext:self.managedObjectContext];
  [fetchRequest setEntity:entity];
  // Set the batch size to a suitable number.
  //[fetchRequest setFetchBatchSize:20];
  // Edit the sort key as appropriate.
  NSSortDescriptor *sortDescriptor =
          [[NSSortDescriptor alloc] initWithKey:@"name"
ascending:YES];
  NSArray *sortDescriptors =
        [[NSArray alloc] initWithObjects:sortDescriptor, nil];
  [fetchRequest setSortDescriptors:sortDescriptors];
  NSFetchedResultsController *aFetchedResultsController =
  [[NSFetchedResultsController alloc]
        initWithFetchRequest:fetchRequest
        managedObjectContext:managedObjectContext
        sectionNameKeyPath:nil
        cacheName:@"Root"];
  aFetchedResultsController.delegate = self;
  self.fetchedResultsController = aFetchedResultsController;
  [aFetchedResultsController release];
  [fetchRequest release];
  [sortDescriptor release];
```

```
  [sortDescriptors release];
  NSError *error = nil;
  if (![[self fetchedResultsController] performFetch:&error]) {
    NSLog(@"Unresolved error %@, %@", error, [error userInfo]);
    abort();
  }
  return fetchedResultsController;
}
```

3. The default implementation of RootViewController also refers to the timestamp attribute of Event in a couple of places, so we'll need to change those references as well before we can run our application. Find the insertNewObject method in RootViewController and change it to set the AKCGroup name and groupDescription instead of the Event's timestamp (Listing 17-5).

Listing 17-5   insertNewObject in RootViewController

```
- (void)insertNewObject {
  // Create a new instance of the entity managed by the
  // fetched results controller.
  NSManagedObjectContext *context =
      [fetchedResultsControllermanagedObjectContext];
  NSEntityDescription *entity =
      [[fetchedResultsController fetchRequest] entity];
  NSManagedObject *newManagedObject =
      [NSEntityDescription insertNewObjectForEntityForName:
      [entity name] inManagedObjectContext:context];
  [newManagedObject setValue:@"A new group" forKey:@"name"];
  [newManagedObject setValue:@"Description of group"
      forKey:@"groupDescription"];
  // Save the context.
  NSError *error = nil;
  if (![context save:&error]) {
    // Replace this implementation with code to
    // handle the error appropriately.
    NSLog(@"Unresolved error %@, %@", error, [error userInfo]);
    abort();
  }
}
```

4. Modify the configureCell method in RootViewController so that it displays the AKCGroup's name and description in the cell instead of the timestamp from the Event entity (Listing 17-6).

(continued)

Listing 17-6 configureCell in RootViewController

```
- (void)configureCell:(UITableViewCell *)cell
        atIndexPath:(NSIndexPath *)indexPath {
  NSManagedObject *managedObject = [self.fetchedResultsController
        objectAtIndexPath:indexPath];
  cell.textLabel.text = [managedObject valueForKey:@"name"];
  cell.detailTextLabel.text = [managedObject
        valueForKey:@"groupDescription"];
}
```

5. Save your changes and run the application. Notice that with hardly any effort, you now have an application that displays a list of AKCGroups and lets you add and delete groups from that list (Figure 17-7).

Figure 17-7 Adding and deleting AKCGroups

Adding Objects

All objects managed by a managed object context are NSManagedObject instances. NSManagedObject is a class that implements the required behavior for a Core Data model object. You do not create NSManagedObject instances, but rather subclasses. These subclasses are usually created from the entities defined in an xcdatamodel file.

The easiest way to create a new managed object is through the NSEntityDescription's class method, insertNewObjectForEntityForName:inManagedObjectContext.

```
+ (id)insertNewObjectForEntityForName:(NSString *) entityName
inManagedObjectContext:(NSManagedObjectContext *) context
```

This method obtains an entity from the model, creates a new NSManagedObject based upon the entity, and inserts it in the current managed object context. For instance, the following code from insertNewObject in Listing 17-5 creates a new AKCGroup from the AKCGroup entity used in this chapter's xcdatamodel file:

```
AKCGroup * newGroup = (AKCGroup *) [NSEntityDescription
        insertNewObjectForEntityForName: @"AKCGroup"
        inManagedObjectContext:self.managedObjectContext];
```

After inserting a new object, you can then set its properties, just as if it were a normal object. The following code sets the newly created AKCGroup's name:

```
newGroup.name = @"A new group";
```

Saving Changes

An application's managed object context does not automatically save changes to a model's data. You must manually save the context to persist changes. For instance, when an application is suspended or terminates, you might want to check the context for changes and, if there were changes, save them.

```
if ([managedObjectContext hasChanges] && ![managedObjectContext
save:&error])
```

The context saves changes using its save method. This method persists the context's changes to its associated persistent data store. The method takes an error as a parameter and returns a Boolean indicating success or failure.

```
- (BOOL)save:(NSError **) error
```

You can also roll back all changes to a context using the rollback method. This method removes everything from something called the undo stack and removes all insertions and deletions, and restores all context-managed objects to their original state.

NOTE

An NSManagedObjectContext can have an NSUndoManager instance assigned to its undoManager property. An NSUndoManager manages undoing actions. When using Core Data, you can use this class to undo changes made to an application's NSManagedModelContext. For more information, refer to the NSUndoManager Class Reference.

Deleting Entities

You use the NSManagedObjectContext's deleteObject method to delete objects from an application's managed object context. This method takes an NSManagedObject instance of the object to delete. For instance, the default code in tableView:commitEditingStyle deletes an AKCGroup for us with the following code:

```
    NSManagedObjectContext *context = [self.fetchedResultsController
managedObjectContext];
    [context deleteObject:[self.fetchedResultsController
objectAtIndexPath:indexPath]];
    // Save the context.
    NSError *error = nil;
    if (![context save:&error]) {
        NSLog(@"Unresolved error %@, %@", error, [error userInfo]);
        abort();
    }
```

Note that the managed object context marks the particular AKCGroup for deletion with the deleteObject call, but it doesn't make the actual change to the persistent store until you call the context's save method.

Updating Entities

Modifying an object from a managed object context is as easy as simply changing its properties and then saving the context. In the next task we'll create a subview for editing an AKCGroup, and when the user taps the Done button, we'll just update the properties of the group from the fields in the view and then save the context with code like the following.

```
self.group.name = nameField.text;
self.group.groupDescription = groupDescriptionField.text;
NSError *error = nil;
if (![self.group.managedObjectContext save:&error]) {
    // Be sure to handle any errors
}
```

Try This Adding Navigation and AKCGroup Editing

1. Open DogBreeds in Xcode.

2. The Xcode template automatically created an Edit button on the left and an Add button on the right for us. Since we're going to eventually extend our application to have another level of navigation (select a group to see all of the breeds in that group), we will need to use the left button for returning back up a level. Open RootViewController.m and change the viewDidLoad method to put the Edit button on the right instead of the Add button (Listing 17-7). Also give the view an appropriate title.

Listing 17-7   viewDidLoad in RootViewController

```
- (void)viewDidLoad {
    [super viewDidLoad];
    // Set up the edit button.
    self.navigationItem.rightBarButtonItem = self.editButtonItem;
    self.title = @"AKC Groups";
}
```

3. When the user taps on the Edit button to edit the list of AKC groups, we want to display the Add button so that they can add new groups as well as delete or edit groups. When the user taps on the Edit button in a UITableView, a setEditing message is sent to the UITableView's delegate (our RootViewController), so we can implement that method and create or remove the Add button when they go into and out of the edit screen (Listing 17-8).

Listing 17-8   setEditing in RootViewController

```
- (void)setEditing:(BOOL)editing animated:(BOOL)animated {
    [super setEditing:editing animated:animated];
    //[tableView setEditing:editing animated:YES];
    if (editing) {
        UIBarButtonItem *addButton = [[UIBarButtonItem alloc]
initWithBarButtonSystemItem:UIBarButtonSystemItemAdd target:self
action:@selector(insertNewObject)];
        self.navigationItem.leftBarButtonItem = addButton;
        [addButton release];
    } else {
        self.navigationItem.leftBarButtonItem = nil;
    }
}
```

(continued)

Figure 17-8 AKCGroups table in editing mode

4. Save your changes and run the application. Notice that the Add button now shows up after we've started to edit the group list, but it still works the way it did before (Figure 17-8).

5. Now we need to create a new view to actually edit the AKCGroup's properties. Add an IBOutlet for the new view in RootViewController.h (Listing 17-9). Don't forget to synthesize the property in RootViewController.m and release it in the dealloc method.

Listing 17-9 RootViewController.h

```
#import <UIKit/UIKit.h>
#import <CoreData/CoreData.h>
@class AKCGroupViewController;
@interface RootViewController : UITableViewController
<NSFetchedResultsControllerDelegate> {
```

```
NSFetchedResultsController *fetchedResultsController;
    NSManagedObjectContext *managedObjectContext;
    AKCGroupViewController *groupEditorVC;
}

@property (nonatomic, retain) NSFetchedResultsController
*fetchedResultsController;
@property (nonatomic, retain) NSManagedObjectContext
*managedObjectContext;
@property (nonatomic, retain) IBOutlet AKCGroupViewController
*groupEditorVC;
@end
```

6. Create a new UIViewController subclass called AKCGroupViewController with an XIB file. Edit the header file and add IBOutlets for the name and groupDescription fields. Also add properties to store the AKCGroup that we're editing and whether or not it's a group insertion (Listing 17-10).

Listing 17-10   AKCGroupViewController.h

```
#import <UIKit/UIKit.h>
@class AKCGroup;
@interface AKCGroupViewController : UIViewController <UITextFieldDelegate,
UITextViewDelegate> {
    AKCGroup *group;
    UITextField *nameField;
    UITextView *groupDescriptionField;
BOOL insertingGroup;
}
@property(nonatomic, retain) IBOutlet UITextField *nameField;
@property(nonatomic, retain) IBOutlet UITextView *groupDescriptionField;
@property(nonatomic, retain) AKCGroup *group;
@property(nonatomic, assign) BOOL insertingGroup;
@end
```

7. Select AKCGroupViewController.xib and add a label and text field for the group name and a label and text view for the description. Connect them to the IBOutlets you created in Step 6 (Figure 17-9).

8. Open RootViewController.xib, create a new view controller, set its class to AKCGroupViewController, and set it to load from that nib. Connect the groupEditorVC outlet from the File's Owner to the new view. Select the table view and check the Allows Selection While Editing option. Save your changes.

(continued)

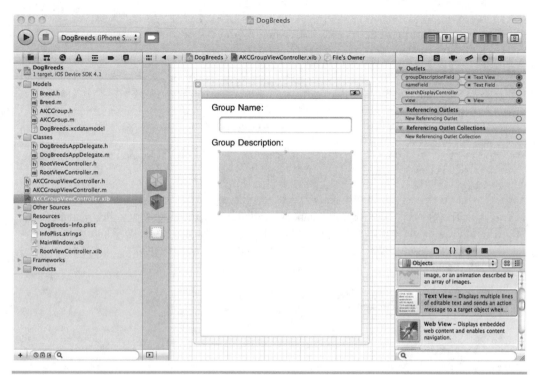

Figure 17-9 Outlets for AKCGroupViewController

9. Open AKCGroupViewController.m and in the viewWillAppear method copy the group name and description from the group to the fields we just created in the XIB file. In the viewDidLoad method you will need to create two navigation buttons: put a Done button on the right and a Cancel button on the left (Listing 17-11).

10. Implement a done method that will be called when the Done button is pressed. It should copy the name and description back into the group object, ask the managedObjectContext to save changes and then pop the view (Listing 17-11).

11. Implement a cancel method that pops the view without saving any changes. If the insertingGroup flag was set, then this was a new group and cancel should delete the group object and ask the managedObjectContext to save changes (Listing 17-11).

Listing 17-11 AKCGroupViewController.m

```
#import "AKCGroupViewController.h"
#import "AKCGroup.h"
@implementation AKCGroupViewController
```

```
@synthesize nameField;
@synthesize groupDescriptionField;
@synthesize group;
@synthesize insertingGroup;

- (void)viewWillAppear:(BOOL)animated {
    [super viewWillAppear:animated];
    self.nameField.text = self.group.name;
    self.groupDescriptionField.text = self.group.groupDescription;
}
- (void)viewDidLoad {
    [super viewDidLoad];
    UIBarButtonItem *doneButton = [[UIBarButtonItem alloc]
         initWithBarButtonSystemItem: UIBarButtonSystemItemDone
         target:self action:@selector(done)];
    self.navigationItem.rightBarButtonItem = doneButton;
    [doneButton release];
    UIBarButtonItem *cancelButton = [[UIBarButtonItem alloc]
         initWithBarButtonSystemItem:UIBarButtonSystemItemCancel
         target:self action:@selector(cancel)];
    self.navigationItem.leftBarButtonItem = cancelButton;
    [cancelButton release];
}
- (void)viewDidUnload {
    [super viewDidUnload];
    // Release any retained subviews of the main view.
    // e.g. self.myOutlet = nil;
}
- (void)done {
    self.group.name = nameField.text;
    [self.nameField resignFirstResponder];
    self.group.groupDescription = groupDescriptionField.text;
    [self.groupDescriptionField resignFirstResponder];
    NSError *error = nil;
    if (![self.group.managedObjectContext save:&error]) {
        // Be sure to handle any errors
    }
    [self.navigationController popViewControllerAnimated:YES];
}
- (void)cancel {
    [self.nameField resignFirstResponder];
    [self.groupDescriptionField resignFirstResponder];
    // If this was a new group that was created, then
    //cancel should get rid of the empty group from the database
```

(continued)

```
            if (insertingGroup == YES) {
                // Delete the managed object for the given index path
                NSManagedObjectContext *context = self.group.managedObjectContext;
                [context deleteObject:self.group];
                // Save the deletion
                NSError *error = nil;
                if (![context save:&error]) {
                    NSLog(@"Failed to save to data store: %@",
                            [error localizedDescription]);
                    NSArray* detailedErrors = [[error userInfo]
                                    objectForKey:NSDetailedErrorsKey];
                    if(detailedErrors != nil && [detailedErrors count] > 0) {
                        for(NSError* detailedError in detailedErrors) {
                            NSLog(@"  DetailedError: %@", [detailedError userInfo]);
                        }
                    }
                    else {
                        NSLog(@"  %@", [error userInfo]);
                    }
                    abort();
                }
            }
        }
        [self.navigationController popViewControllerAnimated:YES];
    }
    - (void)dealloc {
        [group release];
        [nameField release];
        [groupDescriptionField release];
        [super dealloc];
    }
    @end
```

12. Finally, we need to modify insertNewObject in RootViewController and add a few lines at the end to push the group editing view when the user inserts a new group.

```
    self.groupEditorVC.group = (AKCGroup *)newManagedObject;
    self.groupEditorVC.insertingGroup = YES;
    [self.navigationController pushViewController:self.groupEditorVC
    animated:YES];
```

13. When the user taps on a row in a UITableView, the didSelectRowAtIndexPath method is called. Modify that method in RootViewController so that when the user taps on a group while in editing mode, the group editing view is also pushed.

```
    - (void)tableView:(UITableView *)tableView didSelectRowAtIndexPath:
    (NSIndexPath *)indexPath {
        AKCGroup *theGroup = [[self fetchedResultsController]
```

```
objectAtIndexPath:indexPath];
    if (self.editing == YES) {
        self.groupEditorVC.group = theGroup;
        self.groupEditorVC.insertingGroup = NO;
        [self.navigationController pushViewController:
                            self.groupEditorVC animated:YES];
    }
}
```

14. Save all of your changes and run the application. When you put the group list into editing mode, you can now click a group to edit it. When you create a new AKCGroup, you're now immediately taken to the edit view (Figure 17-10). You can polish the view layout and some of the settings like field capitalization, but at this point you have a fairly functional application for manipulating a list of AKC groups.

Figure 17-10 Edit view for AKCGroup

Navigation

You now have a fairly complete application for displaying, adding, deleting, and editing a list of AKC groups. But the groups alone aren't too interesting. When the user taps on an AKC group while not in editing mode, she should see a new UITableView with all of the breeds within that group. Then if she taps on a breed in that list, she should see a detailed view of the breed with a photo and description.

The UITableView with the list of breeds within a group is going to be very similar to the list of AKC groups, so for the Try This task in this section you can largely copy the code from RootViewController and AKCGroupViewController and we will only highlight the differences.

Try This Adding Navigation and Editing
for a List of Breeds

1. Reopen DogBreeds in Xcode. If you have the DogBreeds-Final project downloaded, you might want to also open it so that you can easily refer to the final project if you are uncertain how to complete a step.

2. Using File | New File from the main menus, create a new subclass of UITableViewController (select the check boxes for a subclass of UITableViewController and create a xib file). Call it **BreedsListViewController**.

3. Edit BreedsListViewController.h and add a property to store which group was selected and IBOutlets for sub-views to edit a breed and display breed details. Also add properties for the fetchedResultsController and managedObjectStore like RootViewController. The class will also have to implement the NSFetchedResultsControllerDelegate protocol (Listing 17-12).

Listing 17-12 BreedsListViewController.h

```
#import <UIKit/UIKit.h>
@class AKCGroup;
@class BreedViewController;
@class BreedDetailViewController;
@interface BreedsListViewController :
                    UITableViewController
<NSFetchedResultsControllerDelegate> {
    AKCGroup *selectedGroup;
    BreedViewController *breedEditorVC;
    BreedDetailViewController *breedDetailVC;
    NSFetchedResultsController *fetchedResultsController;
    NSManagedObjectContext *managedObjectContext;
}
```

```
@property (nonatomic, retain) AKCGroup *selectedGroup;
@property (nonatomic, retain) IBOutlet BreedViewController
*breedEditorVC;
@property (nonatomic, retain) IBOutlet BreedDetailViewController
*breedDetailVC;
@property (nonatomic, retain) NSFetchedResultsController
*fetchedResultsController;
@property (nonatomic, retain) NSManagedObjectContext
*managedObjectContext;

@end
```

4. Open BreedsListViewController.m and synthesize the properties you added in Step 3 and be sure to release them in the dealloc method.

5. Copy the fetchedResultsController accessor and all of the NSFetchedResultsControllerDelegate methods from RootViewController, since we'll be fetching the Breed objects for the table in the same way as we did the AKCGroup objects in RootViewController. We do need to change the fetchedResultsController so that it retrieves Breed entities and only those entities in the selected group (using a predicate):

```
NSEntityDescription *entity =
        [NSEntityDescription entityForName:@"Breed"
        inManagedObjectContext:self.managedObjectContext];
[fetchRequest setEntity:entity];
NSPredicate *groupFilter = [NSPredicate predicateWithFormat:
        @"group = %@", self.selectedGroup];
[fetchRequest setPredicate:groupFilter];
```

6. Change viewDidLoad to add the Edit button just like RootViewController. Copy the numberOfSectionsInTableView, numberOfRowsInSection, cellForRowAtIndexPath, and configureCell methods unchanged from RootViewController. Change configureCell to only display the name. Save your changes.

7. Edit RootViewController and add an IBOutlet called breedsListVC for the BreedsListViewController. Modify didSelectRowAtIndexPath so that when not in editing mode, it initializes the new breeds list controller and pushes it onto the view stack:

```
else {
  self.breedsListVC.selectedGroup = theGroup;
  self.breedsListVC.title = theGroup.name;
  self.breedsListVC.managedObjectContext =
        self.managedObjectContext;
  [self.navigationController
        pushViewController:self.breedsListVC
        animated:YES];
}
```

(continued)

8. The BreedsListViewController object is created once, stored in the breedsListVC property of the RootViewController, and then reused as the user taps on different groups to view them. The fetchedResultsController accessor is designed to create the NSFetchedResultsController the first time and then just reuse it. This creates an interesting problem. The second time the user taps on a group, the didSelectRowAtIndexPath method in RootViewController changes the selected group in breedsListVC and changes the view's title. But the fetchedResultsController in BreedsListViewController has already fetched results, and it is simply reused. You can solve this problem by overriding the default setter for selectedGroup and making the other necessary changes within the view when the group changes (Listing 17-13).

Listing 17-13 Overriding the setter for selectedGroup

```
- (void)setSelectedGroup:(AKCGroup *)theGroup {
    if(theGroup != self.selectedGroup) {
        [self.selectedGroup release];
        selectedGroup = [theGroup retain];
        self.fetchedResultsController = nil;
        [self.tableView reloadData];
    }
}
```

9. Save your changes and select RootViewController.xib. Add a ViewController for BreedsListViewController, set its class and NIB, and connect it to the breedsListVC IBOutlet.

10. Save your changes and try running the application. You should be able to tap on an AKCGroup and switch to a new table view with the group's name as the title. The table is empty but would be displaying the breeds in that group if there were any. We can now navigate into and out of the AKC groups.

11. You can now implement the breed editing functionality exactly the same way we did it for the AKCGroup in RootViewController. You'll need to define a BreedViewController class that lets you edit the breed's name, photo URL, and description in exactly the same way you implemented AKCGroupViewController and change didSelectRowAtIndexPath to push it on the view stack when the user taps a row while in editing mode.

12. You will need to add an insertNewBreed method that is very similar to the insertNewAKCGroup method in RootViewController. However, in addition to creating the new Breed entity, it will also need to add it to the selected AKCGroup with addBreedsObject so that Core Data can maintain the relationship between them (Listing 17-14).

Listing 17-14   insertNewBreed in BreedsListViewController

```
- (void) insertNewBreed {

    NSManagedObjectContext *context = [self.fetchedResultsController
                                managedObjectContext];
    Breed *newBreed = [NSEntityDescription insertNewObjectForEntityForName:
                                @"Breed" inManagedObjectContext:context];
    [newBreed setValue:@"" forKey:@"name"];
    [newBreed setValue:@"" forKey:@"breedDescription"];
    [newBreed setValue:@"" forKey:@"photoURL"];
    [self.selectedGroup addBreedsObject:newBreed];

    NSError *error = nil;
    if (![context save:&error]) {
        NSLog(@"Unresolved error %@, %@", error, [error userInfo]);
        abort();
    }
    self.breedEditorVC.breed = newBreed;
    self.breedEditorVC.insertingBreed = YES;
    self.breedEditorVC.selectedGroup = self.selectedGroup;
    [self.navigationController pushViewController:self.breedEditorVC
animated:YES];
}
```

13. Select BreedViewController.xib and add labels and text fields for the breed name and photo
    URL. Add a label and text view for the description. Connect the fields to the IBOutlets
    in the File's Owner. Save your changes and then switch to BreedsListViewController.xib,
    add a view controller and change its class to BreedViewController, set it to load from the
    BreedViewController nib, and connect it to the breedEditorVC IBOutlet.

14. Save all of your changes and run the application. You can now add/edit/delete AKC
    groups, move in/out of AKC groups, and add/edit/delete breeds within any group
    (Figure 17-11). You're getting close to a completed application.

(continued)

Figure 17-11 Editing screens for AKCGroup and Breed

Try This Adding a Breed Detail View

1. Reopen DogBreeds in Xcode and create a new UIViewController subclass called BreedDetailViewController with a xib file.

2. Open BreedDetailViewController.h and add a property to store the selected breed. Add properties and IBOutlets for the breedDescription and photo (Listing 17-15). Save your changes and open BreedDetailViewController.m and synthesize the properties and release them in the dealloc method.

Listing 17-15 BreedDetailViewController.h

```
#import <UIKit/UIKit.h>
@class Breed;
```

```
@interface BreedDetailViewController : UIViewController {
    UITextView *breedDescription;
    UIImageView *photo;
    Breed *selectedBreed;
}
@property(nonatomic, retain) IBOutlet UITextView *breedDescription;
@property(nonatomic, retain) IBOutlet UIImageView *photo;
@property(nonatomic, retain) Breed *selectedBreed;
@end
```

3. Select BreedDetailViewController.xib and add UIImageView and UITextView objects. Connect them to the IBOutlets in the File's Owner.

4. Select BreedListViewController.xib and add a new View Controller object, change its class to BreedDetailViewController, and change its nib file attribute. Connect it to the breedDetailVC IBOutlet of the File's Owner object.

5. BreedDetailViewController.m only needs one small change. When the view will be displayed, we need to use the photo URL and actually retrieve the photo and display it in the UIImageView. iOS makes it easy to retrieve data from a URL and use it to create a UIImage (Listing 17-16).

Listing 17-16   viewWillAppear method in BreedDetailViewController.m

```
- (void)viewWillAppear:(BOOL)animated {
    [super viewWillAppear:animated];
    self.breedDescription.text = self.selectedBreed.breedDescription;
    NSURL* aURL = [NSURL URLWithString:self.selectedBreed.photoURL];
    NSData *imageData = [[NSData alloc] initWithContentsOfURL:aURL];
    UIImage *theImage = [[UIImage alloc] initWithData:imageData];
    [photo setImage:theImage];
    [theImage release];
}
```

6. Save all of your changes and run the application. If you create a couple of breeds with a valid photo URL, you will now be able to tap on a breed and see a description and photo.

7. Delete the DogBreeds application from the iPhone Simulator (which also deletes its Core Data database). Open and run the DogBreeds-Final project. You will find that it comes with all of the AKC groups defined and all of the dogs in the "Herding Group" complete with description and photo (Figure 17-12).

(continued)

Figure 17-12 Finished application with data

Distributing Core Data with Your App

By the end of this chapter you now have a fairly useful iOS application. It needs some more polish, maybe a few more fields in the Breed entity, some search functionality perhaps, but it's well on the way to being useful. However, no one is going to buy your reference application if they have to enter all of the reference material themselves! If you have a Core Data–based application, how do you fill it with useful information and then distribute that with the application in the App Store?

The first step is to get all of your information into Core Data. With the DogBreeds application, we built all of the editing functionality into the app, so to enter the data you could just run it in the iPhone Simulator and type or paste all of the information in to create the 9 AKC groups and 168 recognized breeds. All of that information is readily available in places like Wikipedia.

Of course, using the iPhone Simulator to enter all of the information for your reference application might start to get quite tedious. If the information you want to embed is available in a standard format (e.g., a csv file), you could also add a bit of temporary code to your application that looks for the file and imports it. If you will need to maintain the information over time and release periodic updates, then the easiest thing to do might be to create a Mac OS X application for editing the data. While the topic is beyond the scope of this book, you probably noticed that iOS (Cocoa Touch) and Cocoa for Mac OS X overlap. In particular, Core Data is not specific to iOS. If you want to build a simple desktop application with a few views for entering and editing your information, you can use exactly the same xcdatamodel file. Then you'll be able to directly use the Core Data persistent store database created by Mac OS X in your iOS application.

Once you've filled a Core Data persistent store database with your information, the next step is to find that database so that you can include it in your application's Resources folder for distribution. If you used the iPhone Simulator to enter your data, the easiest way to find that database is to set a breakpoint on the following line in the persistentStoreCoordinator accessor in DogBreedsAppDelegate:

```
NSURL *storeUrl = [NSURL fileURLWithPath:
        [[self applicationDocumentsDirectory]
        stringByAppendingPathComponent:@"DogBreeds.sqlite"]];
```

The storeURL variable will contain the full path to the persistent store for the iPhone Simulator on your development computer. Add that file to the Resources folder of your application so that it will be included in your application when it's built for distribution. If you created a separate Mac OS X application for editing your data, you can use a similar trick to find the database file from that application.

With the default database embedded in the Resources folder, you can make a minor change to the persistentStoreCoordinator accessor in DogBreedsAppDelegate so that the first time your application runs, it copies the default database to the Documents directory:

```
NSString *storePath = [[self applicationDocumentsDirectory]
        stringByAppendingPathComponent: @"DogBreeds.sqlite"];
    NSURL *storeUrl = [NSURL fileURLWithPath:storePath];

    // Copy the default db from resources
    // if it doesn't already exist in documents
    NSFileManager *fileManager = [NSFileManager defaultManager];
    if (![fileManager fileExistsAtPath:storePath]) {
        NSString *defaultStorePath = [[NSBundle mainBundle]
            pathForResource:@"DogBreeds" ofType:@"sqlite"];
        if (defaultStorePath) {
            [fileManager copyItemAtPath:defaultStorePath

                        toPath:storePath error:NULL];
        }
    }
```

The sample DogBreeds application for this chapter included editing functionality so that we could illustrate adding, deleting, and updating objects stored using Core Data. In a typical reference application you probably wouldn't include any editing functionality and the database could be read-only. If that is the case, then you could avoid copying the database to the Documents directory and just open it in the Resources directory (which is read-only).

If you downloaded the DogBreeds-Final project in the sample code for this chapter, you'll see that it includes a default database with some of the dog breeds in the herding group already entered for you. We'll start with that project in Chapter 19 and turn it into a universal application for the iPad, so having some data already present will make it much more interesting on the iPad's large screen.

What Next?

You now have a complete and somewhat useful iOS application. In the preceding section you even learned how to distribute your application with predefined information. It should be fairly easy to repurpose the sample code from this chapter for different reference material by simply changing the data model to have the appropriate entities, attributes, and relationships and then changing the various views to display those attributes. So, what remains to be done before you can proudly submit your reference application to the App Store and start making money? There are several rough edges in our sample application that you would want to polish in order to have a quality application, but none of them are difficult.

The first thing that you might do is remove the editing functionality from the application and build a separate Mac OS X application (using the same data model) for entering and editing your reference material. If it's reference material, you probably don't want your customers changing it anyway. That would also free up the right button location in the navigation bar for an information icon button. At the RootViewController level that button could display a screen of general information about your application, data sources, etc. At the BreedsListViewController level it could display the description of the breed, since we're currently only displaying the first line of it in the table view.

When tapping on the various breeds in the Herding Group in the DogBreeds-Final application, you probably noticed a delay between when you tapped and when the detailed view appeared. The viewWillAppear method loads the photo data synchronously from the Internet, which means the user waits while a potentially large photo downloads. Ideally, the application should have immediately displayed the detail view and then loaded the photo data asynchronously with some indication that the photo was loading.

Even better would be to make your reference application self-contained. When they create a new breed, you could retrieve the photo from the URL and store the actual photo data in the database. Then when the user taps on a breed you can display the detail view quickly and it will work whether the user has Internet access or not.

There are also many ways that you could make the application prettier. For instance, the UITableView that displays the list of breeds within an AKC group could use custom table cells that display a thumbnail photo of the breed alongside its name.

Summary

In this chapter, you learned the basics of Core Data framework. After learning how to model your application's data objects, you learned how to insert, fetch, and delete instances from the data model. But you only scratched Core Data's surface in this chapter. There are so many ways to create an NSPredicate, so many ways to create an NSFetchRequest, and so many variations on the different ways of working with the managed object context that covering them all would result in a several-hundred-page book.

To continue learning more about Core Data, refer to Apple's documentation. Apple has heavily documented the Core Data framework. The first reference you should consult is "Apple's Core Data Tutorial for iOS." Consult Apple's "Creating a Managed Object Model with Xcode" tutorial and also "Xcode Tools for Core Data" for more information on using Xcode's data modeler. Consult Apple's "Predicate Programming Guide" for more information on writing predicates. Finally, for a complete reference on Core Data, consult Apple's "Core Data Programming Guide."

Chapter 18

Multimedia

Key Skills & Concepts

- Playing system sounds

- Playing songs

- Using the Media Player to interact with a device's multimedia

- Playing video

U p until the release of the iOS 3.0, the iPhone was a difficult platform for developing multimedia applications. The capabilities were there, but you had to resort to using low-level C APIs to program audio and video. And as for the multimedia on a device that was placed there by iTunes? Forget it, off limits. Any media you wished playing in your application had to either be packaged as part of your application or be streamed from a server. That restriction changed with iOS 3.0; now you can access and play a user's audio iTunes multimedia, making the iPhone and iPod touch the most programmable portable music players ever released. The vast majority of iOS devices currently in use are running iOS 3.0 or later, so except for a very unusual application, you can assume at least iOS 3.0 in your build settings and feel free to write your application to take advantage of the new APIs.

In this chapter, you explore the basic multimedia capabilities of the iPhone and iPod touch. You first learn how to play system sounds and longer sounds. You then move to the Media Player framework, where you use the framework to select and play a user's iTunes audio multimedia. After learning to play iTunes media, you then learn how to play a video using the Media Player framework's video player.

Playing Sounds

Playing short sounds on an iPhone or iPod touch is easy. Simply load the song as a system sound, obtain the sound's id, and use the AudioServicesPlaySystemSound method to play the sound. Playing a longer sound using the AVAudioPlayer is not difficult, but a little more involved. However, there is one important limitation you must realize when using sound on your device using the AudioServicesPlaySystemSound function or AVAudioPlayer: Any media you play must be packaged as part of your application or must be streamed from a server. So, although these two classes are good for adding sound to your application or for developing an interface to a server that streams multimedia, they are not good classes for developing a music player. Instead, you should use the Media Player Framework, covered later in this chapter.

AudioServicesPlaySystemSound

The AudioServicesPlaySystemSound function plays a short system sound. Although security restrictions prevent your application from playing a device's OS system sounds, you can load and play your own short (30 seconds or less) sounds and play them using this function.

The AudioServicesPlaySystemSound function can only play a sound with the following format: .caf, .aif, or .wav. The sound plays at whatever audio level the device is set to, and the sound plays immediately upon its id being passed to the function. There is no pausing, rewinding, fast-forwarding, or other sound manipulation functionality. You load a sound, and the function plays it.

```
void AudioServicesPlaySystemSound (SystemSoundID inSystemSoundID);
```

The function takes a SystemSoundID as a parameter. A SystemSoundID is an unsigned integer that uniquely identifies the sound. You obtain a SystemSoundID by loading a sound with the AudioServicesCreateSystemSoundID function.

```
OSStatus AudioServicesCreateSystemSoundID (CFURLRef inFileURL,
SystemSoundID * outSystemSoundID);
```

The AudioServicesCreateSystemSoundID function takes a reference to the file's URL and the SystemSoundID to assign the value to. A CFURLRef is simply a lower-level pointer to a URL. You can ignore creating a CFURL (what the CFURLRef points to) and instead cast an NSURL as a CFURLRef. After obtaining a sound's URL, you pass it to the create system sound function. It assigns the value to the system sound ID variable you defined; you pass that ID to the system sound player function; and it plays the sound.

Ask the Expert

Q: What's a CFURLRef? What's an NSURL?

A: A CFURLRef is a reference to a CFURL object. A CFURL is part of the Core Foundation framework, meaning it is C, not Objective-C, and provides functions to create and parse URLs. An NSURL is a higher-level, Cocoa Objective-C class for working with URLs. It encapsulates a URL and provides many functions for manipulating URLs. Refer to the NSURL Class Reference for more information.

You can cast an NSURL * as a CFURLRef because of Apple's "toll-free bridging" functionality. The term "toll-free bridging" refers to certain Core Foundation types being interchangeable with their higher-level Cocoa counterparts. Just remember, a pointer to an NSURL is equivalent to a CFURL reference.

TIP

You can use the AudioServicesPlaySystemSound to vibrate a user's iPhone. Pass the kSystemSoundID_Vibrate identifier constant to the function. All versions of the iPhone can vibrate, but only the latest 4th-generation iPod touch is capable of vibrating; this code does not do anything on an earlier iPod touch.

AVAudioPlayer and AVAudioPlayerDelegate

The AVAudioPlayer plays sounds. The audio player does not have the limitations of the AudioServicesPlaySystemSound function. It can play any length sound, loop a sound, and play multiple sounds at the same time; it also allows control over a sound's volume. Methods you might use include prepareToPlay, play, pause, and stop. Each method's functionality should be intuitive. Notice that prepareToPlay and play return a BOOL, so you can evaluate if the call was successful.

```
-(BOOL)prepareToPlay
-(BOOL)play
-(void)pause
-(void)stop
```

You can initialize an AVAudioPlayer with data or a URL. The initWithData:error: function initializes an audio player using data encapsulated in an NSData object. The initWithContentsOfURL:error: initializes an audio player using the sound file referenced by the URL. That sound file can be in your application's bundle, or it can be a resource on a server and streamed. If it is streamed, note that the prepareToPlay method discussed previously takes more importance, as it buffers the content and helps lessen a user's wait when playing an external resource.

```
-(id)initWithData:(NSData *) data error:(NSError **) outError
-(id)initWithContentsOfURL:(NSURL *) url error:(NSError **) outError
```

Properties you might use include the currentTime, data, delegate, duration, playing, volume, and numberOfLoops. The currentTime property returns the playback in seconds as an NSTimeInterval. The duration property returns a sound's duration in seconds as an NSTimeInterval. The volume returns the player's playback gain as a float between 0.0 and 1.0. The playing property returns a BOOL, while the numberOfLoops property returns an unsigned int. There are also more advanced properties, such as numberOfChannels and peakPowerForChannel. For a more complete listing of AVAudioPlayer's properties and methods, refer to the AVAudioPlayer Class Reference.

An AVAudioPlayer's delegate property refers to an audio player's AVAudioPlayerDelegate protocol. As with all protocols, you implement a custom class that adopts the protocol. Protocol methods you might implement are listed in Table 18-1.

Method	Description
– (void) audioPlayerBeginInterruption: (AVAudioPlayer *) player	Responds to an interruption to an audio player.
– (void) audioPlayerDecodeErrorDidOccur: (AVAudioPlayer *) player error: (NSError *) error	Responds to a decoding error.
– (void) audioPlayerDidFinishPlaying: (AVAudioPlayer *) player successfully: (BOOL) flag	Responds to a sound finished playing.
- (void) audioPlayerEndInterruption: (AVAudioPlayer *) player	Responds to the end of an interruption.

Table 18-1   AVAudioPlayerDelegate Methods

Try This   Playing a Sound and an MP3

1. Create a new View-based Application and name it **AVPlayer**.

2. From the sample code Resources folder, add the mp3, charleston1925_64kb.mp3, to the application's Resources folder. Also add the burp_2.aif file.

3. Add the AudioToolbox.framework to the application's frameworks. Also add the AVFoundation.framework. Remember, you can easily add a framework by control-clicking one of the frameworks already in your project (e.g., UIKit) and selecting Show In Finder. Then drag and drop the new frameworks from the Finder into the Frameworks folder in the project window. Be sure to uncheck the Copy Items Into Destination Group Folder option.

4. Open AVPlayerViewController.h and import the AudioToolbox and AVFoundation header files (Listing 18-1). Have the class adopt the AVAudioPlayerDelegate protocol.

Listing 18-1   AVPlayerViewController.h

```
#import <UIKit/UIKit.h>
#import <AudioToolbox/AudioToolbox.h>
#import <AVFoundation/AVFoundation.h>
@interface AVPlayerViewController : UIViewController
<AVAudioPlayerDelegate> {
SystemSoundID burpSoundID;
AVAudioPlayer * player;
}
- (IBAction) playSound: (id) sender;
- (IBAction) playSong: (id) sender;
@end
```

(continued)

5. Add a SystemSoundID as a variable to AVPlayerViewController; name it burpSoundID. Also add an AVAudioPlayer as a variable and name it player.

6. Add two IBActions to AVPlayerViewController named playSound and playSong. Do not forget to add the actions to AVPlayerViewController's header and implementation (Listing 18-2). Don't implement the actions yet; you do that in Step 9. Save the application.

Listing 18-2   AvplayerViewController.m

```
#import "AVPlayerViewController.h"
@implementation AVPlayerViewController
-(void) viewDidLoad {
  AudioServicesCreateSystemSoundID((CFURLRef)
        [NSURL fileURLWithPath:
            [[NSBundle mainBundle] pathForResource:@"burp_2"
            ofType:@"aif"]], &burpSoundID);
}
-(IBAction) playSound: (id) sender {
  AudioServicesPlaySystemSound (burpSoundID);
}
-(IBAction) playSong: (id) sender {
  NSError *error = nil;
  player = [[AVAudioPlayer alloc] initWithContentsOfURL:
        NSURL fileURLWithPath:[[NSBundle mainBundle]
        pathForResource: @"charleston1925_64kb"
        ofType:@"mp3"]] error:&error];
  player.delegate = self;
  if(error != NULL) {
    NSLog([error description]);
    [error release];
  }
  [player play];
}
-(void) audioPlayerDidFinishPlaying:
        (AVAudioPlayer *) theplayer successfully:(BOOL)flag {
  [theplayer release];
}
-(void)dealloc {
  [player release];
  [super dealloc];
}
@end
```

7. Open AVPlayerViewController.xib in Interface Builder and add two buttons. Connect Touch Up Inside for one button to playSound and for the other button to playSong. Label both buttons appropriately.

Figure 18-1   The finished application in the iPhone Simulator

8. Save and exit Interface Builder.

9. Implement playSound, playSong, and viewDidLoad. Also implement the audioPlayerDidFinishPlaying:successfully: method from the AVAudioPlayerDelegate protocol.

10. Click Run. Tap the button connected to playSong to begin playing the song. After the song starts playing, tap the button connected to playSound, and the iPhone Simulator belches simultaneously (Figure 18-1).

This task is straightforward; first, you loaded the sound and obtained its id. As system sounds are 30 seconds or less, loading it into memory and keeping it there should not tax your device's memory. Notice you do not load the longer song into memory until you actually play it in the playSong method, as it takes more memory.

You initialize the system sound in the viewDidLoad method. Don't let the one line of code be intimidating; it's actually doing something quite simple. It gets the path to the file, creates an NSURL using the path, casts it as a CFURLRef, and creates a system sound from the resource.

The playSong method creates a new AVAudioPlayer instance every time the application calls it. If an error occurs, the method logs the error; otherwise, it plays the song. When the song is finished playing, it calls the audioPlayerDidFinishPlaying:successfully: method and releases the player.

NOTE

The mp3 song is entitled The Charleston, and is a digital copy of the 1925 recording. It was obtained from the Internet Archive's 78RPMS & Cylinder Recordings Collection. The mp3 is licensed under the Creative Commons Commercial license. The burp_2.aif sound is also public domain.

Media Player Framework

Before iOS 3.0, a device's multimedia loaded by iTunes was off limits for application developers. The Media Player framework released with OS 3.0 removes that restriction by providing several classes that work with a device's iTunes-loaded multimedia.

NOTE

Running the Media Player audio application in this chapter requires installing the application on an iPod touch or iPhone running iOS 3.0 or later. The sample application won't run correctly in the iPhone simulator.

Media Data Classes

An MPMediaLibrary class represents a device's multimedia library loaded from iTunes. An MPMediaItem object represents every multimedia item in the media library. The MPMediaItem class contains metadata such as title, artist, and length about a media item.

When working with the MPMediaLibrary, you usually execute an MPMediaQuery that returns an MPMediaItemCollection. Although the Media Player framework offers several methods for accessing a device's media programmatically, another way is by using an MPMediaPickerController. An MPMediaPickerController is a class that presents a view much like the current iPod application. A user can then select one or more media items, and the picker returns an MPMediaItemCollection.

After selecting the media items to play, you pass them to an MPMusicController to play. The MPMusicController class is responsible for playing music, rewinding, forwarding, and other playback functionality.

MPMediaItem and MPMediaItemCollection

An MPMediaItem encapsulates a single audio multimedia element in a device's iTunes multimedia collection. The MPMediaItem contains one method for obtaining a media item's properties, the valueForProperty: method.

```
-(id)valueForProperty:(NSString *)property
```

The valueForProperty: method takes a constant representing the property for which to obtain a value. Notice that the method returns an id; this means the function's return value is tied to the property constant passed to the method. Listing 18-3 lists the properties you might pass to the valueForProperty: method.

Listing 18-3   Media Item properties

```
NSString *const MPMediaItemPropertyPersistentID;
NSString *const MPMediaItemPropertyAlbumTrackNumber;
NSString *const MPMediaItemPropertyAlbumTrackCount;
NSString *const MPMediaItemPropertyDiscNumber;
NSString *const MPMediaItemPropertyDiscCount;
NSString *const MPMediaItemPropertyArtwork;
NSString *const MPMediaItemPropertyLyrics;
NSString *const MPMediaItemPropertyPodcastTitle;
```

You can also use user-defined properties. These properties have a variable value, depending upon a user's multimedia collection use. Listing 18-4 lists the user-defined properties.

Listing 18-4   User-defined properties

```
NSString *const MPMediaItemPropertyPlayCount;
NSString *const MPMediaItemPropertySkipCount;
NSString *const MPMediaItemPropertyRating;
NSString *const MPMediaItemPropertyLastPlayedDate;
```

The MPMediaItemCollection class is a collection of media items. You obtain a collection's media items through its items property. This property returns an NSArray of MPMediaItem objects. Other properties include count, mediaTypes, and the representativeItem properties. The count property returns a count of the collection's multimedia items as an NSUInteger. You use the mediaTypes property and the representativeItem property to obtain a collection's media types.

Selecting Multimedia

Before playing multimedia, a user must select the media items. The easiest way to allow a user to do this is through the MPMediaPickerController. Similar to the UIImagePickerController, it controls a view that is hidden from developers. Also, like the image picker, it enables you to define a delegate for the media picker. That delegate, the MPMediaPickerControllerDelegate, responds to a user's interaction with the media picker.

MPMediaPickerController

The MPMediaPickerController class manages the media picker view. As with the UIImagePickerController, you present this controller's view as a modal view that overlays the currently displaying view.

```
[self presentModalViewController:mediaController animated:YES];
```

You can initialize a media picker to only display certain media types using the initWithMediaTypes method. This method takes an MPMediaType; valid types are MPMediaTypeMusic, MPMediaTypePodcast, MPMediaTypeAudioBook, and MPMediaTypeAnyAudio. Notice there is no MPMediaTypeVideo; you cannot select or play an iTunes-loaded video on devices using MPMediaPickerController. (Note that iPhone 3gs and later devices are capable of selecting video using the UIImagePickerController.)

You can also initialize a media picker to allow a user to select multiple items by setting the allowsPickingMultipleItems property to YES. If you don't set this property, its default value is NO.

MPMediaPickerControllerDelegate

A media picker requires an MPMediaPickerControllerDelegate if it is to do anything interesting. An MPMediaPickerControllerDelegate has two methods you implement when adopting this protocol: the mediaPicker:didPickMediaItems: and mediaPickerDidCancel: methods.

```
(void) mediaPicker: (MPMediaPickerController *)mediaPicker
didPickMediaItems: (MPMediaItemCollection *) mediaItemCollection
(void) mediaPickerDidCancel: (MPMediaPickerController *) mediaPicker
```

The mediaPickerDidCancel: method responds to a user canceling the media picker, while the mediaPicker:didPickMediaItems: method responds to a user clicking the Done button after selecting media in the media picker.

Playing Multimedia: MPMusicPlayerController

A user will probably want to play a multimedia object after selecting it. You play an MPMediaItemsCollection using the MPMusicPlayerController. This class is responsible for playing audio media items. There are two player types to choose from: an iPodMusicPlayer and an applicationMusicPlayer. An iPodMusicPlayer replaces an iPod's state, while an applicationMusicPlayer is independent of a user's iPod. For instance, if you are using iPodMusicPlayer and set it to shuffle mode, the user's iPod application will be in shuffle mode the next time he or she uses it. When using the applicationMusicPlayer, this does not happen because it does not modify the iPod's state.

You initialize a music player's media collection using the setQueueWithQuery:, setQueueWithItems:, or setQueueWithItemCollection: method. The set with query method takes an MPMediaQuery, the set with items method takes an NSArray of MPMediaItems, and the set with collection method takes an MPMediaItemCollection.

You can initialize a media player's state using the repeatMode and shuffleMode properties. If you do not set these properties, your player's state is the user's iPod application state. Other properties you can use to obtain information about a media player are the nowPlayingItem, currentPlaybackTime, and playbackState properties. The nowPlayingItem property is an MPMediaItem that represents the currently playing media item. The currentPlaybackTime is an NSInterval containing the now-playing item's playback location in seconds. The playbackState property returns the music player's playback state as an MPMusicPlaybackState. Valid values for these states include MPMusicPlaybackStateStopped, MPMusicPlaybackStatePlaying, MPMusicPlaybackStatePaused, MPMusicPlaybackStateInterrupted, MPMusicPlaybackState SeekingForward, and MPMusicPlaybackStateSeekingBackward.

Methods you can use to control a media player are play, pause, stop, beginSeekingForward, beginSeekingBackward, endSeeking, skipToNextItem, skipToBeginning, and skipToPreviousItem. The play, pause, and stop methods should be self-explanatory. The beginSeekingForward and beginSeekingBackward methods are for fast-forwarding and rewinding, respectively, while the endSeeking method stops fast-forwarding or rewinding. The skipToNextItem, skipToPreviousItem, and skipToBeginning methods should also be self-explanatory.

The MPMusicPlayerController has no delegate protocol for responding to its events. Instead it provides two notifications: the MPMusicPlayerControllerPlaybackStateDidChange and MPMusicPlayerControllerNowPlayingItemDidChange notifications. The first notification posts when an MPMusicPlayerController's playback state changes. The second notification posts when an MPMusicPlayerController's now-playing media item changes. By using these two notifications, your application can respond to the media player's state, as the next example task illustrates.

Try This · Using the Media Picker and Media Player

1. Create a new View-based Application; name it **iPodSongs**.

2. Add the Media Player framework (MediaPlayer.framework) to the project's frameworks.

3. Add the player_stop.png, player_pause.png, player_play.png, player_rew.png and player_fwd.png images from the sample code Resources folder to the project's Resources folder.

4. Open iPodSongsViewController and add four IBOutlets: three for UILabels and one for a UIView. Name the outlets currentTitle, currentArtist, currentLengthInSeconds, and volumeView.

5. Add an IBAction named selectSongs. Don't implement selectSongs yet. Add an IBAction named changeState (Listings 18-5 and 18-6).

(continued)

Listing 18-5   iPodSongsViewController.h

```
#import <UIKit/UIKit.h>
#import <MediaPlayer/MediaPlayer.h>
@class MyMediaPickerDelegate;
@interface iPodSongsViewController : UIViewController {
  MyMediaPickerDelegate * mediaControllerDelegate;
  MPMediaLibrary * mediaLib;
  UILabel * currentTitle;
  UILabel * currentLengthInSeconds;
  MPMusicPlayerController * player;
  UIView * volumeView;
  MPVolumeView * mpVolumeView;
}
@property (nonatomic, retain) MyMediaPickerDelegate
*mediaControllerDelegate;
@property (nonatomic, retain) MPMediaLibrary * mediaLib;
@property (nonatomic, retain) IBOutlet UILabel * currentTitle;
@property (nonatomic, retain) IBOutlet UILabel * currentArtist;
@property (nonatomic, retain) IBOutlet UILabel * currentLengthInSeconds;
@property (nonatomic, retain) MPMusicPlayerController * player;
@property (nonatomic, retain) IBOutlet UIView * volumeView;
- (IBAction) selectSongs : (id) sender;
- (IBAction) changeState: (id) sender;
@end
```

Listing 18-6   iPodSongsViewController.m

```
#import "iPodSongsViewController.h"
#import "MyMediaPickerDelegate.h"
@implementation iPodSongsViewController
@synthesize mediaControllerDelegate;
@synthesize mediaLib;
@synthesize currentTitle;
@synthesize currentArtist;
@synthesize currentLengthInSeconds;
@synthesize player;
@synthesize volumeView; int currentItem = 0;
-(void) viewDidLoad {
  [MPMediaLibrary defaultMediaLibrary];
  [[NSNotificationCenter defaultCenter] addObserver:self
      selector: @selector(songsPicked:)
      name:@"SongsPicked" object:nil];
  [[NSNotificationCenter defaultCenter] addObserver:self
      selector: @selector(songChanged)
      name: @"MPMusicPlayerControllerNowPlayingItemDidChangeNotification"
      object:nil];
```

```objc
    mpVolumeView = [[MPVolumeView alloc] init];
    [mpVolumeView setFrame:[self.volumeView bounds]];
    [self.volumeView addSubview:mpVolumeView];
}
-(void) songsPicked: (NSNotification *) notification {
    player = [MPMusicPlayerController applicationMusicPlayer];
    player.repeatMode = MPMusicRepeatModeNone;
    player.shuffleMode = MPMusicShuffleModeOff;
    [player setQueueWithItemCollection:(MPMediaItemCollection *)
    [notification object]];
    [player beginGeneratingPlaybackNotifications];
    [player play];
}
-(void) songChanged {
    MPMediaItem * tempMediaItem = (MPMediaItem *)player.nowPlayingItem;
    [self.currentTitle setText:[tempMediaItem valueForProperty:
        MPMediaItemPropertyTitle]];
    [self.currentArtist setText: [tempMediaItem valueForProperty:
        MPMediaItemPropertyArtist]];
    [self.currentLengthInSeconds setText: [NSString stringWithFormat:@"%i",
    [tempMediaItem valueForProperty:MPMediaItemPropertyPlaybackDuration]]];
}
-(IBAction) changeState: (id) sender {
    NSInteger num = ((UIControl*)sender).tag;
    switch (num) {
      case 1: [player pause]; break;
      case 2: [player play]; break;
      case 3: [player stop]; break;
      case 4: [player skipToPreviousItem]; break;
      case 5: [player skipToNextItem]; break;
    }
}
-(IBAction) selectSongs: (id) sender {
    MPMediaPickerController * mediaController =
          [[MPMediaPickerController alloc] init];
    mediaController.allowsPickingMultipleItems = YES;
    mediaController.delegate = [[MyMediaPickerDelegate alloc] init];
    [self presentModalViewController:mediaController animated:YES];
}
-(void)dealloc {
    [[NSNotificationCenter defaultCenter] removeObserver:self];
    [mediaControllerDelegate release];
    [player stop];
    [mpVolumeView release];
    [super dealloc];
}
@end
```

(continued)

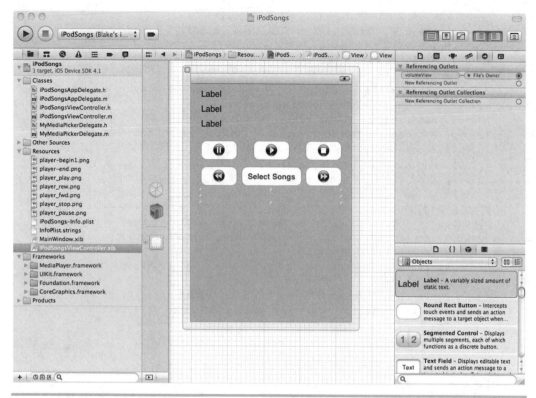

Figure 18-2 The application's canvas in Interface Builder

6. Save your changes and open iPodSongsViewController.xib. Create a button and connect its Touch Up Inside event to the selectSongs method.

7. Create five buttons and add an image to each button (Figure 18-2). Assign each button a unique tag in the Inspector. Connect the five buttons to the changeState action.

8. Add three labels to the canvas. Also add a UIView to the view's canvas and connect it to the volumeView outlet.

9. Connect the three labels to the currentTitle, currentArtist, and currentLengthInSeconds outlets.

10. Exit Interface Builder and return to iPodSongsViewController.

11. Create a new Objective-C class that is a subclass of NSObject named MyMediaPickerDelegate and have it adopt the MPMediaPickerControllerDelegate protocol (Listings 18-7 and 18-8). Don't forget to import the MediaPlayer header file.

Listing 18-7   MyMediaPickerDelegate.h

```
#import <Foundation/Foundation.h>
#import <MediaPlayer/MediaPlayer.h>
@interface MyMediaPickerDelegate : NSObject
<MPMediaPickerControllerDelegate> {
}
@end
```

Listing 18-8   MyMediaPickerDelegate.m

```
#import "MyMediaPickerDelegate.h"
@implementation MyMediaPickerDelegate
-(void) mediaPicker: (MPMediaPickerController *) mediaPicker
        didPickMediaItems: (MPMediaItemCollection *)
mediaItemCollection {
  NSArray * mediaItems = [mediaItemCollection items];
  NSEnumerator * enumer = [mediaItems objectEnumerator];
  id myObject;
  while (myObject = [enumer nextObject]) {
    MPMediaItem * tempMediaItem = (MPMediaItem *) myObject;
    NSLog(@"Title: %@", [tempMediaItem valueForProperty:
          MPMediaItemPropertyTitle]);
    NSLog(@"id: %@", [tempMediaItem
          valueForProperty:MPMediaItemPropertyArtist]);
    NSLog(@"id: %i", [tempMediaItem valueForProperty:
          MPMediaItemPropertyPersistentID]);
    NSLog(@"----------------------");
  }
  [mediaPicker.parentViewController dismissModalViewControllerAnimated
:YES];
  [mediaPicker release];
  [[NSNotificationCenter defaultCenter] postNotificationName:
          @"SongsPicked" object: mediaItemCollection];
}
-(void) dealloc {
  [[NSNotificationCenter defaultCenter] removeObserver: self];
  [super dealloc];
}
@end
```

12. Open iPodSongsViewController and add properties for the MyMediaPickerDelegate, MPMediaLibrary, and MPMusicPlayerController. Name the properties mediaPickerDelegate, mediaLib, and player.

13. Add a variable for MPVolumeView named mpVolumeView.

14. Be certain that iPodSongsViewController imports MyMediaPickerDelegate, and do not forget to synthesize the three properties.

15. Return to MyMediaPickerDelegate and implement the didPickMediaItems delegate methods.

16. Return to iPodSongsViewController and implement the selectSongs and changeState methods.

17. Implement the viewDidLoad method and the songsPicked method, paying particular attention to the NSNotification.

18. The application runs, displays the controls, and allows selecting multimedia. Click Select Songs, choose a few songs from your iPod and then tap Done. The music player starts playing and displays the currently playing item in the labels (Figure 18-3).

Figure 18-3 The application running on an iPod touch

When you think about how long it took us to write this application, it is perhaps the coolest application in the entire book. The user interface isn't pretty, but the application works well as a simple music player. In fact, with a little polish you might even like it better than the iPod touch's Music application because you can quickly select all the songs you're interested in and then play them.

In the viewDidLoad method, notice the code for initializing a volume control. Although the MPVolumeView class provides a sizeThatFits method, it is better to do it the way presented here. Simply add a UIView as a subview, size it to the desired size, and then add the volume view to the subview. Easy, and it is guaranteed to size correctly.

```
mpVolumeView = [[MPVolumeView alloc] init];
[mpVolumeView setFrame:[self.volumeView bounds]];
[self.volumeView addSubview:mpVolumeView];
```

As the MPMediaPlayerController does not have a delegate, you made the iPodSongsViewController a listener for the MPMusicPlayerControllerNowPlayingItemDid ChangeNotification event. When a player's now-playing item changes, the player fires this event. You set the songChanged method as the method called when the event fires. After being called, the songChanged method obtains the now-playing item and updates the view's labels.

The changeState method handles any one of the five control buttons being tapped. Because each button has a different tag, the method can distinguish which button fires the Touch Up Inside event and handle the message appropriately. In a real-world application, you would disable the buttons as appropriate. For instance, when paused, the Pause button should be disabled and only the Play button enabled. Here, however, the extra code would have detracted from the example's intended purpose.

In addition to the player's notification, you created your own notification in MyMediaPickerDelegate. Upon selecting an MPMediaItemCollection using the media picker, this notification is fired. The songsPicked method in iPodSongsViewController responds to this notification. The method takes the NSNotification as a parameter; remember notifications can contain an object. Here, that object is the selected MPMediaItemCollection. After initializing the media player with the collection, the songsPicked method tells the media player to begin generating playback notifications and then starts playing.

MPMoviePlayerController

The MPMoviePlayerController plays video bundled as part of your application. It can also stream video from a server. However, despite its name, it cannot use video loaded on a user's device by iTunes.

In versions of iOS prior to 3.2, MPMoviePlayerController always presents a modal, full-screen video when it plays and you can only minimally modify its appearance using properties. With iOS 3.2 and later, MPMoviePlayerController can also play video in a portion of the screen or even in portrait orientation. This is particularly helpful on the iPad, where the display is large enough to display video in a portion of the screen alongside other information. If you want to remain compatible with devices running iOS 3.1 and earlier, then the player runs full screen and you can change the movie player's background color, a movie's scaling, and the controls presented to the user when playing a movie. You change a movie's background color using the backgroundColor property. You change a movie's scaling using the scalingMode property, and you change the controls presented using the movieControlMode property.

The backgroundColor property changes the movie player's background color when playing a movie. For instance, when you watch a video using the Video application on an iPod touch, the background is black. If you wish, you can change that color using this property.

The scalingMode property changes a movie's scaling. Valid values for scalingMode are MPMovieScalingModeNone, MPMovieScalingModeAspectFit, MPMovieScalingModeAspect Fill, and MPMovieScalingModeFill.

The movieControlMode property determines the visible controls when a movie plays. For instance, when playing a movie using the Video application, if you tap the screen, it presents a control showing the volume, a control showing the location in the video, a scaling control, and a Done button. You can modify which control a player presents using this property. Valid values are MPMovieControlModeDefault, MPMovieControlModeVolumeOnly, and MPMovie ControlModeHidden.

You initialize a movie player using the initWithContentURL: method. This method takes an NSURL to the movie's location. This location must be within your application's sandbox or available via an Internet server (it's a URL). After initializing the player, you call the prepareToPlay and play methods. If you wish to be notified that the player has stopped playing, you register as a notification listener, listening for the player's MPMoviePlayerPlay backDidFinishNotification notification.

Try This Play a Video

1. Create a new View-based Application called **MoviePlayer**. Add the Media Player framework to the application.

2. Add the movie short.3gp from the sample code Resources folder to the project's Resources folder.

3. Open MoviePlayerController and add an MPMoviePlayerController as a property; name it moviePlayer (Listings 18-9 and 18-10). Do not forget to import the MediaPlayer.

Listing 18-9 MovieplayerViewController.h

```
#import <UIKit/UIKit.h>
#import <MediaPlayer/MediaPlayer.h>
@interface MovieplayerViewController : UIViewController {
  MPMoviePlayerController * movieplayer;
}
@property (nonatomic, retain) MPMoviePlayerController * movieplayer;
-(IBAction) playMovie: (id) sender;
-(void) playingDone;
@end
```

Listing 18-10   MovieplayerViewController.m

```objc
#import "MovieplayerViewController.h"
@implementation MovieplayerViewController
@synthesize movieplayer;
-(void) viewDidLoad {
  [[NSNotificationCenter defaultCenter] addObserver:self selector:
          @selector (playingDone)
          name:MPMoviePlayerPlaybackDidFinishNotification object:nil];
}
-(IBAction) playMovie: (id) sender {
  movieplayer = [[MPMoviePlayerController alloc] initWithContentURL:
          [NSURL fileURLWithPath:[[NSBundle mainBundle]
          pathForResource:@"short" ofType:@"3gp"]]];
  // Only iOS 3.2 and above respond to the loadState selector
  if ([movieplayer respondsToSelector:@selector(loadState)]) {
    // Our application runs in portrait orientation,
    // so on iOS 3.2 and later, the movie player will also
    // display in portrait mode by default.
    // The next few lines change the orientation to landscape
    [[UIApplication sharedApplication]
            setStatusBarOrientation:UIInterfaceOrientationLandscapeRight
            animated:NO];
    // Rotate the view for landscape playback
    [[self view] setBounds:CGRectMake(0, 0, 480, 320)];
    [[self view] setCenter:CGPointMake(160, 240)];
    [[self view] setTransform:CGAffineTransformMakeRotation(M_PI / 2)];
    // Set frame of movie player
    [[movieplayer view] setFrame:CGRectMake(0, 0, 480, 320)];
    // Add movie player as subview
    [[self view] addSubview:[movieplayer view]];
    // Play the movie
    [movieplayer play];
  } else {
    // Prior to iOS 3.2, this was enough to play the movie correctly
    [movieplayer play];
  }
}
-(void) playingDone {
  [movieplayer release];
  movieplayer = nil;
}
-(void)dealloc {
  [[NSNotificationCenter defaultCenter] removeObserver:self];
  [movieplayer release]; [super dealloc];
}
@end
```

(continued)

4. Add a method called playingDone and an IBAction called playMovie to MoviePlayerView Controller. Implement both methods the same as in Listing 18-10. Also implement the viewDidLoad method.

5. Save your changes and open MovieplayerViewController.xib.

6. Add a button to the canvas and connect it to the playMovie action.

7. Save your changes and click Run. Click the play movie button and an old B&W movie will play in landscape orientation.

Like the music player, you register to listen to the finished playing event in the viewDidLoad method. Notice that unlike the previous task, you didn't place the event's name in quotations. This omission was intentional. The event and the event's NSString name are the same, and you can use either. The viewDidLoad method also initializes the movie player with the short.3gp movie's location. In a real-world application, loading a movie when a view loads is probably not a good idea, as movies are usually quite large.

When a user taps the button, the movie player begins playing the movie in landscape mode (Figure 18-4). Upon tapping the Done button, the user returns to the application's view in portrait mode. The controller also receives the notification that the player stopped playing and releases the player.

Figure 18-4 The application running in iPhone Simulator

Summary

In this chapter, you learned how to play system sounds, sounds, a device's audio multimedia loaded from iTunes, and video. You first played a system sound. System sounds are 30 seconds or less and are designed as audible alerts. You also played an MP3 using the AVAudioPlayer. The AVAudioPlayer is for playing longer sounds, including your application's multimedia, such as MP3s. However, the audio player is limited to sounds bundled with your application or streamed from a server. It cannot play iTunes-loaded multimedia.

The newer media player can play iTunes multimedia, provided it is audio. You learned how to use the media player and how to use a controller to select music and a player to play it. After learning about the Media Player framework's newer features, you then learned about its movie player. Despite being part of the Media Player framework, you can only play video bundled as part of your application or video streamed from a server.

In the next chapter we will return to the MoviePlayer example and look at how to play video in a subview on the iPad's larger display.

Chapter 19

Universal Applications
for the iPad

Key Skills & Concepts

- Understanding the key differences of the iPad
- Creating a universal application
- Creating a Split View Controller
- Popover views
- Understanding of other iPad and iOS 4 features

It's important to understand that the iPad isn't just an iPhone with a bigger screen. Somehow, the larger screen completely changes the experience. When you're designing for the iPad, don't just think about spreading out your content so that it more or less fills the screen. Instead, think about how you could completely reimagine what you're presenting given the freedom of the iPad's large screen. Information that had to be spread over multiple tabs on an iPhone can be elegantly displayed on a single screen. Or you can include a variety of controls alongside your content. While the iPhone and iPod touch were best suited to consuming content, the iPad is also great for creating it—think about applications that you could design that would let the user create new content while on-the-go. The iPad provides whole new opportunities for innovative applications.

Everything that you've learned about iOS programming in the previous chapters also applies to the iPad, and all of the example applications should run just fine on an iPad. However, because they were designed and built for the smaller display of the iPhone, without modification they will run in a small area in the center of the iPad's much larger display—not a particularly compelling experience for the user (Figure 19-1). Fortunately, the changes necessary to make a typical application run full screen on the iPad are quite easy. In this chapter you will begin by looking at the minimum changes necessary to create a universal application.

However, making your app run full screen as a universal application on the iPad is only the start. Unless your primary audience will be using an iPhone or iPod touch, you'll want to go well beyond the minimum and design your information layout for the larger screen. You'll also want to incorporate new iOS functionality added just for the iPad. For instance, the larger screen of the iPad makes it possible to display two levels of the hierarchy in a navigation-based application at once, making it faster and easier for the user to move around in your content. We will incorporate Split View Controllers and popovers into the DogBreeds app from Chapter 17.

The movie player from Chapter 18 used the full screen of the iPhone when playing video, which made sense on a small device. However, when video is supplementing other information in an iPad application, it will often make more sense to display it in only part of the screen so that you can display additional information or controls around the video. Later in this chapter you will convert the MoviePlayer application from Chapter 18 into a universal application and then modify it to play the video in the center of the screen.

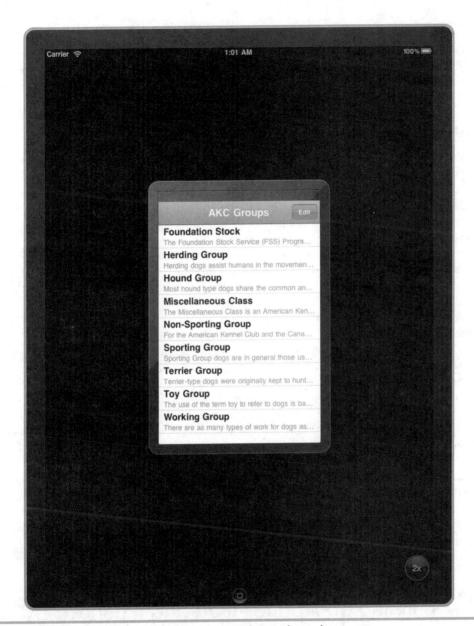

Figure 19-1   DogBreeds application running in the iPad Simulator

Finally, we will briefly take a look at some of the other new iOS functionality that showed up in iOS 3.2 on the iPad and then in iOS 4.0 on the iPhone and iPod touch. We don't have enough space in an introductory book to try examples for each of these new features, but we'll give you a taste for what they can do and point you at the Apple documentation if you decide they make sense for your applications.

Creating a Universal Application

In all of the Try This examples up to this point, the Targeted Device Family has always been set to iPhone (which includes the iPod touch). If you reopen the DogBreeds app from Chapter 17 and select iPad Simulator from the pull-down next to the Run button, and then click Run, the app will launch in the iPad Simulator in a small window in the center of the larger iPad display (Figure 19-1). Technically, it's compatible with the iPad, but since it wasn't built with any knowledge of the iPad's different hardware, the iPad is just emulating an iPhone.

To take full advantage of the larger screen and other unique features of the iPad, your application will have to be built for the iPad. You essentially have two choices when starting a project that will run on the iPad. Your first option is to create a universal application that will run well on both the iPad and the iPhone, detecting which device it's on and adjusting as necessary. This is best for users, since they can buy it once in the App Store and use it on both their iPhone and their iPad.

If the iPhone and iPad versions would sell to different audiences or your application contains a lot of predefined graphics that take up a lot of space and need to be different for each screen size (e.g., game backgrounds), it might be more practical to build separate versions for each device. That allows you to include only the graphics needed for the device, or to charge for both versions separately. If the code is largely the same, you can do this with a single project and two build targets. However, if your iPad and iPhone versions will have significantly different functionality, it might make sense to create two separate projects that share any common source files but implement different views and controllers.

In the next Try This example, we will turn the DogBreeds app from Chapter 17 into a universal application. The functionality will be very similar between the iPad and iPhone versions, and it's the sort of reference application that users would expect to only pay for once. This will require us to check which device we're running on and layout views accordingly, but it is usually worth complicating the code a bit to have a single application that is distributed to everyone.

Try This Building an App for iPad and iPhone

1. Select the DogBreeds project in the Navigation pane. Make sure the Deployment Target is set to range from 3.2 through the latest version of the iOS.

2. Click Build Settings tab and select iPhone/iPad in the pull-down menu next to Targeted Device Family (Figure 19-2).

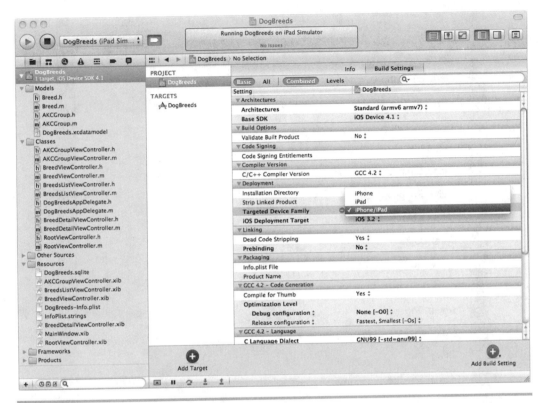

Figure 19-2   Changing the targeted device family

3. Make sure the iPad Simulator is still selected in the pull-down next to the Run button and then click Run. The DogBreeds app will launch in the iPad Simulator and use the full screen (Figure 19-3).

4. Click in and out of the groups and look at a breed or two in the Herding group. Notice that the app more or less works, but as you look at the details for a specific breed, it only uses one corner of the display. You will also notice that when you rotate the iPad, the app continues to display in portrait mode.

(continued)

Figure 19-3 DogBreeds running full-screen in the iPad Simulator

Handling Orientation Changes

If you've had the opportunity to handle an iPad in person, one of the first things that you probably noticed is that you are just as likely to use it in landscape as portrait orientation. You may also find yourself rotating the iPad often while using it. This behavior is different than what is typical with the iPhone or iPod touch. With those devices, you could get away with creating an application that ignores device orientation and only functions in portrait mode. In fact, except for games that were designed for landscape orientation, most of the iPhone applications in the App Store ignore rotation and display in portrait orientation only.

When running on the iPad, your application will have to react to rotations and draw accordingly. Fortunately, reacting to changes in orientation and redrawing the standard UI components is very easy. When an iOS device is rotated, the shouldAutorotateToInterfaceOrientation method is called in the current view controller. If you don't implement that method, then it defaults to NO.

Try This · Reacting to Orientation Changes

1. Reopen the DogBreeds project.

2. Add the shouldAutorotateToInterfaceOrientation method in Listing 19-1 in all of the view controllers in the application (AKCViewController, BreedViewConroller, BreedsListViewController, BreedDetailViewController, and RootViewController).

Listing 19-1   shouldAutorotateToInterfaceOrientation method

```
-(BOOL)shouldAutorotateToInterfaceOrientation:
(UIInterfaceOrientation)orientation {
    if (UI_USER_INTERFACE_IDIOM() == UIUserInterfaceIdiomPad)
      return YES;
    return NO;
}
```

3. Save all of your changes and click Run. In the Hardware menu of the iPad Simulator, there are menu commands to rotate the device left or right. Play with rotating it while on each of the DogBreed screens, and you will notice that it now rotates and redraws as necessary.

NOTE

The orientation argument to shouldAutorotateToInterfaceOrientation can have one of four values: UIInterfaceOrientationPortrait, UIInterfaceOrientationPortraitUpsideDown, UIInterfaceOrientationLandscapeLeft, UIInterfaceOrientationLandscapeRight. If you have an application that will only work in certain orientations (e.g., portrait and portrait upside down), you can use that argument to decide when to allow rotation.

In the preceding example, we simply allowed rotation when on the iPad and iOS took care of everything else for us, redrawing all of the subviews as necessary. That's great for UITableViews, but for views where you're presenting a lot of data in an elegant format, you will probably need to shift around or resize elements to make them continue to fit and look good. You can override the willRotateToInterfaceOrientation:duration method on any view controllers where you want a chance to change the content of the view before it rotates into the new orientation.

In Listing 19-1 you will also notice that the application needed to determine if it was currently running on an iPad and used the following test:

```
(UI_USER_INTERFACE_IDIOM() == UIUserInterfaceIdiomPad)
```

This is the Apple-preferred way of determining whether you're running on an iPad or on an iPhone/iPod touch. As you modify various parts of the DogBreeds application to make it display differently on an iPad, you will find yourself using that test fairly often. It's a judgment call, but when you find yourself having to test whether you are on an iPad over and over in the same view controller, it may make sense to define two view controllers and then instantiate and push one for the iPad and the other one for the iPhone.

Icons and Default Screens

We haven't bothered creating icons for our sample iPhone applications in previous chapters, but that's a step that you have to take care of before submitting your application to the App Store. With an iPhone application, you only needed to create a 57 × 57 pixel icon. When creating a universal application, you will also need three more sizes:

- A 72 × 72 icon named "icon-ipad.png" for the home screen

- A 50 × 50 icon named "icon-small-50.png" for Spotlight on the iPad

- A 29 × 29 icon named "icon-small.png" for Spotlight on the iPhone

After you've created your icons and added them to the Resources folder, control-click DogBreeds-Info.plist and select Open As Source Code. Replace the two lines:

```
<key>CFBundleIconFile</key>
    <string></string>
```

with the following lines to reference all of the icons:

```
<key>CFBundleIconFiles</key>
    <array>
        <string>icon.png</string>
        <string>icon-ipad.png</string>
        <string>icon-small-50.png</string>
        <string>icon-small.png</string>
    </array>
```

If you include a default screen in your application's resources, iOS will use it to display a splash or startup screen while your application is launching. Our sample apps start up very quickly, so we haven't bothered to create a splash screen. However, when your application is larger or needs to do a lot of initialization at startup, it's nice to give your user something to look at while it launches. For an iPhone application, the screen would be 320 × 460 and added to your Resources folder as "Default.png." If you're creating a universal application, then you also need to include portrait (768 × 1004) and landscape (1024 × 748) screens named "Default-Portrait.png" and "Default-Landscape.png."

Applications on the iPhone always launch in portrait orientation, but if you want your iPad application to be able to launch in any orientation, you'll also have to add the following entry to the plist we were editing earlier:

```
<key>UISupportedInterfaceOrientations~ipad</key>
<array>
   <string>UIInterfaceOrientationPortrait</string>
   <string>UIInterfaceOrientationPortraitUpsideDown</string>
   <string>UIInterfaceOrientationLandscapeLeft</string>
   <string>UIInterfaceOrientationLandscapeRight</string>
</array>
```

Split Views

The DogBreeds application now runs full screen on the iPad, but it has a lot of wasted space. In a typical navigation-based application, the larger display of the iPad is ideally suited to displaying navigation and item details at the same time. When the iPad is in landscape orientation, a table view from the iPhone easily fits alongside a detail area that's still much larger than it is on the iPhone. Apple calls this a split view, and iOS 3.2 on the iPad added the UISplitViewController to make it easy to implement a navigation view on the left that controls a detail view on the right.

When the iPad is in portrait orientation, there's not quite enough width to display a standard table view alongside a reasonably-sized detail area, so when in portrait orientation, the Split View Controller uses the full display for the detail view and pops up a navigation view on top of it when the user taps a button. UISplitViewController automatically takes care of hiding the popover navigation view as you rotate the iPad.

Try This Add a Split View

iOS lets you define a second main window xib that will be used when the application is running on the iPad. We start by creating that window and placing a Split View Controller in it instead of the Navigation Controller.

1. Open the DogBreeds project. Control-click the project in the Navigation pane and select New Group, naming it **Resources-iPad**. Drag the new folder down next to the Resources folder. This will give us a convenient place to keep all of our iPad-specific resources.

2. Control-click the Resources-iPad folder and select New File | Select User Interface from the column on the left and Application as the template. Select iPad from the Device Family pull-down (Figure 19-4). Name the new file **MainWindow-iPad**. This creates a new xib file that is sized specifically for the iPad.

(continued)

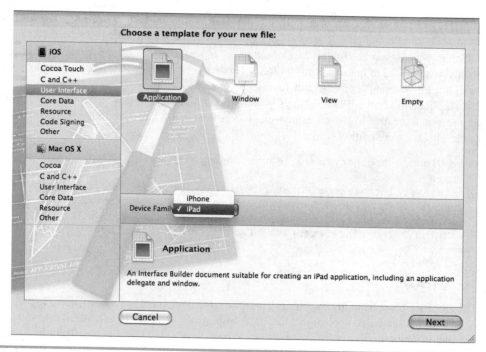

Figure 19-4 Creating a new window xib

3. Now we need to tell the application about the new MainWindow file. Select DogBreeds-Info.plist and add a new entry with key NSMainNibFile~ipad and the string value "MainWindow-iPad".

4. Select MainWindow-iPad.xib. Drag a Split View Controller into the main window.

5. Select the View Controller on the left (under the Root View Controller title). In the Identity subpane of the Utilities pane, change the class of this View Controller to RootViewController. Select the right pane in the Split View Controller and change its class to BreedDetailViewController. In the Attributes subpane, set each of them to load from their respective NIB files. Save your changes.

6. Go to DogBreedsAppDelegate.h and define a new instance variable and IBOutlet property:

```
UISplitViewController *splitVC;
@property (nonatomic, retain) IBOutlet UISplitViewController
*splitVC;
```

7. Synthesize the property in the .m file and release it in the dealloc method.

8. Switch back to MainWindow-iPad.xib. Select the App Delegate and set its class to DogBreedsAppDelegate. In the Connections subpane, connect the navigationController outlet to the Navigation Controller, the splitVC outlet to the Split View Controller, and the window outlet to the Window (Figure 19-5).

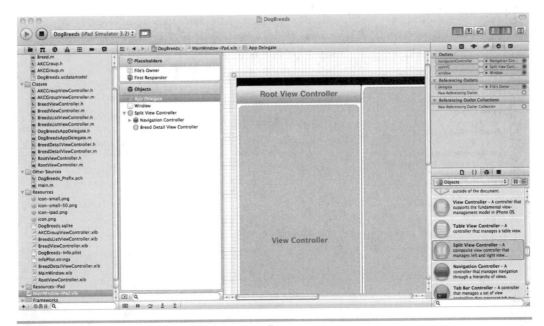

Figure 19-5   Setting up the Split View Controller

9. Now when the application launches, we need to use the appropriate view based on whether we're running on the iPhone or iPad. Select DogBreedsAppDelegate.m and change the application:didFinishLaunchingWithOptions method to match Listing 19-2.

Listing 19-2   application:didFinishLaunchingWithOptions method

```
- (BOOL)application:(UIApplication *)application
    didFinishLaunchingWithOptions:(NSDictionary *)launchOptions {
  if (UI_USER_INTERFACE_IDIOM() == UIUserInterfaceIdiomPad) {
    [window addSubview:[splitVC view]];
  } else {
    [window addSubview:[navigationController view]];
  }
  [window makeKeyAndVisible];
  return YES;
}
```

10. Save your changes and click Run. If the iPad is in portrait orientation, rotate it to landscape orientation. You should see the dog groups navigation along the left and an empty details view on the right (Figure 19-6). If you stop the application and switch to running it in the iPhone Simulator, you'll find that everything still works as expected on the smaller iPhone screen.

(continued)

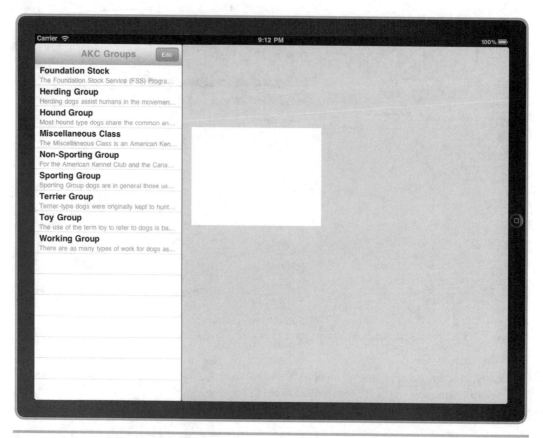

Figure 19-6 DogBreeds with a split view

You will notice that clicking a group takes you to the breeds list as expected, but clicking a breed displays its details in the navigation pane rather than the details area. This is because the two panes don't know anything about each other yet.

You will also notice that when you rotate the iPad Simulator to portrait orientation, the navigation view slides out of sight as expected. However, there's no button to make the navigation appear as a popover. Let's solve this problem first, and then we'll worry about connecting the detail pane to the navigation pane.

We will need to add a toolBar to the Breed Detail View in order to have some place to draw the button. But the catch is that the iPhone version already has a navigation bar and we don't want to add an additional toolbar there. Since we still want the rest of the behavior of the Breed Detail View, the easiest way to solve this will be to subclass BreedDetailViewController. Adding this subclass will also give us the opportunity to change the layout of the photo and description in the nib file to make better use of the larger iPad display.

1. Create a new file, making it a UIViewController subclass with Targeted for iPad selected. Make sure a XIB is created too (Figure 19-7). Name the new file **BreedDetailViewController_iPad**.

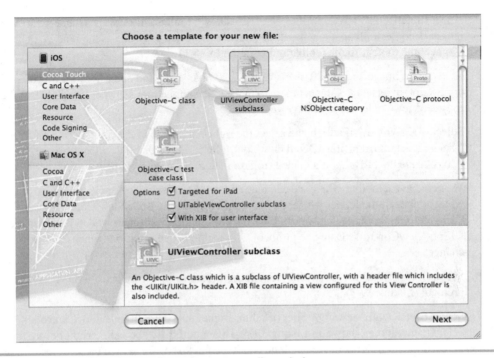

Figure 19-7   Creating a BreedDetailViewController subclass

2. Edit BreedDetailViewController_iPad.h and change the class to inherit from
   BreedDetailViewController. Add an instance variable and IBOutlet property called toolbar
   to keep track of the toolbar we will be adding. Also create a property to keep track of the
   popover that we will be implementing a little later (Listing 19-3). Be sure to synthesize
   the properties and release them in BreedDetailViewController_iPad.m

Listing 19-3   BreedDetailViewController_iPad.h

```
#import <UIKit/UIKit.h>
#import "BreedDetailViewController.h"
@interface BreedDetailViewController_iPad : BreedDetailViewController
<UISplitViewControllerDelegate> {
  UIToolbar *toolbar;
  UIPopoverController *popover;
}
@property(nonatomic,retain) IBOutlet UIToolbar *toolbar;
@property(nonatomic, retain) UIPopoverController *popover;
@end
```

(continued)

3. Select BreedDetailViewController_iPad.xib. Drag a toolbar into Edit pane and remove the button from the toolbar, since it will be added/removed in our code as the iPad is rotated. Connect the toolbar to the toolbar outlet in the File's Owner.

4. Also add an Image View (500 pixels wide × 350 pixels tall) and add a Text View (600 pixels wide × 560 pixels tall). Connect them to their outlets in the File's Owner (it will be similar to BreedViewController.xib). Save your changes.

5. Select MainWindow-iPad.xib and select the right-hand pane of the Split View Controller. Change its class from BreedDetailViewController to BreedDetailViewController_iPad. Also change the NIB that it's loaded from to match. Save your changes.

   We now have a toolbar where we can place a button to display the navigation popover when in portrait mode, but we need to be notified when the Split View Controller is changing orientation so that we can hide/show the button. Fortunately, iOS provides the UISplitViewControllerDelegate protocol with methods that are called when orientation changes.

6. Select BreedDetailViewController_iPad.h. Add the UISplitViewControllerDelegate protocol (Listing 19-3).

7. Select BreedDetailViewController_iPad.m. Implement the willHideViewController delegate method as shown in Listing 19-4. This method will be called right before the navigation controller is hidden and the detail view resized. We set the name of the button and then keep track of the popover so that we can delete it later, when the iPad rotates back to landscape orientation. We also take this opportunity to resize the photo and description fields to fit nicely in the portrait layout.

Listing 19-4   willHideViewController in BreedDetailViewController_iPad.m

```
- (void)splitViewController:(UISplitViewController*)svc
willHideViewController:(UIViewController *)aViewController
        withBarButtonItem:(UIBarButtonItem*)barButtonItem
forPopoverController:(UIPopoverController*)pc {
    if (self.selectedBreed != nil)
        barButtonItem.title = self.selectedBreed.group.name;
    else
        barButtonItem.title = aViewController.title;
    [self.toolbar setItems:[NSArray arrayWithObject:barButtonItem]
animated:YES];
    self.popover = pc;
    CGRect portraitPhotoFrame = photo.frame;
    portraitPhotoFrame.origin.x = 135;
    portraitPhotoFrame.origin.y = 50;
    photo.frame = portraitPhotoFrame;
    CGRect descFrame = breedDescription.frame;
```

```
    descFrame.size.height = 560;
    descFrame.origin.x = 85;
    descFrame.origin.y = 410;
    breedDescription.frame = descFrame;
}
```

8. Select MainWindow-iPad.xib. Select the Split View Controller and connect its delegate outlet to the BreedDetailViewController_iPad in the left pane of the view controller.

9. Save all of your changes and click Run. DogBreeds should now display a button when rotated to portrait orientation. Clicking the button brings up the group list or the breeds list if a group has already been selected.

10. You'll notice that the button remains in the toolbar after switching back to landscape orientation. Implement the willShowViewController delegate method as shown in Listing 19-5. When the navigation view is about to reappear when the iPad rotates to landscape orientation, it removes the button and releases the popover view. We also take the opportunity to change the position and size of the photo and description fields to make them fit nicely in the landscape layout.

Listing 19-5   willShowViewController in BreedDetailViewController_iPad.m

```
- (void)splitViewController: (UISplitViewController*)svc
willShowViewController:(UIViewController *)aViewController
  invalidatingBarButtonItem:(UIBarButtonItem *)barButtonItem {
    [self.toolbar setItems:[NSArray array] animated:YES];
    self.popover = nil;
    // Adjust the photo and description to fit nicely in landscape mode
    CGRect portraitPhotoFrame = photo.frame;
    portraitPhotoFrame.origin.x = 100;
    portraitPhotoFrame.origin.y = 20;
    photo.frame = portraitPhotoFrame;
    CGRect descFrame = breedDescription.frame;
    descFrame.size.height = 360;
    descFrame.origin.x = 50;
    descFrame.origin.y = 375;
    breedDescription.frame = descFrame;
}
```

11. Run the application again and the button now disappears when you rotate back to landscape orientation.

We still have one major issue outstanding in our split view. Clicking a breed in the navigation view displays the details in the navigation view instead of the detail view. This is the desired behavior on the iPhone, but on the iPad the navigation view needs to be able to find the separate

(continued)

detail view and update it. We can do this by first ensuring that rootViewController has a reference to the detail view and then passing that reference on to the BreedsListViewController when it's pushed so that it has access to the detail view when a breed is selected.

1. First add an IBOutlet property to RootViewController.h to store a reference to the BreedDetailViewController (and remember to synthesize it and release it in the dealloc method):

```
BreedDetailViewController *breedDetailVC;
@property (nonatomic, retain) IBOutlet BreedDetailViewController
*breedDetailVC;
```

2. Now we have to make sure it's connected to the detail half of the Split View Controller. Open MainWindow-iPad.xib, select the left pane of the split view (the RootViewController) and in the Connections pane, connect breedDetailVC to the right hand pane of the split view (the BreedDetailViewController). Save your changes.

3. Select RootViewController.m and edit the didSelectRowAtIndexPath method and set the breedDetailVC property of breedsListVC to the breedDetailVC property of the RootViewController (Listing 19-6).

Listing 19-6   didSelectRowAtIndex in RootViewController.m

```
- (void)tableView:(UITableView *)tableView didSelectRowAtIndexPath:
(NSIndexPath *)indexPath {
    AKCGroup *theGroup = [[self fetchedResultsController]
objectAtIndexPath:indexPath];
    if (self.editing == YES) {
        self.groupEditorVC.group = theGroup;
        self.groupEditorVC.insertingGroup = NO;
        [self.navigationController pushViewController:
self.groupEditorVC animated:YES];
    } else {
        self.breedsListVC.selectedGroup = theGroup;
        self.breedsListVC.title = theGroup.name;
        self.breedsListVC.managedObjectContext =
self.managedObjectContext;
        if (UI_USER_INTERFACE_IDIOM() == UIUserInterfaceIdiomPad)
            self.breedsListVC.breedDetailVC = self.breedDetailVC;
        [self.navigationController pushViewController:
self.breedsListVC animated:YES];
    }
}
```

4. Select BreedDetailViewController.h and add two new method declarations:

```
- (void)updateDetails;
- (void)updateBreed: (Breed *)theBreed;
```

5. Switch to BreedDetailViewController.m and implement the methods as shown in
   Listing 19-7. We're adding a handy method for changing the breed associated with the
   BreedDetailViewController and a separate method for loading the values for the details
   fields (photo and description) into their subviews. We'll call updateBreed from the
   navigation controller when the user selects a specific breed.

Listing 19-7   Changes to BreedDetailViewController.m

```
- (void)viewWillAppear:(BOOL)animated {
    [super viewWillAppear:animated];
    [self updateDetails];
}
- (void)updateDetails {
    self.title = selectedBreed.name;
    self.breedDescription.text = self.selectedBreed.breedDescription;
    NSURL* aURL = [NSURL URLWithString:self.selectedBreed.photoURL];
    NSData *imageData = [[NSData alloc] initWithContentsOfURL:aURL];
    UIImage *theImage = [[UIImage alloc] initWithData:imageData];
    [photo setImage:theImage];
    [theImage release];
}
- (void)updateBreed: (Breed *)theBreed {
    self.selectedBreed = theBreed;
}
```

6. When running on the iPhone, updateBreed doesn't update the subviews because that will
   have to wait until the view is ready to appear. However, on the iPad updateBreed should
   update the details immediately and notify the view that something has changed so that
   it will redraw. Switch to BreedDetailViewController_iPad.m and add an override of the
   updateBreed method (Listing 19-8).

Listing 19-8   Changes to BreedDetailViewController_iPad.m

```
- (void)updateBreed: (Breed *)theBreed {
    self.selectedBreed = theBreed;
    [self updateDetails];
    [self.view setNeedsDisplay];
}
```

7. Select BreedsListViewController.m and edit the didSelectRowAtIndexPath method to
   match Listing 19-9. We can now call updateBreed regardless of what device the application
   is running on. If the application is running on the iPhone we also need to push the detail
   view onto the stack.

(continued)

Listing 19-9 didSelectRowAtIndexPath in BreedsListViewController.m

```
-(void)tableView:(UITableView *)tableView
                  didSelectRowAtIndexPath:(NSIndexPath *)indexPath {
    Breed *theBreed = [[self fetchedResultsController]
                            objectAtIndexPath:indexPath];
    if (self.editing == YES) {
        self.breedEditorVC.breed = theBreed;
        self.breedEditorVC.insertingBreed = NO;
        [self.navigationController pushViewController:
self.breedEditorVC animated:YES];
    } else {
        [self.breedDetailVC updateBreed:theBreed];
        if (UI_USER_INTERFACE_IDIOM() != UIUserInterfaceIdiomPad) {
            [self.navigationController pushViewController:
                            self.breedDetailVC animated:YES];
        }
    }
}
```

8. Save all your changes and run the application (Figure 19-8).

Everything should be more or less working, but you'll notice that in portrait orientation, when you select a breed and the details update behind the navigation popover, it remains visible. It would be nice if the popover disappeared once we've selected a breed so that you can easily see the breed information.

1. Select BreedDetailsViewController_iPad.m and edit the updateBreed method and add the following lines:

```
if (self.popover)
        [self.popover dismissPopoverAnimated:YES];
```

2. Save your changes and run the application. In portrait orientation, when you select a breed, the navigation popover will now disappear to let you see the breed information.

3. You will notice that when you stay in portrait orientation, the button to bring up the navigation popover doesn't change to reflect the group of the currently selected breed. The updateBreed method can update the button title, but it will need a reference to the button first. Edit BreedDetailViewController_iPad.h and add a UIBarButtonItem property called navButton. Be sure to synthesize and release it.

4. Edit the willHideViewController method in BreedDetailViewController_iPad and set the navButton property to the button:

```
self.navButton = barButtonItem;
```

5. Edit the willShowViewController method and set navButton to nil, since it's going away.

6. Finally, edit the updateBreed method and, if the button is non-nil, then update its title to match the group of the newly selected breed (Listing 19-10).

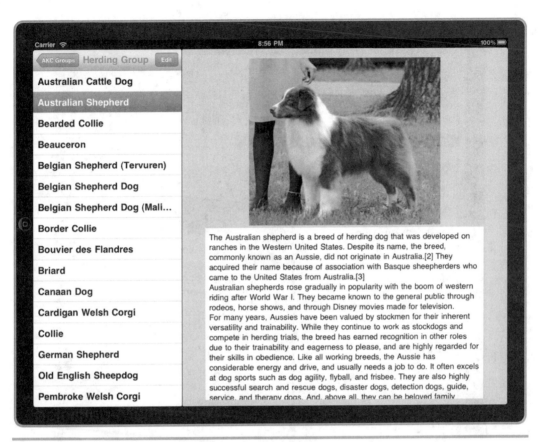

Figure 19-8   DogBreeds running in landscape orientation

Listing 19-10   Updating the button title in updateBreed

```
-(void)updateBreed: (Breed *)theBreed {
    if (self.popover) {
        [self.popover dismissPopoverAnimated:YES];
        if (self.navButton != nil) {
            self.navButton.title = theBreed.group.name;
            [self.toolbar setNeedsDisplay];
        }
    }
    self.selectedBreed = theBreed;
    [self updateDetails];
    [self.view setNeedsDisplay];
}
```

(continued)

Figure 19-9 DogBreeds running in portrait orientation

7. Run the application and note that the button updates its title as you switch between breeds in different working groups (Figure 19-9).

Note that because we load the breed photo over the Internet before redrawing the detail view, there will be a delay between tapping the breed name and the details appearing. When the Internet connection is slow, this delay will be long enough that the user won't think that their tap worked. Immediate feedback is especially important in navigation controls, and if we were creating a polished application ready for submission to the App Store, the photo would need to be loaded asynchronously so that the rest of the details can show up immediately.

You have now converted the DogBreeds application from Chapter 17 into a fully functional universal app that still works the same way it did on the iPhone but also looks good on the iPad. If you were planning to submit this application to the App Store, there's still a lot of polishing you could do, but the basic functionality is all there. With the much bigger details view, you could store and display a lot more information about the breeds. To fit that extra information in the iPhone version, you might want to switch to a tabbed interface for the details screen and spread what fits in one screen on the iPad over several tabs on the iPhone.

Other iPad Features

The iPad and iOS 3.2 brought new functionality to iOS, and in this section we'll briefly cover the most significant new features. It's beyond the scope of this book to cover all of them in detail with complete Try This examples, but we will at least introduce the new features, describe when you might want to use them, and then point you toward excellent Apple documentation that you can leverage to add advanced functionality to your own applications.

Using Popovers for Information or Editing

The popover view that is used by UISplitViewController for navigation in portrait orientation can also be used independently on the iPad. Popovers work well in any situation where the user might want to tap on a visible item on the screen and then see more information or quickly edit some aspect of the item. They have the advantage of being quick and unobtrusive, while leaving the rest of the screen (the overall context) still visible to the user. However, popovers should not be used in situations where you must have an answer from the user. When using the popover, the user should always be able to tap outside the popover and have it disappear. If you need to get the attention of your user, or must have an answer to some question or choice, you will want to use a modal view instead.

Displaying a popover is quite easy. You will want to begin by creating a view controller that contains the information you want to display or the controls needed for editing an item that you are displaying on the screen. Make sure that view controller is accessible via an outlet in the enclosing view so that you can refer to it when the user taps on an item.

Popovers are ideal for situations where the user taps on an object in the display, or even just an obvious area of the screen. Assuming you detect that tap and then call a method to handle it, the implementation of that method will look something like the following:

```
-(void) handleUserTap: (id)sender {
UIPopoverController *thePopover = [[UIPopoverController alloc]
        initWithContentViewController: myInfoVC];
  thePopover.popoverContentSize = myInfoVC.view.frame.size;
```

```
[thePopover presentPopoverFromRect: ((UIView *)sender).bounds
        inView: (UIView *)sender
        permittedArrowDirections:UIPopoverArrowDirectionAny
animated:YES];
}
```

This assumes *sender* is the subview that was tapped by the user and the contents to be displayed in the popover are in an outlet called *myInfoVC*. If you need to know when the popover shows and hides in order to adjust its content, you can implement the UIPopoverControllerDelegate protocol. Apple's "iPad Programming Guide" has a good description of using popovers for content, and Apple's ToobarSearch sample application shows how to use a popover to display search results.

Movies in a View

On the iPad with its larger screen, it will often make sense to display video in a smaller view, leaving room on the screen for additional information or controls. As we mentioned in Chapter 18, with iOS 3.2 and later, the movie player does not need to take over the full screen. In the next Try This example, we will convert the MoviePlay application from Chapter 18 into a universal application. While it will behave the same as before on the iPhone, you will be modifying it to play the movie in the center of the screen on an iPad. You can easily imagine how a reference application could be particularly useful on the iPad when you can continue to display information while playing a video in only part of the screen.

Try This MoviePlayer Centered on the iPad Screen

1. Open the MoviePlayer project from Chapter 18. You will convert it to a universal application by following steps similar to the first Try This example. Begin by changing the build settings so that the targeted device family is iPhone/iPad.

2. Create a new UIViewController subclass with the name MoviePlayerViewController_iPad. Make sure that Targeted for iPad and With XIB are checked.

3. Edit MoviePlayerViewController_iPad.h and make it a subclass of MoviePlayerViewController (you will need to import MoviePlayerViewController.h).

4. Create MainWindow_iPad.xib and add a View Controller with class MoviePlayerViewController_iPad, loaded from the MoviePlayViewController_iPad nib. Change the class of the App Delegate to MoviePlayerAppDelegate. Connect the window and view controller outlets of the App Delegate to the window and new view controller.

5. Select MoviePlayerViewController_iPad.xib and add a Play Movie button connected to the File's Owner playMovie action. Set the button's geometry so that its size is fixed and it centers horizontally and vertically (Figure 19-10).

6. Add an entry to MoviePlayer-Info.plist with key NSMainNibFile~ipad and string value MainWindow-iPad, the same as you did when converting DogBreeds to a universal app.

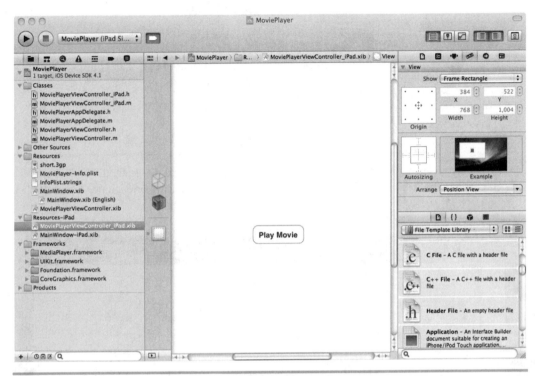

Figure 19-10 Changing the geometry of the Play Movie button

7. Save all of your changes and run the application. The Play Movie button should show up and tapping it should start the movie in one corner of the display. It works, but it doesn't look pretty on an iPad.

8. Override the playMovie method in MoviePlayerViewController_iPad using the implementation in Listing 19-11.

Listing 19-11   playMovie in MoviePlayerViewController_iPad.m

```
-(IBAction) playMovie: (id) sender {
  movieplayer = [[MPMoviePlayerController alloc]
      initWithContentURL: [NSURL fileURLWithPath:
      [[NSBundle mainBundle]
      pathForResource: @"short" ofType:@"3gp"]]];
  [[NSNotificationCenter defaultCenter]
      addObserver:self
      selector:@selector(playingDone)
      name:MPMoviePlayerPlaybackDidFinishNotification
      object:nil];
```

(continued)

```
CGPoint center =
    ([UIDevice currentDevice].orientation ==
        UIDeviceOrientationPortrait) ?
        CGPointMake(384,512) : CGPointMake(512,384);
[[movieplayer view] setFrame:CGRectMake(center.x - 240,
    center.y - 160, 480, 320)];
[[self view] addSubview:[movieplayer view]];
[movieplayer play];
}
```

9. Save your changes and run the application. Now the button and movie should both appear centered in the display, whether the iPad is in landscape or portrait orientation (Figure 19-11).

Figure 19-11   MoviePlayer on the iPad with video in a subview

You have now had practice converting a second application to be a universal application that runs well on the iPad but still runs correctly on the iPhone. On the iPad with its larger screen, it will often make sense to display video in a smaller view leaving room for additional information or controls. We successfully converted the MoviePlayer application from Chapter 18 so that on an iPad the video plays in an iPhone-sized view with plenty of room for additional information or controls.

External Display

A little known feature of the iPad is the ability to connect an external display. Apple sells an adapter cable that will plug into the connector on the bottom of the iPad and connect to any VGA display or projector. It's important to note that the monitor or projector becomes a second display for the iPad; it doesn't mirror the contents of the iPad screen. This is actually very useful behavior if you're writing something like a presentation application where the second screen displays the content and the iPad displays controls or presentation notes. There aren't very many applications in the App Store that take advantage of an external display, so if you have a clever idea for a new application that leverages two screens, it could be a great opportunity.

To use the external display, you have to add code to your application to detect the display, get a reference to it, and then add views to it. This is actually surprisingly easy to do. You can detect a second screen by registering to be notified when an external display is connected and disconnected:

```
NSNotificationCenter *center = [NSNotificationCenter defaultCenter];
[center addObserver:self selector: @selector(screenConnected:)
name:UIScreenDidConnectNotification object:nil];
[center addObserver:self selector: @selector(screenDisconnected:)
name:UIScreenDidDisconnectNotification object:nil];
```

If an external display is already connected when your application launches, no notifications are sent, so you will also need to check for a second screen on launch. You can check for the second screen and get a reference to the screen using the UIScreen class:

```
NSAray *allTheScreens = [UIScreen screens];
if ([allTheScreens count] > 1) {
  // external display attached
}
```

The first screen in the array is always the iPad's built-in display. Any additional screens will be external (at present only one is supported, but who knows what the future holds).

To draw on the external screen, you need to create a UIWindow, set its screen to the reference to the external screen and then add a view to the window. For example:

```
UIScreen *secondScreen = [[UIScreen screens] objectAtIndex:1];
UIWindow *externalWindow = [[UIWindow alloc] initWithFrame:[secondScreen
bounds]];
[externalWindow setScreen: secondScreen];
externalView = [[UIView alloc] initWithFrame: [externalWindow bounds]];
[externalWindow addSubview:externalView];
[externalWindow makeKeyAndVisible];
```

The *externalView* is just like any other view, and you add subviews to it or draw in it. The main thing to remember is to watch for notifications when the external screen appears or disappears, since the user can unplug it at any time and you will need to react and move controls or information back onto the main display as needed.

It's also worth noting that while you've become accustomed to working with a fixed screen size on the iPhone and then the iPad, that isn't necessarily the case with the external screen. Depending on the device attached, it could be one of several different sizes (at least 640 × 480, 800 × 600, and 1024 × 768 are supported by the iPad). You may need to examine the bounds of the second screen and adjust the layout of your content accordingly.

Working with Documents

With iOS 3.2 on the iPad and then iOS 4.0 on the iPhone and iPod touch, iOS devices gained some functionality for working with documents. The details are beyond the scope of this book, but if you're writing a document-based application that would benefit from sharing documents with other applications, this new functionality can be extremely useful. Apple's "iPad Programming Guide" has more details, but we will provide a brief introduction to the key features.

Your application has always had a Documents directory where it could store information, but prior to iOS 3.2, it was largely hidden from the user. Now, if you add the key *UIFileSharingEnabled* with value *true* to YourApplicationName-Info.plist, then your users can use iTunes to add files to the Documents folder and retrieve documents that were created or edited on the iPad.

You can also register your application to deal with specific types of documents. You will need to edit your application's plist and add a key like the following:

```
<key>CFBundleDocumentTypes</key>
<array>
  <dict>
    <key>LSItemContentTypes</key>
    <array>
      <string>public.plain-text</string>
    </array>
  </dict>
</array>
```

Each dictionary entry is a type of document that your application can handle. In addition to registering the types that you can handle, your application will also need to handle opening the document when requested. In the application:didFinishLaunchingWithOptions method, you will need to check the options dictionary that is passed in for an NSURL that specifies a document that another application has requested you open. Again, see the "iPad Programming Guide" for more information.

Finally, if you write an application that handles documents that it doesn't necessarily know how to open (e.g., productivity applications), then it can use a UIDocumentInteractionController object to work with those documents. The document interaction controller works with the system to preview files in place and determine if they can be opened by another application.

Summary

In this chapter, you learned how to take an iPhone/iPod touch application and convert it to a universal application that handles rotation and takes advantage of the larger iPad display. You then learned how to use a split view on the iPad to enhance that application so that it provided easy navigation on the iPad while still retaining the standard navigation on the iPhone. All of these same techniques would be used when creating a universal application from scratch.

You also learned how to make MPMoviePlayerController use only part of the screen on the iPad so that there is space to place additional information or controls around the video. While working with the movie player you also got practice creating a second iPad application.

We also briefly introduced some of the other features that became available with the iPad initially and then in iOS 4 on the iPhone and the iPod touch when it was released in the summer of 2010.

With the completion of this chapter, you should be fairly comfortable creating your own universal applications or an iPad-specific application. iOS has a very rich feature set, so there are many things that we didn't cover in this book, but you've had a chance to work with all of the main functionality that is needed for a typical application. For the more advanced features, explore Apple's documentation and sample applications and you'll have everything you need to create the next big hit in the iTunes App Store. Have fun!

Index

D

N